Television, Audiences and Cultural Studies

Television, Audiences and Cultural Studies presents a multifaceted exploration of audience research, in which David Morley draws on a rich body of empirical work to examine the emergence, development and future of television audience research.

In addition to providing an introductory overview of the development of audience research from a cultural studies perspective, David Morley questions how class and cultural differences can affect how we interpret television, the significance of gender in the dynamics of domestic media consumption, how the media construct the 'national family', and how small-scale ethnographic studies can help us to understand the global-local dynamics of postmodern media systems.

Morley's work reconceptualizes the study of ideology within the broader context of domestic communications, illuminating the role of the media in articulating public and private spheres of experience and in the social organization of space, time and community.

The collection contributes both to current methodological debates – for instance, the possible uses of ethnographic methods in media/cultural studies – and to new debates surrounding substantive issues, such as the functions of new (and old) media in the construction of cultural identities within a postmodern geography of the media.

David Morley is Reader in Media Studies at Goldsmith's College, University of London. He is the author of *The 'Nationwide' Audience* (1980) and *Family Television* (1986).

Television, Audiences and Cultural Studies

David Morley

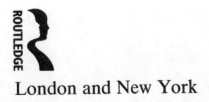
ROUTLEDGE

London and New York

First published 1992
by Routledge
11 New Fetter Lane, London EC4P 4EE

Simultaneously published in the USA and Canada
by Routledge
29 West 35th Street, New York, NY 10001

Typeset in 10 on 12 point Times by Florencetype, Avon
Printed in Great Britain by Clays Ltd, St Ives plc.

British Library Cataloguing in Publication Data
Morley, David
    Television, Audiences and Cultural Studies
    I. Title
    302.23

Library of Congress Cataloging in Publication Data
Morley, David
    Television, audiences, cultural studies / David Morley.
        p. cm.
    Includes bibliographical references.
    1. Television viewers – Research.   2. Television broadcasting – Social
aspects.   I. Title.
    PN1992.55.M65   1992
    302.23′45–dc20   92–10404

ISBN 0–415–05444–3   ISBN 0–415–05445–1 (pbk)

Contents

Acknowledgements

In so far as this book has some basis in empirical research, I should like to thank Ed Buscombe of the British Film Institute and Bob Towler (sometime Head of Research at the Independent Broadcasting Authority) for being prepared to fund *The 'Nationwide' Audience* and *Family Television* projects respectively – in each case, when no other institution would do so. My thanks go also to all the members of the Centre for Contemporary Cultural Studies Media Group 1972–8, but especially to Ian Connell, in those early days. My thanks to Ellen Seiter and Jane Armstrong, who both helped me out, perhaps more than they realized, at a difficult moment. I would like to thank Roger Silverstone, both for inviting me to participate in the research project on 'The Household Uses of Information and Communication Technology' at Brunel University from 1987 to 1990, and for granting his permission for me to reprint material here (Chapter 9) which we wrote jointly. My thanks to Ien Ang and Kevin Robins who have both, in their different ways, made our intellectual collaborations serious fun. Last, and most particularly, my thanks to Stuart Hall and Charlotte Brunsdon, for their insight and encouragement throughout.

Much of the material collected in this volume has seen previous publication in earlier forms. Chapter 1 draws on material originally published in D. Morley, *The 'Nationwide' Audience*, London: British Film Institute, 1980. Chapter 2 draws on material from my 'Changing paradigms in audience studies', in E. Seiter *et al.* (eds) *Remote Control*, London: Routledge, 1989, and also from 'Texts, readers, subjects', in S. Hall *et al.* (eds) *Culture, Media, Language*, London: Hutchinson, 1981. Chapter 3 is an edited version of a course unit, *Interpreting Television*, published by the Open University Press (1981) as part of the OU's 'Popular Culture' course. Chapter 4 was originally published in *Screen Education* (1981). Chapter 5 draws on material from my *Family Television* (1986). Chapter 6 was published in an earlier version 'Domestic relations: the framework of family viewing', in J. Lull (ed.), *World Families Watch Television* (© 1988 Sage Publications, Inc.). Chapter 8 draws on some material which also appears in an article, 'Communication and context' (jointly written with

Roger Silverstone), which appears in N. Jankowski and K. Jensen (eds), *A Handbook of Qualitative Methodologies for Mass Communication Research*, Routledge, 1991. A differently edited version of Chapter 9 appeared in *Media, Culture and Society* 12(1) (1990). An earlier version of Chapter 12 appeared in D. Swanson and D. Nimmo (eds), *New Directions in Political Communication* (© 1990 Sage Publications, Inc.). Chapter 13, again in an earlier version, appeared in *Screen* 32(1) (1991).

I am grateful to all those concerned for their permission to reprint these materials here.

My thanks go to Dave Mason and to Sue Field Reid, for helping me to convert a mountain of cut-and-paste into a finished (?) product.

Introduction

The sequence of the materials in this book is organized in an attempt to offer a particular reading of the trajectory of my research, as it has moved from the analysis of the ideological structure of factual television programmes, through a concern with the wider field of popular programming, towards the multifaceted processes of consumption and decoding in which media audiences are involved. This work has also involved an attempt to reframe the study of ideology within the broader context of domestic communications, entailing the interdiscursive connections of new technologies, broadcast media and family dynamics. Most recently, the work has been concerned with the fundamental role of the media in articulating the public and private spheres, and in the social organization of space, time and community. This, I would argue, is the proper context in which current debates about the role of the media in the construction of cultural identities can most usefully be situated (see Morley and Robins 1989, 1990 and 1992).

I am aware both of the dangers of hindsight, and of the dangers of claiming an over-coherent trajectory to this work. It has simply been a case of returning, again and again, to the same old questions about cultural power, sometimes reformulating those questions in different ways, and at various points shifting the angle of vision from which the questions have been asked.

The work can be said to have involved a series of shifts in its principal foci of interest, moving from a concern with questions of ideology and the analysis of televisual messages, through a set of questions concerning class structure and the decoding process, towards an emphasis on gendered viewing practices within the context of the family. From this point on, the work has been engaged in two principal shifts, one concerning the decentring of television as the focus of interest (towards a more inclusive concern with the uses of various information and communication technologies in the domestic sphere), and the other involving a broader consideration of the functions of such media in the construction of national and cultural identities within the context of a postmodern geography of the media.

There is not only a degree of repetition between chapters, but also a certain unevenness of tone, given that they were originally written for a variety of readerships. It has, none the less, seemed best to leave the material largely in its original form.

This Introduction is intended to offer (section 2) some reflections on the intellectual context in which the trajectory of this work originated, a retrospective view (section 3) of the significance (both positive and negative) which has been attributed to the work (especially the *Nationwide* audience study), and an intervention (section 4) in current debates as to the direction which audience studies should take in the future. However, by way of preamble, it seems necessary to offer also some explanation of the significance (at least to me) of the words in the book's title.

1 WHAT'S IN A TITLE

To give a book the title *Television, Audiences and Cultural Studies* is clearly to stake a number of claims and, in effect, to offer a number of hostages to fortune in respect of what each of the terms in the title (and their syntactic relations) might be taken to imply. I shall take them in reverse order, beginning with the last term, 'cultural studies'. A number of critics have rightly pointed not only to the dangers of the installation of a particular orthodoxy, as this field is increasingly codified and institutionalized, but also to the dangers of the international export of British cultural studies, as offering a ready-made template for work in this field, in other contexts than that (England in the 1960s and 1970s) in which it was originally developed.

Ang and I have argued elsewhere (Ang and Morley 1989) against the dangers of the transplanting of British cultural studies, through the publishing export industry, into a free-floating transnational academic paradigm for the field as a whole. As we noted there, cultural studies is not helpfully seen as 'a fixed body of thought that can be transplanted from one place to another, and which operates in similar ways in diverse national or regional contexts'. Rather,

> the place and relevance of cultural studies varies from context to context, and has to be related to the specific character of local forms of political and intellectual discourse as culture . . . it is the context-dependence of cultural studies which we need to keep in mind, and indeed reinforce, if we are to resist tendencies towards the development of orthodoxies and the temptations of a codified vocabulary.
>
> (Ang and Morley 1989: 135–6)

In a similar vein Turner (1990b) rightly points to a regrettable tendency both to present what is in effect English cultural studies (from which the question of ethnicity was, at least for many years, entirely left out: cf.

Hall 1988b) as British cultural studies (whatever happened to Wales, Scotland and Northern Ireland?) and, further, to 'exnominate' the British element itself, so that, for instance, the 'enquiry in the signifying practices of the British media is assumed to be an enquiry into the signifying practices of the media in general' – as if the British case was, in some way, essentially (rather than, in specific cases, historically, through processes of imperialism) the 'standard around which the rest of the world provide(s) variants' (ibid., 5). What follows from this clearly is a further tendency towards the improper 'homogenising of TV texts and audiences, across cultural and political borders' rather than a properly conjunctural analysis of these issues in their own specific contexts (Turner 1990b: 7). Thus, for example, Turner notes that the export of British cultural studies perspectives to the USA, 'to a context where the notion of the popular occupies a very different place with dominant cultural definitions' (25) has, among other things, exacerbated the problematic tendency towards cultural optimism which he sees as enshrined in much of this British work.

Turner goes on to discuss the quite different cultural significance in Australia, as opposed to Britain, of an ethos of masculinist, anti-authoritarian, nationalist values which 'honours manual labour, is sceptical of the intellect and . . . proudly sees itself as essentially working class' (12). If, in the analysis of Willis (1978), this can be seen as a subordinate (or even implicitly oppositional) discourse within British culture, it would be quite wrong to imagine that it functioned in the same way within the context of post-colonial Australian culture, where it can rather be seen as part of a dominant nationalist mythology. Clearly, in different places and at different times the same things do not always have the same significance, and this is a danger to which any improperly universalizing tendency within cultural studies will always be prey.

It would seem that today, especially in the context of the North American Academy, cultural studies not only has become almost synonymous with a certain kind of postmodern theorizing but also is now often referred to (in my experience, especially by graduate students there) simply as 'theory'. This fetishization of a rather abstract idea of theory is quite at odds with what Stuart Hall has described as the 'necessary modesty' which academic work in this field should properly display. This process of fetishization has both a number of explanations and a number of consequences. As to the former, in the first place, as O'Connor (1989) puts it, there is the simple 'difficulty, in the USA, of reading the cultural studies style of theorising through concrete examples, when most of the examples are specific to British society'. As he aptly notes, 'How many students in the USA . . . have seen a *Nationwide* TV show?' (O'Connor 1989: 407). There is also the question of the effect of publishing economics on the development of the field. The point here is a quite banal but ultimately crucial one, to the effect, crudely, that higher levels of abstraction ('theory') can be sold in a more extensive (and not nationally specific) market, and thus tend towards both higher levels of profitability for the publisher, and a wider reputation for the theorist. In short, 'theory' travels best.

To move to the question of the consequences of this process, and their significance: as O'Connor notes, one of the crucial features of the American appropriation of British cultural studies has been a loss of the sense of the rootedness of communication processes in social reproduction and politics (see also Byars 1991, for a useful account of the development of cultural studies in America). As he notes, by way of example, in the circulation and appropriation of his work in the USA, Hall often is presented as 'a theoretician of the superstructures, of communication effectively isolated from material and political limits and pressures' in such a way that 'under the rubric of postmodernism . . . the sense of culture as practice, form and institution has been lost' (O'Connor 1989: 408). As Hall himself has put it, in this transformation, one runs the risk of losing hold of what he argues to be one of the defining commitments of cultural studies – to holding 'theoretical and political questions in an ever-irresolvable but permanent tension . . . [which] . . . constantly allows the one to bother and disturb the other' (Hall 1990: 17), at the necessary cost of avoiding any final theoretical stabilization. (See also the comments in Hall 1986 on the American take-up of his work in connection with debates on postmodernism).

I would concur with Murdock when he notes that the task facing us, in the development of any adequate form of cultural studies, is 'to conceptualise the relation between [the] two sides of the communications process – the material and the discursive, the economic and the cultural – without collapsing either one into the other' (Murdock 1989a: 436). I would further agree with him that much cultural studies work (especially in the recent period, and particularly in its North American variant) seems to fall short on precisely this point, in so far as the discursive process of the construction of meanings is frequently analysed without reference to its institutional, economic or material settings, so that, as Murdock notes, we are frequently offered 'an analysis of the cultural industries which has little or nothing to say about how they actually work, as industries' (436).

By way of explaining the widespread failure to incorporate the necessary insights of political economy into cultural studies analyses, Murdock (ibid.) makes the simple but telling point that, almost without exception, the key figures in cultural studies came originally from backgrounds in literary criticism and the humanities and that, consequently, their own primary concerns (and competences) lie with the analysis of texts of one kind or another, while they tend to have, on the whole and with the significant exception of Hall (see Hall 1980, for an account of the early engagement with sociology of the Centre for Contemporary Cultural Studies), neither corresponding competence nor interest in matters of economics and social science (notwithstanding the frequent references to Marxism). As Murdock notes, this unfortunate limitation is, increasingly, enhanced by the tendency for newly institutionalized Departments of Cultural Studies to be mainly housed in faculties of arts and humanities and to have few institutional links to the social sciences.

This insight is of particular interest to me, as one trained initially as a sociologist who has, by virtue of that fact, always felt somewhat marginal to the successive dominant paradigms (whether in their culturalist, structuralist, psychoanalytic, post-structuralist or postmodern variants) within cultural studies. Thus, from within cultural studies, the major critique of much of my own work has been that it is too essentialist or reductionist. From my own point of view, the prime objective of the work has been to analyse processes of culture and communication within their social and material settings. I am personally much more worried by what I see as the tendency towards the 'textualization' of cultural studies, which often allows the cultural phenomena under analysis to drift entirely free from their social and material foundations.

To be precise, most of the initial impetus for my own interest in questions of media audiences was derived from two early strands of sociological literature, neither of which has, to my mind, ever been properly integrated into the mainstream (if that is not an oxymoron), of cultural studies work, and the neglect of which, I believe, continues to have a debilitating effect on the development of the field. The first of these strands was work in the sociology of education and in sociolinguistics which is concerned with the relation of linguistic and cultural codes and social structures: it is represented crucially by the work of Bernstein (1971), Rosen (1972), Labov (1970), Keddie (1973), Bourdieu (1972), Giglioli (1973), Pride and Holmes (1972) and Hymes (1964). The second strand was that concerned with the complex relations of class, culture and consciousness, as represented not simply by the early work of Parkin (1971) – which tends to be the only example of this trajectory referred to (usually dismissively) within cultural studies debates – but also by Harris (1971), Parkin (1974 and 1979) Mann (1970 and 1973), Moorhouse and Chamberlain (1974), Bulmer (1975), Beynon (1973), Nicholls and Armstrong (1976), Beynon and Nicholls (1977), and all the debates surrounding the question of *embourgeoisement* engendered by the publication of Goldthorpe and Lockwood *et al.*'s seminal analysis, *The Affluent Worker* (1968).

To be sure, these were only starting-points, and to reinvoke them now cannot be to claim that we could turn back to this earlier work as a source of ready-made answers to contemporary questions. Rather, my aim is (a) to make clear the sociological origins of my own work; and (b) to argue for the continuing relevance of the questions necessarily posed (if not the answers given) by the sociological cast of this work, as a necessary part of the kind of cultural studies which I, for one, would wish to be understood to be engaged in.

I take these issues to be of particular pertinence as we confront what Hall has recently described as a 'moment of profound danger', as cultural studies, especially in America, is rapidly professionalized and institutionalized around a 'theoretical fluency' of deconstructionist formalism, in which the current 'overwhelming textualisation of cultural studies' own discourses . . . constitutes power and politics as exclusively matters of language' (Hall 1990).

Again, the simple economics of publishing itself, in conjunction with the exigencies of academic life, are material to the (theoretical) point. In a burgeoning, and originally interdisciplinary, field, where new courses are set up each term, students (and publishers) understandably require textbooks, which quickly acquire a kind of canonical status, delimiting and defining the field. One example of this is Allen's *Channels of Discourse* (Allen 1987), which offers an introduction to a range of (principally American) cultural studies perspectives on television, and which has, in so doing, undoubtedly performed a useful function for many students. My own interest lies in identifying the particular definition of the field which this important collection of essays promotes. In this respect, I would agree with Silverstone (1989), who notes that, despite its recurring gestures towards the need to produce not only a semiology but also a sociology of television, the book finally remains entirely 'text-centric', despite the recurring acknowledgements that television cannot be satisfactorily reduced to a textual phenomenon. As Hall notes, in this respect, 'textuality is never enough' and cultural studies must learn to live with 'the . . . tension which Said describes as its affiliations with institutions, offices, agencies, classes, academies, corporations, groups, ideologically defined parties and professions, nations, races and genders . . . questions that . . . can never be fully covered by critical textuality and its elaborations' (Hall 1990: 16–17).

In bringing this section to a conclusion, I should first note that if this book offers itself as operating within (across?) the field of cultural studies, it is already clear that mine is a quite particular (and in some ways, perhaps, marginal) perspective within that field, in respect of my continuing commitment to a sociological perspective on the questions at issue in the analysis of communications and culture.

Equally, if it is not really a 'cultural studies' book, nor is it a book about audiences as they have traditionally been understood – mainly as the (rather tedious) empirical (or empiricist) province of mass communications research. Rather, to run ahead of the book's argument, it offers various ways of reconceptualizing media audiences; these have been, to some extent, constructed by 'poaching' (cf. de Certeau 1984) on the territory of mass communications research, while mobilizing perspectives borrowed from a range of other disciplines – originally sociolinguistics and the sociology of education, more recently family studies, anthropology and geography. My own experience has been that it is precisely the interfacing of these different perspectives that has always been the most productive.

To take the first term in the book's title last: nor is the book about television in any essentialist way (whether the definitions of the medium posed by McLuhan 1964, Heath and Skirrow 1977 or Ellis 1982, for example). Rather, I am interested in what Andrew Ross (1988) has usefully described as 'TV' or 'television – as-it-is-used' – what television means to different kinds of people, watching different kinds of programmes, in different contexts and at different times. In my work with Roger Silverstone (Chapter 9 below) I have also been concerned to begin to break out of the television-centric focus of media studies, and to relocate television in the broader contexts both of a fuller range of information and communication technologies and of domestic consumption in its various aspects.

So much for the denials, disavowals and alibis.

2 STARTING-POINTS

If, in the British context, media studies was reinvigorated in the early 1970s by what Stuart Hall (1982) has characterized as the 'rediscovery of ideology', this rediscovery led, in the first instance, to a focus on the analysis of the ideological structure of news (both on television and in the press) and, more generally, to a focus on the analysis of media coverage of politics, particularly media coverage of explicitly controversial issues such as industrial and race relations. Some of this work was framed within a more (or less) sophisticated concern with bias (see Morley 1976, and Glasgow Media Group 1976, *et seq.*), while other studies mobilized concepts of ideology derived from the work of Gramsci and Althusser (see, *inter alia*, Hall *et al.* 1981). However, while internally differentiated in this respect, much of this work shared two key premises: first, that it was in the field of explicitly political communications that the concern with the reproduction of ideology (and the presumed consequence of the maintenance of social order or hegemony) would be most productively focused; and second (partly inscribed in the theoretical model of ideology underpinning the first premise – see Abercrombie and Turner 1978; Abercrombie *et al.* 1984), that the (ideological) effects of the media could, in effect, be deduced from the analysis of the textual structure of the messages they emitted. To this extent, the media audience was largely absent from these analytical discourses, and the power of the media over their consumers was often taken for granted (see Connell 1985).

As is well known, both of these premises have been severely questioned in recent years. In the first case, there has been a growing recognition of the considerable political significance of a much wider realm of cultural products (partly owing to the influence of feminist and anti-racist perspectives on the symbolic process of construction of personal and cultural identities), and a consequent concern with the ideological structure of entertainment media, popular fiction and music. In the second place, there has been a growing recognition (dating notably from Hall's seminal paper (Hall 1973a) on the encoding and decoding of television) of the complex and contradictory nature of the process of cultural consumption of media products – both within the realm of television (see, for example, Morley 1980), and within the broader field of popular culture (see Hebdige 1979 and 1988a). I wish to consider, briefly, each of these shifts and to try to trace their implications for contemporary work in the field of political communications.

The significance of the 'popular'

From the late 1970s onwards, researchers within the media/cultural studies traditions in Britain began to explore the political and ideological significance of the structure of media products outside the 'news' category. These studies focused on issues such as the construction of gender identities in soap opera (see Hobson 1982; Ang 1985), the presentation of racial stereotypes in drama and light entertainment (see Cohen and Gardner 1984), the political and cultural values embedded in popular fiction and drama (see McCabe 1981; McArthur 1981; Bennett and Woollacott 1987) and the presentation of knowledge itself in quiz shows (Mills and Rice 1982). In Britain much of this work was collected and summarized in the Open University's influential course on 'Popular Culture' (1981). These studies demonstrated that any concern with the influence of the media in the construction of political culture needed to operate with a wider and more inclusive definition of the kind of media texts considered to be relevant. In this context, the study of news and explicitly 'political' media products was then seen to be but a small part of the overall field. This shift of interest towards the broader field of fictional and dramatic programming was paralleled by another shift, this time in relation to the study of television news and current affairs programming itself. In this context the Media Studies Group at the Centre for Contemporary Cultural Studies, during the period 1975–7 took as the focus for its analysis the BBC's early evening magazine programme *Nationwide* (successor to the 'flagship' programme of British television magazine programming, *Tonight*). The point of interest in the *Nationwide* programme lay partly in its pivotal position in the BBC's scheduling policy – as an explicit attempt to build a large audience early in the evening, through a form of popular magazine programming which at once ignored and transcended politics. At one level the programme's ambitions were quite limited, and certainly eschewed any commitment to serious programming, on the premise that this simply was not what the audience wanted. As the editor of the programme, Michael Bunce, put it:

> you need to be unpredictable; you need to mix the chairman of the Post Office with a tattooed lady. Most people have had a hard day's work, and when they sit down they don't want a remorseless, demanding 'hard-tack' diet every night.
>
> (Interview in the *Sunday Times*, 2 March 1975)

However, while the programme certainly prioritized the attempt to engage (and hold) the interest of its audience with its entertaining mixture of items, it also became clear, as the CCCS Media Group's analysis of the programme developed, that at another level the programme, for all its seemingly quirky emphasis on the variety and eccentricities of 'everyday folk', could in fact be seen to be heavily implicated in the transmission of a quite definable set of political values, precisely through its 'common-sensical', no-nonsense style of presentation. If the presenter's bluff, 'man (*sic*) of the people' stance was one which seemed equally cynical of all politicians and bureaucrats, representing the viewpoint of the 'ordinary person in the street', then the premise was that all of these political issues could in the end be addressed (and presumably resolved) most effectively from the standpoint of commonsense – the totem to which the programme was ultimately and explicitly reverential. The CCCS Media Group's analysis of the programme (Brunsdon and Morley 1978) was concerned to demonstrate how the programme articulated and presented as natural what was in fact a (necessarily) particular definition of what constituted commonsense as the, supposedly, non-political ground from which the antics of the 'the politicians and bureaucrats' could be understood. This (constructed, though seemingly naturalized) definition of commonsense then functions as the implicit yardstick against which all political questions are judged. The process of construction of commonsense is, then, one of the most centrally important ideological (and, of course, ultimately political) processes in which media programmes such as *Nationwide* are engaged as they translate the exotic world of politics into everyday terms ('But Chancellor, what will all this mean for ordinary people?') and thus construct for their audience a quite particular perspective on, and relation to, the world of politics. In brief then, the argument here (outlined in Brunsdon and Morley 1978: ch. 4) is that the analysis of media products which explicitly define themselves as non-political is in fact of central concern to any analysis of political culture. However, it has, of course, not simply been the analysis of media products that has been at stake in my research, but also the readings which different audiences have made of those products. It is also a question of the readings which others have made of the readings I have offered of the audience responses I have gathered.

3 RETROSPECT: *THE 'NATIONWIDE' AUDIENCE* RECONSIDERED

As Radway aptly notes in her 1987 introduction to the British edition of *Reading the Romance*, 'whatever her intentions, no writer can foresee or prescribe the way her book will develop, be taken up, or read' (Radway 1984b (1987): 2). That introduction, in which Radway attempts to explain both the specific context in which her own work developed, and attempts to 'secure a particular reading' (1) for it in the context of its British publication is, to my mind, exemplary, not least for the clarity with which she both addresses what she subsequently perceived as the limitations of that work, and the way in which she forcefully recounts her own sense of the continuing importance of the questions which it was attempting to answer.

For any author to comment on the subsequent interpretations of his or her own work is, evidently, to court the risk of being thought both vain and/or oversensitive to criticism. When that work is itself substantively concerned with the ways in which audiences interpret texts, the irony is manifest. None the less, and despite the arguments of Barthes (1977) concerning the status of the author, I offer below a number of comments on the interpretations (or 'decodings') that have subsequently been made of *The Nationwide* audience study in particular, in an attempt to (re-) establish what I would consider to be the 'preferred reading' of that text. In so far as this procedure needs excusing, my reasons for adopting it can be briefly stated.

While I have, naturally, been gratified by the attention given to *The 'Nationwide' Audience* book (Morley 1980), and by the fact that, a decade after its publication, it is still widely cited, there are aspects of its subsequent mode of circulation which do concern me. In the first place, the book itself has been out of print for some years now and, with the exception of those with access to library copies, most contemporary readers are only familiar with it at second-hand, through the summaries and accounts of that work offered in student texts such as Fiske (1987a) or Turner (1990a). It is for this reason that I decided to include a summary version of that work (see Chapter 2) in this collection, so that, for good or ill, the work could be made available again for discussion, in its own terms. Second, and this may to some extent be explained by the fact that those who ostensibly speak of it actually speak only of others' summaries of that work, some of the secondary accounts are simply inaccurate. Thus, for example, Frow (1991: 60 n. 3) berates me for making in the *Nationwide* project, the 'classic mistake' of confusing 'texts written in the conventional genre of the questionnaire answer with the direct experience of the programme'. The problem here is that the *Nationwide* audience research did not employ a questionnaire to generate audience responses (it employed a version of the 'focused interview', derived from Merton and Kendal 1955).

While simple matters of factual inaccuracy, such as this, can evidently be cleared up relatively easily, more complex questions arise when we turn to broader interpretations of the work and its significance. I offer below (see section 4 of this Introduction) an account of my own anxieties about the way in which the *Nationwide* work has latterly been invoked as the theoretical justification of what we might call the 'don't worry, be happy' school of (principally American) cultural studies (variously labelled as the 'interpretivist' or 'new revisionist' perspective by other critics). For the moment, I wish to focus on the interpretations (and uses) of the *Nationwide* work offered in Fiske 1987a (see also below) and Turner 1990a, given their widespread use as student textbooks.

In particular, I am concerned with how the *Nationwide* work has been retrospectively positioned as 'the point where the encoding/decoding model starts to break down' (Turner 1990a: 136). Thus, Fiske claims of the *Nationwide* work that 'what Morley found was that Hall, in following Parkin (1971), had overemphasised the role of class in producing different readings and had underestimated the variety of determinants of reading' (Fiske 1987: 63). Turner argues that 'Morley's attempt to develop Hall's encoding/decoding model came to demonstrate, instead, that individual readings of television are much more complex than Hall's model would allow' (Turner 1990a: 111). He goes on: 'Morley has to concede that social position "in no way correlates" with the readings he has collected' (135) and that 'Morley admits . . . that the attempt to tie differential readings to gross social and class determinants, such as the audience's occupation group, was a failure' (135), or, as he puts it elsewhere (32) 'a waste of time', an enterprise which was 'the victim of crude assumptions' (136).

The problems here are manifold. Radway (1984a) rightly notes my own retrospective concern (see Morley 1981) with the particular concentration in the *Nationwide* study 'on the single variable of class and the rather simple way in which the concept of class itself was constructed' (Radway 1984a: 9) and points, by way of parallel, in her own study, to what she retrospectively came to see as the corresponding problems of an 'exclusive preoccupation with gender and . . . the use of a rather rigid notion of patriarchy' (9). The point is that any empirical study has to start somewhere, and in order to force issues on to the research agenda, one does sometimes run the risk of overstating one's case (with ample time for *post hoc* regrets). It is no part of my concern to attempt to preserve the *Nationwide* work from legitimate criticism, and I am aware that its faults are many. However, I am concerned to query misrepresentations of the intellectual history involved, and to defend the work against what Richards (1960) defines as 'misreadings' as distinct from 'variant readings'.[1]

Reference to the original sources quickly demonstrates that it is Parkin, rather than Hall, who might appropriately be charged with offering too mechanistic an account of the relationship between (in his terms) 'meaning systems' and class position (Parkin 1971). Equally, it is clearly demonstrable that Hall's own seminal 'encoding/decoding' essay (Hall 1973a) is at some pains not to replicate Parkin's error in this respect, as Hall 'amplifies' the model. Indeed, it is some of my own early formulations, rather than Hall's, that give such distinct analytical priority to class, over and above all other social categories. However, even in that case, matters are not so simple. When Turner quotes Morley as 'conceding' that social position 'in no way correlates with . . . the readings he has collected' (Turner 1990a: 135) he omits one crucial word from the original sentence. The full quotation reads: 'in no way *directly* correlates' (my emphasis). If this seems an inconsequential matter of textual exegesis, I can only apologize to the reader, but to my mind the difference made by the word which Turner omits is fundamental. Had Hall or I been attempting to demonstrate some utterly mechanistic form of social determination, in which decodings were rigidly determined by class, then evidence of a lack of such correspondence would, clearly, have been damning to the whole enterprise. However, that is not what either Hall or I was proposing, but rather a much more complex process, through which structural position might function to set parameters to the acquisition of cultural codes, the availability (or otherwise) of which might then pattern the decoding process. Moreover, while the results of the *Nationwide* study showed that the patterning of decodings was certainly more complex than could be accounted for by class alone, those results did demonstrate a quite significant degree of patterning, which a non-mechanistic theory of social determination can, in fact, help us to account for productively. To this extent I would argue that both Fiske and Turner not only misread the evidence offered in the *Nationwide* study but, more fundamentally, misrepresent the questions to which that evidence was intended to contribute some (if partial) answers.

At a more general level, O'Connor (1989) notes that, in his presentation of British cultural studies for the American audience, Grossberg (1983) presents that work (including both my own and Hebdige's (1979) work) as a series of failed attempts to connect 'culture' and 'society', showing no clear patterning of response by social group, and thus justifying the abandonment of any attempt to trace such connections, in favour of the flux of postmodernism. The point is that the absence of automatic and clear-cut patterns of determination would only be counter-evidence to the most simplistic theory of class (or any other form of) structuring of culture (cf. Bourdieu 1984, for an indication of what such a non-mechanistic theory might look like).

Methodological debates

There has been considerable critical discussion of the methodologies employed in the *Nationwide* and *Family Television* studies. I offer below (Chapter 8) a lengthy account of my own views on these matters, and so will only comment in a preliminary way here on some of the key issues at stake.

My own work has subsequently come to be identified largely with the ethnographic approach to media audiences, partly as a result of my own invocation of that perspective at various points in the work, but also, more recently, in a broader context, in which ethnography has come close to being viewed as the only (politically correct) method for the (post?) modern media researcher (and even then a dangerous one – see Clifford and Marcus 1986; Marcus and Fischer 1986). In the case of American cultural studies, in particular, the identification of qualitative methods with the progressive wing of communications studies seems to be almost complete, and ethnography, as Lull (1988: 242) has argued, has come to be a fetishized 'buzz-word' in the field.

In fact, while I have principally employed qualitative methods, thus far in my own work (though both the *Nationwide* and the *Family Television* projects also included quantitative elements) I hold no brief for their exclusive claim to methodological adequacy. I hold all questions of methodology to be ultimately pragmatic ones, to be determined according to the resources available and the particular type of data needed to answer specific questions, and would further hold that all methodological choices (ethnography included) incur what an economist would call an 'opportunity cost' – in terms of the other possibilities excluded by *any* particular choice of method. Thus, I would entirely agree with Murdock's comments when he observes that, for some purposes, properly constructed social surveys are by far the most appropriate methods of research. As Murdock observes:

> Critical work is not defined by the techniques of enquiry it employs, though a number of commentators have proceeded as though the 'soft' data produced by observation, depth interviewing and personal testimony offer the only permissible evidence, and all forms of 'number-crunching' are to be rejected on principle . . . [as] . . . a compromise with empiricism.
>
> (Murdock 1989b: 226)

Conversely, I would disagree with Nightingale's (1986) argument that ethnographic research, because of its primary commitment to description, is somehow thus intrinsically unsuited to serving the properly critical purposes of cultural studies. My position is not only that no single method has a monopoly on virtue, but the choice of method, in itself, can neither guarantee nor damn a given study. Personally, I would far rather read a good survey than a bad ethnography (and vice versa). Thus, although his remarks are in some part intended as a critique of the particular methodological choices made in the research which Silverstone and I have conducted on ICTs (see Chapter 9 below), I would, in fact, also agree in principle with Corner's comments, when he notes that proponents of the ethnographic approach who are wary of 'even such limited "experimental" procedures as the special screening of video material to generate discussion' all too often 'over-state the extent to which the removal of acts of viewing from the naturalised and fragmented flow of mundane use . . . creates an unacceptable degree of distortion in viewers' responses . . . [given] the continuities . . . of formed personal identity . . . as well as the significatory stabilities of the texts themselves' (Corner 1991: 25–6). To this extent, I would thus reject Turner's argument that the results of the *Nationwide* study are ultimately vitiated by the 'formal and artificial' (Turner 1990a: 140) methods used there, in arranging special screenings to engender discussion. As Fiske (1990: 89) notes, much ethnographic data is produced specifically for an occasion constructed and controlled by the researcher, but while that certainly necessitates a degree of caution and self-awareness in the interpretation of that data, it does not, *per se*, invalidate it. It all depends, finally, on what it is you want to find out.

Turner, drawing on Hartley's (1987) argument that audiences are 'fictions' and have no empirical existence, presses the point further, claiming that the *Nationwide* study was also artificial in that it involved collecting people for interview 'in a group that would not otherwise have been formed, in a place they would otherwise not have occupied' (Turner 1990a: 164). This is simply inaccurate. The groups interviewed in that project already existed, as groups of students following particular courses, and were deliberately interviewed in the educational settings which they routinely inhabited. As I have noted elsewhere (Morley 1981), this was hardly a procedure without its own costs and limitations, but these are quite other than the ones Turner adduces. I argue below (following Geertz 1988) that Hartley's own position depends on a misappropriation of the concept of a 'fiction' (something made) and depends on a confusion of 'making things out' with 'making things up'.

As for the question of my own employment of ethnographic methods, I would entirely accept Turner's observation that their appropriation in the *Nationwide* study was 'anything but thorough' (Turner 1990a: 136) but, given the arguments above, I would not agree that this fact, in itself, has any particular consequences for the validity or otherwise of the study. Only one who believed that ethnography alone had all the methodological answers would conclude thus. Equally, while I am in sympathy with many of Radway's (1988) observations on the problems of ethnographic studies of media audiences which are too narrowly circumscribed (cf. Evans 1990, on the difference between traditional anthropological ethnographies and those customarily conducted in this field), Corner's comments on the corresponding dangers of 'an under-theorised and imprudently comprehensive notion of the contextual' (Corner 1991: 28) should give us pause for thought before we conclude that the inclusion of 'more context' is necessarily, in all cases, the guarantee of methodological adequacy.

To move to a different issue, one recurring criticism of both the *Nationwide* and the *Family Television* studies is that each overstates the degree of inter-group differences (between occupationally based groups in the one case, and between genders in the other). This point I am happy to concede, in so far as it was precisely the objective of the two projects to insert questions of class and gender (respectively) at the heart of the media research agenda, from which starting-point any consequent over-simplification could then be corrected. Surprising as it may now seem, given the taken-for-grantedness of such a transformed agenda nowadays, at the point of writing the *Nationwide* study, despite all the work (quoted earlier) in the sociology of education which had clearly demonstrated the pertinence of class to the communicative process, these issues were largely absent from the study of media consumption. Similarly, at the point of writing the *Family Television* study (Morley 1985), despite all the psycho-analytically based work which had focused on the question of gender in film studies (even if in a rather abstracted way), except in the early work of Brunsdon (1981), Hobson (1982), Modleski (1984), Radway (1984) and Ang (1985), the question of the influence of gender in the reception of television was still relatively marginalized, certainly by comparison to the position it occupies today.

Strategic essentialism and methodological individualism

If the early formulations of the cultural studies tradition of research into media issues, with their primary focus on questions of class, have only been displaced relatively recently by the emergence of feminism and its focus on gender in these matters, it is only more recently (and partially) that this work has begun to be further reshaped and reconstructed by the emergence of anti-racist perspectives and their insistence on questions of race and ethnicity. One key (and much-cited) contribution, in this respect, has been Bobo's (1988) analysis of 'black women as cultural readers' of films such as *The Color Purple*. Bobo sets herself the task of understanding 'the overwhelming positive response from Black female viewers' to the film (in contradiction to the film's largely negative reception among many radical reviewers and critics), 'why people liked . . . [it] . . . in spite of its sometimes clichéd characters' within the more general context of the issue of how 'a specific audience creates meaning from a mainstream text and uses the reconstructed meaning to empower themselves and their social group' (Bobo 1988: 92–3).

If Bobo's invocation of the category 'Black women' can be faulted for an implicit essentialism, which would too automatically derive decoding strategies from structural position (cf. 'an audience member from a marginalised group (people of colour, women, the poor, and so on) has an oppositional stance as they participate in mainstream media'), this is only an instance of the same criticism as can be levelled against, for example, the insistence on class in the *Nationwide* study or that on gender in Radway's (1984b) analysis. As argued above, I would likewise here want to defend Bobo's analysis against criticisms, on these kind of theoretical grounds, in so far as, in inserting the question of race and ethnicity into the fundamental framework of media analysis, she achieves far more than her critics would seem to recognize. Clearly, there is much to be gained from subsequent theoretical work on the need to develop a non-reductive analysis of the articulation of structures of race, ethnicity and gender with those of culture (in the British context, see the debate in the pages of *Third Text* between Mercer (1990) and Gilroy (1989), for example). However, whatever its theoretical shortcomings in this respect, it is the great virtue of Bobo's work to offer us a clearly grounded analysis of the specificities of the responses of (at least some) Black women viewers to mainstream material of this kind.

The point, as Bobo argues, is that

a Black audience, through a history of theatre-going and film-watching, knows that at some point an expression of the exotic primitive is going to be offered to us. Since this is the case, we have one of two options . . . One is never to indulge in media products, an impossibility in an age of media blitz. Another option, and I think this is more an unconscious reaction to and defence against racist definitions of Black people, is to filter out that which is negative and select from the work, elements we can relate to.

(Bobo 1988: 101)

If Bobo's use of the category 'we' may be argued to be somewhat problematic, her central and substantive point remains pertinent, when she argues that the motivation for Black women's positive responses to *The Color Purple* was grounded in an overwhelming sense of relief at being offered, for once, portrayals of Black women on screen in non-marginal roles, in the context of a historical situation in which, as Bobo puts it, 'we understand that mainstream media has never rendered our segment of the population faithfully. We have as evidence our years of watching film and TV programmes and reading plays and books. Out of habit, as readers of mainstream texts, we have learnt to ferret out the beneficial and put up blinders against the rest' (96). Or, as Christian puts it, 'Finally, somebody says something about us' (quoted in Bobo 1988: 101).

Substantive questions of 'essentialism' in relation to race or any other category clearly also involve questions of methodology. In terms of methodological procedures, the question of inter- and intra-group differences (and of my own tendency to privilege the former over the latter, in the *Nationwide* study in particular) is also raised by the critiques of Lewis (1983) and of Brunt and Jordin (1986), which, in different ways, query the wisdom of my choice to work with group rather than individual interviews in that project. The basic reasons for that choice are outlined below (see Chapter 3), though it is worth observing that the *Nationwide* project was initially designed to utilize both types of interview, and was only conducted as it was because of subsequent funding limitations. In a parallel vein, Turner argues that the lack of attention to intra-group variations in the responses of the groups in the *Nationwide* project 'should make us question those readings' in so far as 'it is likely that a consensualising process was engendered by the grouping itself' and my own interviewing practice 'may also have reinforced any consensualising process' (Turner 1990a: 135). The problem here concerns the methodologically individualist conception of culture which seems to lie, implicitly, behind Turner's criticism. His point would seem to be that the use of group interviews prevented the individuals within each group from expressing their individual responses and differences. The problem here concerns the way in which this perspective fails to recognize Durkheim's (1938) fundamental point that social facts are *sui generis* and cannot be reduced to being a mere 'summation' of individual facts.

The fundamental difficulty with Turner's position was identified by Pollock (1955), in his critique of mainstream empirical research into public opinion. As Pollock notes, the 'very assumption that there exists the opinion of every individual is dubious', in so far as 'individual opinion, which appears to current opinion research to be the elementary unit, is in actual fact an extremely derivative, mediated thing' (Pollock 1955: 228, 233). Pollock's central point, which was the rationale for allowing the most forceful individuals in each group in the *Nationwide* project to dominate the discussions and to articulate the outline of a 'group consensus' (as they presumably did, routinely, in other situations in which the group was together), is, as he puts it, that 'the procedure of opinion research, which enumerates and appraises all individuals as having equal rights, as dots without qualities, so to speak, ignores the real differences of social power and social impotence' (231) – differences which are as crucial in the collective consumption and discussion of media programmes as they are in any other field of social life. As Pollock cautions, we should not think of every individual as a monad whose opinions crystallize in isolation, or as being in a social vacuum (from which processes of group dynamics, for example, are absent). Rather, 'realistic . . . research would have to come as close as possible, in its methods of research, to those conditions in which actual opinions are formed, held and modified' (230) – the conditions within the groups of which the individual is a member, for instance.

4 AUDIENCE STUDIES, NOW AND IN THE FUTURE?

It certainly seems that, over the last few years, things have changed in the world of media studies. As we all know, in the bad old days television audiences were considered as passive consumers, to whom things happened as television's miraculous powers affected them. According to choice, these (always other) people were turned into zombies, transfixed by bourgeois ideology or filled with consumerist desires. Happily, so the story goes, it was then discovered that this was an inaccurate picture, because in fact these people were out there, in front of the set, being active in all kinds of ways – making critical/oppositional readings of dominant cultural forms, perceiving ideological messages selectively/subversively, etc., etc. So, it seems, we needn't worry – the passively consuming audience is a thing of the past. As Evans (1990) notes, recent audience work in media studies can be largely characterized by two assumptions: (a) that the audience is always active (in a non-trivial sense); and (b) that media content is 'polysemic', or open to interpretation. The question is what these assumptions are taken to mean exactly, and what their theoretical and empirical consequences are.

The 'new audience research'

In an essay on the problems of the 'new audience research', Corner identifies a number of the key issues at stake in current debates about the 'activity' of the media audience. He argues that, in recent years, the question of media power as a political issue has tended to slip off the research agenda of this burgeoning field of 'demand-side' research. In his analysis, this new research is seen to amount largely to 'a form of sociological quietism . . . in which increasing emphasis on the micro-processes of viewing relations displaces . . . an engagement with the macro-structures of media and society' (Corner 1991: 4).

For my part, while in sympathy with much of Corner's argument (see below), I find this particular formulation problematic, in so far as it malposes the relation between macro and micro, effectively equating the former with the 'real'. Corner's analysis fails to recognize, among other things, the articulation of the divisions macro/micro, real/trivial, public/private, masculine/feminine – which is what much of the work which he criticizes has, in various ways, been concerned with. More centrally, Corner seems to invoke a notion of the macro which is conceptualized in terms of pre-given structures, rather than (to use Giddens's phrase) 'structuration' (Giddens 1979) and which fails to see that macro-structures can only be reproduced through micro-processes. Unless one deals in a reified sense of 'structure' such an entity is, in fact, simply an analytical construct detailing the patterning of an infinite number of micro-processes and events (cf. Saussure 1974, on the status of *langue*). It was precisely for this reason that the work of the media group at CCCS in a formative period (see Hall *et al.* 1981) turned to an engagement with ethno-methodological perspectives: not in order to abandon the macro in favour of the micro (as many ethno-methodologists themselves seemed to do) but, rather, the better to articulate the analysis of the one to that of the other.

In this connection Gledhill offers a useful formulation when she points to the central role of the concept of 'negotiation' of meanings in allowing us to avoid 'an overly deterministic view of cultural production, whether economic . . . or cine-psychoanalytic' (Gledhill 1988: 67). Gledhill's central point concerns the homology between the substitution of the concept of 'negotiation' for that of 'effects' at the micro-level, and the corresponding substitution of the concept of 'hegemony' (as a necessarily unstable and incomplete process) for that of the imposition of a 'dominant ideology' (as a given and guaranteed effect) at the macro-level. The point precisely is that the general macro-process can only operate through myriad micro-performances of power, none of which can be guaranteed in advance, even if the general pattern of events is subject to the logic of probabilities. As Giddens (1979) argues, structures are not external to action, but are only reproduced through the concrete activities of daily life, and must be analysed as historical formations, subject to modification – as structures constituted through action, as much as action is constituted structurally.

In this connection Murdock rightly points to the usefulness of Bourdieu's conception of the 'habitus' as a way of grasping the articulation of the two dimensions of structure and action – as a matrix of dispositions and competences capable of generating and underwriting a wide variety of specific practices but where, as Murdock puts it, 'habituses are not habits. They do not entail the application of fixed rules and routines. Rather, they provide the basis for structured variations in the same way that jazz musicians improvise around a . . . theme' (Murdock 1989b: 243). At the same time, while Murdock stresses the positive aspects of Bourdieu's overall theory, he is rightly critical of the exclusive stress that Bourdieu lays on early family socialization as the sole source of cultural capital and competences. As Murdock notes, while we must recognize that people's initial socialization will play a key role in structuring their access to cultural codes, to see this process as necessarily irreversible is over-deterministic:

clearly if, in later life, someone joins . . . a . . . political party or . . . religious cult, they will have access to additional discourses with the potential to restructure their interpretative activities in powerful ways.

The 'prison house of language' may be a high-security installation, but escape is always possible.

(Murdock 245)

Corner's critique, unfortunately, seems to conflate two different issues: on the one hand the conceptual shift from a model of dominant ideology as a given structure to a processual model of hegemony (and the consequent interest in the micro aspect of macro-processes); and, on the other, the substantive reworking of the field under the impact of feminist theory and research, decentring the former principal concerns with class in favour of a concern with the articulation of structures of gender and class, especially in relation to the media's role in public/private interface. This certainly is a research agenda with a transformed concept of media power (rather different from that of classical Marxism, for example), but it is hardly a research agenda from which power has slipped. In so far as it is a perspective, as Corner puts it, which has 'revised downwards' notions of media power, it is one which takes on board the critique made by Abercrombie *et al.* (1984) of the excesses of the 'dominant ideology thesis' (but see also my critical comments on this position below). This, then, is to follow neither the Parsonian reading of Durkheim (attributing all signs of social stability to the 'conscience collective' or the 'value-system' of society) nor the Frankfurt School reading of Marx (with its neglect of the role of the 'dull compulsion of the economic', in Marx's phrase, and the sheer facticity of economic interdependence, in any society with a complex division of labour). To argue thus is to avoid over-emphasizing the role of ideology or, more prosaically, in Connell's (1985) phrase, to avoid 'blaming the meeja' for everything.

None the less, I do share Corner's concern that much recent work in this field is marred by a facile insistence on the polysemy of media products and by an undocumented presumption that forms of interpretative resistance are more widespread than subordination or the reproduction of dominant meanings (cf. Condit 1989, on the unfortunate tendency towards an over-drawn 'emphasis on the polysemous qualities of texts' in media studies). To follow that path, as Corner correctly notes, is to underestimate the force of textual determinacy in the construction of meaning from media products, and not only to romanticize the role of the reader improperly but to neglect all the evidence of the relatively low level of ambiguity, at some levels of meaning, of widespread systems of signification, such as those purveyed by the mass media. As Corner notes, to follow this primrose (and perhaps postmodern) path in giving such emphasis to the polysemic qualities of media messages, is to risk falling into a 'complacent relativism, by which the interpretive contribution of the audience is perceived to be of such a scale and range as to render the very idea of media power naive' (Corner 1991: 29).

Conversely, while taking many of the points raised by critics such as Corner with reference to the inherent problems and limitations of the 'preferred reading' model developed by Hall (1973a), I remain convinced that the model, while needing development and amendment in various respects, still offers the best alternative to a conception of media texts as equally 'open' to any and all interpretations (usually derived from Barthes 1972) which readers wish to make of them. While I would agree that Hall's original model tends to blur together questions of recognition, comprehension, interpretation and response which may ultimately need to be separated analytically, there is a considerable body of work in the sociology of reading and literacy (see Hoyles 1977) which would argue that, given the context-dependent mode of understanding which readers ordinarily employ, too radical a separation of these issues will leave us with a neat but unrealistic model of what readers do when they read a text. Further, while it is true that the preferred reading model was originally developed for the analysis of news and current affairs journalism, and is easiest to employ directly in the analysis of material of that type, it is not as difficult as some critics (including Corner 1991) would seem to suggest to apply it to other materials. Thus, for example, given the hierarchies of discourse routinely offered by fictional texts, usually centring around the point of view of one or more privileged character(s), it is clearly possible to transpose the model to the analysis of the classical realist text and its derivatives in the fictional realm (see p. 122 below).

The interventions of Brunsdon (1989) and Gripsrud (1989), cautioning against current tendencies entirely to dissolve the text into its readings can, with hindsight, be seen to have been foreshadowed by Counihan's critique (Counihan 1973) of Chaney (1972), who decried the usefulness of any analysis of the message in itself – on the grounds that the 'content is not meaningful in itself . . . [but] is only meaningful in its interaction with an audience'. As Counihan remarks, in the context of Chaney's relentless dissolution of the message into the audiences' perceptions, uses and manipulations of it, 'It is as if the assertion of the necessity for a formal analysis of media "texts" as a distinct region of communications research involved a radical denial of the inalienable rights of audiences to constitute all meaning' (Counihan 1973: 43). The analysis of the text or message remains, of course, a fundamental necessity, for the polysemy of the message is not without its own structure. Audiences do not see only what they want to see, since a message (or programme) is not simply a window on the world, but a construction. While the message is not an object with one real meaning, there are within it signifying mechanisms which promote certain meanings, even one privileged meaning, and suppress others: these are the directive closures encoded in the message. The message is capable of different interpretations depending on the context of association.

This was the point of the analytic procedure employed in the first part of the *Nationwide* project (see Brunsdon and Morley 1978), which was not designed to discover the 'real meaning' of the messages analysed, but simply to follow the 'directive closures' (in the form of headlines, high-status views, etc.) so as to reproduce the reading of the message achieved by operating within the dominant decoding framework. This is not to imply that this is the only reading possible: the analysis is, of necessity, interpretative; its significance ultimately was to be investigated by the subsequent empirical work examining how messages were 'read' and which sections of the audience did make this kind of reading of the message, rather than a 'negotiated' or 'oppositional' reading.

The 'new revisionism' and its critics

In a similar vein to Corner, Curran (1990) offers a highly critical account of what he describes as the 'new revisionism' in mass communications research on media audiences. In brief, his charge is that while 'this . . . "revisionism" . . . presents itself as original and innovative, as an emancipatory movement that is throwing off the shackles of tradition . . . [it] . . . is none of these things' (Curran 1990: 135), but rather amounts to 'old pluralist dishes being reheated and presented as new cuisine' (151). In Curran's view, 'revisionists' (such as myself) are presenting 'as innovation what is in reality a process of rediscovery' (146) and, as far as Curran is concerned, misrepresenting this 'revisionism' in 'assertive terms as an example of intellectual progress' in which 'those hitherto mired in error have been confounded and enlightened' (146) when, in fact the 'revisionists' are actually 'engaged . . . in an act of revivalism – reverting to the discredited wisdom of the past' (153), in so far as most of the claimed 'advances' achieved by this new work are clearly pre-dated and pre-figured, according to Curran, by earlier work within both the 'effects' and the 'uses and gratifications' traditions – of which the 'revisionists' are, in Curran's view, naively ignorant. To some extent, Curran's argument is also supported by Evans (1990), who claims that authors within the interpretivist tradition ('new revisionists', in Curran's terms) have tended to set up the faults of the earlier 'hypodermic effects' model of communications rather as a 'straw man', by contrast to which other positions would more easily seem sophisticated.

Curran's own principal tactic is to bolster his argument by quoting the work of hitherto neglected figures within the mainstream traditions of audience research who argue against any simple hypodermic theory of 'effects', or who stress issues such as the social setting of media reception, thus demonstrating that recent emphasis on such issues is no more than old wine in new bottles. There are two key problems with this argument: one a matter of historiography, concerning the status of history as *histoire* (or story), the other concerning the status of 20/20 vision-in-hindsight.

In the first case, Curran fails to address the issue, which has been central to much recent historical debate, and which was placed on the agenda some years ago by P. Wright (1985), among others, concerning the role of (any) history in the present. As Wright argues, the past is no simple thing to be referred to; rather we must attend to the crucial role played by different constructed narratives and invocations of the past, in contemporary cultural, political (or academic) debates – as legitimating this or that opposing view or strategy in the present. While I am happy to regard Curran's own analysis as an intervention (and a very interesting one at that) in a contemporary debate about how the future trajectory of audience research should be conceptualized, its central thrust is to mobilize his own version of history in support of a very particular set of claims as to how audience research should be conducted. This is simply to note that Curran's history is, inevitably, involved in doing something rather more than he claims; rather than simply 'setting the record straight' in the face of any 'breath-taking . . . caricature of the history of communications research' (Curran 1990: 146) produced by the 'revisionism' Curran decries, it is advancing a particular (and partly unacknowledged) agenda of its own, which equally can be accused of 'writing out' particular problems and issues from the agenda of future research. I will return to the blind spots in Curran's analysis below.

The second problem concerns hindsight. The history Curran offers is an informative one, alerting us to the achievements of scholars whose work has been unrecognized or neglected by many (myself included) thus far. However, my contention is that this is a particular history which could not have been written (by Curran or anyone else) fifteen years ago, before the impact of the 'new revisionism' (of which Curran is so critical) transformed our understanding of the field of audience research, and thus transformed our understanding of who and what was important in its history. I would argue that it is this transformation that has allowed a historian such as Curran to go back and re-read the history of communications research, in such a way as to give prominence to those whose work can now, with hindsight, be seen to have prefigured the work of these 'new revisionists'. The point is that it is only now, after the impact of 'revisionist' analyses, that the significance of this earlier work can be seen. Previously, much of it was perceived as marginal to the central trajectory of mainstream communications research. As Seiter *et al.* note, if the 'academic pendulum swings along the fine line between re-seeing and revisionism' (Seiter *et al.* 1989a: 14), then the work of 're-visioning' (or reconceptualizing, and always newly revising our perspectives), is central to the dynamic through which the field develops. In the nature of the case, it is difficult to accuse others of falsely imagining that history was simply that which led up to them, without, in the event, ending up in the unhappy position of making that claim (explicitly or implicitly) for one's own arguments.

According to Blumler, Gurevitch and Katz (1985: 257), the 'interpretivist focus on the role of the reader in the decoding process should be ringing bells with gratificationists . . . because . . . they are the most experienced in dealing with a multiplicity of responses'. Similarly, Rosengren claims that Radway's (1984b) work 'indirectly offers strong validation of the general soundness of uses and gratifications research', and he goes on to claim that 'in her way, Radway has reinvented . . . gratifications research' (Rosengren 1985: 278). As Evans (1990) notes, the first question, in this connection, is perhaps whether, rather than constituting evidence of a genuine unity between cultural studies and uses and gratifications perspectives, what we see here is in fact a misguided attempt to reduce interpretivist concepts to gratificationist terms. The second (and, as Schroder notes, rather embarrassing) question is 'why has it required a cultural studies scholar to excavate a lost sociological tradition?' (Schroder 1987: 13). The answer that Schroder offers, and with which I, for one, incline to agree, is that in spite of the tributes now paid by Curran and others to those who can, retrospectively, be identified as the forgotten 'pioneers' of qualitative media audience research, 'the fact remains that, until the 1980s, their qualitative work . . . [was] . . . the victim of a spiral of silence, because they attempted to study what mainstream sociology regarded as unresearchable, i.e. cultural meanings and interpretations' (ibid., 14).

There are a number of further substantive problems with Curran's formulation of the issues at stake. In the first instance, in setting up a simple polarity between 'Marxist' and 'Pluralist' perspectives, he unhelpfully blurs together the Gramscian and Althusserian perspectives within the Marxist tradition. His analysis replicates the confusions (in this respect) of Abercombie et al.'s (1978 and 1984) critique of the 'dominant ideology thesis' (see my comments above on the importance of the distinctions between Althusser and Gramsci with reference to the relationship between the analysis of micro- and macro-processes in media analyses). Further, Curran fails to grasp the significance of the encounter with semiology, within the cultural studies perspective, in transforming the concept of the message, away from a conveyor belt model of the transmission of content, towards one more fully informed by the insights of linguistics (notwithstanding the problems of formal semiotic models and the need to move beyond them to a social semiotics).

As I argue below, some of the early work of the American mass communications researchers (see Merton 1946) was highly sophisticated in many respects, and did begin to open up questions about the 'actual processes of persuasion' and the 'processes involved in resistance to persuasive arguments' (quoted in Morley 1980: 3) which can now be seen to have foreshadowed the later contributions of semiology in the close analysis of these issues. Thus Merton insisted on the need to interpret messages within the cultural contexts of their occurrence. However, subsequent work in that tradition largely failed to develop Merton's insights effectively. In this connection, Geertz has argued that the key problem for American communications researchers was that, despite their sophistication in other respects, they lacked anything more than the most rudimentary conception of the processes of symbolic communication. As a result, he argued:

> The links between the causes of ideology and its effects seem adventitious, because the connective element – the autonomous process of symbolic formulation – is passed over in virtual silence. Both interest theory and strain theory go directly from source analysis to consequence analysis without ever seriously examining ideologies as systems of interacting symbols, as patterns of interworking meanings. Themes are outlined, of course; among the content analysis they are even counted. But they are referred for elucidation not to other themes, not to any sort of semantic theory, but either backward to the effect they presumably mirror, or forward to the social reality they presumably distort. The problem of how ideologies transform sentiment into significance, and so make it socially available, is shortcircuited.
>
> (quoted in Hall 1974: 278–9)

It was precisely this issue, I would contend, that the encounter with semiology enabled cultural studies researchers to open up, and thus, long afterwards, to begin to advance Merton's original insights, which had been largely neglected in mainstream research.

Finally, it seems necessary to distinguish between the different traditions which Curran lumps together under the rubric of the 'new revisionism'. It is hardly incidental that Curran and Gurevitch's new edition of *Mass Communication and Society* (1991) is structured around a set of arguments concerning the hypothetical 'convergence' (see also Schroder 1987; Jensen and Rosengren 1990) of radical and mainstream traditions in media research. In the context of that volume, the post-structuralist work of scholars such as Ang and Hermes (1991) is implicitly recruited in support of an argument which, to put it crudely, ultimately claims that Foucault's main significance was to demonstrate that liberal-pluralists were right (or, at least, more right than the Marxists) all along about the 'dispersion' of power. In my view, and despite the problems of post-structuralist tendencies to regress towards a form of methodological individualism, to conflate these traditions is in the end unhelpful.

Curran is, however, right to point to the ambivalence of the Foucauldian legacy in recent media studies, in so far as the predominant (and rather partial) reading of Foucault has promoted a decentring of media research in which, as Curran puts it 'the role of the media is reduced to a succession of reader–text encounters in the context of a society which is analytically dissaggregated into a series of concrete instances . . . or in which power external to discourse is wholly evacuated' (Curran 1990: 140). As Curran rightly observes, such a perspective (in which power is seen as being not so much diffused as defused) is, in reality, not very different from that of the American liberal-pluralist tradition. However, while Curran's proclaimed target is the rather broad (if undefined) one of the 'new revisionism', the central focus of this critique seems to fall on a recent (and principally American) inflection of cultural studies, heavily influenced by the work of Fiske (cf. also Schudson 1987).

Towards a 'semiotic democracy'?

While Fiske's work has undoubtedly had the great value of introducing cultural studies to a whole generation of (principally American) students, Curran is correct, in my view, in pointing to the problems attendant on this particular version of cultural studies (see Fiske, 1987b). Recent reception studies which document audience autonomy and offer optimistic/redemptive readings of mainstream media texts have principally been invoked not simply as a challenge to a simple-minded effects model, but, rather, as in themselves documenting the total absence of media influence in the semiotic democracy of postmodern pluralism. The implicit valorization of audience pleasure in this work leads easily into a cultural relativism which, as Curran notes, is readily incorporated into a populist neo-liberal rhetoric which would abandon any concern with cultural values – or 'quality' television (see Brunsdon 1990b) – and functions to justify the positions of the deregulators who would destroy any version of public service broadcasting. As Seiter *et al.* state pithily, 'in our concern for audiences' pleasures . . . we run the risk of continually validating Hollywood's domination of the worldwide television market' (Seiter *et al.* 1989a: 5), which certainly would seem to be an odd destination for the trajectory of cultural studies media work.

As Curran (1990: 148) observes, Fiske's celebration of a 'semiotic democracy' in which people drawn from a vast shifting range of subcultures and groups construct their own meanings within an autonomous cultural economy is problematic in various respects, but not least because it is readily subsumable within a conservative ideology of sovereign consumer pluralism. To argue thus is by no means to deny the force of many of Fiske's insightful formulations into the complexities of the making and re-making of meanings in popular culture (cf. Seaman 1992 for a misunderstanding of Fiske's arguments). As I have argued elsewhere (Morley 1989), alongside Fiske's work, the work of Bennett and Woollacot (1987) and of Browne (1984) has usefully alerted us to the interdiscursive nature of textual meaning and to the difficulty of ever isolating, in any simple sense, a single text for analysis.

Grossberg has argued that 'not only is every media event mediated by other texts, but it's almost impossible to know what constitutes the bounded text which might be interpreted or which is actually consumed' (Grossberg 1987: 33). This is because the text does not occupy a fixed position, but is always mobilized, placed and articulated with other texts in different ways. However, it can be objected that this new emphasis upon intertextuality runs several risks, notably that contextual issues will overwhelm and overdetermine texts and their specificity. The question is whether, in following this route, we run the danger of arriving at a point in which the text is simply dissolved into its readings.

Fiske has called for a re-theorization of the televisual text, which would allow us to investigate its openness by mobilizing Barthes's distinction between 'work' and 'text'. Barthes argued that the work is the physical construct of signifiers, that it becomes a text only when read. The text, in this formulation, is never a fixed or stable thing, but is continually being recreated out of the work. Indeed, Fiske argues that 'there is no such thing as "the television audience" [cf. Hartley 1987] defined as an empirically accessible object . . . we have now collapsed the distinction between "text" and "audience" . . . There is no text, there is no audience, there are only the processes of viewing' (Fiske 1989: 56–7). None the less, curiously, in his analysis of television quiz shows, Fiske ends up reasserting the centrality of the text, explaining that he has found it necessary to make 'no empirical audience investigation' of the reasons for the popularity of such shows, because 'my theory of popularity . . . is one that is best arrived at by a study of the text itself' (Fiske 1984: 5).

In his discussion of the 'encoding/decoding' model, Fiske suggests that the 'value of the theory lies . . . in its shift away from the text and towards the reader as the site of meaning' and argues that the principal value of ethnographic methods of study is that they 'enable us to account for diversity' (Fiske 1987a: 63). The problems here are (a) that this reading of the encoding/decoding model omits its central stress on strategies of textual closure ('preferred readings' etc.); and (b) that the object of ethnographic study is in fact the discovery of regularities and patterns of behaviour, decoding and response, as much as it is the revelation (or celebration) of diversity. In this respect, I would agree with Ang that ethnography's critical edge does not only reside in 'discovering and validating diversity and difference . . . it can work more ambitiously towards an unravelling of the intricate intersections of the diverse and the homogeneous' (Ang 1990: 257).

Fiske tends to see the textual as the only site of closure, and to equate the social (the site of decoding) exclusively with flux and diversity. Again the problems are twofold. In the first instance, the social is also a site of closure – in so far as it is through social positioning that access to cultural codes (which can be mobilized in decodings) is regulated (cf. Corner 1991). In the second place, this attribution of negative (reactionary) values of fixity to the text, and the corresponding positive valuation of flux and diversity as the source of resistance ('the people still are uncomfortable, undisciplined, intransigent forces') is itself problematic. Behind this formulation lies a conceptual model which seems to be derived from a particular libertarian reading of Barthes's early essay 'Myth today' (Barthes 1972), in which ideology is defined as the (bad) process of the fixing (and reification) of (dominant) meanings, while (good) resistance is seen to lie essentially in the unfixing and destablizing of meanings. Curiously, and despite their obvious substantive differences, there are interesting parallels here with the problem of psychoanalytic theories of spectatorship.

One central problem with what Gledhill (1988) describes as the cine-psychoanalytic critique of the effects of the classical realist text – in producing an ideological sense of fixed and stable identity for the spectator – is that in its (usually implicit) celebration of flux and instability it naively abandons our necessary concern with the positive dimensions of the production of such identities. As Gledhill puts it:

> social out-groups seeking to identify themselves against dominant representations . . . need clearly articulated, recognisable and self-respecting self-images. To adopt a political position is of necessity to assume, for the moment, a consistent and answerable identity. The object of attack should not be identity as such, but its dominant construction as total, non-contradictory and unchanging.
>
> (Gledhill 1988: 72)

To argue thus is simply to recognize that the absence of a coherent sense of identity (whether at the individual level, as in the case of mental illness, or at the socio-cultural level, on the part of oppressed groups) is at least as problematic, in political terms, as is the ideological 'fixing' of such identities by dominant cultural forms. Many years ago sociologists routinely (if crudely) distinguished between social critics who could be described as 'integration-fearers' (clearly, the cine-psychoanalytic school are included here) and those better described as 'incoherence-fearers' (cf. Mann 1970). Any progressive cultural (or political) strategy must avoid the dangers of the Charybdis of incoherence as much as those of the Scylla of reification.

To return to the difficulties of Fiske's position, it is worth noting that Fiske extends his argument towards the idea of a 'readers liberation movement', involving a theory of audience reading which

> asserts the reader's right to make, out of the programme, the text that connects the discourses of the programme with the discourses through which he/she lives his/her social experience, and thus for programme,

society and reading subject to come together in an active, creative living
of culture the moment of reading.

(Fiske 1986: 207–8)

While I sympathize with this concern with 'readers' rights', I would
argue that the concept of 'rights' in this context is problematic, in so far as
it is perhaps less a question of the readers' rights to make out of a
programme whatever meaning they wish (which presumably involves
a moral or philosophical discourse concerning rights in general) than a
question of power – for example, the presence or absence of the power or
cultural resources necessary in order to make certain types of meaning,
which is, ultimately, an empirical question (cf. Gripsrud 1989, for a
further critique of the dangers of any model of 'reader's liberation' which
fails to deal with the social structuring of the distribution of cultural
competences).

In some of his recent writing, Fiske has turned to the work of de Certeau
(1984), and in particular de Certeau's concept of the 'tactics' of the weak in
poaching symbolic and material advantage in the interstices of dominant
structures and institutions controlled by the strategies of the powerful.
While de Certeau's work is evidently of great interest, the dangers of a
partial interpretation of that work, which over-stresses (if not romanti-
cizes) the element of popular resistance, have been clearly identified by,
among others, Frow (1991).

Evans (1990) rightly points to one other crucial development in what he
calls the 'interpretivist' tradition of audience research. Hall's original
formulation of the encoding/decoding model contained, as one of its central
features, the concept of the preferred reading (towards which the text
attempts to direct its reader), while acknowledging the possibility of alternative, negotiated or oppositional readings. As Evans notes, this model has
subsequently been quite transformed to the point where it is often maintained that the majority of audience members routinely 'modify or deflect'
any dominant ideology reflected in media content (cf. Fiske 1987a: 64).

Affirmative and 'redemptive' readings

Budd, Entman and Steinman (1990) argue that current audience research
now routinely assumes that 'people habitually use the content of dominant
media against itself, to empower themselves', so that, in their analysis, the
crucial 'message' of much contemporary American cultural studies media
work is an optimistic one: 'Whatever the message encoded, decoding
comes to the rescue. Media domination is weak and ineffectual, since the
people make their own meanings and pleasures'; or, put another way, 'we
don't need to worry about people watching several hours of TV a day,
consuming its images, ads and values. People are already critical, active

viewers and listeners, not cultural dopes manipulated by the media' (ibid., 170). While I would certainly not wish to return to any model of the audience as 'cultural dopes', the point Budd *et al.* make is a serious one, not least because, as they note, this 'affirmative' model does tend then to justify the neglect of all questions concerning the economic, political and ideological forces acting on the construction of texts (cf. Brunsdon 1989), on the (unfounded) assumption that reception is, somehow, the only stage of the communications process that matters in the end (cf. also Frith 1990). Apart from anything else, and at the risk of being whimsical, one might say that such an assumption does seem to be a curiously Christian one, in which the sins of the industry (or the message) are somehow seen to be redeemed in the 'after-life' of reception.

One crucial question concerns the significance that is subsequently given to often quite particular, ethnographic accounts of moments of cultural subversion in the process of media consumption or decoding. Thus, Budd *et al.* note that, in his account of the ways in which Aboriginal Australian children have been shown to reconstuct television narratives involving Blacks in such a way as to fit with and bolster their own self-conceptions, Fiske (1986) shows a worrying tendency to generalize radically from this (very particular) instance, so that, in his account, this type of alternative response, in quite particular circumstances, is decontextualized and then offered as a model for 'decoding' in general, so that, as Budd *et al.* put it, 'the part becomes the whole and the exception the rule' (see also Schudson 1987, quoted below).

It is in matters of this kind that some of Curran's (1976) earlier observations on the shortcomings of qualitative forms of media analysis are, in my view, borne out, in so far as the rejection of all forms of quantification (as a kind of methodological-ethical principle) precisely allow this kind of unguarded and unwarranted generalization. In a similar vein, Schroder argues:

> one of the tasks ahead will consist in conceptualising a method which makes it possible to incorporate and preserve qualitative data through a process of quantification, enabling the researcher to discern the demographic patterning of viewing responses, for instance the proportions of 'preferred' or 'aberrant' responses within demographic groups and in the general population.
>
> (Schroder 1987: 27)

Along the way, Budd *et al.* raise a number of other problems about what they characterize as the 'affirmative trend in American cultural studies' and the burgeoning tendency to find (and celebrate) traces of 'opposition' everywhere. As they note, even if instances of such readings can be identified, 'we still need to ask what difference [do they] make to relations of power? . . . Surely . . . watching television in itself can have an oppositional kick. But it does nothing outside itself' (Budd, Entmann and Steinman 1990: 176). In a similar vein, Jensen argues:

> oppositional decodings are not in themselves a manifestation of political power . . . the wider ramifications of opposition at the textual level depend on the social and political uses to which opposition may be put, in contexts beyond the relative privacy of media reception.
>
> (Jensen n.d.: 3)

The further problem here is that identified by Evans, who notes that 'intepretivists' often make overblown claims that their perspective, in itself, involves an empowering of the audience, a privileging of the reader which is in fact quite illusory. As Evans puts it, such phrases seem to suggest that a given scholarly approach can empower or privilege 'the people' simply by dint of an analytic characterization, whereas in reality 'as scholars, our own desire to have current ideological systems resisted may produce romanticised, even utopian visions of the people we study, enacting our wishes' (Evans 1990: 12). The point is well taken, and chimes with Frow's argument that we should beware of any tendency towards a kind of populist ventriloquism, in which there is an unacknowledged 'substitution of the voice of a middle-class intellectual for that of the users of popular culture' (Frow 1991: 60), or in which the latter are invoked as bit-part players, only to speak the script constructed and shaped (implicitly) by the analyst. As Ang (1990) notes, in some versions of cultural studies, the researcher is often presented as no longer a critical outsider but, rather, a fellow-participant, a conscious fan, giving voice to and celebrating consumer cultural democracy. The problem, as Ang goes on to argue, is that while 'audiences may be active, in myriad ways, in using and interpreting media . . . it would be utterly out of perspective to cheerfully equate "active" with "powerful"' (Ang 1990: 247).

The equivalence that Newcomb and Hirsch (1984: 69) assert between the producer and the consumer of messages, in so far as the television viewer 'matches the creator [of the programme] in the making of meanings', is in effect a facile one, and ignores de Certeau's (1984) distinction (see above) between the strategies of the powerful and the tactics of the weak (or, as Silverstone and I have argued, elsewhere (Morley and Silverstone 1990) the difference between having power over a text and having power over the agenda within which that text is constructed and presented). The power of viewers to reinterpret meanings is hardly equivalent to the discursive power of centralized media institutions to construct the texts which the viewer then interprets; to imagine otherwise is simply foolish.

While we should not fall back into any forum of simplistic textual determinacy, none the less we must also avoid the naive presumption that texts are completely open, like 'an imaginary shopping mall in which audience members could wander at will, selecting whatever suits them'

(Murdock 1989b: 36). By analogy, as Murdock notes, commenting on his research on the uses of home computers, most domestic users of such machines are still confined to software whose range of options has been designed by someone else:

> People playing adventure games on a home computer, ordering goods from a television shopping show, or responding to an electronic opinion poll certainly have choices, but they are carefully managed. Once again the crucial question to ask is not simply 'What kinds of pleasures do these technologies offer?' but 'Who has the power to control the terms on which interaction takes place?'.
>
> (Murdock *et al.* 1989: 234)

Identification, difference and the position of the analyst

The social identities of academic researchers and their ('our'?) television-viewing subjects, are not only different, but differently valued, and those differences are in play both in the interviewing process and in subsequent editing work that the researcher does in preparing the 'data' for presentation. As Seiter notes, self-reflexively, of her own practice in writing up an interview for publication, the researcher does extensive editing, attributes feelings and intentions to their subjects and bolsters generalizations with the 'authenticity' of 'the real empirical subject' (Seiter 1990: 68–9).

If, as Fiske (1990: 91) notes, it is sometimes possible for the ethnographer to become part of the community of viewers or readers being researched, and to participate in some of their cultural experiences, the dangers of too easy an identification of researcher and researched yet remain. If television audience research offers a particular fascination, in so far as it seems to provide access to the 'other' (the working-class, the female or Black audience, for example), it will not suffice to imagine ourselves to be part of this other audience, or simply to identify with this 'other' and adopt the position of the enthusiastic fan, in so far as this manoeuvre merely obscures the researcher's dominant relation to their subjects in terms of access to cultural capital (cf. Seiter 1990: 69; cf. also Gripsrud 1989).

As Schudson puts it, 'the fact that an anthropologist or literary critic (who is trained for that task) can read an item of popular culture as indexical or as a meta-commentary on cultural forms (*pace* Geertz and Turner) does not mean that all participants in the culture (or the anthropologist or critic at other times, in other roles) will necessarily read the texts that way' (Schudson 1987: 64). He goes on to argue that we should resist the temptation inadvertently to romanticize the semiotic process itself, and to analyse it outside the overall contexts of social relations of power. The case against this kind of formalist semiotics was made cogently by Hall some years ago. He argued:

> In so far as ideologies . . . function like a language they exhibit an absolutely privileged 'formal mode of appearance', which it has been semiology's great contribution to specify. In so far as ideologies arise in the mediate social practices, however, they cannot be structured by the formal rules of their production alone, but by their position within a social formation.
>
> (Hall 1973b: 5)

A purely formal analysis of the codes which made signification possible is not adequate. For, as Dreitzel argues,

> studies of communicative behaviour should be open to the fact that rules of interpretation are not invariant essences of the social life-world, but are themselves subject to other social processes . . . [and] . . . the social world is structured not only by language but also by the modes and forces of material production and by the systems of domination.
>
> (Dreitzel 1972: 16–17)

We cannot study language simply as a closed system, a technical instrument of communication: it is inevitably situated in the whole field of socio-political relations within which communication occurs. It was from this perspective that Iain Chambers criticized Barthes and his more formalist disciples:

> by putting between brackets, or simply failing to acknowledge, the material conditions of the practices they examine, and treating them and society solely as a sign system, structuralism and semiotics have remained caught in the very ideology they claim to have exposed
>
> (Chambers 1974: 50)

He remarked then,

> Codes, like ideas, do not drop from the skies, they arise within the material practices of production. However, Barthes reduces that production to a single moment in the process: the Text; and turns that moment into a self-reflexive totality divorced from its material existence.
>
> (ibid., 52)

Popular audiences and cultural criticism

As Schudson notes, while 'it is right to observe that audiences do not absorb culture like sponges', in so far as 'the popular audience can be attentive, reflective and constructive of culture . . . this is not to suppose that the popular audience is always critical or creative in its responses, any more than élite audience are' (Schudson 1987: 64), for these matters are both variable and dependent on the social context in which the relevant semiotic codes are operative. Moreover, it is perfectly possible that 'very critical and searching readers of fiction may let music wash right over them at a concert . . . people who are discriminating consumers of theatre may rely on "name brands" for dance' (ibid., 64–5).

There is also the question of what bearing any of these observations should have on ultimate questions of cultural value – and the conclusion should not necessarily be a relativist one. As Schudson puts it, 'the fact that popular audiences respond actively to the materials of mass culture is important to recognise and understand, but it is not a fact that should encourage us to accept mass culture as it stands'. The fact that different sub-groups in the population respond in different ways to common cultural objects or have developed refined critical temperaments, with regard to some local or provincial cultural form unrecognized by elites, is important to understand and should lead us to recognize a wide variety of connoisseurships and a plurality of educational forms that lead to them, 'but this is not . . . to admit all cultural forms equal, all interpretations valid, all interpretative communities self-contained and beyond criticism' (Schudson 1987: 66).

In this connection Modleski has also argued that we face a danger of collusion between mass-culture critics and consumer society. Modleski's argument is that:

> the insight that audiences are not completely manipulated, but may appropriate mass cultural artefacts for their own purposes, has been carried so far that it would seem that mass culture is no longer a problem for some Marxist critics . . . . If the problem with some of the work of the Frankfurt School was that its members were too far outside the culture they examined, critics today seem to have the opposite problem: immersed in their culture, half in love with their subject, they sometimes seem unable to achieve the proper critical distance from it. As a result, they may unwittingly wind up writing apologies for mass culture and embracing its ideology.
>
> (Modleski 1986: 11)

Modleski claims that the stress on the active role of the audience/consumer has been carried too far. However, she is also concerned that the very activity of studying audiences may somehow turn out to be a form of collaboration with the (mass culture) industry. More fundamentally, she quotes, with approval, Terry Eagleton's comments to the effect that a socialist criticism 'is not primarily concerned with the consumer's revolution. Its task is to take over the means of production' (quoted in Modleski 1986: 12).

It seems that, from Modleski's point of view, empirical methods for the study of audiences are assumed to be tainted, simply because many of them have been (and are) used within the realms of commercial market research. Moreover, in her use of the quotation from Eagleton, she finally has recourse to a traditional mode of classical Marxist analysis, the weakness of which is precisely its blindspot in relation to issues of consumption – and, indeed, its tendency to prioritize the study of production to the exclusion of the study of all other levels of the social formation. The problem is that production is only brought to fruition in the spheres of circulation and exchange; to that extent, the study of consumption is, I would argue, essential to a full understanding of production (cf. Marx 1973).

Modleski's reading of the *Nationwide* research is mainly concerned to raise methodological questions that might 'temper the optimism with which Morley's work is imbued' (Modleski 1990: 38). The methodological questions she raises are discussed below (Chapter 8). My own concern here is with the function of methodological critiques of empirical work in justifying, by contrast, the worst forms of introspection and speculative criticism, in which the analyst's own reading of a given text is, without recourse to any empirical investigation, simply projected on to the audience category which he or she takes themselves to 'represent'. My further interest lies in determining whence Modleski derives the 'optimism' with which she sees the *Nationwide* text as imbued. Not being, by nature, an optimist, I can only assume that Modleski's own predilections are so pessimistic as to regard the kind of limited evidence of decoding variations adduced in the *Nationwide* work as grounds for surprise; as if such empirical variations, in themselves, represented evidence of anything more than the fact that the hegemonic process is always, necessarily, insecure and incomplete. That the *Nationwide* project offers counter-evidence to a very simple-minded dominant ideology thesis I would readily agree; but if that makes me an optimist, then I think Modleski and I must be dreading quite different things.

I would argue that the critical (or political) judgement which we might wish to make on the popularity of any commercial product is a quite different matter from the need to understand its popularity. The functioning of taste, and indeed of ideology, has to be understood as a process in which the commercial world succeeds in producing objects, programmes (and consumer goods) which do connect with the lived desires of popular audiences (cf. Miller 1988 and Fiske, *passim*). To fail to understand exactly how this works is, in my own view, not only academically retrograde but also politically suicidal. To argue thus is by no means necessarily to fall into the trap identified by Williamson, among others, who warns against the temptations of an uncritical celebration of popular culture, which operates with 'a crude sort of logic that runs . . . the people/the masses/ordinary working class consumers . . . are "good" (i.e. not stupid); these people like TV/fashionable clothes/consuming . . . etc. therefore those things are "good"' (Williamson 1986: 15). As Williamson notes, it is one thing for academics to make 'redemptive' readings of items of popular culture, from their privileged position, in which they have access to a number of codes and competences, at different levels of the established hierarchies of cultural taste, but this is a poor basis for a generalized account of consumption. Williamson's argument, in effect, replicates that of Bernstein, who claims that while the middle classes may have access to both elaborated and restricted codes (in his terms), which they choose to operationalize in different contexts, the working class only has access to the restricted code. Williamson's point, in a parallel sense, is that while the middle-class analyst of popular culture is likely to have access to a variety of cultural forms, 'all this is very different for people for whom it [popular culture] is their only culture' (Williamson 1986: 14).

Certainly, I would agree with Murdock (1989b) that the celebration of audience creativity and pleasure can all too easily collude with a system of media power which actually excludes or marginalizes most alternative or oppositional voices and perspectives. As Murdock argues, 'because popular programmes . . . offer a variety of pleasures and can be interpreted in different ways, it does not follow . . . that attempts to maximise the diversity of representations and cultural forms within the system are redundant' (Murdock 1989b: 229).

However, it remains necessary to analyse and to understand the pleasures that popular culture offers its consumers if we are to understand how hegemony operates through the processes of commercial popular culture. It is clearly inadequate to conceive the relationship between the hegemonic and the popular in terms of mutual exteriority. As Martin-Barbero argues, 'the hegemonic does not dominate us from without, but rather penetrates us' and the popular should not be identified with a corresponding form of intrinsic or spontaneous resistance. Rather, the question is how to understand the 'texture of hegemony/subalternity, the interlacing of resistance and submission, opposition and complicity' (Martin-Barbero 1988: 462). For me, it is in this context that Foucault's (1980) strictures on the necessity of understanding systems of power as being not so much imposed from above as irrigated from below have their pertinence.

Polysemy and its limits

Anderson and Avery (1988: 362) argue that interpretative research is 'distinguished by its move to empower the audience', and Barkin and Gurevitch (1987: 18) describe television as 'an empty vessel that can be all things to all people'. The problem is that these kind of interpretative studies often improperly privilege audience activity, as Carragee puts it, 'over both the production processes that structure media content and the textual properties of that content . . . [failing] to place media audiences within their proper contexts' (Carragee 1990: 84) and largely ignoring the organizational and economic factors that influence media texts, reducing them to autonomous signifying systems cut off from their origins in organizational routines and procedures.

More generally, much of this work, given its (often unacknowledged) roots in phenomenology and symbolic interactionism, can be argued to fail to grasp the significance of the institutional forces which shape the subjectivities, interpretative communities or values which are adduced as the explanation of different individual (or collective) decodings, without proper reference to the connections between these phenomena and their own historical and structural determinations. In Bernstein's terms, to attend to these matters is to do no more than is necessary in order properly to recognize the mediation of groups and classes and 'the role of history and the sedimentation of past experiences in shaping how an individual constitutes his social world' (Bernstein 1978: 16) – and thus how he or she is likely to decode media material. Thus, one of the key problems with Liebes and Katz's much-cited study of *Dallas* (1991) concerns the way in which they mobilize a rather uninterrogated concept of their respondents' 'cultural values' – implicitly derived from their membership of interpretative (cultural) communities – as the explanation of the differential decodings generated in their research. In this connection, as Barrington-Moore argued,

> cultural values do not descend from heaven to influence the course of history. They are abstractions by an observer, based on the observation of certain similarities in the way groups of people behave, either in different situations, over time, or both. Even though one can often make accurate predictions about the way groups and individuals will behave over short periods of time, on the basis of such abstractions, as such they do not explain the behaviour.
>
> (Barrington-Moore 1967: 486)

As he observes, the claim to explain (viewing or any other form of) behaviour by simple reference to the existence of different cultural values is to short-circuit the analysis, unless we also offer an account of the social origins of those 'values' themselves.

To transpose the argument to another context – that of the role of cultural values or cultural codes in explaining the educational success or failure of children from different social backgrounds – if we notice that working-cass children have a set of negative predispositions towards the school (Bernstein 1971; Rosen 1972; Keddie 1973; Willis 1978), such as self-depreciation, devaluation of the school and its sanctions, a resigned attitude to failure, and that if they are the carriers of certain cultural traditions which make them hostile to the school and result in their virtual self-elimination from the education system, then the further problem is to

determine out of what past and present experience these cultural values
and traditions arise and maintain themselves.

Similarly, as Carragee notes, much recent audience work has

> failed to place media texts and media audiences within meaningful
> historical, social and cultural contexts, [and] while properly emphasising
> the significance of understanding audience decodings of media mess-
> ages, interpretative researchers have neglected the contexts and press-
> ures that influence these intepretations. As a result, they fail to explore
> troubling questions relating to political and social power . . . [problems
> which] . . . include the failure to address media texts as products of
> organisations, the scant attention devoted to the texts' properties and
> structure [and] the often unsupported characterisation of media texts as
> polysemic.
>
> (Carragee 1990: 87)

In relation to the last point, as Carragee notes, at the very least this
'polysemy' must be demonstrated, rather than assumed, and its range, in
the case of different types and genres of texts, consumed in different
circumstances, needs to be much more clearly specified. Condit (1989)
suggests that the term 'polyvalence' (which she defines as occurring 'when
audience members share understandings of the denotation of a text, but
disagree about the value of these denotations to such a degree that they
produce notably different interpretations') may, on the whole, be more
useful and apt in accounting for variable decodings of a given message than
the more widely used concept of 'polysemy', in so far as, she argues, in
many cases, 'it is not a multiplicity or instability of textual meanings, but
rather a difference in audience evaluations of shared denotations, that best
account for . . . viewers' discrepant interpretations' (Condit 1989: 106–7).
In this respect one of the key problems with Liebes and Katz's (1991)
analysis of cultural variation in decodings of *Dallas* is their apparent
uncertainty as to whether it is the programme or its elements that are
'polysemic' (or perhaps 'polyvalent'), and as to whether the 'openness' of
meaning they identify in their study is a characteristic of the programme, of
the story or of the audience's responses (for a fuller analysis, see Morley
1991).

Evans (1990) rightly argues that 'when we are presented with an example
of a "resistant" (or "oppositional") reading, we must ask: what is being
resisted?' – in so far as it is only against the backdrop of some conception of
a dominant ideology or set of meanings, however conceived, that any
notion of 'resistance' or 'opposition' makes sense. However, in many
analyses it is in fact quite unclear what an 'oppositional reading' actually
consists in. In his discussion of Fiske's much-cited example of the readings
of Madonna made by teenage girls (Fiske 1987b), Evans raises an interest-

ing point of logic, concerning the very definition of what constitutes an oppositional reading. As he puts it,

> without very careful contextualisation, any given reader's variation from other readers (or from what the analyst expects) cannot be labelled as anything but variation. If a particular cultural group, say adolescents, is typified by rebelliousness, then it would be sociologically inconsistent to label a rebellious adolescent reading as oppositional; indeed, given this contextualisation, it would be the non-rebellious response that would be resistant.
>
> (Evans 1990: 159)

To transpose the argument once more to a different context, an example of the complexity of these matters is given by Bassett and Wiebe (1991), who offer the example of a single-parent household, where the mother, a committed feminist, was in the habit of watching *Blind Date* on television with her adolescent daughters, and felt compelled to give a running commentary on the patriarchal and sexist nature of the programme – much to the chagrin of her daughters, who felt that their mother's critical commentary rather spoiled their enjoyment of the programme. Quite apart from the evident psychic complexity of the dynamics of this situation, it is a nice point as to what, in this instance, then constitutes the dominant discourse, or the preferred reading, and what constitutes an oppositional reading or moment of 'resistance', and to what.

Carragee is right to be anxious about the burgeoning tendency to romanticize and sentimentalize media audiences as 'semiological guerillas', consistently producing oppositional readings, without reference to the various ways in which such readings always have to operate against the delimiting forces of the 'culture industry'. To conceive of audiences as composed of 'free-floating ahistorical actors . . . busily engaged in the social construction of realities' is indeed to ignore 'the textual, historical and material influences on audience interactions with the media', because, as Carragee notes, paraphrasing Marx, if media audiences are engaged in the construction of meanings, 'their constructions are set within and, in part, determined by wider pressures and contexts' (Carragee 1990: 92).

The politics of ethnographic research

In his comments on the work on the *Household Uses of Information and Communication Technology* which Roger Silverstone and I were engaged in at Brunel University (see Part V below), Corner (1991) identifies what he sees as a major problem in the shift from the emphasis (see Part II below, on the *Nationwide* study) on the interpretation of single media texts, to the emphasis on the constitutive role of the contexts and settings of media use. The problem, in Corner's view, is the risk that any strong theory of context-dependency runs: 'What do you include in context and where does it stop?' (Corner 1991: 23). While I would entirely agree with Corner's stricture that 'an understanding of the scale and subtlety of the "life-worlds" within which acts of viewing are set must inform but cannot replace attention to these' (26) and indeed would agree with his criticism of recent tendencies to fetishize the strengths of ethnographic research into context, I would reject the polarity that Corner's argument sets up between this type of ethnographic work and the primary concern with media power, which is the fulcrum of his own argument. For my part, I would argue that this work is of value precisely in so far as it can inform our understanding of media power as it operates in the micro-contexts of consumption – without divorcing those issues from those of macro-structural processes. If micro-studies alone suffer from the 'So what?' problem, if they just pile up an endless set of ethnographic descriptions, then, equally, any theory of hegemony which is not grounded in an adequate analysis of the process of consumption will always tend to be so over-schematic as to be ultimately of little use (cf. Chapter 13 below).

Carragee (1990), in parallel with Corner, criticizes some of the recent work which has focused on the domestic consumption of mass-media products, arguing that this focus on the domestic has often been rather limited in scope and has largely failed to locate the family within any broader social context. As he rightly notes, 'notwithstanding Lull's characterisation of the family as a "private social unit" (Lull 1980: 199), families are embedded in social and political environments that inform their interaction and link their members to broader collectivities' (Carragee 1990: 89). It is precisely for this reason that I have attempted to frame the analyses below of *Family Television* and of the *Household Uses of Information and Communication Technology* within a broader framework of the role of various media in articulating the private and public spheres, which (hopefully) allows us to articulate these micro-analyses to broader perspectives on macro-social issues of politics, power and culture.

It is in this context that we should heed Foucault's injunction: 'A whole history remains to be written of *spaces* – which would at the same time be the history of *powers* . . . from the great strategies of geopolitics to the little tactics of the habitat' (Foucault 1980: 149). I have, with Kevin Robins, elsewhere (see Morley and Robins 1989, 1990 and 1992) begun an exploration of the issues at stake once we try to think of communications processes within the terms of a postmodern geography (cf. Harvey 1989; Soja 1989; Massey 1991b) and once we begin to consider the role of communications in the ongoing construction and reconstruction of social spaces and social relations.

The central point, for my present purposes, concerns the fact that media industries are implicated in these socio-spatial processes in significant and distinctive ways. Thus, as Robins argues, 'issues around the politics of communication converge with the politics of space and place: questions of communication are also about the nature and scope of community' (Robins 1989: 146). The further point is that such theoretical work as has begun to take on board these questions has done so at a very abstracted level, principally in the context of international geopolitics. However, the force of Foucault's remarks, quoted above, is, of course, to remind us that the 'geographical imagination' and its refocusing of the relation of communications and geography, needs to be applied, as he puts it, to the 'little tactics of the habitat' (cf. Moores 1988) every bit as much as to the 'great strategies of geopolitics'. If one of the central functions of communications systems is to articulate different spaces (the public and the private, the national and the international) and, necessarily, in so doing to transgress boundaries (whether the boundary around the domestic household, or that around the nation) then our analytical framework must be capable of being applied at both the micro- and the macro-level. Such is the ambition, if not the achievement, of the perspectives offered in the essays that follow.

Part I

Theoretical frameworks

Chapter 1

Television audience research:
a critical history

It is not my purpose to provide an exhaustive account of mainstream sociological research in mass communications. I do, however, offer a resumé of the main trends and of the different emphases within that broad research strategy, essentially for two reasons: first, because my own work has been framed by a theoretical perspective which represents, at many points, a different research paradigm from that which has dominated the field to date; second, because there are points where this approach connects with certain important 'breaks' in that previous body of work, or else attempts to develop, in a different theoretical framework, lines of enquiry which mainstream research opened up but did not follow through.

Mainstream research can be said to have been dominated by one basic conceptual paradigm, constructed in response to the 'pessimistic mass society thesis' elaborated by the Frankfurt School. That thesis reflected the breakdown of modern German society into Fascism, a breakdown which was attributed, in part, to the loosening of traditional ties and structures and seen as leaving people atomized and exposed to external influences, especially to the pressure of the mass propaganda of powerful leaders, the most effective agency of which was the mass media. This 'pessimistic mass society thesis' stressed the conservative and reconciliatory role of 'mass culture' for the audience. Mass culture suppressed 'potentialities' and denied awareness of contradictions in a 'one-dimensional world'; only art, in fictional and dramatic form, could preserve the qualities of negation and transcendence.

Implicit here was a 'hypodermic' model of the media, which were seen as having the power to 'inject' a repressive ideology directly into the consciousness of the masses. Katz and Lazarsfeld, writing of this thesis, noted:

> The image of the mass communication process entertained by researchers had been, firstly, one of 'an atomistic mass' of millions of readers, listeners and movie-goers, prepared to receive the message; and secondly . . . every Message [was conceived of] as a direct and powerful stimulus to action which would elicit immediate response.
>
> (Katz and Lazarsfeld 1955: 16)

The emigration of the leading members of the Frankfurt School (Adorno, Marcuse, Horkheimer) to America during the 1930s led to the development of a specifically 'American' school of research in the forties and fifties. The Frankfurt School's 'pessimistic' thesis, of the link between 'mass society' and Fascism, and the role of the media in cementing it, proved unacceptable to American researchers. The 'pessimistic' thesis proposed, they argued, too direct and unmediated an impact by the media on their audiences; it took too far the thesis that all intermediary social structures between leaders/media and the masses had broken down; it didn't accurately reflect the pluralistic nature of American society; it was – to put it shortly – sociologically naive. Clearly, the media had social effects; these must be examined, researched. But, equally clearly, these effects were neither all-powerful, simple nor even direct. The nature of this complexity and indirectness too had to be demonstrated and researched. Thus, in reaction to the Frankfurt School's predilection for critical social theory and qualitative and philosophical analysis, the American re-searchers developed what began as a quantitative and positivist method-ology for empirical radio audience research into the 'sociology of mass persuasion'.

It must be noted that both the 'optimistic' and the 'pessimistic' para-digms embodied a shared implicit theory of the dimensions of power and influence through which the powerful (leaders and communicators) were connected to the powerless (ordinary people, audiences). Broadly speaking, operating within this paradigm, the different styles and strategies of research may then be characterized as a series of oscil-lations between two different, sometimes opposed, points in this chain of communication and command: on the one hand, message-based studies, which moved from an analysis of the content of messages to their effects on audiences; and, on the other, audience-based studies, which focused on the social characteristics, environment and, sub-sequently, needs which audiences derived from, or brought to, the message.

Many of the most characteristic developments within this paradigm have consisted either of refinements in the way in which the message/effect link has been conceptualized and studied, or of developments in the ways in which the audience and its needs have been examined. Research following the first strategy (message/effects) has been, until recently, predominantly behaviourist in general orientation: how the behaviour of audiences re-flects the influences on them of the messages they receive. When a concern with cognitive factors was introduced into the research, it modified without replacing this behavioural orientation: messages could be seen to have effects only if a change of mind was followed by a change in behaviour (e.g. advertising campaigns leading to a change in commodity choices). Research of the second type (audience-based) has been largely structural–

functional in orientation, focusing on the social characteristics of different audiences, reflecting their different degrees of 'openness' to the messages they received. When a cognitive element was introduced here, it modified without replacing this functional perspective: differences in audience response were related to differences in individual needs and 'uses'.

We will look in a moment at the diverse strategies through which this basic conceptual paradigm was developed in mainstream research. It is not until recently that a conceptual break with this paradigm has been mounted in the research field, one which has attempted to grasp communication in terms neither of societal functions nor of behavioural effects, but in terms of social meanings. This latter work is described here as the 'interpretative' as against the more dominant 'normative' paradigm, and it does constitute a significant break with the traditional mainstream approach. My own approach shares more with the 'interpretative' than with the traditional paradigm, but I wish to offer a critique, and to propose a departure from, *both* the 'normative' and the 'interpretative' paradigm as currently practised.

The 'normative' paradigm

Post-war American mass-communications research made a three-dimensional critique of the pessimistic mass society thesis: refuting the arguments that informal communication played only a minor role in modern society, that the audience was a mass in the simple sense of an aggregation of socially atomized individuals, and that it was possible to equate directly content and effect.

In an early work which was conceptually highly sophisticated, Robert Merton (1946) first advanced this challenge with his case study (*Mass Persuasion*) of the Kate Smith war bond broadcasts in America. Though this work was occasionally referred to in later programmatic reviews of the field, the seminal leads it offered have never been fully followed through. Merton argued that research had previously been concerned almost wholly with the 'content rather than the effects of propaganda'. Merton granted that this work had delivered much that had been of use, in so far as it had focused on the 'appeals and rhetorical devices, the stereotypes and emotive language which made up the propaganda material'. But the 'actual processes of persuasion' had gone unexamined, and as a consequence the 'effect' of the materials studied had typically been assumed or inferred, particularly by those who were concerned with the malevolent effect of 'violent' content. Merton challenged this exclusive reliance on inference from content to predicted effects.

This early work of Merton is singular in several respects, not least for the attempt it made to connect together the analysis of the message with the analysis of its effects. Social psychology had pointed to 'trigger phrases which suggest to us values we desire to realise'. But, Merton asked, 'Which trigger phrases prove persuasive and which do not? Further, which people are persuaded and which are not? And what are the processes involved in such persuasion and in resistance to persuasive arguments?'. To answer these questions Merton correctly argued that we had to 'analyse both the content of propaganda and the responses of the audience. The analysis of content . . . gives us clues to what might be effective in it. The analysis of responses to it enables us to check those clues'. Merton thus retained the notion that the message played a determining role for the character of the responses that were recorded, but argued against the notion that this was the only determination and that it connected to response in a simple cause-and-effect relationship; indeed, he insisted that the message 'cannot adequately be interpreted if it is severed from the cultural context in which it occurred'.

Merton's criticisms did not lead to any widespread reforms in the way in which messages were analysed as such. Instead, by a kind of reversal, it opened the road to an almost exclusive preoccupation with receivers and reception situations. The emphasis shifted to the consideration of small groups and opinion leaders, an emphasis first developed in Merton's own work on 'influentials' and 'reference groups', and later by Katz and Lazarsfeld. Like Merton, they rejected the notion that influence flowed directly from the media to the individual; indeed, in *Personal Influence* (1955) they developed the notions of a 'two-step flow of communication' and of the importance of 'opinion leaders' within the framework of implications raised by small-group research. From several studies in this area it had become obvious, according to Katz and Lazarsfeld, that 'the influence of mass media are not only paralleled by the influence of people . . . [but also] . . . refracted by the personal environment of the ultimate consumer'.

The 'hypodermic model' – of the straight, unmediated effect of the message – was decisively rejected in the wake of this 'rediscovery of the primary group' and its role in determining the individual's response to communication. In *The People's Choice* (Lazarsfeld *et al.* 1944) it was argued that there was little evidence of people changing their political behaviour as a result of the influence of the media: the group was seen to form a 'protective screen' around the individual. This was the background against which Klapper (1960) summed up: 'persuasive communications function far more frequently as an agent of reinforcement than as an agent of change . . . reinforcement, or at least constancy of opinion, is typically found to be the dominant effect'.

From 'effects' to 'functions' . . . and back again

The work outlined above, especially that of Merton, marks a watershed in the field. I have discussed it in some detail because, though there have been many subsequent initiatives in the field, they have largely neglected the possible points of development which this early work touched on.

The intervening period is, in many ways, both more dismal and less fruitful for our purposes. The analysis of content became more quantitative, in the effort to tailor the description of vast amounts of 'message material' for the purposes of effects analysis. The dominant conception of the message here was that of a simple 'manifest' message, conceived on the model of the presidential or advertising campaign, and the analysis of its content tended to be reduced, in Berelson's (1952) memorable phrase, to the 'quantitative description of the manifest content of communication'. The complexity of Merton's Kate Smith study had altogether disappeared. Similarly, the study of 'effects' was made both more quantitative and more routine. In this climate Berelson and others predicted the end of the road for mass-communications research.

A variety of new perspectives was suggested, but the more prominent were based on the 'social systems' approach and its cousin, 'functional analysis' (Riley and Riley, 1959), concerning themselves with the general functions of the media for the society as a whole (see R. Wright's (1960) attempt to draw up a 'functional inventory'). A different thread of the functionalist approach was more concerned with the subjective motives and interpretations of individual users. In this connection Katz (1959) argued that the approach crucially assumed that 'even the most potent of mass media content cannot ordinarily influence an individual who has no "use" for it in the social and psychological context in which he lives. The "uses" approach assumes that people's values, their interests . . . associations . . . social roles, are pre-potent, and that people selectively fashion what they see and hear'. This strand of the research work, of course, re-emerged in the work of the British 'uses and gratifications' approach, and was hailed, after its long submergence, as the road forward for mass-communications research.

These various functionalist approaches were promulgated as an alternative to the 'effects' orientation; none the less, a concern for effects remained, not least among media critics and the general public. This concern with the harmful effects or 'dysfunctions' of the media was developed in a spate of laboratory-based social-psychological studies which, in fact, followed this functionalist interlude. This, rather than the attempt to operationalize either of the competing functionalist models, was the approach that dominated mass-media research in the 1960s: the attempt to pin down, by way of stimulus-response, imitation and learning-theory psychology approaches, applied under laboratory conditions, the small but quantifiable effects which had survived the optimistic critique.

Bandura (1961) and Berkowitz (1962) were among the foremost exponents of this style of research, with their focus on the message as a simple, visual stimulus to imitation or 'acting-out', and their attention to the consequences, in terms of violent behaviour and delinquency, of the individual's exposure to media portrayals of violence of 'filmed aggressive role models'. Halloran's study of television and violence in this country took its point of departure from this body of work.

During the mid- to late sixties research on the effects of television portrayals of violence was revitalized and its focus altered, in the face of the student rebellion and rioting by Blacks in the slum ghettoes of America (see *National Commission on Causes and Prevention of Violence: the Surgeon-General's Report*). Many of the researchers and representatives of the state who were involved in this work, in their concluding remarks suggested that television was not a principal cause of violence but, rather, a contributing factor. They acknowledged, as did the authors of the National Commission Report, that 'television, of course, operates in social settings and its effects are undoubtedly mitigated by other social influences'. But despite this gesture to mitigating or intervening social influences, the conviction remained that a medium saturated with violence must have some direct effects. The problem was that researchers operating within the mainstream paradigm still could not form any decisive conclusions about the impact of the media. The intense controversy following the attempt of the Surgeon-General to quantify a 'measurable effect' of media violence on the public indicated how controversial and inconclusive the attempt to 'prove' direct behavioural effect remained.

The interpretative paradigm

In the same period, a revised sociological perspective was beginning to make inroads on communications research. What had always been assumed was a shared and stable system of values among all the members of a society; this was precisely what the 'interpretative' paradigm put into question, by its assertion that the meaning of a particular action could not be taken for granted, but must be seen as problematic for the actors involved. Interaction was thus conceptualized as a process of interpretation and of 'mutual typification' by and of the actors involved in a given situation.

The advances made with the advent of this paradigm were to be found in its emphasis on the role of language and symbols, everyday communication, the interpretation of action, and an emphasis on the process of 'making sense' in interaction. However, the development of the interpretative paradigm in its ethno-methodological form (which turned the 'normative' paradigm on its head) revealed its weaknesses. Whereas the normative approach had focused individual actions exclusively as the reproduction of shared stable norms, the interpretative model, in its ethno-methodological form, conceived each interaction as the 'production' anew of reality. The problem here was often that although ethno-methodology could shed an interesting light on micro-processes of interpersonal communications, this was disconnected from any notion of institutional power or of structural relations of class and politics.

Aspects of the interactionist perspective were later taken over by the Centre for Mass Communications Research at Leicester University, and the terms in which its director, James Halloran, discussed the social effects of television gave some idea of its distance from the normative paradigm; he spoke of the 'trend away from . . . the emphasis on the viewer as tabula-rasa . . . just waiting to soak up all that is beamed at him. Now we think in terms of interaction or exchange between the medium and audience, and it is recognised that the viewer approaches every viewing situation with a complicated piece of filtering equipment' (Halloran 1970a: 20).

This article also underlined the need to take account of 'subjective definitions of situations and events', without going over fully to the 'uses and gratifications' position. Halloran recast the problematic of the 'effects of television' in terms of 'pictures of the world, the definitions of the situation and problems, the explanations, alternative remedies and solutions which are made available to us'. The empirical work of the Leicester Centre at this time marked an important shift in research from forms of behavioural analysis to forms of cognitive analysis. *Demonstrations and Communications* (Halloran 1970b) attempted to develop an analysis of 'the communication process as a whole', studying 'the production process, presentation and media content as well as the reactions of the viewing and reading public'. This latter aspect of the research was further developed by Elliott in his study *The Making of a Television Series* (1972), especially the notion of public communication as a circuit relaying messages from 'the society as source' to 'the society as audience'.

Uses, gratifications and meanings

The realization within mass-media research that one cannot approach the problem of the 'effects' of the media on the audience as if contents impinged directly on to passive minds, that people in fact assimilate, select from and reject communications from the media, led to the development of the 'uses and gratifications' model. Halloran advised us: 'We must get away from the habit of thinking in terms of what the media do to people and substitute for it the idea of what people do with the media'. This approach highlighted the important fact that different members of the mass-media audience may use and interpret any particular programme in a quite different way from how the communicator intended it, and in quite different ways from other members of the audience. Rightly, it stressed the role of the audience in the construction of meaning.

However, this 'uses and gratifications' model suffers from fundamental defects in at least two respects:

1 As Hall (1973a) argues, in terms of its overestimation of the 'openness' of the message,

> Polysemy must not be confused with pluralism. Connotative codes are not equal among themselves. Any society/culture tends, with varying degrees of closure, to impose its segmentations . . . its classifications of the . . . world upon its members. There remains a dominant cultural order, though it is neither univocal or uncontested.
>
> (Hall 1973a: 13)

While messages can sustain, potentially, more than one reading, and 'there can be no law to ensure that the receiver will "take" the preferred or dominant reading of an episode . . . in precisely the way in which it has been encoded by the producer' (ibid.) yet still the message is 'structured in dominance' by the preferred reading. The moment of 'encoding' thus exerts, from the production end, an 'over-determining' effect (though not a fully determined closure) on the succeeding moments in the communicative chain.

As Elliott rightly argues, one fundamental flaw in the 'uses and gratifications' approach is that its implicit model of the communication process fails to take into account the fact that television consumption is

> more a matter of availability than of selection . . . [In this sense] availability depends on familiarity . . . The audience has easier access to familiar genres partly because they understand the language and conventions and also because they already know the social meaning of this type of output with some certainty.
>
> (Elliott 1973: 21)

Similarly, Downing has pointed to the limitations of the assumption (built into the 'uses and gratifications' perspective) of an unstructured mass of 'differential interpretations' of media messages. As he points out, while in principle a given 'content' may be interpreted by the audience in a variety of ways,

> In practice a very few of these views will be distributed throughout the vast majority of the population, with the remainder to be found only in a small minority. [For] given a set of cultural norms and values which are very dominant in the society as a whole (say the general undesirability of strikes) and given certain stereotypes (say that workers and/or unions initiate strikes) only a very sustained and

carefully argued and documented presentation of any given strike is likely to challenge these values and norms.

(Downing 1974: 111)

2 The second limitation of the 'uses and gratifications' perspective lies in its insufficiently sociological nature. Uses and gratifications is an essentially psychologistic problematic, relying as it does on mental states, needs and processes abstracted from the social situation of the individuals concerned – and in this sense the 'modern' uses and gratifications approach is less 'sociological' than earlier attempts to apply this framework in the USA. The earlier studies dealt with specific types of content and specific audiences, whereas 'modern' uses and gratifications tend to look for underlying structures of need and gratification of psychological origin, without effectively situating these within any socio-historical framework.

As Elliott argues, the 'intra-individual' processes with which uses and gratifications research deals 'can be generalised to aggregates of individuals, but they cannot be converted in any meaningful way into social structure and process' (Elliott 1973: 6), because the audience is still here conceived of as an atomized mass of individuals (just as in the earlier 'stimulus-response' model) abstracted from the groups and subcultures which provide a framework of meaning for their activities.

This is to argue for the essentially social nature of consciousness as it is formed through language much in the way that Voloshinov does:

> Signs emerge after all, only in the process of interaction between one individual consciousness and another. And the individual consciousness itself is filled with signs. Consciousness becomes consciousness only once it has been filled with ideological (semiotic) content, consequently only in the process of social interaction.
>
> (quoted in Woolfson 1976: 168)

As Woolfson remarks of this, the sign is here seen as vehicle of social communication, and as permeating the individual consciousness, so that consciousness is seen as a socio-ideological fact. From this position Woolfson argues that

> speech utterances are entirely sociological in nature. The utterance is always in some degree a response to something else. It is a product of inter-relationship and its centre of gravity therefore lies outside the individual speaker him/herself.
>
> (ibid., 172)

Thus utterances are to be examined not as individual, idiosyncratic expressions of a psychological kind, but as sociologically regulated, both by the immediate social situation and by the surrounding socio-historical context; utterances form a 'ceaseless stream of dialogic inter-change [which is the] generative process of a given social collective' (172).

What Woolfson argues here in relation to the need to redefine the analysis of 'individual' speech utterances – as the analysis of the communicative utterances of 'social individuals' – I would argue in relation to the analysis of individual viewing patterns and responses. We need to break fundamentally with the uses and gratifications approach, its psychologistic problematic and its emphasis on individual differences of interpretation. Of course, there will always be individual, private readings, but we need to investigate the extent to which these individual readings are patterned into cultural structures and clusters. What is needed here is an approach which links differential interpretations back to the socio-economic structure of society, showing how members of different groups and classes, sharing different 'cultural codes', will interpret a given message differently, not just at the personal, idiosyncratic level, but in a way systematically related to their socio-economic position. In short we need to see how the different sub-cultural structures and formations within the audience, and the sharing of different cultural codes and competences amongst different groups and classes, determine the decoding of the message for different sections of the audience.

Halloran has argued that the 'real task for the mass communications researcher is . . . to identify and map out the different sub-cultures and ascertain the significance of the various sub-codes in selected areas governed by specific broadcasting or cultural policies'. This is necessary, Halloran argues, because we must see that 'the TV message . . . is not so much a message . . . [but] more like a message-vehicle containing several messages which take on meanings in terms of available codes or subcodes. We need to know the potential of each vehicle with regard to all the relevant sub-cultures' (Halloran 1975: 6). This is to propose a model of the audience, not as an atomized mass of individuals, but as a number of sub-cultural formations or groupings of 'members' who will, as members of those groups, share a cultural orientation towards decoding messages in particular ways. The audience must be conceived of as composed of clusters of socially situated individual readers, whose individual readings will be framed by shared cultural formations and practices pre-existent to the individual: shared 'orientations' which will in turn be determined by factors derived from the objective position of the individual reader in the class structure. These objective factors must be seen as setting parameters to individual experience, although not 'determining' consciousness in a mechanistic way – people understand their situation and react to it through the level of sub-cultures and meaning-systems.

This brings us, in the first instance, to the problem of the relationship between social structure and ideology. The work of Bernstein (1971) and others in the field of educational sociology is of obvious relevance here, and some extrapolations on the possible significance of that work for media audience research are made in Morley (1974). Rather than rehearse that argument in detail I will attempt in the next section simply to outline the notorious problem of the relation of classes and codes.

Classes, codes and correspondences

One of the most significant interventions in the debate about the problem of 'determination', or the relation of class structure and ideology, has been that made by Hirst (1976) and his associates. They have argued that the attempt to specify this determination is doomed to incoherence, on the grounds that either the determination must be total, in which case the specificity of the ideological or the level of signifying practices is denied; or alternatively that the proper recognition of this autonomy precludes the specification of any such form of determination of the ideological. The argument is, of course, premised on the rejection of the concept of 'relative autonomy' derived from Althusser, and in particular on the rejection of the use of that concept within the field of cultural studies (cf. Coward 1977).

Ellis (1977) takes up this point, following Hirst's arguments. He denies the sense of attempting to derive expectations as to ideological/political practices from class position, and denies the validity of any model of 'typical positions' (such as those embedded in the encoding/decoding model derived from Parkin). He argues that this is illegitimate, since: 'According to the conjuncture, shopkeepers, for example, can be voting communist, believing in collective endeavour' (Ellis 1977: 58) So presumably, according to the 'conjuncture', shopkeepers can be decoding programmes in any number of different frameworks/codes, in an unstructured way.

This 'radical' formulation of the autonomy of signifying/ideological practices seems inadequate in two respects. First, by denying the relevance of cultural contexts in providing for individuals in different positions in the social structure a differential range of options, the argument is reduced, by default, to a concern with the (random) actions (voting, decoding) of individuals abstracted from any socio-historical context except that of the (unspecified) conjuncture. This return to methodological individualism must be rejected if we are to retain any sense of the audience as a structured complex of social collectivities of different kinds.

Second, and more importantly, the Ellis/Hirst approach simply seems to throw out the baby with the bathwater. The argument against a mechanistic interpretation in which 'it is assumed that the census of employment category carries with it both political and ideological reflections' is of course, perfectly correct, precisely because this approach 'eliminates the need for real exploration of ideological representations in their specificity (Ellis 1977: 65) by assuming that members of category X hold beliefs of type Y as a function of their economic situation.

However, there is no licence for moving from this position, as Ellis and Hirst do, to an argument that therefore *all* attempts to specify determination by class structure are misconceived. The argument here becomes polarized into an either/or, both poles of which are absurd: either total determination or total autonomy.

The problem is that shopkeepers do not act as Ellis hypothesizes. The reason that bourgeois political science makes any kind of sense at all, even to itself, is precisely because it is exploring a structured field in which class determinations do, simply on a level of statistical probability, produce correlations and patterns. Now, simply to count these patterns may be a fairly banal exercise, but to deny their existence is ludicrous; the patterns are precisely what are to be explored, in their relation to class structures.

It is interesting to compare the Ellis/Hirst intervention with that of Rosen (1972), who begins to provide precisely the kind of non-mechanistic, non-economistic account of the determination of language by class and the action of language on class formation that Ellis and Hirst seem to consider impossible. Rosen attacks Basil Bernstein exactly for providing a mechanistic, economistic analysis. The working class is, in Bernstein's work, an undifferentiated whole, defined simply by economic position. Factors at the level of ideological and political practice which 'distinguish the language of Liverpool dockers from that of . . . Coventry car workers' (Rosen 1972: 9) are ignored. However, Rosen precisely aims to extend the terms of the analysis by inserting these factors as determinate. He rejects the argument that linguistic code can be simply determined by 'common occupational function' and sees the need to differentiate within and across class categories in terms of ideological practice: 'history, traditions, job experience, ethnic origins, residential patterns, level of organisation' (6).

Yet the central concern remains. The intervention is called *Language and Class* and its force is produced directly by the attention paid (as against Bernstein's mechanistic/economistic account) to the levels of ideological, discursive and political practice. These factors are here inserted with that of class determination, and their extension into the field of decoding is long overdue – but the relative autonomy of signifying practices does not mean that decodings are not structured by class. *How* they are so structured – in what combinations for different sections of the audience, the relation of language, class and code – is 'a question which must be ethnographically investigated' (Giglioli 1972: 10).

The question is really whether this is an irretrievably essentialist or mechanistic problematic. I would argue that a charge of mechanism cannot be substantiated. Indeed, the formulation of structures, cultures and biographies (outlined in Critcher 1978) clearly evades the polarity of either total determination or total autonomy, through the notion of structures setting parameters, determining the availability of cultural options and responses, not directly determining other levels and practices. This problematic, then, clearly is concerned with some form of determination of cultural competences, codes and decodings by the class structure, while avoiding mechanistic notions.

The problem which the *Nationwide* audience project was designed to explore was that of the extent to which decodings take place within the limits of the preferred (or dominant) manner in which the message has been initially encoded. However, the complementary aspect of this problem is that of the extent to which these interpretations or decodings are inflected by other codes and discourses which different sections of the audience inhabit. We are concerned here with the ways in which decoding is determined by the socially governed distribution of cultural codes between and across different sections of the audience: that is, the range of different decoding strategies and competences in the audience.

To raise this as a problem for research is already to argue that the meaning produced by the encounter of text and subject cannot be 'read off' straight from textual characteristics; rather, 'what has to be identified is the use to which a particular text is put, its function within a particular conjuncture, in particular institutional spaces, and in relation to particular audiences' (Neale 1977: 39–40). The text cannot be considered in isolation from its historical conditions of production and consumption.

Thus the meaning of the text must be thought of in terms of which set of discourses it encounters in any particular set of circumstances, and how this encounter may restructure both the meaning of the text and the discourses which it meets. The meaning of the text will be constructed differently according to the discourses (knowledges, prejudices, resistances, etc.) brought to bear on the text by the reader and the crucial factor in the encounter of audience/subject and text will be the range of discourses at the disposal of the audience. Here, of course, 'individuals do have different relations to sets of discourses in that their position in the social formation, their positioning in the real, will determine which sets of discourses a given subject is likely to encounter and in what ways it will do so' (Willemen 1978: 66–7).

Clearly Willemen is here returning to the agenda a set of issues about the relation between social position and discursive formation which were at the core of the work in educational sociology generated by Bernstein's intervention, and developed in France by Bourdieu, Baudelot and Establet. Moreover, Willemen's work can be seen as a vital element in the development of such a theory. As he argues, determination is not to be conceived as a closed and final process:

Having recognised the determining power of the real, it is equally necessary to recognise that the real is never in its place, to borrow a phrase from Lacan, in that it is always and only grasped as reality, that is to say, through discourse . . . the real determines to a large extent the encounter of/with discourses, while these encounters structure, produce reality, and consequently in their turn affect the subject's trajectory through the real

(ibid., 67–8)

– or, as Neale would have it, 'audiences are determined economically, politically *and ideologically*' (Neale 1977: 20; my emphasis).

Chapter 2

Psychoanalytic theories: texts, readers and subjects[1]

One key perspective on the audience which has been developed in recent years is the body of work, principally within film theory, based on psychoanalytic theory concerned with the positioning of the subject by the text.

Despite the theoretical sophistication of much of this work, in offering a more developed model of text/subject relations it has, until now, contributed little to the empirical study of the audience. This is for the simple reason that those working in this tradition have, on the whole, been content to deduce audience responses from the structure of the text. To this extent, and despite the theoretical advances achieved by this work in other respects, I would argue that the psychoanalytically based work has ultimately mobilized what can be seen as another version of the hypodermic theory of effects – in so far as it is, at least in its initial and fundamental formulations, a universalist theory which attempts to account for the way in which the subject is necessarily positioned by the text. The difficulty, in terms of audience studies, is that this body of work, premised as it is on universalist criteria, finds it difficult to provide the theoretical space within which one can allow for, and then investigate, differential readings, interpretations or responses on the part of the audience. This is so quite simply because the theory, in effect, tries to explain any specific instance of the text/reader relationship in terms of a universalist theory of the formation of subjects in general.

From within this perspective emphasis falls on the universal, primary, psychoanalytic processes through which the subject is constituted. The text is then understood as reproducing or replaying this primary positioning, which is then the foundation of any particular reading. My argument would be that in fact we need to question the assumption that all specific discursive effects can be reduced to, and explained by, the functioning of a single, universal set of psychic mechanisms – which is rather like a theory of Platonic forms, which find their expression in any particular instance. The key issue is that this form of psychoanalytic theory poses the problem of the politics of the signifier (the struggle over ideology in language) exclusively at the level of the subject, rather than at the intersection between constituted subjects and specific discursive positions – i.e. at the site of interpellation, where the discursive subject is recognized to be operating in interdiscursive space.

In making this argument, I follow Hall's critique of the Lacanian perspective. Hall argues that 'without further work, further specification, the mechanisms of the Oedipus complex in the discourse of Freud and Lacan are universalist, trans-historical and therefore essentialist' (Hall 1978: 11). To that extent, Hall argues, these concepts, in their universalist forms, cannot usefully be applied without further specification and elaboration to the analysis of historically specific social formations.

This is to attempt to hold on to the distinction between the constitution of the subject as a general (or mythical) moment and the moment when the subject in general is interpellated by the discursive formation of specific societies. That is to insist on the distinction between the formation of subjects for language, and the recruitment of specific subjects to the subject positions of discursive formations through the process of interpellation. It is also to move away from the assumption that every specific reading is already determined by the primary structure of subject positions and to insist that these interpellations are not given and absolute but, rather, are conditional and provisional, in so far as the struggle in ideology takes place precisely through the articulation/disarticulation of interpellations.

One major problem with the influential theoretical position advanced by *Screen* during the 1970s was that it operated with what Neale (1977) has characterized as an 'abstract text–subject relationship'. The subject is not conceived as already constituted in other discursive formations and social relations. Also, it is treated in relation to only one text at a time (or, alternatively, all texts are assumed to function according to the rules of a single 'classic realist text'). This is then explicated by reference to the universal, primary psychoanalytic processes (Oedipus complex, 'mirror phase', castration complex and its resolution and so on), through which, according to Lacan's reading of Freud, 'the subject' is constituted. The text is understood as reproducing or replaying this primary positioning, which is the foundation of any reading.

Now, apart from the difficulty of trying to explain a specific instance of the text/reader relationship in terms of a universalist theory of the formation of subjects-in-general, this proposition also serves to isolate the encounter of text and reader from all social and historical structures *and* from other texts. To conceptualize the moment of reading/viewing in this way is to ignore the constant intervention of other texts and discourses, which also position the subject. At the moment of textual encounter other discourses are always in play besides those of the particular text in focus – discourses which depend on other discursive formations, brought into play through the subject's placing in other practices – cultural, educational, institutional. And these other discourses will set some of the terms in which any particular text is engaged and evaluated. 'Screen theory' may be assumed to justify its neglect of the interplay of other discourses on the text/reader encounter by virtue of its assumption that all texts depend on the same set of subject positions, constituted in the formation of the subject, and therefore that they need be accorded no other distinctive effectivity of their own. Here, however, I wish to put in question this assumption that all specific discursive effects can be reduced to, and explained by, the functioning of a single, universal set of psychic mechanisms.

Pêcheux has provided us with the useful and important concept of interdiscourse. As explicated by Woods, he argues:

> The constitution of subjects is always specific in respect of each subject . . . and this can be conceived of in terms of a single, original (and mythic) interpellation – the entry into language and the symbolic – which constitutes a *space* wherein a complex of continually interpellated subject forms interrelate, each subject form being a determinate formation of discursive processes. The discursive subject is therefore an interdiscourse, the product of the effects of discursive practices traversing the subject throughout its history.
>
> (Woods 1977: 75)

Interdiscourse and interpellation

The important point about this formulation is the distinction it holds between the constitution of the subject as a general (original and mythic?) moment – constituting a space – and the (second) moment when the subject-in-general is interpellated in the subject forms (the discursive subject positions) which are provided by the existing complex of discourses that make up the discursive formation (the interdiscourse) of specific social formations. Pêcheux therefore opens out what precisely 'Screen theory' is at pains to close up – the space, the difference, between the formation of subjects-for-language and the recruitment of specific subjects to the subject positions of discursive formations through the process of interpellation. Thus whereas 'Screen theory' poses the problem of the 'politics of the signifier' (the struggle over ideology in language) exclusively at the level of the subject, Pêcheux locates it at the intersection between constituted subjects and specific discursive positions – that is, at the site of interpellation. This is a critical distinction.

In 'Screen theory' there can be no struggle at the site of the interface between subject and text (discourse), since contradictory positions have already been predetermined at the psychoanalytic level. Pêcheux takes over some part of this theory of the formation of the subject, without, however, assuming that the struggle over meaning/interpretation in any subject/text encounter is already determined outside the conditions of reading itself. To put this in Althusserian terms, whereas 'Screen theory' assumes every specific reading to be already determined by the primary structure of subject positions, Pêcheux treats the outcomes of a reading as an over-determination. The two structures involved (constitution of the subject/interpellation into specific discursive positions) are articulated, but are not identical, not mere replications of each other.

This links closely to the argument advanced by Laclau concerning the centrality of interpellation to the functioning of ideological discourses and the struggle in ideology to disarticulate/rearticulate the interpellative structure of particular discourses. The term 'interpellation' itself is an ambiguous one and has been subject to variable formulations. Althusser (1971) introduced it in the 'Ideology and ideological state apparatuses' essay, as a sort of 'loan' from Lacan, without making clear the status of the borrowing in relation to Lacanian theory. That is, Althusser did not clarify to what extent he accepted the argument as derived from Lacan: that interpellation could be explained exclusively by reference to the primary psychoanalytic processes. Althusser proposed, in the controversial second part of his essay, that 'there is no ideology except for concrete subjects', adding that ideology always functions through 'the category of the subject'. But he gave the constitution of that category not to the psychoanalytic level but to the functioning of ideological discourses themselves – that is, at this stage in his argument the subject is a discursive category: 'at the same time and immediately I add that the category of the subject is only constitutive of all ideology in so far as ideology has the function (which defines it) of "constituting" concrete individuals as subjects'. And when, later, he advanced the more Lacanian proposition that the 'individuals' hailed by ideological discourses are always-already in ideology – 'individuals are always-already subjects' – he still leaves somewhat ambiguous the degree of determinacy accorded to this proposition. The unborn child already has an ideological destination and destiny awaiting him/her: but Althusser only goes so far as to say:

> it is clear that this ideological constraint and pre-appointment, and all the rituals of rearing and then education in the family, have some relationship with what Freud studied in the forms of the pre-genital and genital 'stages' of sexuality . . . . But let us leave this point, too, on one side.

Laclau (1977) is more openly agnostic than Althusser when he adopts the term 'interpellation'. He never refers the subjects of interpellation to the psychoanalytic level, and he makes no reference to the Lacanian hypothesis. Instead, following Althusser's lead, he locates it at the level of the discourse: 'what constitutes the unifying principle of an ideological discourse is the "subject" interpellated and thus constituted through this discourse'. Certainly, Laclau cannot mean that this structure of interpellations is already pre-constituted at the moment when the infant becomes a subject in the Lacanian sense, because the whole thrust of his argument is that these interpellations are not given and absolute but conditional and provisional. The struggle in ideology takes place precisely through the articulation/disarticulation of interpellations: 'How are ideologies transformed? The answer is: through the class struggle which is carried out through the production of subjects and the articulation/disarticulation of discourses'. The position, then, seems to be that Pêcheux adopts part of the Lacanian argument but treats the constitution of the space of the subject as only one, predetermining, element in the functioning of specific ideological discourses. Laclau locates interpellation exclusively at the level of the play in and struggle over discourses. Both locate ideological struggle at the level of the interplay between the subject and the discursive.

The concept of contradictory interpellations can be employed to clarify and modify the sociological approach of Parkin (1971) and others, who refer to workers who grant legitimacy to a 'dominant ideology' in the abstract but inhabit a 'negotiated' or 'situationally defined' ideology at the level of concrete practice. That is, it can be used to clarify the problem of contradictory ideological positions, and specifically forms of corporate or sectional class-consciousness, without recourse to the premises of 'false consciousness'. Parkin refers to this evidence as showing 'split levels of consciousness'. However, if we introduce the concept of interpellation, we get rid of the presumption that there is a prescribed, unitary, homogeneous form of class-consciousness. This allows us to specify the articulation of different, contradictory subject positions or interpellations, to which the same individual worker (a contradictory subject, traversed by different discursive practices) is 'hailed': for example, he/she can be interpellated as 'national subject' by the television discourses of the dominant news media, but as 'class/sectional' subject by the discourses of his/her trade union organization or co-workers. In this approach the relative dominance of these contradictory interpellations and the political practices with which they are articulated are not given elsewhere (for instance, at the level of the formation of the subject) but vary with the conjuncture in which the subject is interpellated.

This stress on contradictory interpellations emphasizes the unstable, provisional and dynamic properties of positioning, rather than falling (as Parkin does, with his conception of 'split levels of consciousness') towards a static sociological ascription. The latter simply separates out into fixed proportions – where the subject identifies with the dominant discourses, and where he/she is in potential opposition to them. Again, Laclau's conception of the ideological work of disarticulation – especially his argument about the way discourses can convert opposition and contradiction into mere difference, thereby neutralizing a potential antagonism – is of crucial relevance. The stress now falls on the ideological process and struggle itself, thus making once more problematic a prescribed text/ reader/subject relation.

By 'interdiscourse' Pêcheux appears to mean the complex of discursive formations in any society which provide already available subject positions (the 'pre-constructed') as a necessary category of their functioning. It is clear that the concept of interdiscourse transforms the relation of one text/one subject to that of a multiplicity of texts/subjects relations, in which encounters can be understood not in isolation but only in the moments of their combination.

A further consideration, not taken into account in 'Screen theory', is that subjects have histories. If it is correct to speak not of text/subject but of texts/subjects relations with reference to the present, it must also be the case that past interpellations affect present ones. While these traditional and institutionalized 'traces' (to use Gramsci's term) cannot in themselves determine present interpellations, they do constitute the well-established elements of the interdiscourse and frame successive new encounters. Gramsci speaks of the weight of traditional elements and Laclau of the 'relative continuity' of popular traditions. Indeed, Laclau may not have gone far enough in examining how these elements of the 'pre-constructed' may help to delay and impede the process of articulating/disarticulating the existing interpellative structures of ideological discourses. Consequently, he may offer a picture of too open a struggle between discourses which is not sufficiently attentive to the weight of traditional elements.

Since 'Screen theory' does not make any distinction between how the subject is constituted as a 'space' and specific interpellations, it deduces subjects from the subject positions offered by the text and identifies the two. Thus the 'classic realist text' recapitulates, in its particular discursive strategies, the positions in which the subject has been constituted by the primary processes. There is a fixed identity and perfect reciprocity between these two structures, which in 'Screen theory' are, in effect, one and the same structure. The realist text is therefore not so much 'read' as simply consumed/appropriated straight, via the only possible positions available to the reader – those reinscribed by the text. This forecloses the question of reading as itself a moment in the production of meaning. In the 'Screen theory' account this moment is doubly determined – by the primary subject positions which inscribe the subject in language and by those positions as they are reinscribed in the text through the strategies of realism. Since these are posed as very general mechanisms, 'Screen theory' is not required to address either the possibility of different, historically specific 'realisms' or the possibility of an inscribed realist reading being refused. Readers here appear merely as the bearers or puppets of their unconscious positionings, reduplicated in the structure of the realist discourse (singular). But this runs counter to two of the most important advances previously established by structural linguistics: the essentially polysemic nature of signs and sign-based discourses, and the interrogative/expansive nature of all readings. In many ways, 'Screen theory', which insists on the 'productivity of the text', undermines that concept by defining the realist text as a mere replay of positions established elsewhere.

In contradiction to this argument, I would still want to retain some of the ideas expressed through the concept of 'preferred readings'. This suggests that a text of the dominant discourse does privilege or prefer a certain reading. We might now expand this to say that such texts privilege a certain reading in part by inscribing certain preferred discursive positions from which its discourse appears 'natural', transparently aligned to 'the real' and credible. However, this cannot be the only reading inscribed in the text, and it certainly cannot be the only reading which different readers can make of it. The theory of the polysemic nature of discourse must hold to the possibility of establishing an articulation between the 'encoding' and 'decoding' circuits, but it should not adopt a position of a 'necessary correspondence' or identity between them. What we may call the 'reality effect' is not the product of the required reduplication of the empiricist subject in the discourse of realism, but the effect of an achieved alignment between subjects and texts which the discourse itself accomplishes.

Ideological problematic and mode of address

Even in the case of the 'classic realist text', the subject positions inscribed by the text, as a condition of its intelligibility, may be inhabited differently by subjects who, in the past (as the result of interpellations by other texts/discourses/institutions) or in the present, are already positioned in an interdiscursive space. It does not follow that because the reader has taken the position most fully inscribed in the text, sufficient for the text to be intelligible, he/she will, for that reason alone, subscribe to the ideological problematic of that text. The text may be contradicted by the subject's position(s) in relation to other texts, problematics, institutions, discursive formations. This means that we must establish a distinction between inhabiting inscribed subject positions, adopting an ideological problematic and making a dominant reading of a text. We cannot, then, assume that one text inscribes a required subject, but only that specific text/subject relations will depend, in part, on the subject positions given by a multiplicity of texts that produce (and have produced) contradictory subjectivities which then act on and against each other within 'the space of the subject'.

Neale draws an important distinction between ideological problematic and mode of address. His examination of the two Nazi propaganda films *Der Ewige Jude* and *Jud Suss* suggests that they both share broadly the same ideological problematic but differ in their modes of address. Neale argues that 'If *Der Ewige Jude*, then, can be seen to share with *Jud Suss* a common problematic in terms of race, order and their representation, it nonetheless articulates that problematic in a different way: it has a different mode of textual address'. Neale extends this argument to take into account the effect of the interdiscursive; thus:

> address is not synonymous with textual address . . . although the latter can be analysed and has an effectivity; particular positions and modalities of position are a product of textual address in conjunction with the immediate discourses that necessarily surround it within the apparatuses that support it, and . . . these in turn owe their character, the particular modalities of position that they produce in interaction with a text, to ideological practices – the state of ideological struggle – within the conjuncture as a whole.
>
> (Neale 1977: 34)

Ideological problematic, here, must be understood not as a set of contents but rather as a defined set of operations: the way a problematic selects from, conceives and organizes its field of reference. This is constituted by a particular agenda of issues and themes, premises and propositions which are visible/invisible, or by a repertoire of questions (proposing answers) which are asked/not asked. This matrix of propositions constitutes it as a relatively coherent space of operations. A problematic can define the dominant or preferred themes of a text. But texts may also be structured by more than one problematic, though one or a restricted set will tend to be in dominance.

Neale employs 'mode of address' specifically with reference to the positioning of the subject:

> To speak of representation in discourse in relation to ideology is also to speak of subject positions: each discursive representation constitutes a subject position, a place for the production and configuration of meaning, for its coherence, or, occasionally, for its critical rupture;
>
> (ibid., 18)

but, he adds, 'they are not necessarily marked by a single, specific mode of address'. The term may, however, be more usefully defined in relation to all those discursive operations which seek to establish and define the form of the text/reader relation. But we must beware of arguing that the positions of knowledge inscribed in the textual operations are obligatory for all readers. We must also distinguish between the positions which the text prefers and prescribes in its discursive operations and the process by which concrete individuals, already constituted as subjects for a multiplicity of discourses, are (successfully or inadequately) interpellated by any single text. Individuals are not merely subjects for/by leave of a single text.

A successfully achieved correspondence must be understood as an accomplishment, not a given. It is the result of an articulation; otherwise it could not be disarticulated.

'Screen theory' constantly elides the concrete individual, his/her constitution as a 'subject-for-discourse', and the discursive subject positions constituted by specific discursive practices and operations. These need to be kept analytically distinct, otherwise we will fail to understand the relation subjects/texts within the terms of 'no necessary correspondence'. Of course, specific combinations – for example, between specific problematics and specific modes of address – may exist historically as well secured, dominant or recurring patterns in particular conjunctures in definite social formations. These may be fixed in place by the institutionalization of practices within a particular site or apparatus (for example, Hollywood cinema). Nevertheless, even these correspondences are not 'eternal' or universal. They have been secured. One can point to the practices and mechanisms which secure them and which reproduce them, in place, in one text after another. But unless one is to accept that there is no ideology but the dominant ideology, which is always in its appointed place, this naturalized correspondence must constantly be deconstructed and shown to be a historically concrete relation. It follows from this argument that there must be different realisms, not a single 'classic realist text' to which all realist texts can be assimilated. And there is no necessary correspondence between these realisms and a particular ideological problematic.

Individuals, subjects, 'subjects'

In an important contribution, Willemen has identified an unjustified conflation, in a great deal of 'Screen theory' of the subject of the text and the social subject. He argues:

> There remains an unbridgeable gap between 'real' readers/authors and 'inscribed' ones, constructed and marked in and by the text. Real readers are subjects in history, living in social formations, rather than mere subjects of a single text. The two types of subject are not commensurate. But for the purposes of formalism, real readers are supposed to coincide with the constructed readers.
>
> (Willemen 1978: 48)

Hardy, Johnston and Willemen (1976) also mark the distinction between the 'inscribed reader of the text' and the 'social subject who is invited to take up this position'. Gledhill (1978) has opened up this question of the psychoanalytic and the historical 'subject'; in response Johnston (1979) called for a move away from a notion of the text as an autonomous object of study, and towards the more complex question of subjectivity seen in historical/social terms. Feminist film practice can be seen no longer simply in terms of the effectivity of a system of representation, but rather as a production of and by subjects already in social practices, which always involve heterogeneous and often contradictory positions in ideologies.

In their earlier paper Hardy, Johnston and Willemen proposed a model of 'interlocking subjectivities', caught up in a network of symbolic systems, in which the social subject 'always exceeds the subject implied by the text because he/she is also placed by a heterogeneity of other cultural systems and is never coextensive with the subject placed by a single fragment (i.e. one film) of the overall cultural text' (Hardy, Johnston and Willemen 1976: 5). The subjects implied/implicated by the text are thus always already subjects within different social practices in determinate social formations – not simply subjects in the symbolic in general. They are constituted by specific, historical forms of sociality:

> this subject, at its most abstract and impersonal, is itself in history: the discourses . . . determining the terms of its play, change according to the relations of force of competing discourses intersecting in the plane of the subject in history, the individual's location in ideology at a particular moment and place in the social formation.
>
> (Willemen 1978: 66–7)

Nowell-Smith rightly points to the particularity of Neale's approach, breaking, as it does, with the ahistorical and unspecified use of the category of the subject. In his summary of Neale's position, Nowell-Smith points out that '[propaganda] . . . films require to be seen, politically, in terms of the positionality they provide for the socially located spectator' (Nowell-Smith 1977: 5). This is 'on the one hand, a question of textual relations proper, of mode of address'; but it is also a question of 'the politico-historical conjuncture', because 'the binding of the spectator takes place' (or, I would add, fails to take place) 'not through formal mechanisms alone but through the way social instructions impose their effectivity at given moments across the text and also elsewhere'. This argument has consequences for how both texts and subjects are conceptualized. It gives the level of the discursive its proper specificity and effectivity; but it does not treat the text as autonomously signifying, nor does it accord signification an all-inclusive effect. It qualifies what can be meant by the term 'the productivity of the text'.

Willemen returns to the agenda – but now from a position within the discursive – a set of questions about the relations between the social position of the reader and discursive formations. These questions, in a more sociological form, were at the centre of Bernstein's early (1971) work. Their disappearance from the discussion is, no doubt, attributable to that general critique of sociological approaches common in 'Screen theory', where the mere ascription of the qualifier 'sociological' is enough to consign a text so stigmatized to the scrap-heap of theory (cf. Coward 1977). Bernstein did invite criticisms by the over-deterministic way in which the relation between class and language was posed in his early work. The position was extensively criticized, and there has been some modification on his part since then. The terms of the argument can be extensively faulted. But the questions addressed are not without their rational core. The basic problem with the sociological formulations is that they presumed a too simple, one-to-one correspondence between social structure and discourse: they treated language as ascribed by and inscribed in class position. This position cannot be defended or sustained. It is based on a too simple a notion of how classes are constituted, and on the ascription of fixed ideologies to whole classes. There is no conception of signifying practices, their relative autonomy and specific effects.

The weaknesses in the position need not be elaborated at length. Class is not a unitary category with effective determination at the level of the economic only. There is no simple alignment between the economic, the political and the ideological in the constitution of classes. Classes do not have fixed, ascribed or unitary world views. In Poulantzas's (1971) phrase, they do not carry their world views around like number plates on their backs. Laclau argues that even 'ideological elements, taken in isolation, have no necessary class connotation and this connotation is only the result of the articulation of those elements in a concrete ideological discourse' (Laclau 1977: 99), and the articulation of these discourses with class practices in specific conjunctures. However, the essentialism and class-reductionism which tend to characterize positions such as those of Parkin (1971), for example, have generally been countered by its simple opposite or inversion: the premise, in essence, of an absolute autonomy, and the assumption that any relationship between discursive formations and class formations must be, by definition, reductionist. This is not acceptable either. The problem can only be resolved if we are able to think through the full implications of two apparently contradictory propositions: first, discourses cannot be explained by or reduced to classes, defined exclusively at the level of the economic; second, nevertheless, 'audiences *are* determined economically, politically and ideologically'. The first proposition suggests that classes, understood economically, will not always be found 'in place' in their proper discursive position. The second proposition, however, insists that the economic and political constitution of classes will have some real effectivity for the distribution of discourses to groups of agents. (I deal here exclusively with the question of the reduction of discourses to classes. But it must be remembered that other structures and relations – for example, those of gender and patriarchal relations, which are not reducible to economic class – will also have a structuring effect on the distribution of discourses.)

In short, the relation classes/meaning-systems has to be fundamentally reworked by taking into account the full effectivity of the discursive level. Discursive formations intervene between classes and languages. They intervene in such a way as to prevent or forestall any attempt to read the level of the operation of language back in any simple or reductive way to economic classes. Thus we cannot deduce which discursive frameworks will be mobilized in particular reader/text encounters from the level of the socio-economic position of the readers. But position in the social structure may be seen to have a structuring and limiting effect on the repertoire of discursive or decoding strategies available to different sectors of an audience. They will have an effect on the pattern of the distribution of discursive repertoires. What is more, the key elements of the social structure which delimit the range of competences in particular audiences may not be referable in any exclusive way to class understood in the economic sense. The key sites for the distribution of discursive sets and competences are probably – following some of the leads of Bernstein and Bourdieu – the family and the school, or, as Althusser (following Gramsci) argued (1971), the family/school couplet. This is the key institutional site or articulation for the distribution of cultural capital, in Bourdieu's terms. Other formations – for example, gender and immediate social context or cultural milieu – may also have a formative and structuring effect, not only on which specific discourses will be in play in any specific text/reader encounter, but also in defining the range and the repertoire of performance codes. The distribution of the discourses of the media and other cultural apparatuses will also have a structuring effect on the differentiated discursive competences of socially structured audiences.

This proposition now requires to be elaborated at a more concrete level. But the direction in which further work must proceed is already clear. In effect, what is required is to work through more fully the consequences of the argument that the discourses mobilized by readers in relation to any text cannot be treated as the effect of a direct relation between discourses and 'the real'. It must be analysed, instead, in terms of the effects of social relations and structures (the extra-discursive) on the structuring of the discursive space – that is, of the 'interdiscourse'. These structured relations cannot produce a reading (and no other) in any specific instance. But they do exercise a limit on (that is, they determine) the formation of the discursive space, which in turn has a determinate effect on the practice of readings at the level of particular text/reader encounters. This approach undermines any notion of the automatic or 'unquestioned performance of the subject by the text' – an approach which merely replaces a sociological determinism by a textual one. It provides the theoretical space in which the subject may be placed in some relation to the signifying chain other than that of a 'regulated process'.

These then are, in my view, the main difficulties with much recent psychoanalytic work, in so far as it is a theoretical perspective which presumes a unilateral fixing of a position for the reader, imprisoning him or her in its structure, so as to produce a singular and guaranteed effect. The text, of course, may offer the subject specific positions of intelligibility, it may operate to prefer certain readings above others; what it cannot do is to guarantee them – that must always be an empirical question.

If we are to theorize the subject of television, it has to be theorized in its cultural and historical specificity, an area where psychoanalytic theory is obviously weak. It is only thus that we can move beyond a theory of the subject which has reference only to universal, primary psychoanalytic processes, and only thus that we can allow a space in which one can recognize that the struggle over ideology also takes place at the moment of the encounter of text and subject and is not 'always already' predetermined at the psychoanalytic level.[2]

Part II

Class, ideology and interpretation

Chapter 3

Interpreting television: the *Nationwide* audience

In considering the process of how meaning is generated in communications I employ here two distinct modes of analysis (semiotics and sociology) to analyse two distinct types of constraints on the production of meaning. These are: (a) the internal structures and mechanisms of the text/message/ programme which invite certain readings and block others (and which can be elucidated through semiotics); and (b) the cultural background of the reader/recipient/viewer, which has to be studied sociologically. The inter-action of these two constraining structures will define the parameters of a text's meaning – thus avoiding the traps of either the notion that a text can be interpreted in an infinite number of (individual) ways or the formalist tendency to suppose that texts determine meaning absolutely.

In order to bring these theoretical problems into sharper focus, some evidence will be presented from a research project conducted at the Centre for Contemporary Cultural Studies, University of Birmingham, between 1975 and 1979, in which I was involved. This project began by analysing, in some detail, the way in which the television programme *Nationwide* was characterized by particular formal devices, particular modes of address to its audience, particular forms of textual organization. The second stage of the project explored how that programme material was interpreted by individuals from different social backgrounds, with a view to establishing the role of cultural frameworks in determining individual interpretations of the programmes in question. Below I present material from audience interviews undertaken in this second stage of the research project which, I hope, will demonstrate some of the relations between socio-demographic factors (such as age, sex, race, class) and differential interpretations of the same programme material.

This research project focused on the analysis of one particular pro-gramme (*Nationwide*) within one particular mode or genre (magazine/ current affairs) of one particular medium (television). In attempting to generate any principles of wider applicability, we must take care to allow for the specificity of the programme, genre and medium. However, while allowing for such specificities, we must also consider the extent to which

the structural factors invoked here to account for differential interpretations of the same signs will be factors which need to be taken into
consideration in any analysis of text/audience interaction: although the
specific form of their effectivity may vary from one area of communications
to another.

I am concerned here with the everyday experience of reading newspapers, or watching television programmes, and the question of what we
make of those messages, how we interpret the messages that we consume
through the mass media. If we raise the question of audience interpretation
of messages, we are already rejecting the assumption that the media are
institutions whose messages automatically have an effect on us as their
audience. As against that assumption I am raising to the central place in my
analysis the question of how we make sense of the sense of the world that
the media offer to us. This is to pose our activity in our sitting-rooms,
watching the television, as an active process of decoding or interpretation,
not simply a passive process of 'reception' or 'consumption' of messages.
For us to make any sense at all of the images and sounds that we see and
hear, we have to be engaged in an active work of interpretation. In the first
instance, we have to learn to see the particular combination of dots on a
screen as representing objects in the world – people, houses, fields, trees.
We have all had to learn the basic codes of interpreting television – codes
which we unconsciously operate. These are the rules by which we give
meaning to the fact that a person is dressed in a particular way, speaks with
a particular kind of accent, is sitting in a certain kind of chair, in a certain
kind of setting. Such signs tell us something about the person and his or her
status.

It is often assumed (certainly by the broadcasters) that watching television is something done by the family together at home. While this is
certainly a fair assumption, it often tends to carry with it a further and
more questionable one – namely that 'family viewing' is a passive affair in
which we all sit there and soak up the messages that our television sets
emit. In fact, you can probably think of plenty of instances of arguments
that have broken out with the other people in the room with whom you are
'watching telly'. What one may find interesting may bore another. One
person may respond positively to the government spokesman's latest
announcement about economic policy while another may feel like throwing
the cat at the television (or vice versa).

In my experience, and probably in yours, it takes only a few moments of
watching a news broadcast with friends or other members of your family
for discussion (at least of some of the points) to break out. It might well be
a discussion 'sparked off' by the messages seen on the screen, which then
goes off on a totally different route. But this is to stress the audience's
potential to respond actively and even argumentatively to the messages of
the media. Because we all bring to our viewing those other discourses and

sets of representations with which we are in contact in other areas of our lives, the messages that we receive from the media do not confront us in isolation. They intersect with other messages that we have received – explicit and implicit messages, from other institutions, people we know, or sources of information we trust. Unconsciously, we sift and compare messages from one place with those received from another. Thus, how we respond to messages from the media depends precisely on the extent to which they fit with, or possibly contradict, other messages, other viewpoints that we have come across in other areas of our lives.

Pêcheux (1982) has named this the phenomenon of inter-discourse. This is to say that we, as people existing in a field of different discourses, different message systems, are situated between those different systems. We experience a multiplicity of discourses, and the space in which we exist is crossed by a number of different discourses, some of which support each other, are in alignment with each other, some of which contradict each other, some of which we relate to positively, some negatively. But the basic point to bear in mind is that in the process of decoding and interpreting the messages of the media, other messages, other discourses are always involved, whether or not we are explicitly conscious of it. We cannot understand the process of media communications if we think about the moment in which, say, we switch on the television at 9 o'clock and listen to the news, as an isolated event. That is but one moment in a complex field of communications, and we have to understand the nature of the relationship between that moment and all the other strands of communication in which we are involved. We have to understand how one message relates to the other sets of representations, images, stereotypes that the audience is familiar with. Media communications have to fit into the fields of personal and institutional communications in which the people who constitute the audience also exist as voters, housewives, workers, shoppers, parents, roller-skaters or soldiers. All those institutions, all those roles within which people are situated, produce messages which intersect with those of the media. The person watching the news is situated within that complex field of communication, and is involved in a process of decoding media material in which one set of messages or discourses feeds into, or is deflected by, another.

THE CIRCUIT OF MASS COMMUNICATIONS

A full analysis of the process of mass communications would seem to involve at least three different elements: first, the study of the production of media artefacts; second, the study of the products – the study of television programmes as constructed sets of sign units which carry a message; third, the process of decoding or interpreting those signs which the audience is actively engaged in.

The material below is concerned with the way in which the same television programme is decoded by people from different social and cultural backgrounds. Any understandings of mass communications will be inadequate if we consider the elements of that process (production, programme, audience) in isolation from each other. In fact it might be said that media research has been dominated over quite a long period by a kind of 'pendulum effect' in which attention has been focused either exclusively on the message or exclusively on the audience, but rarely on the two in combination. In some cases, researchers have simply concentrated on the analysis of messages on the assumption that these messages automatically have large and direct effects on those who see and hear them – effects which can be assumed, or deduced directly, from the nature of the message. If we make these assumptions, then we are freed from the necessity of researching directly into the process of audience decodings. That might be called the 'hypodermic' model of the media's powerful effect, a model in which all media messages are assumed to have a direct effect on their audience. From this it seems to follow logically that what is needed is simply a more and more refined method of message analysis which will reveal the true nature of the media's messages. Counihan, in a review of the field, summarized the development of mass communications research as follows:

Once upon a time . . . worried commentators imputed a virtual omnipotence to the newly emerging media of mass communication. In the 'Marxist' version . . . the media were seen as entirely manipulated by a shrewd ruling class in a bread and circuses strategy to transmit a corrupt culture and neo-fascist values – violence, dehumanised sex, consumer brain-washing, political passivity, etc. – to the masses . . . . These instruments of persuasion on the one hand, and the atomised, homogenised, susceptible masses on the other, were conjoined in a simple stimulus–response model. However, as empirical research progressed, survey and experimental methods were used to measure the capacity of the media to change 'attitudes', 'opinions' and 'behaviour'. In turn, the media–audience relationship was found to be not simple and direct, but complex and mediated. 'Effects' could only be gauged by taking account of other factors intervening between the media and the audience member. Further, emphasis shifted from 'what the media do to people' to 'what people do to the media', for audiences were found to 'attend to' and 'receive' media messages in a selective way, to tend to ignore or to subtly reinterpret those messages hostile to their particular viewpoints. Far from possessing autonomous persuasive and other anti-social power, the media were now found to have a more limited and, implicitly, more benign role in society; not changing, but 'reinforcing' prior dispositions, not cultivating 'escapism' or passivity, but capable of satisfying a great diversity of 'uses and gratifications'; not instruments of a levelling of culture, but of its democratisation.

(Counihan 1973: 43)

From this perspective the 'effects' of mass communications were seen to be highly variable, depending on the individual's response to, and interpretation of the message. Further, the media were thought to have little direct effect on their audience, beyond that of reinforcing already existing attitudes and options. Communications research from this perspective was then principally concerned with the role of the media as part of the ritual of daily life.

Some of the most important evidence for this perspective came from a study conducted by Nordenstreng in Finland. His research showed that while 80 per cent of Finns watch at least one news broadcast per day, when interviewed the next day they could remember hardly any specific information given during the broadcast: the main impression retained was that 'nothing much had happened'. On this basis Nordenstreng argued that the 'content of the news is indifferent to the audience' (Nordenstreng 1972: 390). He concluded that watching television news was a 'mere ritual' for the audience which had little effect on their attitudes or opinions (see below, p. 252).

While it would be foolish to deny the ritual aspects of 'watching the news' at fixed points in the day for most of us, it may be equally wrong to reduce the watching of news purely to its ritual aspect, and to claim that beyond this it is of no significance. Everything depends on how you conceive the question of 'effect'.

It may be that to think of 'effects' purely in terms of immediate effects on attitudes or levels of information is to pose the problem badly. Hartmann and Husband argue that:

to look for effects in terms of simple changes of attitude may be to look in the wrong place. Part of the high incidence of null results in attempts to demonstrate the effects of mass communications lies in the nature of the research questions asked . . . it may be that the media have little immediate impact on attitudes as commonly assessed by social scientists, but it seems likely that they have other important effects. In particular they would seem to play a major part in defining for people what the important issues are and the terms in which they should be discussed.

(Hartmann and Husband 1972: 439)

One cannot argue that just because an audience cannot remember specific content – names of ministers, etc. – that therefore a news broadcast has had 'no effect'. The important point is that while an audience may retain

little in terms of specific information, they may well retain general 'definitions of the order of things' – ideological categories embedded in the
structure of the specific content. Indeed Hartmann and Husband's research
on race and the media precisely focused on the impact of the media on
definitional frameworks, rather than on specific attitudes or levels of
information. These researchers found that while the media seemed to have
a low level of impact on the attitudes of the media audience towards Blacks
in their area, the media did have a very large impact on the ways in which
people thought about 'race' issues. Thus media impact was seen as 'operating on interpretative frameworks – the categories people use when
thinking about race-related matters – rather than on attitudes directly'
(ibid., 440). This, then, is to conceive of the media as having 'effects' at the
level of 'defining the issues', setting the agenda of social problems, and
providing the terms in which those problems can be thought about.

As indicated in Chapter 1, an influential perspective on these questions
has been that provided by the 'uses and gratifications' approach, which
might be said to imply a more benevolent view of the media – seeing them
not so much imposing messages on the audience, as providing the audience
with stimuli which can be used in different ways, to obtain different forms
of gratification. However, within the uses and gratifications perspective the
main interest tends to fall on individual differences in the interpretation of
messages. Thus a certain message (for instance, a sketch in *Not the 9
O'Clock News*) might mean one thing to me and another to you, simply
depending on our personalities (e.g. whether or not we are attracted to
extrovert comedians), whether or not the message related to our different
hobbies or interests (e.g. whether or not we are interested in politics or
gardening). However, it can be argued that the question of different
interpretations of messages is not quite such a purely individual question as
this. I want to suggest that it is not simply a question of the different
psychologies of individuals, but is also a question of differences between
individuals involved in different sub-cultures, with different socio-
economic backgrounds. That is to say, while of course there will always be
individual differences in how people interpret a particular message, those
individual differences might well turn out to be framed by cultural differences. This is to stress the significance of the differences between the
cultural frameworks available to different individuals – so that if I, say, as a
Durham coalminer, interpret a message about government economic
policy differently from you, say, as an East Anglian bank manager, this is
not a difference which is simply attributable to our different psychologies.
The difference between our responses to this message has also to be related
to our different social backgrounds, to the way in which they provide
us with different kinds of cultural tools, different kinds of conceptual
frameworks through which we relate to the media. Murdock makes
this point well:

In order to provide anything like a satisfactory account of the relation-ship between people's mass media involvements and their own social situation and meaning system, it is necessary to start from the social setting rather than from the individual; to replace the idea of personal 'needs' with the notion of structural contradiction; and to introduce the concept of sub-culture . . .

Sub-cultures are the meaning systems and modes of expression devel-oped by groups in particular parts of the social structure in the course of their collective attempt to come to terms with the contradictions in their shared social situation. More particularly, sub-cultures represent the accumulated meanings and means of expression through which groups in subordinate structural positions have attempted to negotiate or oppose the dominant meaning system. They therefore provide a pool of available symbolic resources which particular individuals or groups can draw on in their attempt to make sense of their own specific situation and construct a viable identity.

(Murdock 1973: 213–14)

The analysis of messages

This study of programme structure takes its examples from the BBC television programme *Nationwide*. This clearly invites the question 'Why study a programme such as *Nationwide*?' Why put a great deal of energy into analysing and discovering the structure of a programme which doesn't take itself seriously? A programme which, to quote a former producer, 'does the things that don't matter, at least not to us'. It is a programme for which the broadcasters make no large claims. They see it as a teatime show addressed to an audience which is busy putting children to bed, coming in from work, having tea, and correspondingly they feel that the main point is to provide 'entertainment' and 'human interest'. While the programme may at times attempt to find a way of dealing with the 'serious issues' which face us as a nation, and as individual subjects of that nation, these are exceptional within the basic perspective of the programme.

I want to argue that, despite the programme-makers' self-denigrating remarks, programmes such as *Nationwide* can play a crucial ideological role in the process of communication and that, in consequence, it is particularly important for us to analyse them. Indeed, in some ways, it may be even more important to understand a programme such as *Nationwide* than to understand the more evidently 'controversial' or 'serious' pro-grammes, such as *Panorama*, because through the varied individual reports of 'human life' in our times which constitute *Nationwide*'s stock in trade, a very important set of implicit messages about basic attitudes and social values is also transmitted. These values and attitudes, taken together, tend to constitute what we might think of as a set of 'base-line' assumptions about life in contemporary Britain and about what are the 'sensible' attitudes for us to take towards various 'social problems'. This is not to do with explicit statements in the programme; it is, rather, to do with a set of assumptions that one can deduce from the particular content of the programme. The important point is that this set of assumptions constitutes the ground on which the more serious broadcasting, the *Panorama*s, the news broadcasts can be said to stand. These explicitly non-serious programmes constitute the framework within which the more explicitly controversial messages are to be situated.

This is to argue that there is, in television, no such thing as 'an innocent text' – no programme which is not worthy of serious attention, no programme which can claim to provide only 'entertainment' rather than messages about society. Even though the explicit content of a programme may seem to be of a rather trivial nature – for instance, Tom and Jerry cartoons – it may well be that a number of very important messages about social attitudes and values are built into the programme's texture. For example, in their study of the Donald Duck comics the sociologists Armand Mattelart and Aerial Dorfmann point to the way in which the seemingly innocent antics of the inhabitants of 'Duckburgh' are framed by ideological assumptions about individuality, freedom and 'how to get rich', and also about sexuality and the 'nature' of the family (Mattelart and Dorfmann 1979).

Any programme presents various kinds of explicit information – facts, stories, pictures. Further, the broadcasting institutions provide us with certain kinds of 'frames' into which to fit this 'information' – the programme is billed in the *Radio Times* or the *TV Times* in a certain way, introduced to us by a familiar presenter – and these 'framing devices' link the particular programme into the flow of broadcasting and give us clues as to what expectations to have of it – whether it will principally be concerned to inform or to entertain us, for instance.

However, programmes communicate more than their explicit (manifest) content – they also contain latent messages through implication, assumption or connotation. To understand this level of latent or implicit communication we need to go beyond commonsense observation. At this point we confront a set of questions about methodology – about how we can construct a method of analysis that will enable us to understand these more complex levels of communication.

When we ask the question 'What is a programme saying?', we need also to ask a further question: 'What is taken-for-granted (what 'doesn't need saying') within the programme?'. This brings into focus the question of what kinds of assumptions are made, what kinds of things are *in*visible in the programme, what kinds of questions can*not* be raised within the framework of the programme. This is to start to look not simply at what is present in a programme, but at the relationship between what is explicitly presented and what is absent. It is to enquire whether there are certain characteristic blind spots, silences within the discourse of the programme. If this is so, then we need to understand this pattern of presences/absences if we are to understand the significance of any particular item which does appear in the programme. Here we become involved in a set of problems about methodologies of analysis. There are various competing kinds of methodological approach to the analysis of messages within the media. However, despite the differences in approach offered by content or structural analysis, for example, the two methods tend to have a common misconception of the message/audience relation. That is, both these methods tend to operate with a 'hypodermic' model of the media/audience interaction. Both perspectives tend to assume that all you need to know are the characteristics of the message, from which you can then predict audience effects, and that this knowledge is to be produced by ever more sophisticated methods of textual analysis. The problem is that here we may be involved in something rather akin to the search for the unicorn, an endless quest for a mythical object – the 'real' or 'ultimate' meaning of the message.

However, certain forms of semiological analysis may provide us with a more useful approach in so far as they concentrate not so much on establishing the 'real' or 'ultimate' meaning of a message as on examining the basic conditions of meaningful communication. This approach turns our attention towards examining the codes which are implicit and explicit in the messages – which make it possible for the message to have any meaning at all for the audience. Indeed, later developments in semiological analysis have moved away from the notion of a message being sent to an already positioned subject, to explore the process through which an individual subjectivity is itself constructed. This is to accept the fundamental principle (derived from Voloshinov 1973) that a message is, inevitably, polysemic – a message is always capable of producing more than one meaning, or interpretation, and can never be reduced simply to one 'ultimate' or 'real' meaning. This form of analysis can also be aligned with some of the insights derived from the uses and gratifications approach as to the different possible uses or interpretations which different people may make of any one message.

However, the situation is more complex than that, for we must also attend to the way in which, because of their necessary concern with 'clarity' and 'effective' communication, the broadcasters cannot simply leave the messages as equally open to *any* interpretation. Here we part company with the uses and gratifications approach, which treats the message simply as if it were an empty box, a stimulus, which the decoder is free to use as he or she wishes. We must attend to the way in which the broadcasters, constrained as they are by their desire to communicate 'effectively', are bound to attempt to provide 'direction' or 'closures' within the structure of the message, which attempt to establish *one* of the several possible readings as the 'preferred or dominant reading'.

There are various forms in which these closures can exist within the structure of a programme: for instance, the headline, the caption to a photograph or the commentary to a film report which tell us how to interpret the significance of the images we see. There are also questions about the differential status of speakers within a programme, and the way in which particular contributions are framed by the presenters. There are further questions about the way in which the aim of the presenters within the programme might be to secure a kind of identification between them and the audience and so gain the audience's complicity or assent to the preferred reading which is suggested by the framing and linking discourse of the programme. However, we must not assume that these strategies of closure are necessarily effective. It is always possible to read against the grain, as it were, to produce an interpretation which goes against the grain of that 'preferred' by the programme discourse.

In analysing programmes it cannot be enough simply to look at the content of what is said. We have also to look at the assumptions that lie behind that content. There will be assumptions about us as audience, and these assumptions need to be made visible if we are to understand the implicit 'messages' which a programme may transmit over and above what is explicitly said in it. Thus, we need to be concerned with the modes in which programmes address us, as audience, and with how these 'modes of address' construct our relation to the content of the programme, requiring us to take up different positions in relation to them. This emphasizes the role of television discourse not just in reinforcing pre-established subject positions but rather in actively constructing these viewing positions. Thus, *Panorama* might be said to address us directly as individual citizens of the national political community. *Mr and Mrs* or *The Generation Game* seem to assume that we all live as families, and they address us principally as members of a family. Other programmes seem to address us principally as private individuals, relating to our private interests and hobbies (*Gardener's World*); other programmes address us as consumers, taking up our complaints, examining difficulties and problems in the marketplace.

Mr and Mrs and *The Generation Game* are not preceded by a sociological preamble, which explains that we are going to be addressed on the assumption we all live in families. Rather, no other possibility than that we exist in families is considered. We have to make explicit what assumptions are being made – as these are the grounds on which the programme stands, the taken-for-granted framework within which particular things are said. The concept of mode of address can help us to be more precise in considering what might be called, say, within the framework of literary criticism, the particular 'style' of a programme. I am using 'mode of address' to designate what is distinctive about the specific communicative forms and practices of a programme. Crucially, we are concerned here with the way a programme attempts to establish, through its manner of presentation, a particular form of relation with its audience. However, we should not assume that any programme is necessarily successful in 'positioning' its audience. In the case of a current affairs programme, for example, we need to ask to what extent the audience identifies with the image of itself, presented on the one hand via 'vox pop' material, and on the other hand by more implicit assumptions about what the 'ordinary person's/common-sense' viewpoint on X would be. How far do the different presenters secure the popular identifications to which they (implicitly) lay claim? Which sections of the audience accept which presenter styles as 'appropriate' points of identification for them? Does acceptance or identification mean that the audience will then take over the frameworks of understanding within which the presenters encapsulate the reports? How much weight do a presenter's 'summing-up' comments carry for the audience in terms of what code of connotation they 'map' particular reports into? How far do which sections of the audience align themselves with the 'we' assumed by the presenter/interviewer? To what extent do different sections of the audience identify with interviewers and feel that they are 'lending' him/her their authority to investigate figures in public life 'on their behalf'?

In the end, these are all empirical questions, and in order to throw some light on them we shall need to consider some empirical evidence from research into the audience. However, before doing this, we need to formulate more clearly the theoretical framework within which we are trying to conceptualize the audience.

The message: encoding and decoding

The premises on which this approach is based are:

(a) the same event can be encoded in more than one way;

(b) the message always contains more than one potential 'reading'. Messages propose and prefer certain readings over others, but they can never become wholly closed around one reading: they remain polysemic;

(c) understanding the message is also a problematic practice, however transparent and 'natural' it may seem. Messages encoded one way can always be read in a different way.

In this approach, then, the message is treated neither as a unilateral sign, without ideological 'flux', nor, as in the uses and gratifications approach, as a disparate sign which can be read *any* way, according to the psychology of the decoder. Reference can usefully be made here to Voloshinov's distinction between sign and signal, and his argument that structuralist approaches tend to treat the former as if they were the latter – i.e. as if they had fixed meanings. The television message is treated as a complex sign in which a preferred reading has been inscribed, but which retains the potential, if decoded in a manner different from the way in which it has been encoded, of communicating a different meaning. The message is thus a structured polysemy. It is central to the argument that *all* meanings do not exist 'equally' in the message: it has been structured in dominance, despite the impossibility of a 'total closure' of meaning. Further, the 'preferred reading' is itself part of the message, and can be identified within its linguistic and communicative structure.

Thus, when analysis shifts to the 'moment' of the encoded message itself, the communicative form and structure can be analysed in terms of what the mechanisms are which prefer one, dominant reading over the other readings; what the means are which the encoder uses to try to 'win the assent of the audience' to his preferred reading of the message.

Before messages can have 'effects' on the audience, they must be decoded. 'Effects' is thus a shorthand, and inadequate, way of marking the point where audiences differentially read and make sense of messages which have been transmitted, and act on those meanings within the context of their situation and experience. We assume that there will be no necessary 'fit' or transparency between the encoding and decoding ends of the communication chain (cf. Hall 1974). It is precisely this lack of transparency, and its consequences for communication that we need to investigate.

We have established that there is always a possibility of disjunction between the codes of those sending and those receiving messages through the circuit of mass communications. The problems of the 'effects' of communication can now be reformulated, as that of the extent to which decodings take place within the limits of the preferred (or dominant) manner in which the message has been initially encoded. However, the complementary aspect of this problem is that of the extent to which these interpretations, or decodings, also reflect, and are inflected by, the codes and discourses which different sections of the audience inhabit, and the ways in which this is determined by the socially governed distribution of cultural codes between and across different sections of the audience: that is, the range of different decoding strategies and competences in the audience.

To raise this as a problem for research is already to argue that the meaning produced by the encounter of text and subject cannot be 'read off' straight from 'textual characteristics'. The text cannot be considered in isolation from its historical conditions of production and consumption: 'What has to be identified is the use to which a particular text is put, its function within a particular conjecture, in particular institutional spaces, and in relation to particular audiences' (Neale 1977: 39–40). As Hill puts the point, an analysis of media ideology could not rest with an analysis of production and text alone; but must in fact include a theory of readership and analysis of consumption:

> The meaning of a film is not something to be discovered purely in the text itself, but is constituted in the interaction between the text and its users . . . The early claim of semiology to be able to account for a text's functioning through an immanent analysis was essentially misfounded in its failure to perceive that any textual system could only have meaning in relation to codes not purely textual, and that the recognition, distribution, and activation of these would vary socially and historically.
>
> (Hill 1979: 122)

Thus the meaning of the text must be thought of in terms of which set of discourses it encounters in any particular set of circumstances – and how this encounter may re-structure both the meaning of the text and the discourses which it meets. The meaning of the text will be constructed differently according to the discourses (knowledge, prejudices, resistances) brought to bear on the text by the reader: the crucial factor in the encounter of audience/subject and text will be the range of discourses at the disposal of the audience. Thus social position may set parameters to the range of potential readings, through the structure of access to different codes (e.g. a Black working-class man is unlikely to be 'educated' in the codes of opera; equally, a White upper-class man is unlikely to be 'educated' in the codes of reggae or ska) – certain social positions allow access to wider repertoires of available codes, certain others to narrower ranges.

Whether or not a programme succeeds in transmitting the preferred or dominant meaning will depend on whether it encounters readers who inhabit codes and ideologies derived from other institutional areas which correspond to and work in parallel with those of the programme, or whether it encounters readers who inhabit codes drawn from other areas or institutions which conflict to a greater or lesser extent with those of the programme.

If a notion such as a 'preferred reading' is to have any value, it is not as a means of an abstracted 'fixing' of one interpretation over and above others, but as a means of accounting for how, under certain conditions, in particular contexts, a text will tend to be read in a particular way by (at least some sections of) the audience.

Reconceptualizing the audience

It might be best to think of the audience less as an undifferentiated mass of individuals than as a complicated pattern of overlapping sub-groups and sub-cultures, within which individuals are situated. While we cannot take a

determinist position and assume that someone's conceptual/cultural framework will be automatically determined by their social position, we do need
to bear in mind the way in which social contexts provide the resources, and
set the limits within which individuals operate.

Members of a given sub-culture will tend to share a cultural orientation
towards decoding messages in particular ways. Their individual readings of
messages will be framed by shared cultural formations and practices, which
will in turn be determined by the objective position of the individual in the
social structure. This is not to say that a person's objective social position
determines his consciousness in a mechanistic way; people understand
their situation and react to it through the level of sub-cultures and
meaning-systems.

We need to break fundamentally with the 'uses and gratifications'
approach, and its exclusive emphasis on individual psychological differences of interpretation. What is needed is an approach which links differential interpretations back to the socio-economic structure of society –
showing how members of different groups and classes, sharing different
cultural codes, will interpret a given message differently, not just at the
personal/idiosyncratic level, but in a way systematically related to their
socio-economic position. In short, we need to see how the different sub-
cultural structures and formations within the audience, and the sharing of
different cultural codes and competences amongst different groups and
classes, structure the decoding of the message for different sections of the
audience.

We need to divide and categorize the myriad individual variations in
audience responses to media messages if we are to achieve a social perspective on the process of mass communication. A useful way to do this is
provided by Frank Parkin's theory of the way in which members of the
different social classes within a society can be expected to inhabit what he
calls different 'meaning-systems' or ideological frameworks (Parkin, 1971).
By extension we can apply this model to try to account for the way in which
members of different classes decode media messages.

Parkin argues that within 'Western societies' we can usefully distinguish
three major meaning-systems; that each derives from a different social
source; and that each promotes 'a different moral interpretation of class
inequality'. Parkin claims that these are:

1 the dominant value-system, the social source of which is the major
   institutional order; this is a moral framework which promotes the endor-
   sement of existing inequality, in deferential terms;
2 the subordinate value-system, the social source or generating milieu of
   which is the local working-class community; this framework promotes
   accommodative responses to the facts of inequality and low status;
3 the radical value-system, the source of which is the mass political party

based on the working class; this framework promotes an oppositional interpretation of class inequalities.

Following but adapting Parkin, we can suggest three positions in which the decoder may stand to the encoded message. He or she may take the meaning fully within the interpretative framework which the message itself proposes and prefers; if so, decoding proceeds within, or is aligned with, the dominant code. Second, the decoder may take the meaning broadly as encoded, but by relating the message to some concrete or situated context which reflects his/her position and interests, the reader may modify or partially inflect the given preferred meaning. Following Parkin, we can call this a 'negotiated' decoding. Third, the decoder may recognize how the message has been contextually encoded, but may bring to bear an alternative frame of reference which sets to one side the encoded framework and superimposes on the message an interpretation which works in a directly 'oppositional' way. Such readings cannot be regarded as 'wrong'. They are rather more appropriately understood as a running critique of the preferred reading.

Parkin elaborated his model as a way of understanding the typical positions of members of different classes in relation to the dominant ideology of a society. We are more directly concerned with the question of the range of possible positions in which different sections of the audience may stand in relation to a given message. Parkin's schema, as adapted above, allows us to account for the three logical possibilities: that the decoder will either share, partly share, or reject the code in which a given message has been encoded. This is, evidently, only a very rough schema, and the broad categories – dominant, negotiated and oppositional code – will need to be broken down internally to account for the variations which can occur within this basic schema; for instance, in terms of different forms or variants of, say, the dominant code. Whatever shortcomings Parkin's schema may have, it does allow us to conceive of a socially structured audience and, as such, constitutes a considerable advance on any model which simply conceives of the audience as an unstructured aggregate of individuals.

It may be as well to try to make clear here what is not being said or implied by this framework. In insisting that individual decodings of messages must be considered within their socio-cultural context, I am not implying that individual thought and action are simply determined by, and therefore directly 'explicable' in terms of social position. This would be a crude form of determinism which effectively obliterated the category of the individual – as actor in a social world – and replaced it with the category of social class – as if all the facts about an individual (and in particular the way in which an individual decoded messages) could be reduced to the question of which social class he or she belonged to. We do not need to think of this as an either/or problem: i.e. that decoding is *either* infinitely variable as between all individuals *or* directly predictable for all members of a given social class as a direct and determined consequence of their social position. Rather, we need to understand the relation of the two dimensions – that of individual, varied, experience and response, as it exists in a particular social context, working with the cultural resources available in that context. This is to conceive of the social individual – the individual decoder in a given structured social context.

This leads on to a further point. There is one critical problem with the attempt to incorporate the sociological work of authors such as Parkin into a theory of communications. The problem can be described as that of a tendency towards sociolog*ism* – by which I mean the attempt immediately to convert social categories (e.g. class) into meanings (e.g. ideological positions) without paying due attention to the specific factors involved in this 'conversion'. That is to say that it is inadequate to present social factors – such as age, sex, race, class – as determinants of decoding without specifying how these factors intervene in the process of communication. We must pay attention to the specific mechanisms through which social factors are articulated into discourses. Social factors cannot be treated as if they somehow directly 'intervened' in the communication process. These factors can only have an effect on communication as they are articulated through discourses – through the meaning-systems or codes within which the members of a given class live and understand their experience.

Thus, to take an example, you cannot 'explain' why a member of one particular class decodes a particular message differently from a member of another class directly in terms of class background or position. A person's class position does not 'intervene' in the process of decoding in the manner of the Lone Ranger, riding straight in and fighting off the enemy. Indeed class position can only be of relevance to the decoding process as it is articulated at the level of signs and discourses.

INVESTIGATING AUDIENCE RESPONSES – THE *NATIONWIDE* RESEARCH PROJECT

In order to bring the theoretical questions outlined so far into sharper focus, the remainder of this chapter will present some evidence from the *Nationwide* research project referred to earlier. The first stage of this project was an analysis of *Nationwide*, which involved collective viewing and discussion of the programme over a period of months to establish its recurrent themes and presentational formats, supplemented by an analysis in detail of the internal structure of one particular edition of the programme.[1] By dealing with the specific textual structure of the programme and with empirical investigation of differential interpretations of that same programme material by different groups, we hoped to highlight the nature of the interaction through which audiences produce meanings from the material (words, images) presented to them in the organized form of the text.

Specifically, the project attempted to relate the analysis of practices of 'decoding' of media material to the theoretical problematic centring on the concept of hegemony. In brief, the concept of hegemony enables us to understand the process of meaning-construction as occurring, within any society, in the context of a set of power relations, in which different groups are in competition for the 'power to define' events and values. However, this is usually posed as a rather abstracted process – not really grounded in the analysis of any particular set of communicative exchanges within the society in question. Our concern in the *Nationwide* research project was to connect the theoretical question of the maintenance of hegemony with the empirical question of how a particular programme acts to 'prefer' one set of meanings or definitions of events.

We also wanted to investigate the different forms of negotiation and resistance that the programme met from different groups – i.e. to investigate the extent (or the limits) to which the 'hegemonic' definitions articulated by the programme were taken up and accepted by its audience. Thus we were concerned with the conditions under which counter-hegemonic, or oppositional, meanings were produced within the communicative exchanges initiated by the programme. The project was then concerned to investigate empirically some particular forms of communication through which potentially hegemonic meanings were in passage. We showed videotapes of two *Nationwide* programmes to a range of groups from very different social backgrounds and interviewed them to establish their interpretations of the programmes.

The first programme was shown to eighteen groups drawn from different levels of the educational system, with different social and cultural backgrounds, some in the Midlands region where the programme was broadcast, some in London. These were school-children and part-time and full-time students, in different levels of further and higher education.

The second programme was shown to eleven groups, some from different levels of the education system, but others from both trade union and management training centres, this time mainly in London. These groups included full- and part-time students in further and higher education, full- and part-time trade union officials and managers from banking and printing institutions.

Our procedure was to gain entry to a situation where the group already had some existence as a social entity – at least for the duration of a course. We then arranged the discussions to slot into their respective courses and showed the videotape of the appropriate programme in the context of their established institutional setting.

The groups were mainly of between five and ten people. After the viewing of the videotape, we tape-recorded the subsequent discussion (usually of about thirty minutes' duration), and this was later transcribed to provide the basic data for the analysis.

When watching television programmes the individual viewer confronts a set of signs which have been organized and structured by professional broadcasters in such a way as to 'prefer' a particular reading, or range of readings. However, the individual viewer does not come to the moment of viewing 'culturally naked' – he comes to the text carrying already, and thinking within, his own set of cultural codes and frameworks – derived from his social and cultural situation and background. In the moment of viewing, the codes and structure of the programme meet and have to be filtered through the codes and discourses at the viewer's disposal. The meaning produced by this encounter will vary systematically (as, I hope, the following extracts from the *Nationwide* research project will show) in relation to the audience members' insertion in various kinds of discourses and codes. The meaning or 'reading' of the programme generated by the viewer then depends both on how the programme has been structured by the broadcasters and on what codes of interpretation the viewer brings with him or her to the text.

Research design and methodology

The overall plan of this research project can be seen to have been adapted from that proposed by Umberto Eco (1972):

1 Theoretical clarification and definition of the concepts and methods to be used on the research.
2 Analysis of messages attempting to elucidate the basic codes of meaning to which they refer, the recurrent patterns and structures in the messages, the ideology implicit in the concepts and categories via which the messages are transmitted. (An account of the substantive products of these phases of the research can be found in *Everyday Television: 'Nationwide'*, along with a discussion of some of the problems of programme analysis. Space only allows a brief indication of the main outline of the methods of analysis employed there. The programmes were analysed principally in terms of the way they are constructed: how topics are articulated; how background and explanatory frameworks are mobilized, visually and verbally; how expert commentary is integrated; and how discussions and interviews are monitored and conducted. The aim was not to provide a single, definitive reading of the programmes, but to establish provisional readings of their main communicative and ideological structures. Points of specific concern were those communicative devices and strategies aimed at making the programmes' topics 'intellig-

ible' and filling out their ramifications for the programmes' intended audiences.)

3 Field research by interview to establish how the messages previously analysed have in fact been received and interpreted by sections of the media audience in different structural positions, using as a framework for analysis the three basic ideal-typical possibilities:

(a) where the audience interprets the message in terms of the same code employed by the transmitter – e.g. where both 'inhabit' the dominant ideology;

(b) where the audience employs a 'negotiated' version of the code employed by the transmitter – e.g. receiver employs a negotiated version of the dominant ideology used by the transmitter to encode the message;

(c) where the audience employs an 'oppositional' code to interpret the message and therefore interprets its meaning through a different code from that employed by the transmitter.

4 All the data on how the messages were received having been collected, these were compared with the analyses previously carried out on the messages, to see:

(a) if some receptions showed levels of meaning in the messages which had completely escaped the notice of our analysis;

(b) how the 'visibility' of different meanings related to respondents' socio-economic positions;

(c) to what extent different sections of the audience did interpret the messages in different ways and to what extent they projected freely on to the message meanings they would want to find there. We might discover, for instance, that the community of users has such freedom in decoding the message as to make the influencing power of the media much weaker than one might have thought. Or just the opposite.

The Nationwide audience project: research procedure

The project aims were defined as being:

1 to construct a typology of the range of decodings made;
2 to analyse how and why they vary;
3 to demonstrate how different interpretations are generated;
4 to relate these variations to other cultural factors: what is the nature of the 'fit' between class, socio-economic or educational position and cultural or interpretative competences/discourses/codes?

The first priority was to determine whether different sections of the audience shared, modified or rejected the ways in which topics had been encoded by the broadcasters. This involved the attempt to identify the 'lexico-referential systems' employed by broadcasters and respondents following Mills's proposals for an indexical analysis of vocabularies. He assumes that we can:

> locate a thinker among political and social co-ordinates by ascertaining what words his functioning vocabulary contains and what nuances of meaning and value they embody. In studying vocabularies we detect implicit evaluations and the collective patterns behind them, cues for social behaviour. A thinker's social and political rationale is implicit in his choice and use of words. Vocabularies socially canalise thought.
>
> (Mills 1939: 434–5)

Thus, the kinds of questions to be asked were: Do audiences use the same words in the same ways as broadcasters when talking about aspects of the topic? Do respondents rank these aspects in the same order of priority as the broadcasters? Are there aspects of the topic not discussed by broadcasters which are specifically mentioned by respondents?

Moreover, beyond the level of vocabularies, the crucial questions are: to what extent does the audience identify with the image of itself presented to it via 'vox pop' material (and via other, more implicit, definitions and assumptions about what the commonsense/ordinary person's viewpoint on X is)? How far do the different presenters secure the popular identification to which they (implicitly) lay claim? Which sections of the audience accept which presenter styles as 'appropriate' points of identification for them? And, does acceptance or identification mean that the audience will then take over the meta-messages and frameworks of understanding within which the presenters encapsulate the reports? How much weight do Barratt's 'summing-up' comments on reports in *Nationwide* carry for the audience in terms of what code of connotation they then map the report on to? How far, for events of different degrees of 'distance' from their immediate situation and interests, do which sections of the audience align themselves with the 'we' assumed by the presenter/interviewer? To what extent do different sections of the audience identify with an interviewer and feel that they are 'lending' him/her their authority to interrogate figures in public life on their behalf?

Investigating decodings: the problem of language

Language must be conceived of as exercising a determining influence on the problems of individual thought and action. As Alasdair MacIntyre puts it,

> The limits of what I can do intentionally are set by the limits of the descriptions available to me; and the descriptions available to me are those current in the social groups to which I belong. If the limits of action are the limits of description, then to analyse the ideas current in a

society (or subgroup of it) is also to discern the limits within which
rational, intended action necessarily moves in that society (or
subgroup).

(quoted in Morley 1974: 12)

In these terms, thinking is the selection and manipulation of 'available'
symbolic material, and what is available to which groups is a question of
the socially structured distribution of differential cultural options and
competences. As Mills argues, 'It is only by utilising the symbols common
to his group that a thinker can think and communicate. Language, socially
built and maintained, embodies implicit exhortations and social evaluations' (Mills 1939: 433). Mills goes on to quote Kenneth Burke: 'the
names for things and operations smuggle in connotations of good and bad –
a noun tends to carry with it a kind of invisible adjective, and a verb an
invisible adverb'. He continues:

> By acquiring the categories of a language, we acquire the structured
> 'ways' of a group, and along with language, the value-implications of
> those 'ways'. Our behaviour and perception, our logic and thought,
> come within the control of a system of language. Along with language,
> we acquire a set of social norms and values. A vocabulary is not merely
> a string of words; immanent within it are societal textures – institutional
> and political coordinates

– a modified version of Mead's concept of the 'generalised other',
which is

> the internalised audience with which the thinker converses: a focalised
> and abstracted organisation of attitudes of those implicated in the social
> field of behaviour and experience . . . which is socially limited and
> limiting . . . The audience conditions the talker; the other conditions
> the thinker.

(ibid., 426–7)

However, Mills goes on to make the central qualification (and this is a
point that would apply equally as a criticism of a concept of the 'other'
derived from Lacan): 'I do not believe (as Mead does . . .) that the
generalised other incorporates "the whole society", but rather that it
stands for selected societal segments' (427). This, then, is to propose a
theory not only of the social and psychological, but also of the political,
determinations of language and thought.

'Different languages': project methods

The inadequacy of a purely substantive approach, which assumes that it
makes sense to add up all the 'yesses' and 'noes' given to a particular

question by different respondents, is highlighted once we query the assumption that all these responses mean the same thing. As Deutscher puts it, 'Should we assume that a response of "yah", "da", "si", "oui", or "yes" all really mean the same thing in response to the same question? Or may there be different kinds of affirmative connotations in different languages?' (Deutscher 1977: 244). He goes on to make the point that

> A simple English "no" tends to be interpreted by members of an Arabic culture as meaning "yes". A real "no" would need to be emphasised; the simple "no" indicates a desire for further negotiation. Likewise a non-emphasised "yes" will often be interpreted as a polite refusal.
>
> (244)

However, he argues, these are not simply points which relate to gross lingual differences; these same differences also exist between groups inhabiting different sections and versions of what we normally refer to as the 'same language'. As Mills puts it, 'writings get reinterpreted as they are diffused across audiences with different nuances of meaning . . . A symbol has a different meaning when interpreted by persons actualising different cultures or strata within a culture' (Mills 1939: 435).

Hymes makes the point:

> The case is clear in bilingualism; we do not expect a Bengali using English as a fourth language for certain purposes of commerce to be influenced deeply in world view by its syntax . . . What is necessary is to realise that the monolingual situation is problematic as well. People do not all everywhere use language to the same degree, in the same situations, or for the same things.
>
> (quoted in Deutscher 1977: 246)

Thus, in the first instance, I worked with tapes of respondents' actual speech, rather than simply the substance of their responses, in an attempt to begin to deal with the level of forms of expression and of the degrees of 'fit' between respondents' vocabularies and forms of speech and those of the media (though this aspect of the research is still underdeveloped). For similar reasons I dealt with open discussions rather than pre-sequenced interview schedules, attempting to impose an order of response as little as possible, and, indeed, taking the premise that the order in which respondents ranked and spoke of issues would itself be a significant finding of the research.

The focused interview

The key methodological technique used in this research the focused interview – designed, as Merton and Kendall note, 'to determine responses to particular communications . . . which have been previously analysed by the investigator' (Merton and Kendall 1955) and crucially providing a means of focusing on 'the subjective experiences of persons exposed to the pre-analysed situation in an effort to ascertain their definition of the situation'.

The initial stages of interviewing were non-directive; only in subsequent stages of an interview, having attempted to establish the frames of reference and functioning vocabulary with which respondents defined the situation, did I begin to introduce questions about the programme material based on earlier analysis of it. Again, following Merton, I attempted to do this in such a way that the specific questions introduced did not cut across the flow of the conversation but rather engaged with, and tried to develop, points already raised by the respondents. The movement of the discussion was thus from open-ended prompting (e.g. 'What did you make of that item?') to more specifically structured questions (e.g. 'Did you think the use of that word to describe X was right?'). The initial stages of the discussions enabled the respondents to elaborate, by way of discussing among themselves, their reconstruction of the programme, while the later stages made possible a more direct check on the impact of what, in the programme analysis, had been taken to be the significant points. In short, the strategy was to begin with the most naturalistic responses, and to move progressively towards a more structured probing of hypotheses.

Group interviews

The choice to work with groups rather than individuals (given that limitations of resources did not allow us the luxury of both) was made on the grounds that much individually based interview research is flawed by a focus on individuals as social atoms divorced from their social context.

This project's results confirm the findings of Piepe *et al.* (1975: 163) that while 'people's uses of newspapers, radio and television is varied, it is fairly uniform within subgroups'. While there is some disagreement and argument within the different groups over the decoding of particular items, the differences in decodings between the groups from the different categories is far greater than the level of difference and variation within the groups. This seems to confirm the validity of the original decision to use group discussions – feeling that the aim was to discover how interpretations were collectively constructed through talk and the interchange between respondents in the group situation – rather than to treat individuals as the autonomous repositories of a fixed set of individual 'opinions' isolated from their social context (see earlier, pp. 17–18).

Analysing interview tapes

My concern was to examine the actual speech-forms, the working vocabulary, implicit conceptual frameworks, strategies of formulation and their underlying logics through which interpretations, or decodings, are constructed – in short, the mechanisms of cultural competences. Since there is as yet no one adequate methodology for the analysis of complex, informal discourse, I employed a number of related strategies for the analysis of responses.

At the first level I attempted to establish the visible particularities in the lexical repertoires of the different groups – where particular terms and patterns of phrase mark off the discourses of the different groups one from another. Here it has been of particular interest to establish where, because of differences in overall perspective, the same terms can function in distinct ways within the discourses of the different groups.

At a second level I was concerned to identify the patterns of argumentation and the manner of referring to evidence or of formulating viewpoints which different groups predominantly employ. Here, for instance, an attempt has been made to establish how the central topic areas identified in the programme analysis ('commonsense', 'individuality', 'the family', 'the nation', etc.) are formulated by the different groups. Particularly important here has been the attempt to establish the differential definitions of, on the one hand, 'commonsense' and, on the other, 'good television' operated by the different groups as the points of reference from which evaluations of particular items or aspects of the programme are made. The difficulty here was that of producing explications of such 'taken-for-granted' concepts. The attempt to probe such areas directly often meets with a resistance on the part of respondents, who presumably feel, along with Cicourel, that such attempts at precise definition of 'obvious' terms strips them of 'the kind of vague or taken-for-granted terms and phrases they characteristically use as competent members of that group' (quoted in Deutscher 1977).

At a third level I was concerned with the underlying cognitive or ideological premises which structure the argument and its logic. Here Gerbner's work on proposition analysis (1964) provided the main guide. As Gerbner defines it, the aim of this form of analysis is to make explicit the implicit propositions, assumptions or norms which underlie and make it logically acceptable to advance a particular opinion or point of view. In this way, declarative statements may be reconstructed in terms of the simple propositions which support or underpin them (e.g. in terms of a question in an interview, explicating the assumptions which are probably being held in order for it to make sense to ask that question). Thus, the implied premise of the following question (*Nationwide: Midlands Today*) posed to two academic researchers interviewed on the programme: 'But how will this research help us? What is it going to do for us?' would be constructed as: 'Everyone knows most academic research is pointless. Can you establish your credentials as actually doing research which will have practical use-value?'.

Problems of hypothesis and sample

I attempted to construct a sample of groups who might be expected to vary from 'dominant' through 'negotiated' to 'oppositional' frameworks of decoding. I aimed, with this sample, to identify not only the key points of difference, but also the points at which interpretations of the different groups might overlap one with another – given that I did not assume that there was a direct and exclusive correspondence so that one group would inhabit only one code. Obviously, a crucial point here is that members of a group may inhabit areas of different codes which they operationalize in different situations, and, conversely, different groups may have access to the same codes, though perhaps in different forms.

The research project was designed to explore the hypotheses that decodings might be expected to vary with:

(a) *basic socio-demographic factors*: position in the structures of age, sex, race and class;
(b) involvement in various forms of *cultural frameworks and identifications*, either at the level of formal structures and institutions such as trade unions, political parties, or different sections of the educational system, or at an informal level in terms of involvements in different sub-cultures such as youth or student cultures or those based on racial and cultural minorities.

Evidently, given a rejection of forms of mechanistic determination, it is at this second level that the main concerns are focused. However, the investigation of the relations between levels (a) and (b), and their relations to patterns of decoding, remains important in so far as it allows one to examine, or at least outline, the extent to which these basic socio-demographic factors can be seen to structure and pattern, if not straightforwardly determine, the patterns of access to the second level of cultural and ideological frameworks.

Further, it was necessary to investigate the extent to which decodings varied with:

(c) *topic*: principally in terms of whether the topics treated are distant or 'abstract' in relation to particular groups' own experience and alternative sources of information and perspective, as opposed to those which are situated for them more concretely. Here the project aimed to develop the work of Parkin (1971), Mann (1973) and others, on 'abstract' and 'situated' levels of consciousness. The thesis of these writers is that working-class consciousness is often characterized by an 'acceptance' of dominant ideological frameworks at an abstract level, combined with a tendency at a concrete, situated level to modify and re-interpret the abstractly dominant frameworks in line with localized meaning-systems erected on the basis of specific social experiences. In short, this oscillation in consciousness or conception of contradictions between levels of consciousness is the grounding of the notion of a 'negotiated' code or ideology, which is subordinated, but not fully incorporated, by a dominant ideological framework.

What we need to know is precisely what kind of difference it makes to the decoding of messages when the decoder has direct experience of the events being portrayed by the media, as compared to a situation in which the media account is the audience's only contact with the event? Does direct experience, or access to an alternative account to that presented by the media, lead to a tendency towards a negotiated or an oppositional decoding of the message? If so, might any such tendencies be only short-lived, or apply only to the decoding of some kinds of messages – for instance, messages about events directly concerning the decoders' own interests – or might there be some kind of 'spread' effect such that the tendency towards a negotiated or oppositional decoding applies to all, or to a wide range of messages?

A further level of variation which it had originally been hoped to explore, but from which time and lack of resources ultimately precluded me, was the level of contextual factors – that is, for instance, the extent to which decodings might vary with:

(d) *context*. Of particular concern here were the differences which might arise from a situation in which a programme is decoded in an educational or work context, as compared with its decoding by the same respondents in the context of the family and home.

The absence of this dimension in the study is to be regretted in relation to the investigation of the process by which programmes are, for instance, initially decoded and discussed in the family and then re-discussed and re-interpreted in other contexts. However, I would argue that this absence does not vitiate my results, in so far as I would hypothesize a more fundamental level of consistency of decodings across contexts. The difference between watching a programme in the home, as opposed to in a group at an educational institution, is a situational difference. But the question of which cultural and linguistic codes a person has available to them is a more fundamental question than the situational one. The situational variables will produce differences within the field of interpretations. But the limits of that field are determined at a deeper level, at the level of what language/codes people have available to them – which is not fundamentally changed by differences of situation. As Voloshinov puts it,

The immediate social situation and its immediate social participants determine the 'occasional' form and style of an utterance. The deeper layers of its structure are determined by more sustained and more basic social connections with which the speaker is in contact.

(Voloshinov 1973: 87)

A connected but more serious absence in the research concerns the question of differential decodings, within the family context, between men and women (see Chapter 6 for an exploration of these issues). This is to move away from the traditional assumptions of the family as a non-antagonistic context of decoding and 'unit of consumption' of messages. Interest in this area had originally been stimulated by the results of a project investigating the decoding of media presentation of the Saltley Gate pickets during the miners' strike of 1972 (results kindly made available to me by Charles Parker). That investigation showed a vast discrepancy between the accounts of the situation developed by miners who were at the Saltley picket and those of their wives who viewed the events at home on television, and considerable difficulties for husband and wife in reconciling their respective understandings of the events. This material suggested the necessity of exploring the position of the 'housewife' as a viewer: in so far, for instance, as her position outside the wage-labour economy, and her position in the family, predispose her to decodings in line with what I have defined (Morley 1976) as the media's 'consumerist' presentation of industrial conflict.

Programme outlines

Programme A Nationwide, *19 May 1976*

This programme dealt with a fairly representative mix of *Nationwide* stories – quirky events (a woman revisiting a lion which attacked her), spoofs and parodies (the presenters on a trip down the Norfolk Broads, Americans doing barn dances in Suffolk), mixed with the dubious (a student project making things out of rubbish) and the 'socially useful' (an invention to enable blind people to do three-dimensional drawings). The two items most specifically referred to in the following extracts are two interviews, one with Ralph Nader, the American advocate of consumer rights, and one with Patrick Meehan, released that day from a life-sentence in prison.

Nader is introduced as 'America's leading campaigner on consumer affairs' who is in this country to speak at an Industrial Safety Exhibition; the introduction to the interview notes that 'Mr Nader was paid a fee of £2,000 for speaking'. The interview (three minutes) is held outside the National Exhibition Centre, with the camera alternating between head and shoulders shots of Nader and the interviewer. The interviewer treats Nader with some respect, owing to his accredited 'expert' status, although the questions posed to Nader display some degree of suspicion of his motivation and responsibility. Nader is asked what motivates him to 'get into all these different fields', whether he has the 'degree of expert knowledge to be able to do all this', and how he feels about being described 'as many people would describe you – as an agitator'.

In each case, partly because his 'expert' status means that, within the discourse of the programme, he must be allowed space to develop his points, and partly because of his practised skill at the interview form, Nader manages to turn the questions round, redefine the problem more favourably from his point of view and then give a positive answer. The interview throughout concentrates on his ideas and policies, for instance: 'What are your ideas . . . on industrial safety?'

The interview with Meehan is introduced without any other details about him, or the case he has been involved in, other than that he had spent seven years in prison, 'most of it in solitary confinement as a protest against his conviction'. The point stressed is that it was 'just under two hours ago that he was released' and that *Nationwide* then 'recorded this *exclusive* interview a short time ago'.

The interview lasts four minutes, with the camera continually on Meehan, who is sitting in an armchair, smoking nervously. The interviewer is represented simply as an off-camera voice, and most of the shots are of Meehan's face, much of the time in full close-up, as he recounts his experience.

From the beginning the emphasis is placed on the dramatic, emotional aspects of the situation, and the focus is on Meehan's subjective feelings and responses to his experiences in prison. The questions asked are concerned with Meehan's feelings, to the exclusion of any information about the background of the case. He is asked how he feels now he is 'free and released'; whether 'there was any time during those seven years that you felt you might never get out'; and (twice) 'What was your daily routine in prison?'. As an 'ordinary person' within the categories of the pro-gramme (albeit one who has had an unusual experience), Meehan

(a) is asked about his feelings rather than his ideas;
(b) is not allowed the time to develop any other points;
(c) is not allowed to redefine the questions.

Meehan tries to talk about the political background to the case, but each time he is cut off, and the interviewer brings him back to the question of whether he feels bitter about his experience. (It later transpired that Meehan had at one time been in the employ of British Secret Service, had been sent into the Eastern Bloc and then had come under suspicion of being a double agent. The one reference in the interview to 'British Intelligence' is truncated after those two words.)

Programme B Nationwide, *29 March 1977*

This programme was a 'Budget Special, dealing in the main, and uncharacteristically for *Nationwide*, with the economic and political issues raised by the Budget.

The programme was introduced by Frank Bough as follows:

> And at 6.20, what this 'some now, some later' budget will mean to you. Halma Hudson and I will be looking at how three typical families across the country will be affected. We will be asking . . . union leader Hugh Scanlon and industrialist Ian Fraser about what the budget will mean for the economy.

The main section of the programme examined

> how this budget will affect three typical families, and generally speaking most people in Britain fall into one of the three broad categories represented by our families here . . . the fortunate 10% of managers and professionals, the less fortunate bottom fifth of the population who are the low paid, and the vast majority somewhere in the middle.

The three families were then dealt with, one at a time. Each 'case study' began with a film report which included a profile of the family and their economic situation, and an interview which concluded with the husbands being asked what they would like to see the Chancellor do in his Budget. The families chosen were those of an agricultural labourer, a skilled toolroom fitter, and a personnel manager. The general theme of the programme was that the Budget had simply 'failed to do much' *for anyone*, though the plight of the personnel manager was dealt with at the greatest length.

The other main section of the programme was introduced thus: 'Well now, with one billion pounds' worth of Mr Healey's tax cuts depending upon a further round of pay agreement; we are all now, whether we are members of trade unions or not, actually in the hands of the trade unions'. There then followed a discussion between Hugh Scanlon (AUEW) and Ian Fraser (Rolls Royce), chaired by Frank Bough, which concentrated on the question of the power of the unions to dictate pay policy to the government. Here Scanlon was put on the spot by *direct* questions from both Ian Fraser and Frank Bough in combination ('Well Mr Scanlon *do* you want another round of pay restraint, or don't you?'), whereas Fraser was asked open questions which allowed him the space to define how *he saw* 'the responsibilities of business' ('Ian Fraser, can I ask you how you see Industry's responsibilities in this context?').

THE *NATIONWIDE* AUDIENCE SURVEY

For our purposes here, and in summary form, the twenty-nine groups interviewed in the project can be categorized into four main types:

1 Managers
   (a) Bank managers on an in-service training course; mainly men; age 24–52; all white; middle class.
   (b) Print management trainees; all men; mainly white; age 22–39; middle class.
2 Students
   (a) University arts students; all white; mixed sex; age 19–24; middle class.
   (b) Teacher training college students; mainly white; mainly women; age 19–46; middle class.
   (c) Further-education students; mainly women; mainly black; mainly age 18–25; working class.
3 Apprentices
   All white; mainly men; age 18–24; working class.
4 Trade unionists
   (a) Trade union officials on in-service training; all men; all white; mainly age 35–45; working class.
   (b) Shop stewards; mainly men; all white; age 23–40; working class.

I was concerned with the extent to which individual interpretation of programmes could be shown to vary systematically in relation to the different individual's socio-cultural background. My focus was on the way in which this background provided individuals in the different groups with different cultural repertoires through which they could appropriate and interpret the programme text.

INTERVIEW TRANSCRIPTS

1 Managers

(a) Bank managers (saw programme B)

Question What was the implicit framework [in which the programme presented the Budget]?
Answer I don't think they had one . . . there wasn't a theme . . . like an outline of a Budget.

Question How do you see *Nationwide* as a programme?
Answer It's just a teatime entertainment programme . . . it's embarrassing, patronizing . . . it's exploiting raw emotion and sensationalism . . . In that programme, what have we heard? We've heard opinions from various

people which don't necessarily relate to facts . . . all you've picked up are people's reactions . . . it's not considered . . . I can't bear it . . . I think it's awful . . . you get one thing . . . then chop, chop you're on to the next thing . . . if I'd wanted to find out about the Budget I'd probably rely on the next day's newspaper . . . something like the *Telegraph* . . . or watch *The Money Programme*.

Question How did it come across as a message about the Budget?
Answer It wasn't sufficient, to be quite frank . . . it didn't do anything for me . . . I find that kind of thing . . . quite embarrassing . . . I just squirm in embarrassment for the people they put on.

(b) Print management trainees (saw programme B)

Question What do you think of *Nationwide* in terms of where it stands on the political spectrum?
Answer It's basically socialist. I mean it's BBC and ITV. ITV can't be socialists because it's private enterprise. BBC is a state-owned thing so it's socialist . . . on *Nationwide* they're very subjective . . . the people on it are very pro-Labour . . . they're always biased.

Question How do you, personally, respond to *Nationwide* on the whole?
Answer I come from a very conservative family. Several times I've wanted to pick up the phone and phone *Nationwide*; I have seen people being pulled through the mud there, just because they have too much money . . . now *Nationwide*, for them, those people are 'pigs', the 'pigs' of this society who rob all the money . . . they really drag people through the mud because they're businessmen.

Question Would you say that the discussion in the programme is evenly balanced between management and union interests?
Answer . . . the guy from the union said everything, then they ask something from the man from Rolls Royce and immediately the guy from the union had the last word again . . . they didn't give him a chance, the guy from management.

2 *Students*

(a) University arts students (saw programme B)

Question What would you say a 'typical' *Nationwide* story is likely to be about?
Answer It's supposed to be about something that's happened to the typical lower-middle-class or upper-working-class person . . . but, in fact, if you

watch it, you don't get to know any more about those individuals and what they're doing.

Question What do you think is the significance of the style of presentation that the programme uses?
Answer It's meant to give the impression that we're all in this together. We're a great big happy family as a nation, and we're all doing all these things together . . . the programme tries to give you the impression that Michael Barratt [ex-presenter] is a very nice guy.

Question Would you say that the discussion between the union and the management representatives was balanced or biased?
Answer I don't think they [the programme-makers] have done anything to bias us one way or another . . . the presenter was just saying, just picking up on the implications of what everyone was asking in their own minds.

Question What kind of an audience do you think the programme is aimed at?
Answer It's for women, housewives . . . they're the only people home at 6 o'clock . . . all those bits about budgeting . . . housekeeping, it's surely all directed towards women . . . and just how much money the woman [qua housekeeper] is going to get. In all of those cases, it was always *Mrs* X – there was the wife, not affording this and not affording that . . . even the woman who goes to work . . . they say, how do you spend *his* money – but she's earning too.

(b) Teacher training college students (saw programme A)

Question What kind of an audience do you think *Nationwide* is aimed at?
Answer *Nationwide*'s for general family viewing . . . like the mother rushing around getting the evening meal ready . . . it's for people who don't listen [sic] to current affairs programmes really, and if *Panorama*'s on they switch over to *Starsky and Hutch* or something . . . I suppose at that time of day and with that sort of audience, they don't want to give them anything that might force them to think or anything . . . it's put out for the kind of people who are not interested in the 'in-depth' story . . . [it's] the TV equivalent of the *Sun* or the *Mirror*.

Question How do you respond to the presenters?
Answer They try to make their own personalities, or what they want you to see of it, show through, so that you identify with them; it's like Michael Barratt popping up afterwards . . . If he grins it's supposed to have been funny . . . if he has a straight face, you're supposed to have taken it seriously . . . They're trying to bring . . . their personalities . . . into your home . . . we're supposed to side with them . . . they're trying to get the audience more involved. Unfortunately, it does tend to have the adverse

effect on me, because it irritates the life out of me . . . it gets on your nerves after a while.

Question What did you make of the interview with Patrick Meehan?
Answer That's about the only thing the programme had to offer . . . the . . . Meehan thing . . . that was really newsy and interesting . . . there could have been a lot of potential in that . . . if they'd gone into it . . . it was the only bit of the programme that was interesting . . . and *Nationwide* were skirting round the subject . . . asking about his 'daily routine' . . . they just make it into a 'human profile' of the guy . . . and his feelings . . . there was no detail given about the case, was there? Now, if *Panorama* did that . . . they'd re-enact some of the case . . . and it'd be very, very detailed . . . absolutely full of detail.

(c) Further education students (saw programmes A and B)

Question What did you make of the interview with Patrick Meehan?
Answer All I heard was that he just came out of prison . . . for something he didn't do . . . that's all I heard.

Question Is *Nationwide* a programme made for people like you?
Answer No way, it's for older people, middle-class people . . . affluent people . . . if it's supposed to be for us, why didn't they never interview Bob Marley?

Question Do you find *Nationwide* at all interesting?
Answer *Nationwide* is *so* boring, it's not interesting at all. I don't see how anybody could watch it . . . all of BBC is definitely boring . . . like those 'Party Political Broadcasts' . . . I go to sleep when things like that are on . . . God that's all rubbish . . . it should be banned – it's so boring . . . it doesn't really interest you . . . to me – it's nothing at all.

Question What did you think of the bit in the programme where they said that 'everyone in Britain should fit into one of these three categories' and they showed you some families they said were typical?
Answer It didn't show one-parent families, nor the average family in a council estate – all *these* people they showed seemed to have cars, their own home, property . . . don't they ever think of the average family? . . . and they show it . . . like all the husbands and wives pitching in to cope with problems . . . they don't show conflict, fighting, things we know happen. I mean it's just not, to me it's just not a true picture – it's too harmonious, artificial.

Question What is it that puts you off about the programme?
Answer *Nationwide* gets down more into detail . . . makes it more boring . . . they go into the background . . . down further into it . . . *Nationwide*

goes right down into detail . . . they beat about the bush . . . they say it and then repeat it . . . I was so bored with it . . . *Today*'s shorter . . . less boring . . . and then there's *Crossroads* on after.

3 Apprentices (saw programme A)

Question Do you think the presenters put a slant on the items they introduce?
Answer They're just doing a job, like everyone else . . . I suppose now and then they might slip in the odd comment . . . change it a bit . . . but that's all going a bit deep really, isn't it?

Question How do you respond to the presenter?
Answer It's Barratt, he holds it together . . . a witty remark here and there, thrown in . . . he's a well-known face . . . the news changes from day to day and you're glad to see something that doesn't . . . you walk into the room, you think, 'What's this? . . . someone's fallen in the canal' . . . and then you see Tom Coyne and say, 'Oh, it's *Nationwide* . . .!' . . . it creates the impression that Tom Coyne sort of is your local mate from up the road that's in there on your behalf . . . the presenters have got to be the most authoritative 'cause you see most of them . . . you mistrust the person they're interviewing, straightaway, don't you? I mean, you don't know them, you're suspicious, you know they're out for themselves, the interviewer isn't, he's only presenting the programme.

Question Do you identify with the people on the programme?
Answer I think most people on *Nationwide* . . . the people we see presenting, they all seem to be snobs to me . . . I don't say upper-class, but getting on that way . . . you wouldn't think anyone actually worked in factories – at that time of night: to them, teatime's 6 o'clock and everyone's at home . . . a real middle-class kind of attitude . . . the sort of things they cover are what middle-class people do . . . the audience you can imagine are all office-workers, commuters.

Question What did you think of the interview with Meehan?
Answer It was quite boring really . . . about him being in gaol for seven years . . . that was the most boring thing in the whole programme.

Question What did you think of what the presenter said after the interview with Meehan?
Answer They just said the obvious comment didn't they . . . what he said was pretty obviously OK . . . he just sums up . . . tidies it up.

Question What did you think of what Meehan was saying?
Answer I'm not even sure if he was innocent . . . you know . . . it could be just him *saying* he was . . . when Barratt explained at the end, you know,

the full details . . . I could see, obviously, what had sort of happened; before that . . . I didn't really feel anything about it, because I didn't know enough . . . to say whether he was in the right, or the wrong . . . I didn't know what Meehan was on about and . . . well Barratt's a national figure, so what he says, you know.

Question What did you make of their presentation of Ralph Nader?
Answer Nationwide aren't in it for the money . . . Nader is extremely highly paid . . . *Nationwide* are doing it as a service . . . and they're willing to draw the line . . . say we must accept *some* change . . . but Nader, his attitude is, if you don't do it my way, you don't do it at all . . . he's powerful enough to close firms down . . . Nader's in it for the money . . . it's a kind of racket . . . he says the consumer needs protecting, but the consumer will pay for it in the end . . . he goes to different extremes and causes more money to be spent, and the consumer pays the bill – does this community really need him? *Nationwide* are not so much defending us against people like Nader as showing . . . they're just showing us what people like him are really like.

4 Trade unionists

(a) Trade union officials (saw programme B)

Question Is *Nationwide* a programme that you relate to, and watch at all regularly, yourselves?
Answer I find that quite interesting . . . there's something in that programme for everyone to have a look at . . . it seems to be a programme acceptable to the vast majority of people.

Question What did you make of the presenter's comments and links between items in the programme?
Answer They were basically just saying what many of us thought . . . he was asking the questions millions of other people want to ask as well . . . I thought this was a programme that was fair . . . It was saying there isn't any incentive to try and advance yourself . . . we're talking about incentives . . . and that's going to come to us as well . . . they've increased the income tax in this country to such a degree that it doesn't matter how hard you work . . . let's face it, it's the TUC that's going to make or break any kind of deal . . . basically, what the interviewer was saying, on behalf of you and me and everybody else in the country, was 'Are you going to play ball so we can have our tax reduction?' . . . I mean, it's not even the rich get richer and the poor get poorer . . . any more . . . it's *we* get poorer.

Question What was the implicit framework [in which the programme presented the Budget]?

Answer The whole programme started from the premise that whatever the Budget did it would not benefit the country unless middle management was given a hefty increase – that was the main premise of the programme, they started with that.

Question What did you think of the presentation of the union/ management discussions?
Answer The interviewer was pushing Scanlon [union representative] into a corner . . . getting him into a corner and then the opponent, Fraser [management representative], who was supposed to have been equal . . . more or less came in behind Bough [presenter] to support Bough's attack on Scanlon . . . we've found that . . . with the media . . . y'know, our union . . . we've got good relations with the local media – and yet we're cut all the time, as compared with the management's views.

Question What kind of an audience do you think the programme is aimed at?
Answer Well, it's not for trade union officials! It's for the middle class . . . undoubtedly for what *they* regard as the backbone of the country, the middle class.

(b) Shop stewards (saw programme B)

Question What do you think of *Nationwide*, in terms of where it stands on the political spectrum?
Answer I don't think you can take *Nationwide* in isolation . . . I mean . . . add the *Sun*, the *Mirror*, and the *Daily Express* to it, it's all the same whole heap of crap . . . and they're all saying to the unions '*you're* ruining the country . . .'

Question What do you make of the programme's style of presenting things?
Answer It's quite good entertainment . . . it's easy watching . . . not too heavy . . . but the thing is . . . it's the sort of jolly show-like atmosphere they create . . . all these people laughing at their own misfortunes . . . a sort of jolly, soothing approach . . . as if you can take a nasty problem and just wrap it up . . . you know 'we're all in the same boat together' . . . and there's this 'we' all the time . . . they want the average viewer to all think 'we'.

Question What did you think about the coverage of management and union concerns?
Answer Well it's the Budget, isn't it? And Budgets in the past have always been to do with the level of employment . . . and *they* get through the whole thing without any mention of it – there's no discussion of investment, growth production, creation of employment . . . nobody *mentioned*

unemployment . . . no reference to stocks and shares . . . that are accumulating money all the time without anybody lifting a finger.

Question What was the implicit framework [in which the programme presented the Budget]?
Answer . . . this belief in the entrepreneur's special skill, which makes wealth appear like magic . . . by telling all these idiots what to do, you know it's a special sort of skill . . . it really relates to classical economic theory, the point there is that you see the factors of production as inputs – workers . . . and everything else, and it's only the skill of the overall managers and all their executives who can sort of cream off this exact pool of skill and machinery, and get profit from somewhere, and therefore these individuals are the ones who *create* profit, because it's their judgement and skills who produce it – not the actual graft of the workers . . . you know, that's two totally different interpretations of where wealth comes from – basic stuff.

Question Did you think that the programme was fair in its presentation of issues?
Answer Not at all. Not at all. They had so much more sympathy with the guy from middle management. Even in BBC terms, there wasn't any neutrality in it at all.

Interpreting the transcripts

The next section provides some interpretations of the results of the interviews conducted with the various groups. The interpretations can only be offered as tentative conclusions – the sample of groups interviewed was too small to provide any guarantee that the results are representative. The interpretations should he read critically – how much light do they throw on the transcript material? What differences between the groups remain unaccounted for? What similarities of response and overlaps between different groups remain in need of explanation?

1 Managers

(a) Bank managers

This group proved particularly interesting in one respect – in their responses to the programme they hardly commented at all on its content. It seemed as if they shared the commonsense framework of assumptions of *Nationwide* to such an extent that what was said in the programme was so non-controversial to them as to be almost invisible. This contrasts particularly strongly with the readings made by the trade union group – to whom the programme appeared to have a very particular and highly visible content – a 'theme' of concern for the interests of middle management above all else. Because this 'theme' was unacceptable to the trade union group it was highly visible to them, and most of their comments were focused on it.

Thus the managers focused on the programme's mode of address – which they reject as 'just a teatime entertainment programme, embarrassing, patronizing, exploiting raw emotion, sensationalism'. Their adherence is to a mode of address identifiable as 'serious current affairs' – they mention the *Daily Telegraph* and *The Money Programme* as models of 'good coverage' of these issues, and discuss *Nationwide* in so far as it fails to live up to the criteria established by this framework. By contrast, the shop stewards can accept the programme's mode of address to some extent: what they focus on and reject is *Nationwide*'s ideological formulation of the 'issues'.

(b) Print management trainees

In a sense these young trainee managers were so far to the right of the political spectrum (espousing a hard-line free market version of 'radical conservatism') that they might be said to be making a right-wing 'oppositional reading' of *Nationwide* – which they take to be a 'socialist' programme. To them *Nationwide*'s complex mixture of 'radical populism' resolves itself simply into 'radicalism': in this light they interpret the programme's presentation of management/union problems as heavily biased on the union side; in complete contradiction, of course, with the way this item is interpreted by the union groups – who see it as rabidly anti-union.

In terms of the spectrum of political opinion, these examples of the totally contradictory readings of the same programme item, made by managers and trade unionists, do provide us with the clearest examples of the way in which the 'meaning' of a programme or 'message' depends upon the interpretative code which the audience brings to the decoding situation.

2 Students

(a) University arts students

These groups tended, on the whole, to produce a highly articulate set of negotiated and oppositional readings and redefinitions of the framework of interpretation proposed in the programme. This was certainly true of their readings of the main range of *Nationwide* items on leisure, the home, individuals and their hobbies, etc.

Like the bank managers, these students dismiss *Nationwide*'s style and mode of address. Like the teacher training college students, this group's commitment to the discourse of education leads them to assess *Nationwide* according to criteria of 'relevance' and 'informational value' – criteria derived from 'serious' and 'current affairs' broadcasting. From this perspective *Nationwide* is clearly found to be wanting: it provides an inadequate form of knowledge. As far as they can see, *Nationwide* is only interested in presenting the sensational, the dramatic – the surface forms of events.

Moreover, because of their particular educational background, they consistently produce 'deconstructed' readings – that is to say, they are particularly conscious of the methods through which the *Nationwide* discourse is constructed.

However, when it comes to more directly politico-economic affairs, and in particular *Nationwide*'s presentation of unions and management, their decodings are consistently less oppositional. In relation to these issues these groups tend to accept and take over the framework that *Nationwide* proposes as non-problematic. Rather like the bank managers, they focus their comments on what they see as the programme's 'patronizing' and unacceptably 'trivializing' mode of address – while the framework within which industrial relations is presented is as non-controversial, and therefore as invisible, to them as it is to the bank managers.

While the union groups see *Nationwide*'s presentation of union representatives as heavily biased against them, these student groups deny this ('I don't think they have done anything to bias us one way or another'), and in this respect they accept the *Nationwide* presenters claim to 'speak for us' as the suffering public, caught in the middle of management–union conflicts.

Here we have a clear case of the way in which decoding varies, for a given group, in relation to different topics: i.e. groups do not simply operate different codes from each other – there are also more local and internal differentials to be noted – where decoding will also vary depending on a group's relation to different kinds of subjects or topics. Here we have a case of a group which makes oppositional readings of one category of items along with dominant readings of another category.

(b) Teacher training college students

While these groups share with the apprentices a dominant political affiliation to the Conservative party, their involvement in higher education acts to shift their readings further into the 'negotiated', as opposed to the 'dominant', area.

Taking the involvement in educational discourse as a variable, we can compare the decodings (manifested, for instance, in the differential use of the term 'detail' as a value judgement by which programmes are assessed) of these groups with those of the Black further education students.

These trainee teachers have a high estimation of 'serious', 'educational' television, and are concerned about the provision of information and 'detail'. These are the criteria by which they distinguish 'good' or 'worthwhile' programmes from those which are 'trivial'.

The Black further education groups can be seen as on the one hand resistant to the terms of this discourse (in so far as it would then seem to pass negative judgement on their own cultural involvements) or, more patronizingly, as not having access to the cultural (elaborated? or racist?) codes of the educational system. From the Black students' perspective *Nationwide* is seen to go 'right down into detail' – and, as a consequence is 'boring'. The programme fails to live up to their criteria of 'good television' – as being principally entertaining and enjoyable. For the teacher training students *Nationwide* fails because it does not have *enough* detail or information and is not serious/worthwhile. The teacher-training student groups and the Black 'non-academic' student groups' differential involvement in the discourse of formal education can thus be seen to be a factor of some importance in accounting both for their differential responses to the programme and for the different framework within which they articulate and justify these responses.

The comparison of perspectives is at its sharpest in the case of these groups, because they stand at opposite ends of the spectrum of involvement in educational discourse. As trainee teachers these groups are probably those most committed to that discourse in the whole sample, while the working-class Black groups are probably those most alienated from the discourse of formal education.

(c) Further education students

These students were almost exclusively drawn from a Black (predominantly West Indian) inner-city, working-class community – and their readings of the programme material directly reflect the disjunction between the cultural codes of that community and the cultural codes of *Nationwide*.

These groups are so totally alienated from the discourse of *Nationwide* that their response is in the first instance 'a critique of silence', rather than an oppositional reading: indeed, in so far as they make any sense at all of the items, some of them at times come close to accepting the programme's own definitions. In a sense they fail, or refuse, to engage with the discourse of the programme enough to deconstruct or re-define it. There is simply a disjunction between the set of representations with which the programme works and those generated by the students' sub-cultural milieux.

The Black students made hardly any connection with the discourse of *Nationwide*. The concerns and the cultural framework of *Nationwide* are simply not the concerns of their world. They are clear that it's not a programme for them; it doesn't deal with their specific interests and fails to live up to their standards of 'good TV' – defined in terms of enjoyment and entertainment (in which terms *Today* and ITV in general are preferred to *Nationwide* and BBC).

To this group *Nationwide* is 'so boring, it's not interesting at all: [they] don't see how anyone could watch it'. This is a disjunction between the discourses of their own culture and those not simply of *Nationwide* in particular, but of the whole field of 'serious' television and of party politics. Moreover, these groups reject the 'descriptions' of their life offered by the programme. They can find no 'point of identification' within the programme's discourse about the problems of families in Britain today – a discourse into which the programme presenters have claimed 'most people in Britain' should fit. Their particular experience of family structures among a Black, working-class, inner-city community is simply not accounted for. The programme's picture of family life is as inappropriate to them as that offered in a 'Peter and Jane' reading scheme.

3 Apprentices

These working-class groups inhabit a discourse dominated on the one hand by Conservatism and on the other by a populism which rejects the whole system of party politics. The tone of their overall response to the programme is one of cynicism and alienation. They reject the programme's mode of address as too 'formal/middle-class/BBC – traditional' – at a general level, but still inhabit the same 'populist' ideological problematic of the programme, and thus decode specific items in line with the preferred reading encoded in the text.

They are also, at times, hostile to the questions asked in the interview – it seems hard for them to articulate things which are so obvious to them. There is also a defensive or strategical aspect to it – judgement words such as 'better'/'boring' are used without explication, and explication is refused because 'it's only commonsense, isn't it?'.

The *Nationwide* team is seen as 'just doing a job' – a job seen in technical terms as dealing with technical or communicational problems. To ask questions about the socio-political effects of *Nationwide*'s practices is seen as going 'a bit too deep, really'.

Of all the groups it was the apprentices that most closely inhabited the dominant code of the programme – and their decodings were, on the whole, 'in line with' the dominant or preferred meanings of *Nationwide*. This seemed to be accounted for by the extent to which the lads' 'commonsense' ideological position was articulated through a form of populist discourse which was quite compatible with that of the programme. Although the dominant tone of this group's responses to *Nationwide* was one of cynicism, a resistance to anyone 'putting one over' on them, most of the main items in the programme were, in fact, decoded by these groups within the dominant framework, or preferred reading, established by the programme, and they tended to accept the perspectives offered by and through the programme's presenter. What is commonsense to the programme's presenters seems 'pretty obviously OK' to these groups too, and *Nationwide*'s questions are justified as 'natural', 'obvious' and therefore unproblematic.

4 Trade unionists

I have already suggested that patterns of decoding should not be seen as being simply determined by class position, but by the way in which social position articulates with the individual's positioning in different discursive formations. In this particular instance there is a profound difference in decodings between those groups which are non-union, or are simply 'members' of unions, and those groups with an active involvement in the discourses of trade unionism – although the two categories of groups have the same basic working-class background. The groups of union officials tend to produce forms of negotiated decoding; the shop stewards produce a fully oppositional form of decoding – as compared, for instance, with the apprentice groups, who are simply inactive union members and tend to reproduce dominant decodings of the programme. There are, of course, variations within this basic pattern: officials from different kinds of unions produce different readings – but these, I would suggest, are to be seen as variations on a basically consistent theme. That is to say, for example, it is not simply being working class that makes a difference to decodings of television – it is the articulation of that social position through discourse (in this case, the discourse of trade unionism) that 'inflects' the decoding in a particular direction.

Further, there are the significant differences between the articulate, fully oppositional readings produced by the shop stewards as compared with the negotiated readings produced by the union officials. This, I would suggest, is to be accounted for by the extent to which the stewards are not subject so directly to the pressures of incorporation focused on full-time officials and thus tend to inhabit a more 'left-wing' interpretation of trade unionism.

The trade union officials, on the whole, inhabit a populist version of the negotiated code, espousing a right-wing Labour perspective. They are regular *Nationwide* watchers and approve of both the programme's mode of address and its ideological problematic. They accept the individualistic theme of the programme and its construction of an undifferentiated national community which is suffering economic hardship; to this extent they can be said to identify with the national 'we' which the programme discourse constructs. However, this is at an abstract and general level – at a more concrete, local level (that of directly economic 'trade union' issues), they take a more critical stance, and specific items within this category are then decoded in a more oppositional way (cf. Hall 1973, on the structure of 'negotiated' code).

It is the shop stewards that spontaneously produce by far the most articulate, fully oppositional reading of the programme. They reject the programme's attempt to tell us what 'our grouse' is and its attempt to construct a national 'we'. This group fulfils the criteria of an oppositional reading in the precise sense that it redefines the issues which the programme presents. Its members are critical of what they see as 'significant absences' in the discussion of economics. More than that, however, their critical reading also involves the introduction of a new model, outside the terms of reference provided by the programme: at one point they explain *Nationwide*'s implicit 'theory' of the origin of wealth – in terms of classical economics – and then explicitly move on to substitute for it a version of the labour theory of value.

THE PATTERN OF DECODINGS: AN OVERVIEW AND SOME CONCLUSIONS

The overall 'spread' of the groups' decoding strategies is displayed schematically in the figure below. The diagram is presented in this spatial rather than linear form (as in a one-dimensional continuum from oppositional to dominant readings) because the readings cannot be conceived of as being

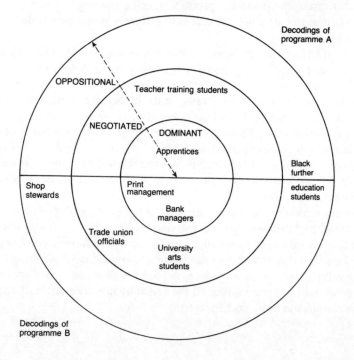

placed along one such continuum. For instance, the Black further education students are not 'more oppositional' than the university students on the same dimension – rather, they are operating along a different dimension in their relation to the programme.

The different responses and interpretations reported here are not to be understood in terms simply of individual psychologies. They are founded on cultural differences embedded within the structure of society – cultural clusters which guide and limit the individual's interpretation of messages. To understand the potential meanings of a given message, we need a 'cultural map' of the audience to whom that message is addressed – a map showing the various cultural repertoires and symbolic resources available to differently placed sub-groups within that audience. The 'meaning' of a text or message must be understood as being produced through the interaction of the codes embedded in the text with the codes inhabited by the different sections of the audience.

To argue that individual 'readings' of messages must be seen in their social context is by no means to opt for a mode of determinist explanation in which individual consciousness is directly explained by social position. As the above transcripts show, class position, for example, in no way directly correlates with decoding frameworks.

The model proposed here does not attempt to derive decodings directly from social class position. It is always a question of how social position plus particular discourse positions produce specific readings, which are structured because the structure of access to different discourses is determined by social position.

We need here to understand the process through which the multiplicity of discourses in play in any social formation intersects with the process of decoding media material. The effect of these discourses is precisely to inflect decodings in a variety of ways – thus, in the case of each of the major categories of decoding (dominant, negotiated or oppositional) we can discern different varieties and inflections of what, for purposes of gross comparison only, is termed the same 'code'. Thus, we would need to make a series of distinctions within and across the crude categories derived from Parkin's schema of meaning-systems in order to develop a more adequate model of the audience.

Moreover, there are always internal differences and divisions within each group, and different groups will operate different decoding strategies in relation to different kinds of material, and in different contexts. The basic dominant, negotiated or oppositional code model will need to be considerably refined before it can provide us with an adequate conceptual framework for accommodating all the relevant sub-divisions and differentiations within the basic code patterns.

Chapter 4

The 'Nationwide' Audience: a critical postscript

This chapter offers an attempt to locate some of the problems and lacunae in *The 'Nationwide' Audience* (Morley 1980) and is offered as an expansion (at points perhaps, merely a reiteration) of the uncertainties expressed in the 'Afterword' to that publication. Although the chapter is centrally concerned to reformulate the framework within which the audience research was conducted, I shall, in the first section, be spending as much time on problems of textual analysis as I later shall on audiences. Evidently, any form of audience research is necessarily engaged in making propositions or assumptions about the nature of the text whose 'effects' or 'uses' or 'decodings' are being investigated. For that reason it seems as well to attempt to clarify the problems with the conception of the text which is proposed or assumed by the *Nationwide* audience work.

My concern in *The 'Nationwide' Audience* book was with two different forms of determination acting on the production of meaning. First, the determinations on meaning produced through particular forms of textual organization of signs. Here I reference the area of semiological study, notions of the effectivity of the text, the specificity of practices of significa-tion, etc. Centrally, in the *Nationwide* project, this involved the concept of the preferred reading of a text: the sense in which a text can be seen to be organized in such a way as to narrow down the range of potential meanings that it can generate – i.e. the notion of textual closure operating on the polysemic potential of the sign. Second, my concern was with the determi-nations on meaning produced by the effectivity of the traditional sociological/structural variables – age, sex, race and class – in terms of the way a person's position in these structures may be seen to determine that person's access to various discourses in play in the social formation. This was an attempt to take up the concerns of Hymes, Bourdieu and Bernstein as to the effectivity of social structures in the *distribution* of different forms of cultural competence throughout the different sections of a social forma-tion. The project was designed to try to study the process of 'decoding' in terms of the way these two dimensions intersected with one another – thus attempting to avoid, on the one hand, a semiological enquiry into processes of signification considered in the abstract, outside of their socio-historical conditions of existence and, on the other, a reductionist sociological approach which would neglect the specificity of practices of signification.

Semiological problems

The encoding/decoding model

First, I would want to register the problems with the encoding/decoding metaphor which informs the project.[1] There are, I think, at least three major points of difficulty:

1 the slide towards intentionality;
2 the notion of television as conveyor-belt for a pre-given message or 'meaning' rather than an understanding of the production of meaning in and through practices of signification;
3 the blurring of what are probably better conceived of as separate processes under the heading of 'decoding'.

Intentionality

The problem here is that the focus of analysis can easily slide away from the examination of textual properties towards the attempt to recover the subjective intentions of the sender or author of a particular message. Thus, insufficient allowance is made for the fact that the meanings of a text frequently escape the conscious mind of its author, and the model implicitly slides towards a confusion of textual meaning with authorial intention. This difficulty reappears around the question of 'preferred readings' (of which, more later) and the sense in which this concept also implicitly invokes a notion of intentionality on the part of broadcasters.[2] The complication is that broadcasters do, indeed, have intentions: intentions to 'communicate effectively', 'ensure balance', 'entertain and inform', etc. We must recognize that this level of conscious intention and activity is itself framed by a whole set of unconscious ideological practices. This is the force of Althusser's argument as to the profoundly unconscious nature of ideology (Althusser 1971). However, as Hall has rightly argued[3] we should remember the end of the much-quoted Althusserian dictum on this point – where he points to the fact that it is 'within this ideological unconsciousness that men [sic] acquire that new form of specific unconsciousness called "consciousness"'. As Hall points out, 'the consciousness of the broadcaster must be an area to be studied, for it exists – the terrain of intention – not as the origin of anything – but precisely as that intentional terrain produced by the field of ideology which is, of course, outside intention'. In the

Nationwide project this field – of the broadcasters' professional ideologies –
is simply left aside, rather uneasily bracketed off.

The conveyor-belt of meaning?

The encoding/decoding metaphor is unhappily close to earlier models of
communication, in so far as it can be taken to imply some conception of a
message which is first formed (in the author's mind?) and then, subsequently, encoded into language for transmission. This raises problems
about the relation of consciousness (to mention only the tip of that iceberg)
and language. In particular, the implicit conception is of language merely
as 'tool' or mechanism for sending messages, rather than of language as the
medium in which consciousness takes shape. Thus, the way in which the
range of expressive possibilities open to consciousness is itself structured
by the available linguistic forms, falls out of focus as an issue.[4] Moreover,
there is an uneasy implication of a separable form and content – where
what is important is the content of the message, which is assumed to be
merely made available to others by its encoding in linguistic form. This is to
neglect the transformational effect of linguistic form – in the sense that the
'same' content encoded through different linguistic forms has different
meanings.

'Decoding'

The notion of decoding may well blur together a number of processes that
would be better addressed separately – it suggests a *single act* of reading
of a text. Perhaps what is involved is a *set* of processes – of attentiveness,
recognition of relevance, of comprehension, and of interpretation and
response – *all* of which may be involved for a single audience member in
front of the screen. Minimally, the model as it stands would seem to blur
the axis of comprehension/incomprehension of signs with that of
agreement/disagreement with forms of propositional meaning generated
from these signs.

Preferred readings

This concept was developed in order to allow connections to be made
between general/theoretical arguments about hegemony and particular/
empirical observations of communicative exchanges. The problem here is
that hegemony has on the whole been treated as an abstract concept –
referring rather widely to the whole field of cultural processes through
which 'dominant meanings' are constructed – without these particular
processes being examined in any detail. Further, the concept was developed as part of an attempt to steer between two equally unsatisfactory

positions – thus, on the one hand, avoiding any notion of a text as containing or imposing one fixed meaning: a conception which runs into difficulties in relation to evidence of differential interpretation of texts. On the other hand, there would also seem to be a need to avoid any notion of the text as completely open to the reader – as merely the site upon which the reader constructs the meaning. This, latter, 'reader as writer' position seems to unite theoretical positions as apparently distant as those of 'uses and gratifications' and those of the Barthes of *The Pleasure of the Text*. In both cases any notion of particular forms of textual organization as constraints on the production of meaning disappears entirely: the text is seen as infinitely and equally open to all interpretations. The attempt to steer between these twin difficulties is effectively guided by a paraphrase of a well-known saying: 'audiences produce meanings, but have to work on material which has been pre-selected and organized in particular ways by producers'. This formulation attempts to take up the stress in uses and gratifications theory on the activity of the reader but to insert that moment into its socio-historical conditions of existence – thus, readers are seen to be engaged in productive work, but under determinate conditions, which are not of their own choosing. However, the concept of 'preferred reading', which has been central to CCCS work on news and current affairs television, gives rise to a number of problems.

The first difficulty arises as soon as one attempts to operate this concept in the analysis of any text outside the realm of news/documentary/current affairs. Thus, for instance, if we attempt to specify the preferred reading of a fictional form – what would be the textual features (comparable to the presenter's framing statements in *Nationwide*) through which we could argue that the preferred reading of a soap opera was generated? It may be that the concept of preferred reading is most applicable to those texts which explicitly claim to make factual statements about the world. The attempt to transpose the concept to the fictional realm, via the equation of 'preferred reading' and 'narrative closure' (or hierarchy of discourse), always runs the risk of reducing a fictional text to the mere vehicle of a banal substantive proposition which can then be labelled as 'ideological'. Evidently meaning is not carried exhaustively at the level of substantive propositions. Thus, the preferred reading generated by the narrative closure of a television drama may well be in tension with the various other scenes and elements in the text which operate to undercut this 'closure'.

There is the further problem of the status of the concept of a preferred reading. Is the preferred reading a property *of* the text *per se*? Or is it something that can be generated *from* the text (by a 'skilled reading'?) via certain specifiable procedures? Or is the preferred reading that reading which the analyst is predicting that most members of the audience will produce from the text? In short, is the preferred reading a property of the text, the analyst or the audience?

Further, we have to consider whether the preferred reading is attributable to a set of particular textual practices (directive closures etc.) – i.e. a set of separable elements in the text. Can one make a clear distinction between text and closures? Are the signs which go together to make up a text infinitely polysemic except for the operation of these (separable) closures? Here we encounter a problem which arises from the transposition of Voloshinov's concept of multi-accentuality from the level of the sign to the level of the text as a whole. Thus, it can be argued that to say that a text is polysemic is quite a different matter from saying that a particular word or image is polysemic. The latter statement would be quite coherent, and that is why Voloshinov talks of words as signs, with a range of potential meaning, rather than as signals with fixed meanings. This is so in as much as words or images can produce different meanings in different contexts – and the principal context here is that of other words and images. However, to say that a text is polysemic except for the operation of a specified set of (separable) textual closures, is to neglect the fact that a text is a construction (in Saussure's terms, a result of choices from paradigmatic sets and combinations of these chosen elements into syntagmatic units). The construction of syntagmatic relations between the separate signs/words/images already (before the operation of textual closures) must act to narrow down the meaning-potential of the signs as they stand in isolation.

This level, at which polysemy is already structured and limited by the syntagmatic relations established between the separate signs as they are organized in the text seems to be neglected in the present formulation of 'preferred reading' – as operating exclusively throughout a higher level of textual organization – devices of 'framing' etc.[5] Thus to link the words Black/youth/street/crime in a sentence in a news report is already to narrow down the range of potential meaning or reference that each has taken as an individual unit – before you get to the point at which the report is framed in any way. If so, then the preferred reading is not generated, or at least not solely generated, through the separable textual mechanisms outlined in *Everyday Television*.

Linguistic form and ideological meaning

The *Nationwide* project was initially premised on an assumption that it ought to be possible to establish a structured set of relations between particular linguistic forms and particular ranges of ideological meanings. However, the encounter, first with Voloshinov and second with discourse analysis, led to a shift of emphasis towards an understanding of the variability of the relationship between linguistic form and ideological meaning. This shift centrally involved the understanding that the same linguistic form can have different discursive functions in different contexts and, conversely, that different linguistic forms can have the same discursive function in particular contexts. This latter point seems also to underlie Neale's seminal argument[6] as to how two films with different formal characteristics (the one defined as 'propaganda' the other as 'realist') could have an equivalent discursive function (so that both could function as propaganda in the context of Nazi Germany). The problem here is that this argument has itself functioned to legitimate the evasion of the attempt to specify any patterns of connection between form and function/ meaning. That is to suggest that the recognition of the theoretical possibility that a given linguistic (or cinematic, or tele-visual) form could have different functions in different contexts has functioned as a legitimation of the failure to explore the ways in which the field of relations between forms and functions is empirically structured. Thus, while it may be the case that linguistic form X does not have for all time, in all circumstances, ideological meaning Y, it does not follow that linguistic form X is equally likely to mean any number of things. There will be predominant patterns of connection here that need to be explained (cf. the work of Fowler, Trew, *et al.*).[7]

If we now turn to the actual practice of the *Nationwide* audience project, it can be seen that it displays a number of shortcomings which are all related to the difficulties outlined above. First, the project did concentrate on the analysis of responses to isolated elements of particular messages, and in particular on the analysis of isolated moments of ideological resistance to particular messages. In this sense, some of the complexity of the argument in *Everyday TV* (in which we had attempted to identify the generative core of the discourse of *Nationwide*) simply does not receive justice in the audience research. What is defined in the programme analysis as a stylistically definable and ordered system of discourse is to some extent reduced/disarticulated into its constituent elements in the audience interviews – which then provide us with evidence of responses to and interpretations of isolated 'bits' of the *Nationwide* discourse, rather than to that discourse as an ordered system.

These problems become of particular relevance when related back to the *Nationwide* project's self-declared aims. I argued in *The 'Nationwide' Audience* book for the necessity to deal with the actual speech of the respondents as the primary data – rather than simply dealing with the substance of their responses. This was premised on the argument that meaning was dependent on form of expression: crudely, that although they all contain a similarly negative response, the answers 'no', 'not on your life' and 'get knotted' mean rather different things, in response to a given question. Thus, I argued that we needed to explore 'degrees of fit between respondents' vocabularies and forms of speech and those of the media'. However, despite the proclaimed intention to deal with questions of linguistic form, the research slides back to a perspective where the question of form becomes of only marginal interest, and the principal focus is on the degree of fit or dissonance between the ideological problematics in play in the text and those articulated by the different sections of the audience.

Sociological problems

Within the terms of the sociological problematic employed in the audience research, there are, again, a number of difficulties. Although reference is made to the effectivity of the structures of age, sex, race and class, only the latter is dealt with in anything resembling a systematic way. Race is invoked as an explanatory factor on a rather *ad hoc* basis, as is sex/gender; age is mentioned but not explored as a structuring factor. Evidently this is a severe problem – as the age and sex/gender dimensions are particularly important in relation to *Nationwide* and its construction of the domestic sphere in relation to women's position in the family. Minimally, then, this is a case of the overemphasis of one structural factor at the expense of all others.

However, I would not take this recognition to imply the need to accept that the range of factors to be taken into account was infinite, or that all such factors would be of equal effectivity. Thus, it can be argued that there is no *a priori* reason to stop at age, sex, race and class – that there is an infinite range of factors (from religion to geography to biology) which could be taken into account as determinations on decoding practices. But while there is indeed no *a priori* reason against this extension of the list of structural variables to be taken into account, there is considerable empirical evidence to suggest the greater effectivity of the factors selected in determining a range of cultural practices. This is fundamentally a question which cannot be resolved on purely theoretical grounds, but has also to take into account empirical evidence. That the task of investigating the complex pattern of relations between structural factors and cultural practices is one which the *Nationwide* audience study only scratches the surface of, I would agree – for a much more developed account of such relations based on a much stronger corpus of empirical data, see the work of Bourdieu.[8] That such relations are only probabilistic is clear (i.e. it is simply more *likely* that a person in social position X will have access to a particular form of cultural competence than a person in position Y). What we need to know (and can know only through empirical observation) is the structure of probabilities. As Mattelart has put it, 'the observation of empirical facts is too important to be left to the empiricists'.

There are, evidently, significant problems with the formulation of class in *The 'Nationwide' Audience* book. The terms 'middle class' and 'working class' are used, on the whole, merely as descriptive labels which are not explained. This is to some extent attributable to the fact that the project was initially based on, or adapted from, Parkin's model of the class structure – which is, in fact, a model of occupational position (much in the manner of the Registrar-General's formulations). This is an implicitly Weberian notion of class based on the income/market/consumption sphere rather than on any notion of class as defined in terms of relations of production. Furthermore, there is a problem about the relation of empirically observable groups to the concept of class. Within the study the groups are referred to in such a way as to grant them implicitly a representative status: they are taken to stand for segments of society – in this case, classes. Minimally, given the small size of the sample studied, there is a problem about generalizing the conclusions of the study in any way that takes for granted the representative nature of these groups – the groups can only be taken to have a potentially illustrative function.

Reworking the decoding model

The decoding model derived from Parkin's schema of meaning-systems[9] is premised on a number of assumptions which need to be clarified before we can go on to see the extent or limitations of the field to which it might be relevant. First, it assumes that one is dealing with a broadly political form of communication. The range of decoding positions hypothesized is based on the stance of the decoder with respect to the central/dominant values of the society – i.e. how near or far one is from the positions/definitions established by this 'central value system'. The messages which the model assumes it is dealing with are, in the end, designated as instances of this value system.

Richard Dyer first opened up this dimension of the decoding model in his review of *Victim*,[10] where he points to the difficulties of operating the model in relation to texts whose preferred reading would seem not to fall so readily within the dominant code. Further, Dyer points to the sense in which the decoding model focuses on the question of how different sections of the audience are placed in relation to the substantive ideological themes or problematics of a text, without giving due consideration to the question of how these sections of an audience are placed in relation to the text itself – as the form through which these ideological themes are articulated. By introducing this distinction, Dyer rightly corrects the arithmetic of the decoding model derived from Parkin to reveal six rather than three hypothetical 'decoding positions'. This recalculation is founded on the necessity to recognize, in the first instance, the question of the viewers' positive or negative response to the text as a particular cultural form – do they enjoy it, feel bored by it, recognize it as at all relevant to their concerns? These questions, he suggests, need to be asked before one can explore whether or

not they 'agree, or disagree, or partly agree' with the ideological propositions of the text. Thus each of the three categories of the Parkin scheme
must itself be sub-divided across this dimension, allowing positive or
negative versions of dominant, negotiated and oppositional decodings.
Evidently these reformulations only begin to unpack the difficulties hidden
in the 'decoding' model. I want to try to suggest some ways in which, by
translating our concerns from the framework of the decoding model into
that of genre theory, we may be able to develop a model of text/audience
relations which is more flexible, and of wider application than the decoding model derived from Parkin. This would seem to involve two moves.
First, it would involve dropping the assumption that we are principally
dealing with the overtly political dimension of communications. Second, it
would involve us in dealing more with the relevance/irrelevance and
comprehension/incomprehension dimensions of decoding rather than
being directly concerned with the acceptance or rejection of substantive
ideological themes or propositions.

These moves, I would suggest, might allow us to substitute for Parkin's
concept of 'meaning-systems' the more flexible notion of genres of cultural artefacts, as developed for instance, by Tom Ryall.[11] In this respect
Ryall argues for an understanding of genres as sets of rules for the
production of meaning – rules governing the combinations of signs into
specific patterns which regulate the production of texts by authors and the
reading of texts by audiences. This would mean that for the decoding
model's three codes, we could substitute a more developed notion of the
complex repertoire of generic forms and cultural competences in play in
the social formation.

From meaning-systems to genres

It may well be the case that the reformulations offered here amount to no
more than terminological substitutions, rather than conceptual clarifica-
tions. However, having got this far, I shall go on to try to indicate,
provisionally, the shift of emphasis which I think the reformulation involves. I shall try to do this, in the first instance, by drawing on Mattelart's
work on cultural imperialism and then relating that to Cohen and
Robbins's work on youth cultures.[12]

Mattelart argues that the idea that imperialism 'invades' the different
sectors of a society in a uniform way has to be abandoned. He proposes
that we substitute for that approach a more precise analysis where particular sectors or milieux of a society favour or resist 'penetration' by a range of
different particular ideological forms. If we transfer the logic of that
argument to the narrower national context, we can then relate Mattelart's
fundamental point to Cohen and Robbins's work on youth culture. Cohen
and Robbins are concerned to explain the specific popularity of one genre

of texts (Kung-fu movies) among one section of a society – urban/working class/male/youth. Their argument is that the genre is popular to the extent that it 'fits' with the forms of cultural competence available to this group.

Now the authors don't really explain this fit: they merely refer to these kids' 'unconscious recognition that the narrative style or grammar' of these movies is identical with their own so that they can 'read' these movies 'effortlessly'. Clearly, to function as a proper explanation, the concept of 'narrative style' or 'grammar' would have to be specified more exactly. However, we do have the outline of a useful argument here. Cohen and Robbins are not suggesting that it is simply a question of an objective correspondence between the content of the movies and the experience of living in a hard urban environment – which would allow an explanation in terms of 'identification'. Rather, they are arguing that the crucial factor is the linkage of two forms of 'collective representation' – a linkage between the forms of some oral traditions in working-class culture and some genres produced by the media – i.e. a correspondence of form rather than content. The argument is that, in this case, the oral traditions constitute forms of cultural competence available to these kids which make it possible for them to appropriate these movies – without such forms of competence, the popularity of these movies would be inexplicable. The English Studies Group at CCCS has made a parallel argument in relation to 'feminine romance'.[13] In this case, they have attempted to establish some of the forms of correspondence between the 'narrative grammars' of, for instance, some genres of novels and the teaching of English in schools – as 'a particular grammar practised within an historical institution'. This, again, is to attempt to establish the forms of interdiscursive connections which can account for the purchase of particular textual forms on particular categories of readers, under determinate sociohistorical conditions.

This approach to forms of cultural consumption is evidently close to that of Bourdieu. Thus, for instance, Bourdieu argues that without the forms of cultural competence generally acquired through informal bourgeois upbringing, you can't appropriate the contents of art galleries, opera houses, etc. However, that argument has generally been concerned only with the question of how far down the social structure the forms of cultural competence necessary for reading high art are spread. We may now be able to develop a more complex model which could deal with the organization of cultural consumption in a number of different modes or genres – from high art to soap opera. However, before we attempt to outline that argument, it may be as well to clarify the basic terms of the approach (argued for here), to the text/audience relation.

At this point we can perhaps usefully re-examine the notion of the way in which a particular text constructs its own ideal reader. However, I want to qualify this formulation in several ways:

1 to use the notion of 'the reader inscribed by the text' in relation to different genres of texts, rather than in relation to individual texts;
2 to specify this concept of the 'ideal reader' principally in terms of the different forms of cultural competence necessary for reading different genres;
3 it may be that the distinction (derived from Willeman and adopted in *The 'Nationwide' Audience* book) between the subject constructed by the text and the social subject, is itself not adequate. In this respect, the English Studies Group at CCCS has pointed to M. Naumann's work (1973), where a further distinction is made between:

(a) the recipient: the actual historical reader;
(b) the addressee: the author's conception of whom he or she is addressing/will be read by;
(c) the reader: a formal, textually defined entity.[14]

The distribution of cultural competences: soap opera, current affairs, television and their 'reading' publics

Focusing for the moment on these two fields of television, I want to argue that each can be considered as a genre in Ryall's sense. Each requires the viewer to be competent in certain forms of knowledge and to be familiar with certain conventions which constitute the ground or framework within/ on which particular propositions can be made. Thus, as Brunsdon has argued[15] soap opera presumes, or requires, a viewer competent in the codes of personal relations in the domestic sphere. The viewer is required to have a particular form of cultural capital – in this case, in the form of the ability to predict the range of possible consequences attendant upon actions in the spheres of the domestic/familial. Correspondingly, current affairs television presumes, or requires, a viewer competent in the codes of parliamentary democracy and economics. The viewer is again required to have available particular forms of knowledge and expertise, because the assumptions/frameworks within which reports/discussions move will rarely be made explicit within the programmes.

Thus, without prior access to these codes the particular content/items within the programmes will remain incomprehensible. These points can be related back to theories of structural distribution of cultural competence only too readily. While the competences necessary for reading soap opera are most likely to have been acquired by those persons culturally con-structed through discourses of femininity, the competences necessary for reading current affairs television are most likely to have been acquired by those persons culturally constructed through discourses of masculinity (with the added rider that, in this latter case, the other probable conditions of access to these forms of cultural competence are being white and being middle or upper class). Dorothy Hobson's work[16] on differential gender relations to broadcast news and current affairs, and Corrigan and Willis's work on popular culture[17] both provide pointers towards the complex ramifications of what is made here as an evidently simplistic argument. Thus, for instance, one might begin to explore the implications of the proposition that the whole realm of 'popular television' is constructed in relation to the cultural competences available to women and working-class men, while the field of 'serious television' is constructed in relation to the cultural competences of middle-class men. Clearly, these are only sketches/outlines of the factors that would need to be taken into consideration – so far dealing only (and not adequately) with the role of class and gender in the construction of audience categories. Crucially these categories are to be defined in terms of forms of cultural competence; however, what is then to be explored is the way in which these cultural forms are distributed in relation to the social-structural position of these different sections of the audience.

Interestingly, in this respect, some developments in literary studies have focused anew on the 'role of the reader', and we can usefully refer here to a literary formulation of this same problem:

> The individual reader is seen, in this perspective, as part of a reading public; the relationship between specific reading publics . . . and either specific works or genres . . . then becomes the focus of enquiry . . . One rather elementary question is 'Who reads what?' In more formal terms, how does membership in a given social group at a given time influence, or even determine, one's reading habits and taste?[18]

My own concern is with the development of what might be termed as 'ethnography of reading'. The implications of this position can perhaps be brought out by turning to Hymes's formulation of what would be involved, from the opposite perspective (that is, production rather than reception) in an 'ethnography of speaking':

> 'Speaking' has been regarded as merely implementation and variation outside the realm of language and linguistics proper. Linguistic theory has mostly developed in abstraction from contexts of use and sources of diversity. But by an ethnography of speaking I . . . understand a . . . theory of speech as a system of cultural behaviour . . . necessarily concerned with the organisation of diversity.[19]

The theoretical underpinnings of this position are derived, in some large part, from Voloshinov, and in particular from his critique of Saussure's conception of the speech act as an individual rather than as a necessarily social phenomenon. Principally, this position is founded on the premise that the act of 'speaking' and the act of 'hearing' (or reading) is always a social phenomenon, where what is at issue is our ability to understand the cultural rules that organize these diversities.

Part III

Gender, domestic leisure and viewing practices

Chapter 5

Research development: from 'decoding' to viewing context

In this short chapter I attempt to outline the sense in which the *Family Television* project represents a continuation of the work on *Nationwide*. In retrospect, my own principal concerns in relation to the earlier work were, first, the difficulties arising from the fact that the *Nationwide* audience study was conducted by interviewing groups of people outside of their homes – i.e. not in their 'natural' domestic viewing context; second, the problems arising from the fact that the *Nationwide* study allowed too little space for the consideration of the contradictory nature of the 'decodings' which the same person may make of different types of programme material.

Let us take these problems one by one, starting with the question of the viewing context. This is a relatively simple matter in so far as in the *Nationwide* study I recruited groups of individuals for interview in the context either of colleges in which they were studying, or of other public locations where they came together, already constituted as groups. While this approach had the obvious advantage of giving me ease of access to groups of people who already functioned as groups, at the same time this strategy had the disadvantage that I was not talking to people about television in the context in which they normally watch it. The problem is that viewing television is done quite differently in the home as opposed to in public places. Indeed, in her article 'The rules of viewing television in public places', Lemish (1982) goes some way towards accounting for the very different ways in which television is watched outside the home – whether it is a husband watching a football game leaning on a couch which is for sale in a department store while his wife is shopping, or a woman who has lunch in a store cafeteria and watches her favourite soap opera on a set for sale in a shop, or the situation of travellers watching a news programme in the lobby in an airport. All these are quite different contexts for watching television, and the way in which it is viewed in these contexts will be quite different from the way in which it is viewed in the home. My own interests have increasingly come to focus on the *how* of television watching – in the sense of understanding how the process of television viewing is done as an activity. This is to prioritize the understanding of the process of television viewing (the activity itself) over the understanding of particular responses to particular types of programme material (the level at which the *Nationwide* audience study is pitched). It is for this reason that, in the *Family Television* project, the decision was taken to interview families, as family groups, in their own homes – so as to get a better understanding of the ways in which television is watched in its 'natural' domestic context. I would wish to argue that this is the necessary framework within which we must place our understanding of the particularity of individual responses to different types of programming.

Regarding the second problem, that of the contradictory nature of responses which individuals may make to different types of programmes, my concerns are the following. In the *Nationwide* audience study, parallel to the sense in which the particular, empirically observable groups in the survey are to some extent taken to 'represent' classes, there is a further sense in which the *Nationwide* study might be taken to imply that the responses of the individuals in the group – the particular readings which they generate from these programmes in this context – might be taken to 'represent' their fundamental, or essential, positions with respect to the totality of cultural practice. Thus, if a shop steward makes an oppositional reading of the *Nationwide* programme on the Budget, we might be tempted to assume that this is evidence that the other readings he will make of other programmes in other contexts will similarly display oppositional tendencies.

The question at issue here is clearly closely related to the question raised by all the debates about the positioning of the subject and the contradictory nature of our subject positions. In a review of Laclau and Mouffe's book *Hegemony and Social Strategy*, Forgacs (1985) makes a number of interesting points. As Forgacs explains, Laclau and Mouffe are critical of the essentialist view that individuals and classes are coherent, unified subjects whose actions and consciousness reflect their underlying essence. Against this, Laclau and Mouffe maintain that human subjectivity, far from being the source of people's actions and social relations, is the effect of the latter. They argue that it is only in our social relations that we assume 'subject positions', and that, moreover, our subjective identity is multifaceted and 'overdetermined'. That is to say, it is built up out of many different relations which only partly overlap with one another. For instance, the same man may be simultaneously a productive worker, a trade union member, a supporter of a social democratic party, a consumer, a racist, a home-owner, a wife-beater and a Christian. Laclau and Mouffe argue that no one of these 'subject positions' can be logically derived from any of the others. No one of them is the 'essence' underlying the others.

My own view is that, while Laclau and Mouffe point to a very important problem, they perhaps go too far in the direction of disaggregating subjectivity – to a point where there is no coherence to be had anywhere. The fact that no one subject position can be logically derived from any of the others does not mean to say that no one of these subject positions is in fact more powerful or more generative than another. The fact that all these subject positions may be logically on the same plane does not mean to say that they are necessarily, empirically, all equivalent. It remains possible that some of these subject positions will be more powerful than others, and indeed some may be dependent on others. Thus I would not want to go overboard for a position which assumed that people will be likely to produce totally unconnected 'readings' or decodings of cultural objects in different contexts, in so far as this would be to assume that basic structural factors could be totally obliterated by contextual variations. However, we do need to tread carefully here.

Perhaps this issue can be made clearer if we take a hypothetical white, male, working-class trade unionist (such as one of those interviewed in the *Nationwide* project) and try to imagine how he might react to another *Nationwide* programme, this time in his home context. First, it would seem likely that in his domestic context, away from the supportive/regulative mores of the group of fellow shop stewards with whom he viewed the 'news' tape in the *Nationwide* interview, the intensity of his 'oppositional' readings will be likely to diminish. But let us also look at how he might respond to a few items in this hypothetical *Nationwide* on different topics. So, his working-class position has led him to be involved in trade union discourses and thus, despite the weaker frame supplied by the domestic context, he may well still produce an oppositional reading of the first item – on the latest round of redundancies. However, his working-class position has also tied him to a particular form of housing in the inner city, which has, since the war, been transformed before his eyes culturally by Asian immigrants, and the National Front comes closest to expressing his local chauvinist fears about the transformation of 'his' area; so he is inclined to racism when he hears on the news of street crimes by Black youths – that is to say, he is getting close to a dominant reading at this point. But then again his own experience of life in an inner-city area inclines him to believe the police are no angels. So when the next item on the programme turns out to be on the Brixton prison riots he produces a negotiated reading, suspicious both of Black youth and also of the police. By now he tires of *Nationwide*, and switches over to a situation comedy in which the man and woman occupy traditional positions, and his insertion within a working-class culture of masculinity inclines him to make a dominant reading of the programme.

So, we have here a person making different readings of the same material in different contexts, and making different readings of material on different topics – oppositional in some areas, dominant in others. He is indeed a 'subject crossed by a number of discourses', but it is *he*, the particular person (who represents a specific combination/intersection of such discourses), who makes the readings, not the discourses that 'speak' to him in any simple sense. Rather, they provide him with the cultural repertoire of resources with which he works.

This is to stress the point that the Althusserian drift of much early cultural studies work (and it is this that, evidently, underlies much of the *Nationwide* project) tends to reduce the decoder to the status of a mere personification of a given structure, 'spoken' by the discourses which cross the space of his subjectivity. However, it is not simply Althusser who is at issue here; much of the psychoanalytic work on the theory of ideology generates an equally passive notion of subjectivity, in which the subject is precisely 'spoken' by the discourses which constitute that person. I want to try to formulate a position from which we can see the person actively producing meanings from the restricted range of cultural resources to which his or her structural position has allowed access.

Crudely, this is to argue that there is a tendency in the *Nationwide* project to think of deep structures (for instance, class positions) as generating direct effects of the level of cultural practice. That is a tendency which I would want to qualify more now, examining in detail the different ways in which a given 'deep structure' works itself out in particular contexts, and trying to reinstate the notion of persons actively engaging in cultural practice. As Dyer puts the point, 'one cannot conclude from a person's class, race, gender, sexual orientation and so on, how she or he will read a given text (though these factors do indicate what cultural code she or he has access to). It is also a question of how she or he thinks and feels about living her/his social situation' (Dyer 1977). Or, to paraphrase Sartre, it is a question of what we make of what history has made of us.

The further problem with the *Nationwide* project concerns the relative weight given in that research to understanding the responses which individuals make to types of material which can be shown to them, as against the weight given to understanding which types of material they might see as relevant to them in the first place. To understand this, we need to deal more directly with the relevance/irrelevance and comprehension/incomprehension dimensions of interpretation and decoding, rather than being directly concerned with the acceptance or rejection of particular substantive ideological themes or propositions. This is, of course, the fundamental limitation of the encoding/decoding model as derived from Parkin's work – in so far as this framework almost inevitably leads to a focus precisely on the question of whether a particular proposition is decoded in a dominant, negotiated or oppositional way. In retrospect, it seems to me that many of the responses which different groups in the *Nationwide* audience survey make to particular programme items need to be seen in the context of a perspective which would recognize that many of those groups would simply not have been watching the programme in the first place; or that if they had been in the room when the programme was on they would not have been watching this particular item in the programme. In short, what we have at the end of the *Nationwide* project is a series of responses to material which is not necessarily salient to the respondents. In effect we only have an account of their decodings of this material because it was artificially supplied to them. The more interesting question perhaps is precisely that of which kinds of material they would be interested in watching and which kinds of material they would not watch. Clearly the question of whether they would make a dominant, negotiated or oppositional reading of a certain type of programme material is less relevant than the question of whether or not they would choose to watch that type of material in the first place. In this connection Lindlof and Traudt quote from the work of Blumer, who provides a useful scenario for thinking about the interpretative procedures standing between the individual user and the mass media. As Blumer says,

> Their interests, their forms of receptiveness, indifference, or opposition, their sophistication or naivity, and their established scheme of definition set the way in which they initially receive the presentation. Usually there is a further intervening stage before the residual effects of the presentations are set in experience and behaviour. This additional stage is an interpretative process which, through analysis and critical judgement, reworks the presentations into different forms, before assimilation into experience. This process of interpretation in the individual is markedly guided by the stimulations, cues, suggestions, and definitions he secures from other people, particularly those constituting his so called 'reference groups'. Account must be taken of the collective process of definition which, in different ways, shapes the manner in which individuals composing the 'audience' interpret and respond to the presentations given through the mass media.
>
> (quoted in Lindlof and Traudt 1983: 267)

The point here, from my own perspective, lies in the relative weight to. be given to the remarks at the beginning of the quotation about forms of receptiveness or indifference. As I have already suggested, it may well be that this is the fundamental question to be explored, rather than the question of what interpretation people will make of a given type of programme material if they are specifically put in a room and asked to make an interpretation. It is this thread of enquiry that the *Family Television* project attempted to explore. And it is for this reason that the question of the pertinence or salience of different types of programme material to different family members or to members of families from different social backgrounds was prioritized in this research above the question of their tendencies to make oppositional, negotiated or dominant readings or interpretations of particular types of programme material.

Chapter 6

The gendered framework of family viewing

The research reported below concerns two different types of research questions regarding, on the one hand, how television is interpreted by its audiences and, on the other, how television material is used in different families.

Questions of interpretation and questions of use have tended, in the past, to be the exclusive provinces of different research traditions – one within the realm of literary/semiological perspectives, the other within the field of sociological leisure studies. This research project was designed to avoid that unproductive form of segregation, in the belief that only a more holistic perspective – one that takes account of both kinds of issue – could successfully pursue the urgent questions about the television audience.

The central thesis was that the changing patterns of television viewing could only be understood in the overall context of family leisure activity. Previous work in this area has tended to focus too narrowly on one or another side of a pair of interlinked issues which need, in fact, to be considered together: these are the issues of how viewers make sense of the materials they view, and of the social (and primarily familial) relations within which viewing is conducted.

Too often the fact that television is pre-eminently a domestic medium, and that viewing is largely done in the family, is either ignored, or is registered only to be assumed away (as a pre-given backdrop to other activity) rather than being directly investigated itself. Television viewing may be a privatized activity – by comparison with going to the movies, for example – but it is still largely conducted within, rather than outside, social relations (except in the case of those who live in single-person households).

In this research, I took the premise that one should consider the basic unit of consumption of television to be the family/household rather than the individual viewer. This was done to raise questions about how the television set is handled in the home, how decisions are made – by which family members, at what times, what is watched – and how responses to different kinds of materials are discussed within the family, and so on. In short, this represents an attempt to analyse individual viewing activity within the household/familial relations in which it commonly operates.

Audience research that ignores this context cannot comprehend a number of key determinations relating to both viewing 'choices' and responses – those involving questions of differential power, responsibility, and control within the family at different times of the day and night.

My further premise is that the use of the television set has to be understood in the wider context of other competing and complementary leisure activities (hobbies, interests, pastimes) in which viewers engage. Television, clearly, is a primary leisure activity, but previous research has tended merely to investigate leisure options as separate and unrelated activities to be listed, rather than studied in relation to each other.

What does it mean to 'watch television'?

'Watching television' cannot be assumed to be a one-dimensional activity of equivalent meaning or significance at all times for all who perform it. I was, therefore, interested in identifying and investigating differences hidden behind the description 'watching television' – both the differences between choices made by various kinds of viewers in relation to different viewing options, and differences of attention and comprehension between and among viewers' responses to the same viewing materials. One important set of differences explored in the project concerns the different levels of attention given to different programmes by different viewers – differences which are typically masked by the finding that they all 'watched' a given programme.

I wanted to explore both differences within families – between their individual members – and differences between families in different social and cultural contexts. I would argue that it is only in this context (that of the wider fields of social and cultural determinations which frame the practices of viewing) that individual choices and responses can be understood.

In particular, this project was designed to explore in detail within a deliberately limited universe the 'how' and 'why' of questions which lie unexplained behind patterns of viewing behaviour revealed by large-survey work. I aimed to produce a more developed conceptual model of viewing behaviour in the context of family leisure by investigating how such factors as programme-type, family position and cultural background interrelate to produce the dynamics of family viewing.

We are, in short, discussing television viewing in the context of domestic life, which, as we all know, is a complex matter. To expect that we could treat the individual viewer making programme choices as if he or she were a rational consumer in a free and perfect market is surely the height of absurdity when we are talking about people living in families. For most people, viewing takes place within the context of what Sean Cubitt (1985) calls 'the politics of the living room', where, as he puts it, 'if the camera pulls us in, the family pulls us out', and where the people you live with are likely to disrupt, if not shatter, your communion with the 'box in the corner'.

Let us consider the problem from another angle: 'Early in the evening we watch very little TV. Only when my husband is in a real rage. He comes home, hardly says anything and switches on the TV' (Bausinger 1984: 344).

As Bausinger notes, in this case 'pushing the button doesn't signify "I would like to watch this", but rather "I would like to see and hear nothing"'. Conversely, there is the opposite case where 'the father goes into his room while the mother sits down next to her eldest son and watches the sports review with him. It does not interest her, but it is an attempt at making contact' (349).

How much space, and of what types, is available to which family members in the context of television-viewing activity? How is that space organized, and how are the television set(s) and other communication technologies inserted into that space? Is the living-room organized around the television set? Do different family members have characteristic viewing positions within that space? All of these may appear at first to be banal questions; but they do indeed have great significance for an understanding of how television 'works' within a family. As Lindlof and Traudt note, for instance, 'in higher density families . . . TV viewing may function as a way of avoiding conflicts or lessening tensions in lieu of spatial privacy' (Lindlof and Traudt 1983: 262).

Questions of 'what?' and 'how?'

Lindlof and Traudt have also made a very basic point about problems with much media research to date. They note that most researchers have concentrated on 'questions of why, to exclusion of what and *how* . . . [scholars] have attempted to describe the causes and consequences of television viewing without adequate understanding of what it is and how it gets done'. They rightly argue that, in fact, in order for 'many of the central theoretical and policy questions to be satisfactorily framed, let alone answered, a number of prerequisite questions concerning *what the act of TV viewing entails* for all family members, need to be posed and investigated' (Lindlof and Traudt, 1983: 262; my emphasis).

Lindlof and Traudt attempt to develop a model of television viewing that is sensitive to different levels of attentiveness paid to the set by different family members in different roles, in relation to different types of programming. They are trying to get away from any notion of television simply dominating family life for all its members in an equal way while the set is turned on. They also challenge the idea that people are *either* living out their social relations *or* watching television – as if these two activities were mutually exclusive.

Selecting television programmes at home

Another body of research relevant to my concerns is Lull's (1982) work on the selection of television programmes at home. Among other questions, he asks who is responsible for the selection of television programmes at home, how programme selection processes occur, and how these activities are influenced by the roles of family position and family communication patterns. The fundamental point here is that any one individual's viewing is often non-selective, in so far as viewers often watch programmes that are selected by someone else in the family. This is often referred to as 'enforced viewing', hardly an uncommon situation in any context in which there is more than one person in the viewing-group. The point is that programme-selection decisions often are complicated interpersonal communication activities involving inter-familial status relations, temporal context, the number of sets available, and rule-based communications conventions (cf. Lull 1982: 802).

Here we approach the central question of power. And, within any patriarchal society the power at issue will necessarily be that of the father. We must consider the ways in which familial relations, like all social relations, are inevitably also power relations. Lull's central finding in his study of the control of the television set, is that the father was observed, and named by other family members, to be the person who most often controls the selection of television programmes in the US. In essence, as Lull (1982: 809) puts it, 'the locus of control in program selection processes can be explained primarily by family position'. Thus, to consider that ways in which viewing is performed within the social relations of the family is to consider the ways in which viewing is performed within the context of power relations, and in terms of *differential* power afforded to members of the family in different roles encompassing gender and age.

Power and gender relations

The question of power and gender relations is of particular interest. Lull's work provides us with a picture of male power within the family, in relation to television viewing, which is very much borne out by my own research. Moreover, this issue raises the further problem of how difficult it is for most women to construct any leisure-time space for themselves within the home – any space, that is, in which they can feel free of the ongoing demands of family life.

Along these lines, the work of Radway (1984b) on women's reading of romance fiction provides us with a number of helpful parallels. Essentially, Radway found that many of the women she interviewed connected their reading of romance fiction with their rare moments of privacy from the endless demands of family and work life. In effect, her respondents seemed to feel that romance reading was almost a 'declaration of independence' in the sense that by picking up a book the woman was effectively erecting a barrier between herself and the arena of regular family duties. As Radway puts it,

> Because husband and children are told 'this is my time, my space, now leave me alone' they are expected to respect the signal of the book and to avoid interrupting. Book reading allows the woman to free herself from her duties and responsibilities and provides a 'space' or 'time' within which she can attend to her own interests and needs.

Radway concludes: 'Romance reading functions for the woman as a kind of tacit, minimal protest against the patriarchal constitution of women – it enables them to mark off a space where they can temporarily deny the selflessness usually demanded of them'.

Television as the centre of family activity

Goodman (1983) notes that psychologists have often focused on the dining-room table as a way to understand family functioning. She suggests, however, that, given television's acknowledged pervasiveness in the lives of so many families, uses of television may provide us with a better starting-point than dining-room table behaviour for understanding how families develop and negotiate rules or principles governing areas of behaviour. If we look at family eating habits, one might be interested in the way members sit around the table, the rules families have regarding manners, the question of who serves, cooks and prepares food, who carves the meat, and what topics of conversation are allowed while eating. All these questions will give valuable insights into family life. But Goodman suggests that television-viewing behaviour can produce equally interesting insights. Her point is that, given television's central position in the home, rule-making, decision-making, and conflict and dominance patterns will emerge around the set.

Goodman suggests that we look at the family as a rule-governed system whose members act in an organized and repetitive manner, and that this patterning can be analysed so as to discover the governing principles of family life. There are two kinds of family rules – explicit or overt rules, and implicit or covert rules. As she notes, research on the family's experience with television focuses on rules for viewing, particularly the explicit rules that parents may have about content and quantity of programming that their children are allowed to watch. But, she observes, these studies examine outcomes rather than processes of rule-making. They may not have been sufficiently sensitive to the implicit rules that govern family processes. To understand this, one would have to ask how rules about television viewing are made in the family, who formulates and who enforces the rules, and whether these rules are simply articulated and followed, or negotiated.

Research design

The particular research project reported here was designed to investigate the changing uses of television among a sample of families of different types drawn from a range of social positions. It was designed to investigate differences between families of different social positions and between families with children of different ages in terms of:

(a) the increasingly varied use of household television set(s) for receiving broadcast television, video games, teletext, and so on;
(b) patterns of differential commitment and response to particular types of programming;
(c) the dynamics of television use within the family; how viewing choices are expressed and negotiated within the family; the differential power of particular family members in relation to viewing choices at different times of the day; the ways in which television material is discussed within the family;
(d) the relations between television watching and other dimensions of family life – television as a source of information on leisure choices and how leisure interests and work obligations (both inside and outside the home) influence viewing choices.

The project was designed to identify and investigate the differences hidden behind the catch-all phrase 'watching television'. We all watch television, but with how much attention and with what degrees of commitment and response, in relation to which types of shows, at what times?

Moreover, as argued earlier, we are now in a situation where watching broadcast television is only one among various possible uses of the domestic television set. Among the questions I set out to explore were the following ones. Which family members, in which types of families, use their televisions for which purposes at which points in the day? What are the factors that give rise to different patterns, and how are they understood by respondents themselves? Further, how are the priorities and preferences of family members negotiated and resolved in relation to conflicting demands on the use of the television in general and of viewing preferences in particular. In short, how do family dynamics interact with viewing behaviour?

Methodology

The methodology adopted was a qualitative one, whereby each family was interviewed in depth in order to elucidate their various accounts of how they understand the role of television in their overall leisure activities. The aim was to gain insight by this means into the terms within which respondents themselves defined their viewing activities. Centrally, I wanted to generate insights into the criteria used by viewers in making choices and in responding (positively or negatively) to different types of programming and scheduling. I believed that this approach would produce some insights into the criteria lying behind (and generating) particular viewing choices and responses. Thus it was hoped that the project would provide a useful complement to the results of survey work which itself, while usefully detailing the overall pattern of viewing choices that are made, cannot hope to explain why and how these choices and responses take place.

The families were interviewed in their own homes during the spring of 1985. Initially the two parents were interviewed, then later in each interview their children were invited to take part in the discussion along with their parents. The interviews lasted between one and two hours and were audiotape-recorded and later transcribed in full for analysis.

Moreover, the interviewing method – unstructured discussion for a period of between one and two hours – was designed to allow a fair degree of probing. Thus, on points of significance I returned the discussion to the same theme at different stages in the interview from different angles. This means anyone 'putting me on' (consciously or unconsciously) by representing themselves through an artificial/stereotyped persona which has no bearing on their 'real' activities would have to be able to sustain their adopted persona through what could be seen as a quite complex form of interrogation. One powerful safeguard was provided by the presence of other members of the family, who often chipped in with their own queries or sarcastic comments when their husbands or wives seemed to them to be misrepresenting their activities.

Sample design

The sample consisted of eighteen families. All were drawn from one area of south London. All possessed a video recorder. All consisted of households of two adults living together with two or more dependent children up to the age of 18. All were white.

Because of the nature of the area where respondents were recruited, my sample contains a high proportion of working-class/lower-middle-class families – not necessarily in terms of income (my sample includes quite a wide range of income) but in terms of all the other aspects of class (cultural capital, education, etc.). Another limitation is indexed by the fact that the population of the area is very stable. Many of the families in my sample have lived there all their lives (and often their parents before them), and are a particularly stable group geographically, with strong roots in their local community – hence their strong and favourable responses to programmes set in the working-class areas of London with which they identify. Conversely, geographically mobile families are absent from my sample. Doubtless my findings would be very different with a sample recruited from the professional, geographically mobile 'non-nuclear' viewers of a more up-market area.

All of this has an obvious bearing on the strength of gender differentiation within the families in my sample. I am not arguing that all families in the UK repeat this pattern. Indeed, I would be amazed if it were repeated among more highly educated professional families. However, I am claiming that gender differentiation and traditional sex-role stereotyping are very strong among working-class/lower-middle-class families in stable inner-city areas, and that this has consequences to which I refer later in terms of viewing patterns.

Television and gender: the framework of analysis

The following major themes were identified in the interviews. They recur frequently enough with the different families to point to a reasonable degree of consistency of response. Clearly, one structural principle working across all the families interviewed is that of gender. These interviews raise important questions about the effects of gender in terms of:

1 power and control over programme choice;
2 styles of viewing;
3 planned and unplanned viewing;
4 television-related talk;
5 technology: use of video;
6 solo viewing and guilty pleasures;
7 programme-type preferences;
8 national versus local news programming.

Before describing the findings under these particular headings, I would first like to make some general points about the significance of the empirical differences which my research revealed between the viewing habits of the men and women in the sample. As will be seen, men and women offer clearly contrasting accounts of their viewing habits in terms of their differential power to choose what they view, how much they view, their viewing styles, and their choice of particular viewing material. However, I am not suggesting that these empirical differences are attributes of their essential biological characteristics as men and women. Rather, I am trying to argue that these differences are the effects of the particular social roles that these men and women occupy within the home. Moreover, I am not suggesting that the particular pattern of gender relations within the home found here (with all the consequences which that pattern has for viewing behaviour) would necessarily be replicated either in nuclear families from a different class or ethnic background or in households of different types with the same class and ethnic backgrounds. Rather, it is always a case of how gender relations interact with, and are formed differently within, these different contexts.

Aside from these qualifications, there is one fundamental point which needs to be made concerning the basically different positioning of men and of women within the domestic sphere. The dominant model of gender relations within this society (and certainly within that sub-section of it represented in my sample) is one in which the home is primarily defined for men as a site of leisure – in distinction from the 'industrial time' of their employment outside the home – while the home is primarily defined for women as a sphere of work, whether or not they also work outside the home. This simply means that, in investigating television viewing in the home, one is by definition investigating something which men are better placed to do wholeheartedly, and which women seem only to be able to do distractedly and guiltily, because of their continuing sense of domestic responsibility. Moreover, this differential positioning is given a greater significance as the home becomes increasingly defined as the prime sphere of leisure.

When considering the empirical findings that follow, care must be taken to hold in view this structuring of the domestic environment by gender relations, as the backdrop against which these particular patterns of viewing behaviour have developed. Otherwise, we risk seeing this pattern as somehow the direct result of 'essential' or biological characteristics of men and women *per se*.

As Brunsdon has put it, commentating on research in this area, we could:

> mistakenly . . . differentiate a male – fixed, controlling, uninterruptable – gaze, and a female – distracted, obscured, already busy – manner of watching television. There is some empirical truth in these characterisations, but to take this empirical truth for explanation leads to a theoretical short-circuit. . . . Television is a domestic medium – and indeed the male/female differentiation above is very close to the way in which cinema and television have . . . been differentiated. Cinema, the audio-visual medium of the public sphere [demands] . . . the masculine gaze, while the domestic, 'feminine' medium is much less demanding, needing only an intermittent glance. This, given the empirical evidence . . . offers us an image of male viewers trying to 'masculinise' the domestic sphere. This way of watching television, however, seems not so much a masculine mode, but a mode of power. Current arrangements between men and women make it likely that it is men who will occupy this position in the home.

> (Brunsdon 1986: 105)

Ang extends the argument

Women's viewing patterns can only be understood in relation to men's patterns: the two are in a sense constitutive of each other. What we call 'viewing habits' are thus not a more or less static set of characteristics inhabited by an individual or group of individuals; rather they are the temporary result of a . . . dynamic . . . process . . . male/female relationships are always informed by power, contradiction, and struggle.

(Ang 1987: 18–19)

So, as Ang argues, male and female modes of watching television are not two separate, discrete types of experience, clearly defined and static 'objects' of study, or expressions of essential natures. Rather than taking differences between male and female relations to television as an empirical given, one must look to how the structure of domestic power relations works to constitute these differences.

Power and control over programme choice

Masculine power is evident in a number of the families as the ultimate determinant on occasions of conflict over viewing choices. ('We discuss what we all want to watch and the biggest wins. That's me, I'm the biggest.') It is even more apparent in the case of those families who have a remote-control device. None of the women in any of the families uses the remote-control device regularly. A number of them complain that their husbands use the device obsessively, channel-flicking across programmes when their wives are trying to watch something else. Characteristically, the remote-control device is the symbolic possession of the father (or of the son, in the father's absence), which sits 'on the arm of Daddy's chair' and is used almost exclusively by him. It is a highly visible symbol of condensed power relations:

Daughter Dad keeps both of the automatic controls – one on each side of his chair.

Woman Well, I don't get much chance, because he sits there with the automatic control beside him and that's it . . . I get annoyed because I can be watching a programme and he's flicking channels to see if a programme on the other side is finished so he can record something. So the television's flickering all the time, while he's flicking the timer. I just say, 'For goodness sake, leave it alone'. I don't get the chance to use the control. I don't get near it.

Woman I don't get the chance to use the automatic control. I leave that down to him. It is aggravating, because I can be watching something and all of a sudden he turns it over to get the football result.

Daughter The control's always next to Dad's chair. It doesn't come away when Dad's here. It stays right there.

Interestingly, the main exceptions to this overall pattern are those families in which the man is unemployed while his wife is working. In these cases it is slightly more common for the man to be expected to let other family members watch what they want to when it is broadcast while he videotapes what he would like to see in order to watch that later at night or the following day, because his timetable of commitments is more flexible than those of the working members of the family. Here we begin to see the way in which the position of power held by most of the men in the sample (and which their wives concede) is based not simply on the biological fact of being men but rather on a social definition of a masculinity of which employment (that is, the 'breadwinner' role) is a necessary and constituent part. When that condition is not met, the pattern of power relations within the home can change noticeably.

One further point needs to be made in this connection. It has to be remembered that this research is based on people's accounts of their behaviour, not on any form of direct observation of behaviour outside the interview itself. It is noteworthy that a number of the men show some anxiety to demonstrate that they are 'the boss of the household', and their very anxiety around this issue perhaps betokens a sense that their domestic power is ultimately a fragile and somewhat insecure thing, rather than a fixed and permanent 'possession' which they hold with confidence. Hence, perhaps physical possession of the channel-control device has symbolic importance to them.

Styles of viewing

One major finding is the consistency of the distinction made between the characteristic ways in which men and women describe their viewing activity. Essentially, men state a clear preference for viewing attentively, in silence, without interruption, 'in order not to miss anything'. Moreover, they display puzzlement at the way their wives and daughters watch television. The women describe viewing as a fundamentally social activity, involving ongoing conversation, and usually the performance of at least one other domestic activity (ironing etc.) at the same time. Indeed, many women feel that just to watch television without doing anything else at the same time would be an indefensible waste of time, given their sense of their domestic obligations. To watch in this way is something they rarely do, except occasionally, alone or with other women friends, when they have managed to construct a situation in which to watch their favourite programme or video. The women note that their husbands are always 'on at them' to shut up, and the men can't really understand how their wives can follow the programmes if they are doing something else at the same time:

Man We don't talk. They talk a bit.

Woman You keep saying 'sshh'.

Man I can't concentrate if there's anyone talking while I'm watching. But they can, they can watch and just talk at the same time. We just watch it, take it all in. If you talk, you've missed the bit that's really worth watching. We listen to every bit of it. If you talk you miss something that's important. My attitude is sort of 'go in the other room if you want to talk'.

Man It really amazes me that this lot [his wife and daughters] can talk and do things and still pick up what's going on. To my mind it's not very good if you can do that.

Woman Because we have it on all the time it's like second nature. We watch, and chat at the same time.

Woman I knit because I think I am wasting my time just watching. I know what's going on, so I only have to glance up. I always knit when I watch.

Woman I can't think of anything I'll totally watch. I don't just sit and watch. I'll probably sew, maybe knit. I very rarely just sit – that's just not me.

Woman There is always something else, like ironing. I can watch anything while I'm doing the ironing. I've always done the ironing and knitting and that . . . you've got things to do, you know, and you can't keep watching television. You think, 'Oh my God, I should have done this or that.'

Brundson offers a useful way of understanding the behaviour reported here. As she argues, it is not that women have no desire to watch television attentively, but rather that their domestic position makes it almost impossible for them to do so unless all other members of the household are 'out of the way':

> The social relations between men and women appear to work in such a way that although the men feel OK about imposing their choice of viewing on the whole of the family, the women do not. The women have developed all sorts of strategies to cope with television viewing that they don't particularly like. . . . However, the women in general seem to find it almost impossible to switch into the silent communion with the television set that characterizes so much male viewing. Revealingly, they often speak rather longingly of doing this, but it always turns out to require the physical absence of the rest of the family.
>
> (Brundson 1986: 104)

Again, we see that these distinctive viewing styles are not simply characteristics of men and women as such but, rather, characteristics of the domestic roles of masculinity and femininity.

Planned and unplanned viewing

It is men, on the whole, who speak of checking through the paper (or the teletext) to plan their evening's viewing. Very few women seem to do this at all, except in terms of already knowing which evenings and times their favourite series are on and thus not needing to check the schedule. This is also an indication of a different attitude to viewing as a whole. Many of the women have a much more take-it-or-leave-it attitude, not caring much if they miss things (except for their favourite serials):

Man Normally I look through the paper because you [his wife] tend to just put on ITV, but sometimes there is something good on the other channels, so I make a note – things like films and sport.
Woman I don't read newspapers. If I know what's going to be on, I'll watch it. He tends to look in the paper. I don't actually look in the paper to see what's on.

One extreme example of the greater tendency for the men to plan their viewing in advance in this way is provided by one man, who at points sounds almost like a classic utilitarian aiming to maximize his pleasure quotient, in terms of both viewing choices and calculations of programme time in relation to video-tape availability, and so on:

Man: I've got it [the video – D.M.] on tonight on BBC, because it's *Dallas* tonight and I do like *Dallas*, so we started to watch *EastEnders* . . . and then they put on *Emmerdale Farm* because I like that, and we record *EastEnders* so we don't have to miss out. I normally see it on a Sunday anyway . . . I got it all worked out to tape. I don't mark it in the paper, but I register what's in there. Like tonight it's *Dallas* then at 9 o'clock it's *Widows*, and then we've got *Brubaker* on till the news. So the tape's ready to play straight through . . . what's on at 7.30? Oh, *This Is Your Life* and *Coronation Street*. I think BBC is better to record because it doesn't have the adverts. *This Is Your Life* we'll record because it's only on for half an hour, whereas *Dallas* is on for an hour, so you only use half an hour of tape . . . Yeah, Tuesday if you're watching the other programme it means you're going to have to cut it off halfway through. I don't bother, so I watch the news at 9 o'clock . . . yes, there's a film at 9 o'clock on a Tuesday, so what do I do? I record the film so I can watch *Miami Vice*, so I can watch the film later'.

– or, as he puts it elsewhere, 'Evening times, I go through the paper, and I've got all my programmes sorted out'.

Television-related talk

Women show much less reluctance to 'admit' that they talk about television with their friends and workmates. Very few men (see below for the exceptions) say they do this. It is as if they feel that to admit that they watch too much television (especially with the degree of involvement that would be implied by finding it important enough to talk about) would be to put their very masculinity in question (see the section on programme-type preferences below). The only standard exception is where the men say that they talk about sports on television. Some part of this has simply to do with the fact that femininity is a more expressive cultural mode than is masculinity. Thus, even if women watch less, with less intent viewing styles, they are none the less inclined to talk about television more than men, despite the fact that men watch it more attentively:

Woman Actually my Mum and my sister don't watch *Dynasty* and I often tell them bits about it. If my sister watches it, she likes it. And I say to her, 'Did you watch it?' and she says no. But if there's something especially good on one night, you know, you might see your friends and say 'Did you see so and so last night?', I occasionally miss *Dynasty*. I said to a friend, 'What happened?', and she's caught me up, but I tend to see most of the series. Marion used to keep me going, didn't she? Tell me what was happening and that.

Man I might mention something on the telly occasionally, but I really don't talk about it to anyone.

Woman At work we constantly talk about *Dallas* and *Dynasty*. We run them down, pick out who we like and who we don't like, what we think should happen next. General chit-chat. I work with quite a few girls, so we have a good old chat . . . we do have some really interesting discussions about television [at work]. We haven't got much else in common, so we talk a lot about television.

Woman I go round my mate's and she'll say, 'Did you watch *Coronation Street* last night? What about so and so?' And we'll sit there discussing it. I think most women and most young girls do. We always sit down and it's 'Do you think she's right last night, what she's done?', or 'I wouldn't have done that', or 'Wasn't she a cow to him? Do you reckon he'll get . . . wonder what he's going to do?' Then we sort of fantasize between us, then when I see her the next day she'll say, 'You were right', or 'See, I told you so.'

Woman Mums at school will say, 'Have you seen any good videos?' And when *Jewel in the Crown* was on, yes, we'd talk about that. When I'm watching the big epics, the big serials, I would talk about those.

Man I won't talk about television at work unless there's been something like boxing on. I wouldn't talk about *Coronation Street* or a joke on *Benny Hill*.

There is one exception in the sample to this general pattern. In this case, it is not so much that the woman is any less willing than most of the others in the sample to talk about television as that her programme tastes are at odds with those of most of the women on the estate where she lives. However, in describing her own dilemma, and the way in which this disjunction of programme tastes functions to isolate her socially, she provides a very clear account of why most of the mothers on her estate do spend so much time talking about television:

Woman Ninety-nine per cent of the women I know stay at home to look after their kids, so the only other thing you have to talk about is your housework, or the telly – because you don't go anywhere, you don't do anything. They are talking about what the child did the night before or they are talking about the telly – simply because they don't do anything else.

It could be argued that the claims many of the male respondents (see pp. 155–7) make about only watching 'factual' television are a misrepresentation of their actual behaviour, based on their anxiety about admitting to watching fictional programmes. However, even if this were the case, it would remain a social fact of some interest that the male respondents felt the compulsion to misrepresent their actual behaviour in this particular way. Moreover, this very reluctance to talk about some of the programmes they may watch has important consequences. Even if it were the case that men and women in fact watch the same range of programmes (contrary to the accounts they gave me), the fact that men are reluctant to talk about watching anything other than factual programmes or sports means that their viewing experience is profoundly different from that of the women in the sample. Given that meanings are made not simply in the moment of individual viewing, but also in the subsequent social processes of discussion and 'digestion' of material viewed, the men's much greater reluctance to talk about (part of) their viewing will mean that their consumption of television materials is of a quite different kind from that of their wives.

Technology: use of the video

None of the women I interviewed operate the video-recorder themselves to any great extent, relying on their husbands or children to work it for them. Videos, like remote-control devices, are largely the possessions of fathers and sons:

Woman There's been things I've wanted to watch and I didn't understand the video enough. She [the daughter] used to understand it more than us.
Woman I'm happy with what I see, so I don't use the video much. I mean lots of the films he records I don't even watch. He watches them after we've gone to bed.
Man I use it most – me and the boys more than anything – mostly to tape racing and pool, programmes we can't watch when they [the women] are watching.
Woman I can't use the video. I tried to tape *Widows* for him and I done it wrong. He went barmy. I don't know what went wrong . . . I always ask

him to do it for me because I can't. I always do it wrong. I've never bothered with it.

It is worth noting that these findings have also received provisional confirmation in the research that Gray (1987) has conducted. Given the primary fact of women's tangential relation to the video machine, a number of consequences seem to follow. For instance, it is common for the woman to make little contribution to (and have little power over) decisions about hiring video tapes; it is rare for the woman actually to go into a video-tape shop to hire tapes; when various members of the family all have their 'own' blank tape on which to tape time-shifted material, it is common for the woman to be the one to let the others tape over something on her tape when theirs are full, and so on.

Given that many women routinely operate sophisticated pieces of domestic technology, it is clearly these gender expectations – operating alongside and framing any particular difficulties the woman may experience with the specific technology of video – that have to be understood as accounting for the alienation which most of the women in the sample express towards the video recorder.

Clearly there are other dimensions to the problem – from the possibility that the expressions of incompetence in relation to the video fall within the classic mode of dependent femininity which therefore 'needs' masculine help, to the recognition, as Gray points out, that some women may have developed what she calls a 'calculated ignorance' in relation to video, so that operating the video does not become yet another domestic task expected of them.

Solo viewing and guilty pleasures

A number of the women in the sample explain that their greatest pleasure is to be able to watch 'a nice weepie' or their favourite serial when the rest of the family isn't there. Only then do they feel free enough of their domestic responsibilities to indulge themselves in the kind of attentive viewing in which their husbands routinely engage. Here we enter the territory identified by Brodie and Stoneman, who found that mothers tended to maintain their role as 'domestic manager' across programme types, as opposed to their husbands' tendency to abandon their manager/ parent role when viewing materials of particular interest to them (Brodie and Stoneman 1983). The point is expressed most clearly by the woman who explains that she particularly enjoys watching early-morning television at the weekends, because these are the only occasions when her husband and sons 'sleep in' providing her with a rare chance to watch television attentively, without keeping half an eye on the needs of others.

Several of these women will arrange to view a video with other women friends during the afternoon. It is the classically feminine way of dealing with conflict – in this case over programme choice – by avoiding it, and 'rescheduling' the programme (often with someone's help in relation to the video) to a point where it can be watched more pleasurably:

Woman That's one thing we don't have on when he's here, we don't have the game programmes on because he hates them. If we women are here on our own, I love it. I think they're lovely . . . if I'm here alone, I try to get something a bit mushy and then I sit here and have a cry, if I'm here on my own. It's not often, but I enjoy that.

Woman If I get a good film on now, I'll tape it and keep it, especially if it's a weepie. I'll sit there and keep it for ages – especially in the afternoon – if there's no one here at all. If I'm tired, I'll put that on – especially in the winter – and it's nice then, 'cause you sit there and there's no one around.

Woman If he's taped something for me, I either watch it early in the morning about 6 o'clock . . . I'm always up early, so I come down and watch it very early about 6.00 or 6.30 Sunday morning. Now I've sat for an hour this afternoon and watched *Widows*. I like to catch up when no one's here – so I can catch up on what I've lost . . . I love Saturday morning breakfast television. I'm on my own, because no one gets up till late. I come down and really enjoy that programme.

Woman I get one of those love stories if he's not in.

Man Yes, I don't want to sit through all that.

Woman Yes, it's on his nights out. It doesn't happen very often.

What is at issue here is the guilt that most of these women feel about their own pleasures. They are, on the whole, prepared to concede that the drama and soap opera they like is 'silly' or 'badly acted' or inconsequential. They accept the terms of a masculine hegemony which defines their preferences as having low status. Having accepted these terms, they then find it hard to argue for their preferences in a conflict because, by definition, what their husbands want to watch is more prestigious. They then deal with this by watching their programmes, when possible, on their own, or only with their women friends, and will fit such arrangements into the crevices of their domestic timetables:

Woman What I really like is typical American trash, I suppose, but I love it . . . all the American rubbish, really. And I love those Australian films. I think they're really good, those.

Woman When the children go to bed he has the ultimate choice. I feel guilty if I push for what I want to see because he and the boys want to see the same thing, rather than what a mere woman would want to watch . . . if there was a love film on, I'd be happy to see it and they wouldn't. It's like when you go to pick up a video, instead of getting a nice sloppy love story, I think I can't get that because of the others. I'd feel guilty watching it because I think I'm getting my pleasure while the others aren't getting any pleasure, because they're not interested.

Programme-type preferences

My respondents displayed a notable consistency in this area, whereby masculinity was primarily identified with a strong preference for 'factual' programmes (news, current affairs, documentaries) and femininity identified with a preference for fictional programmes. The observation may be banal, but the strength of the consistency displayed here was remarkable whenever respondents were asked about programme preferences, and especially when asked which programmes they would make a point of watching and of doing so attentively:

Man I like all documentaries . . . I like watching stuff like that . . . I can watch fiction but I am not a great lover of it.
Woman He don't like a lot of serials.
Man It's not my type of stuff. I do like the news, current affairs, all that type of stuff.
Woman Me and the girls love our serials.
Man I watch the news all the time, I like the news, current affairs and all that.
Woman I don't like to so much.
Man I watch the news every time, 5.40pm, 6.00pm, 9.00pm, 10.00pm, I try to watch.
Woman I just watch the main news, so I know what's going on. Once is enough. Then I'm not interested in it.

There is a refrain among the men that to watch fiction, in the way that their wives do, is an improper and almost 'irresponsible' activity, an indulgence in fantasy of which they disapprove (compare nineteenth-century views of novel-reading as a 'feminizing' activity). This is perhaps best expressed in the words of the couples below, where in both cases the husbands clearly disapprove of their wives' enjoyment of 'fantasy' programmes:

Woman That's what's nice about it [*Dynasty*]. It's a dream world isn't it?
Man It's a fantasy world that everybody wants to live in, but that – no, I can't get on with that.

The husband quoted below takes the view that watching television in this way is an abrogation of civil responsibility:

Man People get lost in TV. They fantasize in TV. It's taken over their lives . . . people today are coming into their front rooms, they shut their front door, and that's it. They identify with that little world on the box.

Woman To me, I think telly's real life.
Man That's what I'm saying. Telly's taken over your life.
Woman Well, I don't mind it taking over my life. It keeps me happy.

The depth of this man's feelings on this point is confirmed later in the interview when he discusses his general leisure pursuits. He explains that he now regularly goes to the library in the afternoons and comments that he didn't realize the library was so good – 'I thought it was all just fiction.' Clearly, for him 'good' and 'fiction' are simply incompatible categories.

Second, men's programme-genre preference for factual material is also framed by a sense of guilt about the fact that watching television is 'second-best' to 'real' leisure activity, a feeling not shared by most of the women:

Man I'm not usually here. I watch it if there's nothing else to do, but I'd rather not . . . In the summer I'd rather go out. I can't bear to watch TV if it's still light.
Man I like fishing, I don't care what's on if I'm going fishing. I'm not worried what's on the telly then.
Man If it's good weather, we're out in the garden or visiting people . . . I've got a book and a crossword lined up for when she goes out, rather than just watch television.

Moreover, when the interviews move to a discussion of the fictional programmes that the men do watch, consistency is maintained by their preference for a 'realistic' situation comedy (a realism of social life) and a rejection of all forms of romance. These responses seem to fit fairly readily into a crude kind of syllogism of masculine/feminine relationships to television:

MASCULINE	FEMININE
Activity	Watching television
Factual programmes	Fictional programmes
Realist fiction	Romance

It could be claimed that my findings in this respect exaggerate the 'real' differences between men's and women's viewing and underestimate the extent of 'overlap' viewing as between men and women. Certainly my respondents offer a more sharply differentiated picture of men's and women's viewing that is ordinarily reported in survey work, which shows substantial numbers of men watching fictional programmes and equally substantial numbers of women watching factual programmes. However, this apparent contradiction largely rests on the conflation of 'viewing' with 'viewing attentively and with enjoyment'. Moreover, even if it could be demonstrated that my respondents had systematically misrepresented their behaviour to me (offering classic masculine and feminine stereotypes which belie the complexity of their actual behaviour), it would remain as a social fact of considerable interest that these were the particular forms of misrepresentation that respondents felt constrained to offer of themselves. Further, these tendencies – for the men to be unable to admit to watching fiction – themselves have real effects in their social lives (see p. 152 above).

National versus local news programming

As has been noted, it is men and not women that tend to claim an interest in news programming. Interestingly, this pattern varies when we consider local news programming, which a number of women claim to like. In several cases they give very cogent reasons for this. For instance, they say that they do not understand what international economic news is about and, as it has no experiential bearing on their lives, they are not interested in it. However, if there has been a crime in their local area, they feel they need to know about it, both for their own sake and for their children's sakes. This connects directly to their expressed interest in programmes like *Police Five*, or programmes warning of domestic dangers. In both these kinds of case the programme material has a practical value to them in terms of their domestic responsibilities, and thus they will make a point of watching it. Conversely, they frequently see themselves as having no practical relation to the area of national and international politics presented in the main news, and therefore do not watch it.

Conclusion

We need to broaden the framework of our analyses to focus on the contexts in which processes of communication occur, including especially those instances where class and gender considerations are articulated. Among other things, the broader frame required also involves analysis of the physical, as well as the social, contexts in which television is consumed. This argument can perhaps usefully be made, in the first instance, by reference to the development of film theory. Predominantly within film theory, the subject addressed has been the subject of the text – the film. At its simplest, I want to argue that it is necessary to consider the *context of viewing* as much as the *object of viewing*. Simply put, films traditionally had to be seen in certain places, and the understanding of such places has to be central to any analysis of what 'going to the pictures' has meant. I want to suggest that the whole notion of the 'picture palace' is as significant as the question of 'film'. This is to introduce the question of the phenomenology of 'going to the pictures', which involves the 'social architecture' – in terms of decor and ambience – of the context in which films have predominantly been seen. Quite simply, there is more to cinema-going than seeing films. There is going out at night and the sense of relaxation combined with the sense of fun and excitement. The very name 'picture palace', by which cinemas were known for a long time, captures an important part of that experience. Rather than selling individual films, cinema is best understood as having sold a habit, or a certain type of socialized experience. This experience involves a whole flavour of romance and glamour, warmth and colour. This is to point to the phenomenology of the whole 'moment' of going to the pictures – 'the queue, the entrance stalls, the foyer, cash desk, stairs, corridor, entering the cinema, the gangway, the seats, the music, the lights fading, darkness, the screen, which begins to glow as the silk curtains are opening' (Corrigan 1983: 31). Any analysis of the film subject which does not take on board these issues of the context in which the film is consumed is, to my mind, insufficient. Unfortunately a great deal of film theory has operated without reference to these issues, given the effect of the literary tradition in prioritizing the status of the text itself abstracted from the viewing context.

My point is that this argument applies with equal force to the study of television. Just as we need to understand the phenomenology of 'going to the pictures', so we need equally to understand the phenomenology of domestic television viewing – that is, the significance of various modes of physical and social organization of the domestic environment as the context in which television viewing is conducted. There is more to watching television than what is on the screen – and that 'more' is, centrally, the domestic context in which viewing is conducted.

Chapter 7

From *Family Television* to a sociology of media consumption

As with so many pieces of research, the *Family Television* project not only raised more questions than it answered, but also failed to pursue effectively all the possible dimensions of analysis of its own data. Thus, in the early stages, I attempted to outline a new conceptual model for the understanding of television viewing in the domestic context, but in the later analysis I was unable to operationalize effectively all the theoretical consequences of this model. In particular, I am aware that, having earlier argued for the importance of taking the family as the unit of consumption of television (rather than the individual in isolation), there is a tendency in the interviews to slide back towards a kind of parallel analysis of 'gendered individuals' rather than conducting a fully fledged analysis of the dynamics of the family unit.

Moreover, having originally intended to interview parents and children together (precisely in order to pursue these family dynamics), in practice I found it impossible to sustain interviews of this complexity with adults and young children at the same time (not least because, after an initial period of fascination, the young children quite quickly got bored). As a result, in the end I opted for interviewing both parents together, but only occasionally including the older children for the full interview, and simply interviewing the younger children separately at the end. This decision had the regrettable effect of shifting the focus of analysis, so that the children's views and comments (and especially those of the younger children) are much more marginal to the analysis than I would have hoped.

I am aware that the section on television and gender focuses centrally (and almost exclusively) on only one dimension of analysis – the effectivity of gender as an influence on viewing behaviour. Here I can only recognize that I have been unable (owing to both theoretical and practical limitations) to pursue a more developed analysis of the patterning of viewing behaviour as between the different categories of families interviewed, in terms either of the categories of social background or of the categories of family 'life-stage' which constituted the parameters along which the sample was constructed. Thus, in the end, the gender dimension of analysis was prioritized more exclusively than had originally been intended, and the effectivity of this particular factor was isolated from that of the others – such as class and age – alongside which, and in interaction with which, it needs ultimately to be situated.

Problems of gender essentialism

In the end, neither class, nor race, nor gender (nor any other single categorization) ever fully contains a social subject's identity. Ang and Hermes (1991) make the point forcefully, in their critique of current tendencies towards what they designate as a kind of 'gender essentialism' which would reify and absolutize gender differences, eliding the necessary distinctions between gender definitions, gender positions and gender identifications, and positing both a fixed set of differences between gender categories and an illusory coherence within them. As they remark in this connection, 'women do not always live in the prison-house of gender', and any assumption of a continuous field of experience shared by all women and only by women tends to naturalize sexual difference and ignores the force of work by those such as Riley (1988) and Butler (1990) who correctly insist in the historically, discursively constructed nature of the category 'woman' (cf. also *Camera Obscura* 20–1 (1989) on 'The female spectator/ the female gaze', etc.) and on its necessary instability. This emphasis is clearly appropriate if we are to avoid, as Ang and Hermes put it, the liability of too easily connecting particular instances of meaning-attribution to texts with socio-demographic variables, such as gender, in a reductionist form of analysis which takes 'women' as a simple, natural collectivity with a constant identity, its meaning inherent in the (biological) category of the female sex. This would be to obscure the sense in which (cf. de Laurentis 1987) the production and maintenance of gender identities is, rather, a continuous, contradictory and necessarily unstable process. To ignore these complications would also be to fail to take the force of the arguments made both by Seiter *et al.* (1989b) and by Press (1991) as to the pertinence of class differences in explaining, for example, the varying interpretations of fictional television made by different women (*pace* Modleski's (1984) argument in this respect).

The central point of Ang and Hermes's argument is not to deny gender differences, but rather to suggest that their meanings are always relative to particular constructions in specified contexts (cf. Laclau 1977) and that 'only through their articulation in concrete historical situations do media consumption practices acquire meanings that are gender specific' (Ang and Hermes 1991: 319).

As Ang and Hermes put it in their commentary on Bausinger's (1984) work:

Gender is . . . not a reliable predicter of viewing behaviour . . . media
consumption is a thoroughly precarious practice [and] . . . the way
gender is implicated in this practice is consequently equally undecided
at least outside of the context in which the practice takes concrete
shape.

(Ang and Hermes 1991: 307)

In a later paper, Hermes presses the point further, in her critique of
the *Family Television* project, arguing that my analysis there 'so focusses
on family dynamics and gender/power relations that the particularities
of everyday life and everyday interaction are lost sight of. . . . Reducing everyday life to power relations means skipping over the particularities of everyday routines that also, partly, explain media use'
(Hermes 1991: 6). In the earlier paper, Ang and Hermes argue that we
should recognize the 'fundamental instability of the role of gender in
media consumption practices. We cannot presume, *a priori* that in any
particular instance of media consumption, gender will be a basic determining factor' (Ang and Hermes 1991: 308). This point I would fully
accept, in so far as the emphasis on instability and process functions as a
necessary corrective to any simplistic form of reductionism. However,
while we cannot assume that gender will always be a basic determining
factor of viewing practices, I would argue that we can reasonably hypothesize that it will often be one. To be completely 'open-minded' (i.e. to
have no starting hypotheses as to which factors are most likely to be
able to help us to explain which sorts of differences) is to abandon any
form of social analysis, which always depends, ultimately, on categorizations. Categorizations are reductive, by their very nature. The point, for
me, lies in deciding which categorization devices to use (however provisionally) in analysing which types of material. Thus, when Ang and
Hermes argue that the analysis in *Family Television* is too mechanical,
in so far as it is 'not likely that [this] gendered pattern of responses [as
identified by D.M.] will be found in all families, all the time', my reply
would be to agree (cf. my comments below) that it is a pattern which is
highly unlikely to be found in all types of families (e.g. regardless of
class, cultural or educational background) but that it is, precisely, quite
likely to be found in families of the particular type interviewed in
Family Television. That the pattern will not be found in all such families
is no kind of counter-evidence to my argument – probabilities and general patterns do not work without exceptions. My argument offers a
generalization (with all the dangers that generalizations always entail) as
to the pattern of gendered viewing that seems most characteristic of
these particular types of families. Without such generalizations, we risk
floating in an endless realm of contextual specificity, a play of infinite
difference, in which we are reluctant to make any generalization for

fear of crudity. However, as Brecht (1966) reminds us, even crude thinking
has its uses.

Psychoanalytic perspectives[1]

In Chapter 2, I offered a detailed critique of the deficiencies, as I see them,
of the cine-psychoanalytic theorization of spectatorship, and of the particular difficulties of transposing that model to the study of television consumption. My argument here runs in parallel with that of Feuer, who argues that
'the "implied spectator" for television is not the isolated, immobilised, pre-
oedipal individual described by Metz and Baudry in their metapsychology
of the cinema, but rather a post-oedipal, fully socialised family member'
(Feuer 1989: 103). This is also to argue, with Donald, that

> what seems to be called for is a new account of the formation of
> subjectivity which does not see it either as a manifestation of uncon-
> scious drives or as an effect of the demands of the social and symbolic.
> Rather, in the failure of, or resistance to, identity it would recognise a
> complex interaction marked by the dynamics of both the psychic and the
> social.
>
> (Donald 1989: 6)

None the less, from a psychoanalytic perspective, a number of reservations could be expressed about the interpretation of respondents' comments which are made in the *Family Television* analysis. Thus, in relation
to the issue of programme-type preferences and, in particular, the men's
recurrent expressions of a strong preference for 'realistic/factual' programmes, this could be interpreted precisely as a mode of defence against
involvement in fiction, fantasy or emotionality, all of which would constitute the pole of femininity, against which these men could be seen to
construct their sense of identity. The further question, of course, is what
gets to count as real/factual/important, and the 'gendering' of these very
definitions.

In relation to styles of viewing, it could be held that the women's
repeated compulsion always to be busy doing something else as well while
watching television is an index of their involvement in a definition of
themselves and their femininity as 'helpful/selfless', leading both to these
women's inability to indulge in viewing without guilt and to their 'talking
over' their husband's viewing – as a form of 'sabotage' of a form of (selfish)
pleasure which they feel resentful at being themselves incapable of/
excluded from.

The question of power and control in the viewing process (and especially
the struggle for possession of the remote-control device) could be read as
indicating less the extent of masculine power (as I have tended to read it)

than the very fragile and insecure nature of that power (not a secure possession, but something always to be struggled for, an index of an innate fear of 'loss of control' or of a childlike fantasy of omnipotence). Similarly, the 'masculine' trait of planned viewing could be read as a fear of the spontaneous, the unplanned, the 'irrational' – again, classically equated with the feminine.

The women's expressions of unease and 'inability' with technology could also be interpreted in a different way – in which the women could be understood to be making a psychic investment in 'helplessness' – which is itself a form of (indirect) power or manipulation, a form of dependence with its own complexities and satisfactions.

I offer these observations simply to indicate the possibility of other interpretations than those I have made, and thus to open up the field of possible discussion of these issues for further debate.

The problem of 'The Family'

Given that the title of my research project was that of *Family Television*, it is important to note what has been happening, empirically, to the family in Britain, where the research was done. Essentially, the last two decades have seen an overall decline in average household size, resulting both from the increase in the number of single-person households (now 26 per cent overall and particularly high among the elderly) and the decline in the average household size (to 2.46 persons by 1990). Overall, we see a growing fragmentation of family and household types, a much higher percentage of married women going out to work (around 60 per cent of households containing married women), and much higher rates both of divorce (up from 40,000 in 1960 to 160,000 by 1984) and of remarriage (by 1982, 34 per cent of all marriages involved at least one partner who had been previously married). We also see a growing number of single-parent families (by 1990 in Britain one in five of all families with dependent children), a significant number of them in difficult economic circumstances. As the 'baby boom' generation itself moves into the family-formation life-stage, the overall birth rate is expected to rise again by around 10 per cent in Britain. However, we should expect these children not necessarily to grow up in households resembling the classic nuclear family, but rather in an increasingly varied and complex range of household types and structures.

Still, whenever the word 'family' comes up, there remains a strong tendency for us to think of the traditional, nuclear family of two adults and their dependent children living together, with the father going out to work and the mother not working outside the home, but solely responsible for the home and childcare. Of course, this is now quite misleading. In fact, only 13.8 per cent of households in Britain now conform to this 'classic' stereotype. None the less, that traditional image of the family retains much of its political and ideological power.

The key point is that if, empirically, the traditional nuclear family is declining as a proportion of households (and this is already to raise all the difficulties inherent in any equation of 'households' with 'families'), yet it retains its ideological centrality in the culture. It is still, to a large extent, a picture of that traditional nuclear family that constitutes the principal image which broadcasters (and government) hold of the domestic audience for television and which, correspondingly, informs much of broadcasters' scheduling practice and of government policy in this area. To that extent, given the necessity to restrict the *Family Television* research project to one household type (because of the limitations of available funding) it seemed best to address the case of the nuclear family – as representative of the ideological (if not empirical) heartland of the television audience.

Beyond these simple demographic facts and trends, we can also point to one central development within Britain, over the last few years, which very much affects the place of the family/household in the study of patterns of leisure, culture, and television consumption. At its simplest, it seems that Britain is becoming an increasingly home-centred culture. Over the last few years there has been a significant reduction in participation rates in almost all forms of out-of-home leisure. Most notably, this has occurred in relation to cinema, where attendance rates have fallen dramatically throughout the last thirty years, to a point where what was once a genuinely popular form of entertainment throughout the society is now largely (and almost exclusively) the preserve of the young and the highly educated 'specialist' cinema-goer. It is not that films are any less popular among the majority of the population; it is simply that nowadays most films in Britain are watched at home – either on broadcast television or on rented videos (cf. Docherty *et al*. 1987). The boom in the British market for domestic video may now be flattening out, but that market is already established at a very high level – yet another example of the tendency for expenditure of leisure time to be transferred from out-of-home to in-home activities. Ownership of video recorders in Britain is now variously estimated at around 60 per cent of all households.

The overall decline in public participation in out-of-home leisure activities – with only the more affluent and the more highly educated minority of the population showing any tendency to move against this trend – correspondingly means that the study of television use, along with other forms of domestic leisure, becomes all the more critical if we are to understand the patterns of life and leisure adopted now by the majority of Britain's population.

Varieties of domestic context

I would readily agree that to argue for the importance of relocating the understanding of media consumption within the framework of an analysis of the domestic is but the first step in a chain of argument. In itself, this relocation would be quite unsatisfactory, if it were to blind us to the significance of the varieties of forms of organization of domestic space between and within cultures. In the end, the study of patterns of media consumption must, of course, properly be located within an analysis of the varieties of the domestic settings and household types within which the activity is conducted.

As noted earlier, Lindlof and Traudt (1983) point to the enormous significance, for viewing practices, of material factors such as the availability of greater or lesser amounts of physical space in the household. Lull extends the point, arguing that the space in which families live

> has cultural significance that differs from country to country and from family to family, within nations. For families that have much space, and more TV's, viewers need not distract others in the home, since there is more domestic mobility. Consequently, there may be less conflict and friction, since competing personal agendas and TV programme preferences can be worked out by moving to another part of the house. Families with a small amount of space . . . must use the room they have for many purposes . . . These situations require ongoing interpersonal negotiation and constant rearranging of furniture, rescheduling of daily tasks and adjustment of the mental orientations of family members.
>
> (Lull 1989: 9–10)

The point, again, is that the practices of television viewing will be significantly different in these various types of household, and these differences would be incomprehensible except by reference to the determinations exercised by the nature of the domestic space. In a related way, Lull observes that the organization of space for television viewing varies culturally. Thus, he notes in his comments on viewing patterns in India, 'the seating pattern for TV viewing there is replete with meanings related to social class and religious caste' (ibid., 10). I would want to argue that this is simply the most visible tip of a larger iceberg, and that the seating patterns for television viewing in any domestic context will similarly be 'replete with meanings' which we need to explore (cf. Gillespie 1989, on seating patterns and viewing rituals in the case of the consumption of Indian video materials among British south Asian families).

This, then, is, among other things, to argue for the importance of the sociological analysis of the varying material circumstances within which television and other communications technologies are consumed in different households, and to argue for the independent effect of household structure as a determinant of differential modes of television consumption. In this connection Kumar notes, from his research findings, that household type seems to exercise a strong determination on modes of relating to television. He concludes that 'interaction among members of a family while watching TV depended on the structure of the family . . . interaction was most lively and animated in the single parent family and the childless families' (Kumar 1988: 28).

The point is also well made by Medrich (1979), in his analysis of variation of viewing patterns in different types of American household. His fundamental point is that the very idea of an audience which watches specific programmes (rather than simply having the television on as a background accompaniment to social life) is a model which is, on the whole, only really applicable to certain (restricted) types of (nuclear-family, middle-class, higher-educated) households. This, he argues, means that media research may have to make a fundamental shift in focus, away from studying the interpretation of the content of specific television programmes:

> Research may have to shift from its emphasis on TV content, to encompass a notion of TV as a pervasive environment in many American homes. The effects of TV content are often thought to be the principal problem, but TV's role as constant background to daily life may culturally prove to have greater significance.
>
> (Medrich 1979: 172)

His point is that, in relation to concerns about children's viewing 'the world of parentally controlled TV exists primarily in middle class and upper middle class families' (ibid., 176; cf. also Paterson 1987, on this image of 'unsupervised' viewing among working-class children), whereas, in families with lower income levels and, crucially, where the mother has a lower level of education (which category Medrich claims to represent over one-third of American inner-city families) the set is always on and provides a constant backdrop to home life – as a form of 'background noise', whether anyone is watching or not, to almost all family activity. His central point is that 'children living in constant TV households are always to some extent competing with the TV, regardless of what they are doing. This may affect their lives in many ways that may make the questions of *what* they watch of secondary importance' (Medrich 1979: 172).

One central issue which Medrich raises is the empirical finding that children from 'constant TV' households do less well in school. While the causal relations which are actually involved here may be more complex than this 'finding' initially suggests (cf. Bernstein 1971; Rosen 1972), the analysis of the connections between household culture, style of television watching and educational success or failure is of evident importance.

For my present purposes, the significance of Medrich's analysis lies in its attempt to specify the differential significance of television watching within households of different types. Thus, Medrich observes:

The poor and the less well educated – those with fewer material and cultural resources and those who often live with less privacy in crowded homes, represent the majority of constant TV households. Television is an especially powerful force in these circumstances, for the children in these households have generally limited out-of-school opportunities or fewer perceived time-use alternatives in the home.

(Medrich 1979: 175)

In a similar vein to Medrich, Kubey (1986) offers an analysis of the significance of television viewing for a specific group of persons: less educated, less affluent people who are divorced or separated – i.e. a specific type of single-person household. Thus, just as Medrich offers an analysis of the specific importance of television in the lives of children in poor (and often single-parent) families, Kubey argues that less affluent, less educated and divorced or separated respondents are 'more inclined than others to use TV to avoid the negative moods that often coincide with solitude and unstructured time' (Kubey 1986: 108).

Kubey operates from within a individualist and behaviourist form of psychological research, which has no room in its conceptual framework for any adequate analysis of cultural or semiotic processes in communication. Moreover, his research methodology is certainly open to criticism, and the impact of his research in the American popular media has principally functioned simply to confirm the commonsense position – that 'TV is bad for you'. None the less, and despite these reservations, I want to argue that Kubey's research, as reported in the article used here, is worthy of some attention. My own interest in Kubey's analysis lies in the model it offers for an analysis of communication practices in specific circumstances, which attempts to deal simultaneously with the various different dimensions (psychological, economic and social) of determination, within which the practice of television viewing needs to be understood. Thus, Kubey argues:

particular kinds of experiences (moods), occurring among certain types of people (e.g. less privileged and divorced or separated persons) and under certain conditions (solitary and unstructured time) can explain particular uses of media (heavy TV viewing). When people from less affluent, less educated, less privileged and divorced or separated demographic groups . . . feel bad, in unstructured or solitary situation, and TV is available, they are . . . more inclined to watch than are more affluent, more educated, more privileged and married respondents.

(ibid., 119)

Now, as a psychologist, Kubey ultimately interprets these 'inclinations' as mere personal attributes. However, if we relate Kubey's work to that of Lodziak (1987), Golding (1989) and Murdock (1990) a number of interesting points begin to emerge. Lodziak correctly insists on the importance of the seemingly banal observation that the main point about watching television as a leisure activity is that it is very cheap compared with most alternatives, and he goes on to argue (convincingly, in my view) that many working-class (and elderly or otherwise underprivileged) people spend a lot of time watching television for the simple reason that they cannot afford to do anything else. Both Golding and Murdock argue that the choice to watch television has to be understood in the context of the differential access (or lack of it) which potential viewers have to the resources (in the form of cultural and financial capital and transport opportunities) necessary to engage in any alternative form of leisure activity. This is, then, to argue that what appears empirically, at one level, as two instances of the same activity – say, two people of different class positions, in different geographical locations, watching the same television programme at the same time – may in fact need to be differentiated, because their choices are not in fact of the 'same' significance, if the range of alternative options from which they are choosing is substantially different.

Family Television: a turn away from politics?

Some reviewers (e.g. Acland 1989; Peters 1987) have expressed disquiet about the transition from the *Nationwide* to the *Family Television* project, regarding the latter as disappointing, in so far as it is no longer focused directly on questions of ideology. There are those who would argue that, in the shift of emphasis away from textual analysis towards an understanding of television consumption in domestic contexts, the political edge of the work has been blunted. To anticipate an argument made later (see Chapter 13) in relation to the charge that work on media consumption in the domestic sphere involves a 'retreat into the sitting-room', away from the proper ('public') concerns of communications and cultural studies, that seems to me to involve a very restricted conception of what 'politics' is and also to involve a conception of a much less 'political' sitting-room than any that I have ever come across.

In insisting on the necessity of tracing viewing practices through the detail of domestic life, and insisting that programme choice and interpretation must be seen as an important aspect of television viewing or 'television-as-it-is-used' (cf. Ross 1988), which is itself an integral part of the domestic life-pattern, my argument is that this contextual frame has been missing in previous studies (including my own) of programme readings (however sophisticated), as well as from the study of programme 'effects'. In insisting on the pertinence of these contextual issues, concerning the organization of viewing practices, I have also to some extent taken a more positive approach to the insights of the 'uses and gratifications' tradition than I had done previously.

Moreover, in focusing on the importance of seemingly less 'political', more domestic issues, and in returning to a concern with standard sociological variables such as household structure, I am not at all wanting to suggest that we should abandon the broader framework of analysis of the structuring of audience response by class, education and ideology, developed in the *Nationwide* project. Rather, I am suggesting that it is now necessary to try to integrate these sociological dimensions of household structure within that larger framework. The questions at issue, then, concern the manner in which, for example, a factor such as class or income might determine (at least negatively) a factor such as size of home, which might then be the directly operative factor which determines viewing practices (again in the sense of setting parameters, not mechanistically) in a given instance. The question is how to integrate these different levels of analysis. Likewise with gender – to return to my comments on the positions taken by Ang and Hermes (1991) – the question, to my mind, is how to develop a perspective which can recognize the complexity of the issues to which they point. This involves recognizing the necessary instability of all the elements of social structure, not mechanically foreclosing analysis by too easy a recourse to category membership (or 'gender identity') as an explanation of specific viewing practices. Rather, analysis needs to trace precisely *how* gender (or class or race) operates in specific contexts – without falling into an equally unhelpful methodological individualism (even if re-marketed as 'post-structuralism') which will finally debar us from making any analytical connections between different empirical instances, for fear of the charge of 'reductionism'. My argument is that context is important (in this case, the domestic context of viewing) but that, at the same time, we must avoid the disabling impetus of a radical contextualism which, taken to its logical conclusion, can only say, finally, that everything is different from everything else, and which fails to help us to identify the underlying modes of organization of this 'diversity' (cf. Giglioli 1972).

Part IV

Methodological issues

Methodological issues

Chapter 8

Towards an ethnography of the television audience[1]

Introduction

This chapter addresses the potential contribution to the study of media audiences offered by methods of investigation such as participant observation and ethnography, traditionally associated with the discipline of anthropology. These approaches are holistic in emphasis and are fundamentally concerned with the context of actions: thus, the argument runs, an action such as the viewing of television needs to be understood within the structure and dynamics of the domestic process of consumption of which it is but a part.

The limitations of statistically based quantitative survey techniques for the analysis and investigation of 'watching television' are well established. For some years there have been calls for a move towards the investigation of television consumption in its 'natural' setting, as a contextualized activity, though it is only in the recent period that this lead has begun to be followed through in significant ways. Statistical techniques are, by their very nature, disaggregating – inevitably isolating units of action from the contexts that make them meaningful – and much contemporary commercial media-audience research seems to compound the difficulty in its search for a 'technical fix' (people-meters etc.) designed to solve the problem of achieving a reliable form of 'knowing' the audience. The problem is, as Silverstone (1990) has argued, that television watching is, in fact, a very complex activity, which is inevitably enmeshed with a range of other domestic practices and can only be properly understood in this context. My argument is that, in the first instance, the prime requirement is to provide an adequately 'thick' description (cf. Geertz 1973) of the complexities of this activity, and that an anthropological and broadly ethnographic perspective will be of some assistance in achieving this objective.

I offer below a brief critical survey of the work in media studies which has begun to explore the television audience from this kind of perspective. Such anthropological perspectives, I argue, allow us to re-focus television viewing in the broader context of studies of consumption as a symbolic as well as a material process. The concern of qualitative research, then, is with developing a close understanding of the processes through which communication technologies, such as television, acquire meaning, and of the variety of practices in which they are enmeshed.

The trouble with numbers

The tradition of audience studies has long been predominantly one of quantitative empirical investigation. Researchers in the positivist tradition have sought to isolate those factors in the communication process that can be seen to be effective, or to have effects on different groups of people under different circumstances. It is a commonplace observation that the enormous research effort which has developed over the years has only, at best, a modest amount to offer on the basic question of influence. The constitution of the audience as amenable to a kind of clinical empiricism, which substantially involves processes of methodological isolation and abstraction, has led media research up too many blind alleys. It has consistently mistaken rigour for understanding.

In recent years, within the broadcasting industry, the introduction of the automatic channel-control device and of video-recorders into the home has led to concerns with viewer inattentiveness – as a result of 'zapping' and 'zipping' on the part of audience members. The belated recognition of the degree to which people may have the set on while paying it little attention has also led to a concern that the audience ratings may overestimate viewer attention and thus (under pressure from the advertisers) to a concern with developing better (more 'objective') techniques of data collection, most recently with the development of the 'passive people-meter' – a computerized, camera-like device attached to each set in the household, which uses an 'image recognition' system to identify who is actually present in front of which sets, and when. What we have there is the attempt to provide a technical 'solution' to the problems of television audience research. The question is whether the problem is, in principle, amenable to this type of solution. Some years ago, Wober (1981) rightly noted that most audience 'research' is, in fact, measurement – i.e. the quantitative registration of various types of viewing-related behaviour. As he put it, the problem is that 'the data produced by "audimetry" [techniques of audience measurement] provides much raw material for research: but in itself it does not constitute research or even half of research' (Wober 1981: 410).

As Hammersley and Atkinson put it, quantitative research, in so far as it is concerned centrally with the 'mere establishment of a relationship among variables', while providing a basis for prediction, does not constitute a theory: 'A theory must include reference to mechanisms or processes by which the relationship among the variables identified is generated. Moreover, such reference must be more than mere speculation, the existence and operation of these "intervening variables" must be described' (Hammersley and Atkinson 1983: 20).

As Ang (1991) rightly argues, what ratings discourse does is to describe viewers and the differences between and among them exclusively in terms of a few generalized and standardized viewing behaviour variables. All other bases of identity and difference are ignored. Thus the subjective element is minimized and 'watching television' (whatever its meaning to the audience) is reduced to the observable behaviour of having the set on, and is further assumed to be a simple act, having, in principle, the same meaning and salience for everybody. The problem, evidently, is that this is simply a misleading picture of the activities involved. What is needed is not simply improved techniques of audience measurement (*pace* the 'passive people-meters' debate) but improved methods of audience research (Wober's distinction, quoted earlier), so that we can not only measure what different types of audience do, but also understand how and why they do as they do. This centrally involves an understanding of television viewing as a complex and contextualized domestic practice.

As Ang (1991) notes, quantitative research has to treat viewers as numbers – as units of equal value in a calculation of audience size. Thus 'people-watching-television' are taken to be the basic units of audience-measurement. These people are, of course, singular and subjective and all located in particular circumstances – but inclusion of the details of their singularity would, of course, make the production of ratings impossible – hence, the individual and subjective differences have to be suppressed in order to create calculable categories of ratings, emphasizing averages, regularities and generalizable patterns rather than idiosyncratic differences.

Given these considerations, let us retrace our steps, and carefully examine the premises on which the predominant mode of television-audience research is based. First, it does not, in fact, usually measure television viewing as such: it usually measures some other factor (the set being on, presence in the room), which is then assumed to be a reliable indicator of viewing. Second, it assumes that switching the television on is an index of wanting to view the specific programme turned to (rather than, for instance, a reflex action signifying 'getting home'). Bausinger (1984) has pointed to a number of the problems hidden behind this assumption (not least the use of television as an alibi to escape the demands of domestic interaction, regardless of whether attention is actually being paid to the screen). Third, it effectively assumes that all viewing behaviour is the result of individual decision-making processes, whereas we know that much viewing is, in fact, done in groups, where power is unequally distributed and choices must be negotiated – so that much viewing is, for many viewers, 'enforced': they are putting up with what someone else in the viewing group wants to watch, rather than leaving the room (even in multi-set households, there is usually a 'main set', which is the focus of competing demands). Fourth, it assumes that viewing decisions can meaningfully be treated as context-free and equivalent – thus ignoring the different significance given to the 'same' viewing choice by contextual factors such as variations in access to resources (both material and symbolic) enabling alternative leisure choices to be made (e.g. variations in extent of household space, in income, access to transport, etc.).

On the basis of all these *ceteris paribus* assumptions, much audience research assumes that 'watching television' is a one-dimensional activity which has equivalent meaning for all who perform it. However, at the simplest level, we already know, for example, that 'pure' television viewing is a relatively rare occurrence. Thus, Gunter and Svennevig (1987: 12–13) quote surveys showing variously 50 per cent and 64 per cent of viewers as reporting that they usually watch television while doing something else at the same time. Equally, having the set on, or the presence of people in front of the set, can mean, as Towler (1985) notes, 'a hundred different things'. In his lecture to the Royal Television Society (Cambridge, 1985) the then head of the IBA Research Department, Bob Towler, began by claiming: 'we are now beyond head counting', and argued for the urgency of a different type of 'close-up' research, more directly focused on the actual practice of television viewing, examining 'different kinds of viewing' as they occur, at different times of the day in relation to particular types of programme, on the part of different viewers. Perhaps it is now time to substantiate his claim.

In a review of recent quantitative audience research, Jensen has argued along similar lines – stressing the need for the contextualization of research 'findings'. As he puts it:

> What goes on in the reception situation should be understood with constant reference to the social and cultural networks that situate the individual viewer . . . [The ratings] offer few clues for understanding the significance of TV as an integrated element in the viewer's everyday life . . . The audience experience of a particular medium and its content cannot be separated from how it is used . . . if we are to understand the lived reality behind the ratings we need to turn to the context of use, the physical setting where reception takes place, and ask, what is the meaning of TV viewing to the audience.
>
> (Jensen 1987: 25)

In a similar vein, Lull has argued that if interpersonal and mass communication are to be read as texts, the surrounding context is the necessary foundation of meaning. Thus, he argues:

> To invoke the importance of the 'fabric of everyday life' places a responsibility on the researcher to (1) observe and note routine behaviour of all types characteristic of these who are being studied,

(2) do so in the natural settings where the behaviour occurs and (3) draw inferences carefully after considering the details of communication behaviour, with special attention paid to the often subtle, yet revealing, ways that different aspects of the context inform each other.

(Lull 1987: 320)

In this connection Ang (1991) rightly notes that the head-counting which lies at the base of the whole ratings enterprise is based on the simple binary opposition of watching/non-watching of television. However, in the face of all the research evidence quoted above, it can no longer be assumed that having the television set on equals watching or that watching equals paying attention. As Ang points out, it is now increasingly recognized that television watching is a complex and variable mode of behaviour, characteristically interwoven with other, simultaneous activities. At this point, of course, the simple binary 'watching/non-watching' opposition which is the epistemological basis of all the ratings statistics begins to break down. With some justification, Ang thus argues that we may perhaps conclude that: 'the project of audience measurement may have reached a point of no return: it may have definitively lost its hold on its basic assumption: namely, that watching TV is a simple type of behaviour that can be objectively measured' (ibid.).

If we take this argument seriously, then it follows that the kind of research we need to do involves identifying and investigating all the differences hidden behind the catch-all category of 'watching television'. We all watch television at different times, but with how much attention and with what degree of commitment, in relation to which types of programmes and occasions? Only if this kind of qualitative distinction can be established can the aggregated statistical results of large-scale survey work be broken down into meaningful components. Thus, it would seem that we do need to focus on the complex ways in which television viewing is inextricably embedded in a whole range of everyday practices – and is itself partly constitutive of those practices (Scannell 1988). We need to investigate the context – specific ways in which particular communications technologies come to acquire particular meanings and thus come to be used in different ways, for different purposes, by people in different types of household. We need to investigate television viewing (and the rules of its 'accomplishment') in its 'natural' setting.

Problems of empiricism

Ang (1989) raises the essential question of what kind of knowledge empirical research on audiences can produce. In short, what are the politics of audience ethnography? She rightly insists that doing research is itself a discursive practice which can only ever hope to produce historically and culturally specific knowledges which are the result of equally specific discursive encounters between researcher and informants. Research is thus, from her point of view, always a matter of interpreting (or, indeed, constructing) reality from a particular position, rather than the positivist approach of assuming that a 'correct' scientific perspective will finally allow us to achieve the utopian dream of a world completely known in the form of indisputable facts.

Fiske argues that there is no such thing as 'the television audience', defined as an empirically accessible object (Fiske 1989: 56), following Hartley, who pursues the 'constructivist' argument further, arguing that 'there is no "actual" audience that can be separated from its construction as a category – audiences are products of institutions, and don't exist prior to them, or outside them' (Hartley 1987: 125).

Hartley goes on to argue that audiences may be 'imagined' empirically, theoretically or politically, but in all cases the product is a fiction that serves the needs of the imagining institution. The argument is that we must recognize the 'constructivist' character of the research process and drop any ideas of 'capturing' the television audience 'as it is', in its totality. From this perspective, the television audience does not so much constitute an empirical object as exhibit an imaginary status, a realm in which anxieties and expectations, aspirations and fantasies, as to the predicaments of 'modern society' are condensed. Thus, Hartley argues that 'In no case is the audience "real" or external to its discursive construction. There is no "actual" audience that lies beyond its production as a category . . . audiences are only ever encountered . . . as representations' (Hartley 1987: 125). This stress on the institutionalized discursive practices through which television audiences are constructed (e.g. in Hartley's argument, the 'paedocratic discourse' through which the television audience is constituted by broadcasters) is of considerable value as a corrective to any simple-minded 'naive realism' in the research process. However, it is possible to recognize the necessarily constructivist dimension of any research process without claiming that audiences only *exist* discursively. To argue otherwise is to confuse a problem of epistemology with one of ontology. Naturally, any empirical knowledge which we may generate of television audiences will be constructed through particular discursive practices, and the categories and questions present and absent in those discourses will determine the nature of the knowledge we can generate. However, this is to argue, contra Hartley, that while we can only know audiences through discourses, audiences do in fact exist outside the terms of these discourses.

To fail to appreciate this is to misread the point which Gledhill made some years ago:

> Under the insistence of the semiotic production of meaning, the effectivity of social, economic and political practice threatens to disappear

altogether. There is a danger of conflating the social structure of reality with its signification, by virtue of the fact that social processes and relations have to be mediated through language, and the evidence that the mediating power of language reflects back on the social process. But to say that language has a determining effect on society is a different matter from saying that society is nothing but its languages and signifying practices.

(Gledhill 1978; quoted in Morley 1981: 170)

Certainly any kind of empirical research is always, necessarily, caught up in representation (rather than any transparent reflection of a pre-existing reality), and accounts of what people do with television always involve interpretation. As Ang notes, 'the empirical does not offer the answers, as positivism would have it. Answers are to be constructed in the form of interpretations' (Ang 1989: 106). However, none of this, in principle, vitiates the need for empirical work and for argument founded on the assessment of empirical evidence. The parallel can perhaps be exemplified by reference to E. H. Carr's arguments about the nature of history. As Carr puts it,

It does not follow that, because a mountain appears to take on different shapes from different angles of vision, it has objectively either no shape at all or an infinity of shapes. It does not follow that because interpretation plays a necessary part in establishing the facts of history, and because no existing interpretation is wholly objective, that one interpretation is as good as another.

(Carr 1967: 27)

While Ang's criticisms concern the necessary limitations of a particular method (ethnography) of empirical audience research, Feuer (1986) has advanced a much more fundamental argument, which queries the very point of undertaking empirical work with audiences at all. As she notes, from the standpoint of reception theory, the question of what constitutes the text is extremely complex. From this perspective it becomes increasingly hard to separate the text from its contemporary encrustations – fan magazines, the ads., the product tie-ins, the books, the publicity articles and so on – and, indeed, the very sense of attempting this separation is called into question. Feuer's argument is that this approach endlessly defers the attribution of meaning. In relation to Bennett's argument that 'the text is never available for analysis except in the context of its activations', Feuer notes:

the reception theorist is asking us to read those activations, to read the text of the reading formation. Thus, audience response criticism becomes another form of interpretation, the text for which is now relocated. If we take the concept of the 'openness' . . . of a text to its

logical extreme, we have merely displaced the whole problem of interpretation, for the audience responses also constitute a representation, in
this case a linguistic discourse. In displacing the text onto the audience,
the reception theorist constantly risks falling back into an empiricism of
the subject, by granting a privileged status to the interpretations of the
audience over those of the critic.

(Feuer 1986: 7)

In Feuer's formulation, the problem is that when one attempts to combine
this perspective with empirical work:

the authors begin by reacting against theories which assume that the text
has a total determinity over the audience. They then attempt to read
their own audience data. In each case, the critic reads another text, that
is to say, the text of the audience discourse. For the empirical researcher, granting a privileged status to the audience response does not
create a problem. But it does for those reception theorists who acknowledge the textual status of the audience response. They then have to read
the unconscious of the audience without benefit of the therapeutic
situation, or they can relinquish the psychoanalytic conception of the
subject – in which case there is a tendency to privilege the conscious or
easily articulated response.

(ibid.)

Feuer concludes that studies of this type are not necessarily 'gaining any
greater access to the spectator's unconscious responses to texts than do the
more speculative attempts by film theorists to imagine the possible implications of spectator positioning by the text' (ibid.)

Certainly, much of the audience work discussed here (including my own)
is inevitably subject to the problems of reflexivity that Feuer raises. In my
own research, I have offered the reader a 'reading' of the texts supplied by
my respondents – those texts themselves being the respondents' accounts
of their own viewing behaviour. However, in relation to the problems of
the status of any knowledge that might be produced as a result of this
process of 'readings of readings', I would still argue that the interview (not
to mention other techniques such as participant observation) remains a
fundamentally more appropriate way to attempt to understand what
audiences do when they watch television than for the analyst simply to stay
at home and imagine the possible implications of how other people might
watch television, in the manner that Feuer suggests.

In the case of my own research, I would accept that in the absence of any
significant element of participant observation of actual behaviour beyond
the interview situation, I am left only with the stories that respondents
choose to tell me. These stories are, however, themselves both limited by,

and indexical of, the cultural and linguistic frames of reference which respondents have available to them through which to articulate their responses, though, as Feuer rightly notes, these are limited to the level of conscious responses.

However, a number of other points also need to be made. The first concerns the supposedly lesser validity of respondents' accounts of behaviour, as opposed to observations of actual behaviour. The problem here is that observing behaviour always leaves open the question of interpretation. I may be observed to be sitting, staring at the television screen, but this behaviour would be equally compatible with total fascination or total boredom on my part – and the distinction will not necessarily be readily accessible from observed behavioural clues. Moreover, should you wish to understand what I am doing, it would probably be as well to ask me. I may well, of course, lie to you or otherwise misrepresent my thoughts or feelings, for any number of purposes, but at least, through my verbal responses, you will begin to get some access to the kind of language, the criteria of distinction and the types of categorizations through which I construct my (conscious) world. Without these clues my television viewing (or other behaviour) will necessarily remain the more opaque.

The interview method, then, is to be defended, in my view, not simply for the access it gives the research to the respondents' conscious opinions and statements but also for the access that it gives to the linguistic terms and categories (the 'logical scaffolding' in Wittgenstein's terms) through which respondents construct their words and their own understanding of their activities.

The dangers of the 'speculative' approach advocated by Feuer, in which the theorist simply attempts to imagine the possible implications of spectator-positioning from the text, are well illustrated in Seiter et al.'s (1989b) critique of Modleski's work. Seiter et al. argue that Modleski's analysis of how women soap-opera viewers are positioned by the text – in the manner of the 'ideal mother' who understands all the various motives and desires of the characters in a soap opera – is in fact premised on an unexamined assumption of a particular white, middle-class social position. Thus, the subject-positioning which Modleski 'imagines' that all women will occupy in relation to soap-opera texts turn out, empirically, to be refused by many of the working-class women interviewed by Seiter et al. In short, we see here how the 'speculative' approach can, at times, lead to inappropriate 'universalizations' of analysis which turn out to be premised on particular assumptions regarding the social positioning of the viewer. This is precisely the point of empirical work: as Ang puts it, to 'keep our interpretations sensitive to concrete specificities, to the unexpected, to history' – to the possibility of, in Willis's words, 'being surprised, of reaching knowledge not prefigured in one's starting paradigm' (Willis 1981: 90).

Telling stories

We face the difficulty, as qualitative media researchers, of finally telling stories about the stories which our respondents have chosen to tell us. These problems are both irreducible and familiar. As Geertz remarked, long ago,

> what we call our data are really our own constructions of other people's constructions of what they and their compatriots are up to . . . Right down at the factual base, the hard rock, in so far as there is any, of the whole enterprise, we are already explicating: and worse, explicating explications.
>
> (Geertz 1973: 9)

However, as Geertz also notes, rather than giving up and going home, on realization of this, the ethnographer's alternative is to try to pick his or her way through the piled-up structures of inference and implication which constitute the discourse of everyday exchange. For Geertz the point is to analyse these structures of signification in an attempt to determine their social ground and import – and to develop what he, borrowing from Gilbert Ryle (1949), has famously characterized as 'thick descriptions' of this inherently dubious 'data'. At the end of his well-known account (Geertz 1973: 6–7) of the impossibility of distinguishing, at the level of observed empirical data between a 'wink', a 'twitch of the eye' and a 'fake/parody wink', Geertz argues that

> the point is that between what Ryle calls the 'thin description' of what the person (parodist, winker, twitcher) is doing ('rapidly contracting his right eyelids') and the 'thick description' of what he is doing ('practising a burlesque of a friend faking a wink to deceive an innocent into thinking a conspiracy is in motion') lies the object of ethnography: a stratified hierarchy of meaningful structures in terms of which twitches, winks, fake-winks, parodies and rehearsals of parodies are produced, perceived and interpreted.
>
> (ibid., 7)

Towards ethnography

Television as 'text' and television as technology are united by their construction, their recontextualization, within the practices of our daily lives and in the display of goods and cultural competence, both in private and in public. If we are to make some sense of the significance of these activities which after all, are the primary ones for any understanding of the dynamics of the pervasiveness and power of contemporary culture, then we have to take seriously the varied and detailed ways in which they are undertaken. This is the basis for a commitment to ethnography as an empirical method.

What might be involved? There is an emerging literature reporting on work done with television audiences in their natural settings. There is also work on the ethnography of consumption. The starting-point for any such study is the household or the family, for it is here that the primary involvement with television is created, and where the primary articulation of meanings is undertaken. The household or family, itself embedded in a wider social and cultural environment, provides, through its patterns of daily interaction, through its own internal systems of relationships, and its own culture of legitimation and identity formation, a laboratory for the naturalistic investigation of the consumption and production of meaning.

Silverstone (1990b) suggests an analogy. In introducing their recent volume on the modern city, Feher and Kwinter (1987) refer to the Chinese way of drawing a carp:

> To draw a carp, Chinese masters warn, it is not enough to know the animal's morphology, study its anatomy or understand the physiological functions of its existence. They tell us that it is also necessary to consider the reed against which the carp brushes each morning while seeking its nourishment, the oblong stone behind which it conceals itself, or the rippling of water when it springs toward the surface. These elements should in no way be treated as the fish's environment, the milieu in which it evolves or the natural background against which it can be drawn. They belong to the carp itself . . . The carp must be apprehended as a certain power to affect and be affected by the world.
>
> (quoted in Silverstone, 1990b: 3–4)

It is in this connection that Silverstone (ibid.) suggests that 'communication is a carp', and that our understanding of it should be premised on the integration of environment and action in the ways we think about it and research it.

Such an ambition requires a particular methodological response. It is to study the communication process in detail and in so far as it is possible, in real space and time, to take a broadly ethnographic position, and to examine the dynamics of action and constraint in the daily activities and practices of the individuals and groups who are engaged in the socially situated production and consumption of meanings.

This is the specific ambition of an ethnographic and interdisciplinary approach to the study of communication. It rests on an ability to understand how social actors themselves define and understand their own communication practices – their decisions, their choices and the consequences of both for their daily lives and their subsequent actions – as well as on the ability of the researcher to bring into the analysis (and even offer his or her subjects) the benefits of more structural considerations (for more on these points, see Silverstone 1990b); on anthropology as reflexive, see Marcus and Fischer 1986). It also rests on the ability to bring more than one disciplinary perspective to bear. The world of everyday life is not one which can be satisfactorily viewed through a single pair of spectacles, or from a single position. It requires varieties of distance, magnification and position, and it requires to be understood as the dialectical product of inside and outside: of biographies, personalities, meanings, actions, spaces, times, opportunities and material constraints. It is from this perspective, Silverstone (ibid.) suggests, that the ethnographer and the Chinese master-draftsman have the same concerns.

Television and everyday life: the context of viewing

One of the most important advances in recent audience work has been the growing recognition of the importance of the context of viewing. In the case of television this is a recognition of the domestic context. Let us being by noting, with Ang, that

> an audience does not merely consist of the aggregate of viewers of a specific programme, it should also be conceived of as engaging in the practice of watching television as such . . . so decodings must be seen as embedded in a general practice of television viewing.
>
> (Ang 1991)

This activity is, of course, a rule-governed process, and the primary concern of the ethnographer is with explicating the rules which govern and facilitate this practice. Thus, as Anderson argues, we must recognize that:

> the ordinary viewing of television . . . is not an unstructured pastime . . . media use happens within connected skeins of behaviour, accomplished practices . . . which constitute and maintain our social realities. Family viewing, for example, is no more casual and spontaneous than the family dinner. It is accomplished by competent actors with great improvisational skill.
>
> (Anderson 1987: 164)

As we all know from our everyday existence, these quotidian procedures and activities can be deceptively complex and, at times, treacherously so – not least because of their 'vagueness' (resulting from the absence of explication procedures in everyday communication between people who are already familiar with each other). Thus, as Lindlof and Meyer note,

> Much of our ordinary communication behaviour . . . demands a certain amount of vagueness which further impairs [the researcher's] ability to assess what is occurring and why. Ironically, vagueness is the arch villain of positivist science, where clarity and objectivity of interpretation are

the embraced ideals. But vagueness is essential to daily patterns of social interaction. Without it, or worse, with the pursuit of scientific clarity, social interactions as we have come to know and experience them would be nearly impossible.

(Lindlof and Meyer 1987: 25)

Thus, for the researcher to attempt to enter this 'natural world', where communication is vague and meanings implicit, is inevitably to go skating on thin ice. None the less, the corresponding claims that can then be made in terms of 'data validity' (to put it in rather scientistic terms) are considerable. Lindlof and Meyer make a forceful case for the study of media audiences in their 'natural' domestic setting. In the first place, as they argue, 'mediated communication' is a quintessentially domestic activity: 'The fact that media messages are usually received by people in private and familiar settings means that the selection and use of these messages will be shaped by the exigencies of these local environments' (2). Furthermore, they argue, recent technological changes in media delivery-systems mean that, nowadays 'messages can be edited, deleted, rescheduled, or skipped past with complete disregard for their original form. The received notion of the mass communication audience simply has little relevance for the reality of mediated communication' (ibid.).

This returns us to the central focus on the study of everyday communication practices – in support of which we might usefully recall that, for Schutz 'the exploration of the general principles according to which man [sic] in daily life organises his experiences . . . is the first task of the methodology of the social sciences' (Schutz 1963: 59).

This, of course, is to argue for the importance of a phenomenological perspective – for systematically addressing audience activity in its natural setting, using qualitative methods as tools for the collection of naturalistic data, and with some priority given in the analysis to categories that can be derived from the respondents' own conceptual frameworks. Again, as Jensen reminds us, 'meaning is the stuff that the world of everyday life is made of, individual instances of communication make no sense before they have been interpreted in the total context of the audience's lifeworld'.

The central concern, from this perspective, is with the logics-in-use of situated everyday behaviour – in order to understand how communication processes are achieved, in their natural settings, and how, within this context, the various public media are incorporated into and mobilized within these private worlds.

As Anderson puts it, if we approach the study of mediated communication and the mutual implication of the mass-media and family-communication processes from this point of view, then

our intent is to explain the presence, functions and influence of the content and technology within the structures, functions, systems and interaction of the family. When the study is taken from the naturalistic perspective, we seek to document the social action of the situated family for the purpose of understanding the socially constructed meanings of the family's structures, functions, systems and interaction. Our research domain is the situated family, the data reside in the social action, and our explanation illuminates the socially constructed meanings of the members.

(Anderson 1987: 163)

Of course, access to the private sphere of the household is always a matter of degree – there will almost always be some areas of the household which are 'haram'/forbidden (cf. Bourdieu 1972a) to a stranger and, as Anderson notes, some social action will never be manifested in the presence of an outsider to the family. The account which the ethnographer can give must be conscious of its own partiality, incompleteness and structured gaps.

Notes of caution are certainly in order here. Not only is some self-consciousness (or 'reflexivity') needed in relation to the inevitable partiality of any analysis; as Lull (1988) argues, rigorous and systematic forms of data collection and interpretation are just as necessary in qualitative as in quantitative research. As he notes, in recent years the very term 'ethnography' has become totemic (a ritual genuflexion towards a newly instituted tribal deity?) within the field of audience studies. Suddenly everyone is an ethnographer (the ethnographer as fashion victim?); but, as Lull points out, 'what is passing as ethnography in cultural studies fails to achieve the fundamental requirements for data collection and reporting typical of most anthropological and sociological ethnographic research. "Ethnography" has become an abused buzz-word in our field' (Lull 1988: 242).

Problems of ethnography and epistemology

At its simplest, it has traditionally been argued that the ethnographer's task is to 'go into the field' and, by way of observation and interview, to attempt to describe – and inevitably interpret – the practices of the subjects in that cultural context, on the basis of his or her first-hand observation of day-to-day activities.

Qualitative research strategies such as ethnography are principally designed to gain access to 'naturalized domains' and their characteristic activities. The strength of these approaches lies in the possibilities generated for contextual understanding of the connections between different aspects of the phenomena being studied. Clearly, this type of analysis is dependent on various techniques of 'triangulation' in order to reconcile different aspects of the observational work. As Hammersley and Atkinson point out, this may involve

the comparison of data relating to the same phenomenon but deriving
from different phases of the fieldwork, different points in the temporal
cycles occurring in the setting, or, as in respondent validation, the
accounts of different participants in the setting.

(Hammersley and Atkinson 1983: 198)

Thus, according to Hammersley and Atkinson, ethnography can be
understood as

simply one social research method, albeit an unusual one, drawing on a
wide range of sources of information. The ethnographer participates in
people's lives for an extended period of time, watching what happens,
listening to what is said, asking questions, in fact, collecting whatever
data are available to throw light on the issues with which he or she is
concerned.

(ibid., 2)

This, of course, already raises considerable problems – concerning, for
instance, the delimitation of the field research – in establishing which
elements of the (potentially infinite) realm of its 'context' is going to be
relevant to the particular research in hand. Here we return to the familiar
debate concerning the relative advantages and disadvantages of 'open-
ended' or 'closed' research strategies. While researching women's relations
to video technology, Gray (1987) reports that very often, the women she
interviewed wanted to tell her stories ('their stories') and that, at first, she
was anxious lest they should be 'getting away from the point' of her
research project (their uses of video), in so far as the stories involved
complex family histories and extended narratives. However, as Gray
points out, the great value of this open-ended approach lies in the fact that,
in allowing respondents to 'tell it their way', with a minimum of direction,
they offered her the understanding of their video (non-)use in the context
of their own understanding of their social position – without which, whatever they might have said in answer to direct questions on the ostensible
research topic would have been relatively insignificant, as it was how they
saw their lives that explained the extent to which they did (or rather, did
not) use video technology.

The question, however, is not only a pragmatic one – of how much (and
which elements) of the context are necessary to understand any act; it is
also a theoretical (and epistemological) question of the relation between
the particular and the general, the instance and category. In this connection Ang argues that, in the field of media audience research, given the
dominance of the generalizing/categorizing tradition in much previous
work, and given the well-advertised epistemological limitations of these
approaches and their categorizations of 'viewer types', it would be timely

for this emphasis to be, at least, complemented by the opposite concern – with particularization (cf. Billig 1987). As she puts it,

> rather than reducing a certain manifestation of 'viewing behaviour' to an instance of a general category, we might consider it in its particularity, treat it in its concrete specificity, differentiate it from the other instances of the general category . . . Only then can we go beyond statistical 'significance without much signification'.

(Ang 1991: 160)

Ang argues in support of Knorr-Cetina's (1989) concept of 'methodological situationalism' (rather than methodological individualism) – a perspective which would give analytic priority to concrete situations of television viewing rather than to decontextualized forms of viewing behaviour. Thus, she argues, 'the analysis of micro-situations of watching TV should take precedence over either individual "viewing behaviour" or totalised taxonomic collectives such as the "TV audience"' (Ang 1991: 162).

Some years ago, Geertz argued that cultural analysis should be considered not as an experimental science in search of law, but as an interpretative one in search of meaning – attempting to explicate forms of behaviour which may well appear enigmatical (or even banal). Thus, in Geertz's argument, the task of theory in this context is not to

> codify abstract regularities . . . not to generalise across cases but within them . . . Rather than beginning with a set of observations and attempting to subsume them under a governing law, such inference begins with a set of (presumptive) signifiers and attempts to place them within an intelligible frame.

(Geertz 1973: 26)

What defines ethnography, for Geertz, is the attempt to furnish 'thick descriptions' of activities and events – which take the form of 'a multiplicity of complex conceptual structures . . . superimposed upon or knotted into one another' (Geertz 1973: 14), where most of what we want to know is never made explicit (cf. Pêcheux (1982) on the importance of the unspoken premises of any communicative exchange). The task is to render these inexplicit meanings accessible, to dissolve their opacity, by 'setting them in the frame of their own banalities' (ibid.).

Geertz claims that the ethnographer should seek neither to become nor to mimic the 'native/other'. As he puts it, 'only romantics or spies would seem to find any point in that' (13). The research procedure – necessarily, argues Geertz – is that 'we begin with our own interpretations of what our informants are up to, or think they are up to, and then systematise those' (15). The analyst's account is, necessarily, an interpretation (and, notes Geertz, often a second- or third-order one). It is, necessarily, a fiction – in the sense, Geertz argues, that it is 'something made . . . [or] . . . fashioned – the original meaning of 'fiction' – not that . . . [it is] false' (15).

Of course, Geertz points out, what we describe is not 'raw social discourse' to which we do not have full access, 'but only that small part of it which our informants can lead us into understanding' (20). However, as he goes on to note 'this is not as fatal as it sounds, for . . . it is not necessary to know everything in order to understand something'; (ibid.). Ethnographic accounts are, of course, 'essentially contestable' and at its heart cultural analysis is a necessarily incomplete business of guessing at meanings, assessing the guesses and drawing explanatory conclusions from the better guesses. However, as he goes on to argue, the fact that complete objectivity is impossible is not an excuse for letting one's sentiments run loose in untrammelled subjectivity.

Clearly, we can never *simply* describe a social setting – we necessarily interpret it from our own point of view, and we have to make sense of our respondents' words and actions in our research reports. It is around this issue that the recent debates concerning postmodern (or post-structuralist) anthropology have centred, especially in the US. Thus, the central issue has concerned the relationship between the observer and the observed – 'the imperialist ethnographer who descended as a white man [*sic*] into the jungle and bore away back to the white man's world, "meanings" of native life that were unavailable to those who lived it' (Fiske 1990: 90) – and the basis of the ethnographer's 'authority' to convey the cultural experiences of others.[2] Among other commentators, Marcus and Fischer (1986) have talked of a 'crisis of representation' in this connection, and Said (1978) cogently argued for a more reflexive analysis of the process of 'Orientalization' – the process of imaginative geography which produces a fictionalized 'other' as the exotic object of knowledge.[3]

In a similar vein, Rabinow (1977) stressed the irreducible component of 'symbolic violence' at the heart of the ethnographic project and insisted on the need to reinscribe the subjectivity of the 'I-witnessing' author in such 'they-picturing' stories (Geertz 1988). It is in this connection that Clifford (1986) and others have echoed (or, perhaps, more accurately amplified) Geertz's original claim that ethnographic writings must finally be understood as 'fictions' involving complex processes of interpretation and representation. In all this, of course, the object of criticism is a form of naive empiricism or 'ethnographic realism' which would remain insensitive to these issues of reflexivity and would presume both a transparency of representation and an immediacy of the problematic category of 'experience' (cf. Althusser 1972).

For critics like Clifford, there can be no 'place of overview (mountain top) from which to map human ways of life, no Archimedean point from which to represent the world. Mountains are in constant motion . . . we ground things, now, on a moving earth' (Clifford 1986: 22, but see also

Carr, quoted p. 179). This, of course, requires that we specify who writes, about whom and from what positions of knowledge and power. It further requires us to recognize that the 'truths' produced by media researchers, for example, are necessarily relative and partial – they are always interpretations constructed from a particular position. As Clifford puts it,

> Cultures do not hold still for their portraits. Attempts to make them do so always involve simplification and exclusion, selection of a temporal focus, the construction of a self–other relationship, and the imposition or negotiation of a power relationship.

> (ibid., 10)

As Gray has argued, these difficulties require, among other things, that we recognize 'the subjectivity of the researcher and mobilise that in a rigorous way' (Gray 1987b: 10); or, in Angela McRobbie's words, we 'locate our own autobiographies . . . inside the question we might want to ask' (McRobbie 1982: 52). This also means, however, that we need to avoid the dangers of slipping into an infinite regress of self-absorbed concern with our own subjective processes, and to manage our subjectivity, rather than to be paralysed by it. The point is, as Geertz has noted, that if the traditional anthropological attitude to these questions ('Don't think about ethnography, just do it') is the problem, then, equally, to fall into a paralysing (if vertiginously thrilling) trance of epistemological navel-gazing ('Don't do ethnography, just think about it') is no kind of answer.

Clifford and the other contributors to *Writing Culture* (Clifford and Marcus 1986) are concerned to reject any ideology of the transparency of representation and immediacy of experience. They acknowledge that 'even the best ethnographic texts – serious, true fictions – are systems, or economies of truth'; that the ethnographer no longer holds unquestioned rights of salvage ('the ambitious social scientist making off with tribal lore and giving nothing in return') and is necessarily inserted in relations of power, in attempting to speak for the 'others' being studied. Even so, Clifford expresses the hope that this 'political and epistemological self-consciousness need not lead to ethnographic self-absorption, or to the conclusion that it is impossible to know anything certain about other people' (Clifford 1986: 7).

At a more technical (or 'operational') level, of course, that doubt – concerning our ability even to know the 'other' – is often expressed in the critique of any research procedures in which members of category A observe/research members of category B. If that makes the research *ipso facto* invalid, that can only be on the premise of an ultimately solipsistic theory of knowledge, which logically entails an infinite regress – so that one would have to argue that, finally, only a person of exactly the same category (of which there is, logically, only one) could do research: on themselves.[4] The political objections to the idea of members of one social category researching members of another are of a quite different order (though often the political objection is presented as if it were an epistemological one); but, even on those grounds, the objection is finally hard to sustain, as it precludes any possibility of a general interest and logically regresses into a Hobbesian model of the war of all against all, in which difference is presumed to be not simply problematic but necessarily conflictual or exploitative. On these criteria, for example, Marx's research into the position of the working class would be invalidated, on both epistemological and political grounds, on the simple basis that Marx himself was not a member of the working class.

Postmodern ethnography and 'moral hypochondria'

More recently Geertz (1988) has attempted to respond to what he calls the 'pervasive nervousness' and 'moral hypochondria' engendered by 'writing culture' and other post-structuralist and 'postmodern' writing about ethnography. He notes that these 'Jesuits of the Future' or, as he puts it elsewhere, 'diehard apostles of the hermeneutics of suspicion' (1988: 86) start from a quite proper suspicion of the Malinowskian ideal of 'immersionist ethnography' and the naive invocation of the ethnographer's appeal to 'sincerity', 'authenticity' or 'being there' as the founding authority of the ethnographic account. As Geertz notes, nowadays 'Malinowski's happy "Eureka!" when first coming across the Trobrianders – "feeling of ownership: It is I who will describe them . . . [I who will] . . . create them" sounds not merely presumptuous, but outright comic' (133).

For Geertz, it becomes clear, some part of this methodological and epistemological navel-gazing is finally beyond the pale – summed up perhaps in his image of 'the almost unbearably earnest and reflexive fieldworker (Why did I ask that? . . . What does he think I think of him? . . .) burdened with a murderously severe conscience and possessed of a passionate sense of mission'. As he puts it, 'the question that raises, of course, is how anyone who believes all this can write anything at all, much less go so far as to publish it' (96–7).

Massey (1991b) refers, in this connection, to Mascia-Lees et al.'s observation that 'when western white males – who traditionally have controlled the production of knowledge – can no longer define the truth . . . their response is to conclude that there is not a truth to be discovered' (Mascia-Lees et al. 1989: 15). The issue, as formulated by Hartsock (1987), is that

it seems highly suspicious that it is at this moment in history, when so many groups are engaged in 'nationalisms' which involve redefinitions of the marginalised others, that doubt arises in the academy about the possibilities for a general theory which can describe the world, about historical 'progress'. Why is it, exactly at the moment when so many of us who have been silenced begin to demand the right to name ourselves, to act as subjects rather than objects of history, that just then, the concept of subjecthood becomes problematic . . . [that] . . . just when we are forming our own theories about the world, uncertainty emerges about whether the world can be adequately theorised?

(quoted in Massey 1991b: 33)

As Massey further points out, Sangren (1988), writing of ethnography, notes that 'whatever "authority" is created in a text has its most direct social effect not in the world of political and economic domination of the Third World by colonial and neo-colonial powers, but rather in the academic institutions in which such authors participate' (quoted in Massey 1991b: 34). Even more cynically, perhaps, as Mascia-Lees *et al.* argue, 'while postmodern anthropologists such as Clifford, Marcus and Fischer may choose to think that they are transforming global power relations, as well as the discipline of anthropology itself, they may also be establishing first claim in the new academic territory on which this decade's battles for intellectual supremacy and jobs will be waged (quoted in Massey 1991b: 34).

There is, of course, quite another substantive objection which can be raised against the positions advocated by much post-structuralist writing on ethnography, which concerns the reduction of the 'other' to a discursive effect – this is the point of Grossberg's critique of Clifford and Marcus. As Grossberg points out, the post-structuralist perspective finally 'deconstructs the other into the productivity of the ethnographer's subjectivity, a subjectivity which can, in turn, be deconstructed into the productivity of discourses. In this deconstructive move, the very facticity of the other is erased, dissolved into the ethnographer's semiotic constructions' (Grossberg 1988: 381–2). As Gewertz and Errington (1991) argue, it is but a small step then to a position in which, as they put it 'we think, therefore they are'. The irony, as Spivak has argued, is that 'the ones talking about the critique of the subject are the ones who have had the luxury of a subject. The much publicised critique of the sovereign subject thus actually inaugurates a subject' (Spivak 1988: 272).

The point, for Grossberg, is that an adequate reconceptualization of ethnography must recognize 'that there is a "reality", an otherness which is not merely its mark of difference within our signifying systems' and is not reducible to them. Thus, Grossberg rightly argues, following Probyn (unpublished), for any 'epistemological (and political) critique of the ontological assumption that the other is produced as other (i.e. outside of our discourse) from *within* our discourse' (Grossberg 1988: 382). As he notes, it is crucial that we refuse this reduction of material otherness to semiotic difference (cf. Gledhill, quoted earlier).

For Geertz, similarly, there is an important limit to what he is prepared to concede to the post-structuralist argument. To recognize the subjective component of ethnography is no more than commonsense, as it is to recognize that ethnographies are products themselves, 'fictions' of a sort. But, as he notes, 'to argue . . . that the writing of ethnography involves telling stories' could only have ever seemed contentious on the premise of 'a confusion . . . of the imagined with the imaginary, the fictional with the false; making things out with making them up' (Geertz 1988: 140).

What Geertz characterizes here as 'methodological soul searching' has, of course, as he notes, been generated by a widespread decline of faith in 'brute facts, set procedures and unsituated knowledge', not to mention a loss of faith in the very possibility of unconditioned description. In this context, telling it as it is is 'no more an adequate slogan for ethnography than for philosophy since Wittgenstein', and the claim to 'explain enigmatical others on the grounds that you have gone about with them in their native habitat' will always be contestable. None the less for those of us (*pace* Tyler 1986) with a 'lingering affection for facts, descriptions, inductions and truth', these are the kinds of claims we shall still have to find ways to pursue (Geertz 1988: 131–7).

Certainly, within the discipline of anthropology (or at least, within its fashionably postmodern sectors) these are difficult positions to sustain, and in that context the very right to write ethnography seems at risk – and understandably so. The desire to distance oneself from the power assymetries upon which the ethnographic encounter has so often rested has produced an attitude towards the very idea of ethnography which is at least ambivalent. Moreover, given the epistemological crisis produced by the widespread loss of faith in received stories about the nature of representation, anthropologists now 'have added to their "Is it decent?" worry (Who are we to describe them?) an "Is it possible?" one (Can Ethiopian love be sung in French?)' (Geertz 1988: 135).

It is certainly necessary for us to recognize our own authorial role in any ethnography we write – this follows quite simply from the 'un-get-roundable fact that all ethnographical descriptions are home made, that they are the describer's descriptions' (ibid., 145). The point is, of course, that 'once ethnographic texts begin to be looked at as well as though, once they are seen to be made, and to be made to persuade, those who make them have rather more to answer for' (ibid., 138) and in this respect 'the burden of authorship cannot be evaded, however heavy it may have grown, there is no possibility of displacing it onto "method", "language" or "the people themselves" redescribed . . . as co-authors' (ibid., 140).

If, as Geertz argues, ethnography is 'like quantum mechanics or the Italian opera . . . a work of the imagination, less extravagant than the first, less methodical than the second', still, while recognizing the inevitably constructed nature of any ethnography, its primary task, as he puts it, is to

convey 'what it is like to be somewhere specific . . . [because] . . . whatever else it may be . . . [ethnography] is above all else a rendering of the
actual . . . [which] is the basis upon which anything else which ethnography
seeks to do . . . finally rests' (140–3). For Geertz, the status of an ethnographic account finally rests on the degree to which it is able to clarify 'what
is going on' in a particular place – that, for Geertz, is what discriminates a
better from worse account. As he puts it, returning to his earlier example,
'if ethnography is thick description . . . then the determining question for
any . . . [ethnography] . . . is whether it sorts winks from twitches and real
winks from mimicked ones'(16).[5]

The object of study?

As is clear from the argument so far, the strictly methodological considerations to be faced in developing qualitative audience research are formid-
able. If we are not to run the risk of a premature closure of analysis which
allows us to achieve precision only at the price of ripping actions from the
contexts that give them meaning, then the forms and techniques of data
collection, interpretation and analysis which we shall need to develop will
have to demonstrate considerable subtlety.

However, as if this were not enough already, there remains the further
(and fundamental) problem of producing an adequate definition of the
object of study. Silverstone and I have argued elsewhere (Morley and
Silverstone 1990) for the redefinition of the field of media studies to include
a far wider range of technologies than is commonly presumed (or allowed)
by the 'traditional' focus on television in isolation. For this reason the
Household Uses of Information and Communication Technology (HICT)
project at Brunel University (see Silverstone, Morley *et al.* 1989) started
from the premise that television should now be seen not in isolation, but as
one of a number of information and communication technologies, occupying domestic time and space alongside the video-recorder, the computer
and the telephone, as well as the Walkman, the answering-machine, the
stereo and the radio. In this our main objective was to re-contextualize the
study of television in a broader framework.[6] In the HICT project we were
concerned to re-contextualize the study of television consumption within a
wider socio-technical and cultural frame than that which has dominated
research in this area thus far. Our second concern was to draw other
domestic technologies – particularly those involved in the provision of
information and communication – into this same socio-technical frame. At
a conceptual level we were offering what we believed to be a necessary
challenge to many of the conventions (and some of the cornerstones) of
current media and cultural studies, as they bear on an understanding
of the place and significance of television and other communication and
information technologies in the modern world. But, quite clearly, such a

conceptual re-orientation is not, by itself, enough. What is then required is an effort to bring such concepts and ideas to life, and this, in turn, requires a substantial commitment to empirical – and to broadly ethnographic – work, in order to provide a substantive base for understanding the complexity of the issues. Within this formulation, television's meanings – that is, the meanings of both texts and technologies – have to be understood as emergent properties of contextualized audience practices. These practices have to be seen as situated within the facilitating and constraining micro-social environments of family and household interaction. These, in turn, must be seen as being situated in, but not necessarily determined by, those of neighbourhood, economy and culture, in which acts of consumption (of both texts and technologies) provide the articulating dimension.

The problem at issue concerns the adequate contextualization of the activities, for instance, of the audience for any one television programme or programme-type. As Radway has put it, in an auto-critique of her work in this field,

> No matter how extensive the effort to dissolve the boundaries of the textual object or the audience, most recent studies of reception, including my own, continue to begin with the 'factual' existence of a particular kind of text which is understood to be received by some set of individuals. Such studies perpetuate the notion of a circuit [of communication – D.M.] neatly bounded and therefore identifiable, locatable and open to observation.
>
> (Radway 1988: 363)

Radway's argument (and it is one which I would support) is that we need to investigate the ways in which a whole variety of media is enmeshed in the production of popular culture and consciousness across the terrain of everyday life – and that this is fundamental if we are to recognize the interdiscursive patterning (cf. Pêcheux 1982) of communication. As Radway puts it,

> our habitual practice of conducting bounded, regionalised investigations of singular text–audience circuits may be preventing us from investigating, except in a limited way, the very articulations between discourses and practices we deem important, both theoretically and strategically.
>
> (ibid., 366)

It is for this kind of reason that, in the HICT research, we chose to focus on a number of different, but interlinked questions, for example: the relationship between family structure and family relations and the use of communication and information technologies; in the relationship between familial and technological systems; the relationship of the family to the public sphere as mediated by these technologies; the differences of socialization into technological usages and competences, particularly in relation to gender; the culture of technology and the ways in which domestic technologies are constructed not just as material but as symbolic goods; and the dynamics and processes of consumption, both of the technologies themselves and of the content of their communication and information. Our concern was with the place and the dynamics of the texts (the programmes and the software) and the technologies of communication and information in the home and for the family. Technological innovation, social relationships and cultural identities are intimately bound together and the family is often the crucible within which they are resolved. Within the established, and systemic, patterns of most people's domestic lives, the texts and technologies of communication and information are crucially involved in the management of time, in the management of the division of labour, and in the creation and sustenance of social relationships and individual identities. The use of the telephone, the computer, the video, the television, never mind the microwave or the washing-machine, enables social spaces to be organized, linking and separating individuals to and from one another within the family and the household, and also between the family and the household and the outside world.

In her auto-critique, Radway (1988) points to the radically narrowed conception of ethnography which has been imported into media studies. As she notes, in anthropological usage an 'ethnography' is a written account of a lengthy social interaction between a scholar and a culture. Although in the analysis its focus is often narrowed to focus on some specific feature of social life (kinship, initiation rituals, or whatever), that account is rooted in an effort to understand the entire tapestry of social life. By contrast, she notes:

> those of us who have turned to the ethnographic method to understand how specific social subjects interact with cultural forms have nonetheless always begun with a radically circumscribed site, a field surveyed or cordoned off by our preoccupation with a single medium or genre . . . we have remained locked within the particular topical field defined by our prior segmentation of the audience of its use of one medium or genre. Consequently, we have often reified, or ignored totally, other cultural determinants beside the one specifically highlighted . . . Ethnographers of media use have . . . tended to rule out as beyond our purview questions of how (for example) a single leisure practice intersects with or contradicts others.
>
> (Radway 1988: 367)

To follow this trajectory is, then, to argue, for example, that if we are to take the medium of television seriously, then we have to develop approaches which take equally seriously the complexity of its intervening in the daily lives of all of us in contemporary society. It is to argue that the focus on the embedded audience must certainly now be a priority for media research.

To return to the earlier argument, concerning the difficulty of isolating the practice of television watching, this is to note, with Ang, that 'in everyday contexts the distinction between viewing and non-viewing is radically blurred. In day to day reality audience membership is a fundamentally vague subject position; people constantly move in and out of "the TV audience" as they integrate viewing behaviour with a multitude of other concerns and activities in radically contingent ways' (Ang 1989: 163).

Thus, as Ang notes, in common usage 'watching television' is the ill-defined shorthand term for the multiplicity of situated practices and experiences in which television audiencehood is embedded. In a similar vein, drawing on the work of de Certeau (1984), Silverstone has elsewhere argued:

> 'Television is everyday life. To study the one is at the same time to study the other. There are TV sets in almost every household in the western world . . . Their texts and their images, their stories and their stars provide much of the conversational currency of our daily lives. TV has been much studied. Yet it is precisely this integration into the daily lives of those who watch it which has somehow slipped through the net of academic enquiry.
>
> (Silverstone 1989: 77)

Thus, Radway suggests that, instead of 'segmenting' a social formation – by construing it as a set of 'separate' audiences for specific media or types of product – it might be more useful to take a broader canvas, and to begin with the habits and practices of everyday life as they are 'actively, discontinuously, even contradictorily pieced together by historical subjects themselves, as they move nomadically via disparate associations and relations, through day-to-day existence . . .'. This would be to move towards 'a new object of analysis . . . the endlessly shifting, ever evolving kaleidoscope of daily life and the way in which the media are integrated and implicated within it' (Radway 1988: 366).[7]

It is in this spirit that I would suggest that for audience studies, when it comes to television, the key challenge lies in our ability to construct the audience as both a social and a semiological (cultural) phenomenon, and in our ability to recognize the relationship between viewers and the television set as they are mediated by the determinancies of everyday life – and by the audience's daily involvement with all the other technologies in play in the conduct of mediated quotidian communication. It is within such an extended definition of the field of study that qualitative audience research must now be developed.

Part V

Television, technology and consumption

Chapter 9

Domestic communication: technologies and meanings[1]

(with Roger Silverstone)

Television should now be seen, not in isolation, but as one of a number of information and communication technologies, occupying domestic time and space alongside the video-recorder, the computer and the telephone, as well as the Walkman, the answering-machine, the stereo and the radio. In what follows many of the empirical and theoretical references are to work within the field of television studies. While this focus is necessary, given the emphasis in recent years on television within the overall study of communications, our overall objective is to re-contextualize the study of television in a broader framework.

Of course, it is important to remain sensitive to the ways in which the new media do not simply displace but are also integrated with the old. New forms, such as pop videos, are integrated into traditional modes of communication, such as teenage oral cultures and gossip networks.[2] New technologies may simply displace pre-existing family conflicts into new contexts.[3] Equally, we must also note the potential significance of the changing distribution of hardware: the emergence of the multi-set (and even the multi-VCR) household. These technical changes have profound implications for the potential development of domestic life.[4]

In this changed context, a number of our working assumptions about television and its audience will need to be considered afresh.[5] Because of these technical changes in the nature of the medium, it seems increasingly misleading to see television as isolated. Television has to be seen as embedded within a technical and consumer culture that is both domestic and national (and international), a culture that is at once both private and public.

From the point of view of changes in communications technology, these remarks will provide some indication of the framework of our research. But it is one thing to frame a project in this way and another to define and to defend the bases on which such framing is undertaken. And it is yet another to explore its implications for an understanding of the social and cultural significance of television as a communicating medium. Indeed many questions about that significance have already been begged. Why a focus on the household? Why see television as technology? What are the consequences of such a framing for our understanding of television audiences and of their practices as consumers? What are the implications for the future of the family and the future of television? Why, in other words, is there an insistence on seeing television in this broad context at all?

In this chapter we will attempt answers to these questions in the hope of advancing our understanding of television's changing place in contemporary society. We will argue for a position which requires a commitment to empirical work, and above all to ethnographically focused empirical work. And we will seek an approach which defines television as an essentially domestic medium, to be understood both within the context of household and family and within the wider context of social, political and economic realities.

Television and the domestic

Within this formulation television's *meanings*, that is the meanings of both texts and technologies, have to be understood as emergent properties of contextualized audience practices. These practices have to be seen as situated within the facilitating and constraining micro-social environments of family and household interaction. These, in turn, must be seen as being situated within but not necessarily determined by, those of neighbourhood, economy and culture, in which acts of consumption (of both texts and technologies) provide the articulating dimensions.

Why households? In one sense the answer is a simple one. We watch television in our homes. The household and the family are our primary environment. Television is part of our socialization, just as we are socialized to television – in parlours, sitting-rooms and kitchens.[6] We learn from television; television provides the stuff of family talk and neighbourhood gossip. We see other households and other families on television. We take television for granted. But television and the primary culture which it generates, or which we generate around it, have barely been studied. Behind the closed front-doors of Western and other societies, television and other information and communication technologies are consumed and used, one imagines, in ways that are both common and unique. All screens are technically the same, and the same programmes will be seen by millions, but their physical position in these households, their status as the focus of daily ritual, their incorporation into private and domestic lives will be as varied as the individuals and families who attend, and socially significant (or not) in their patterning and their persistence. Television is received in an already complex and powerful context. Households, families, are bounded, conflictful, contradictory. They have their own histories, their own lore, their own myths, their own secrets. They, and the individuals who compose them, are more or less open or closed to outside influences, more or less pervious or impervious to the appeals of advertisers and educators and entertainers to buy, to learn from, and to be entertained by television. Its pleasures are domestic pleasures, and its subjects, of whatever age or gender, are domestic subjects. The audience for television is an embedded audience, and home and hearth[7] are both its product and its precondition.

Over the last few years there has, of course, been a growing recognition that the analysis of broadcasting must be reformulated to take into account its inscription within the routines of everyday life and the interweaving of domestic and public discourses. Our present concern is with how relations to communications technologies are organized in and through the context of domestic social relations. The point is stated, at its simplest, by Lindlof and Meyer, who point out that because media messages are usually received by people in domestic settings 'the selection and use of those messages will be shaped by the exigencies of those environments'.[8] The consequences of this recognition for the development of a viable research strategy are outlined by Bryce: 'Research on technology and social behaviour . . . must begin with a thorough analysis of the interactional system, and then look to see how technology is incorporated within this system'.[9]

In that article Bryce goes on to comment that 'TV viewing is one possible label for a variety of family attitudes'.[10] We are precisely concerned to develop a model of domestic communications that enables us to take into account the various communicative (and other) activities that are likely to co-exist in a situation where a family might simplistically be described as 'watching television'.[11]

We argue, then, for a re-contextualization of the study of television viewing (among other uses of communication technologies) within the broader context of a range of domestic practices. However, in acknowledging audiences as active in a range of ways as they integrate what they see and hear into their domestic lives, we should not romanticize or exaggerate the audience's creative freedoms. There is a difference between power over a text and power over an agenda. Studying television as a domestic technology requires a study of the domestic context within which an audience's activities in relation to it are articulated and constrained. It also requires attention to the similarities and differences between families and households and an understanding of their place in the wider culture and society, where issues of class, ethnicity, ideology and power define (should they be forgotten) the materialities of the everyday-life world.

But the domestic is neither a simple nor an unproblematic category. Households are not families. Families extend beyond households. Our interest is not in an imposed typology but in one that may emerge as a result of empirical work, and also in one which articulates public discourse, particularly in the marketing of domestic technologies and the construction of schedules and programmes. The household has become a major unit of consumption and a major market focus, but we are not particularly well informed about the processes of consumption or the dynamics of the market and of programming as they impinge on domestic time, space and actions. Our interest, therefore, is, first, in the internal dynamics of households, on the patterning of age and gender differences, as they bear on the uses of television and other information and communication technologies; and, second, in the external dynamics of households as their consumption and use of these goods, services and meanings defines a relationship to the outside world.

So far we have suggested re-locating the study of media consumption within its domestic context. In the end, however, this study must be located within an analysis of the varieties of forms of organization of domestic space between and within cultures. This is to argue for the independent effect of the varying material circumstances and household structures as determinants of modes of consumption of television and other communications technologies. We should not overlook, for instance, the determining effects of the physical structure of the home (cf. Lindlof and Traudt 1983).

In a similar way, in his conclusion to a recent cross-cultural study of television viewing, Lull notes that the presence or absence of different types of 'specialized' space within the household will give rise to a variety of different modes of viewing.[12]

Technology reconsidered

Close inspection of technological development reveals that technology leads a double life, one which conforms to the intentions of designers and interests of power and another which contradicts them – proceeding behind the backs of their architects to yield unintended consequences and unanticipated possibilities.[13]

Why technology? We have already suggested that the use of television cannot be separated from everything else that is going on around it. And, in particular, it cannot be separated from the use of other technologies. There is a history of displacement of media technologies in the household, but that displacement is neither complete nor simple. Radio survives. Videos and computers and cables are plugged into the television, converting it into a VDU or an instrument for narrowcasting or interactive communication. It is reasonably clear that the last forty years have seen a major increase in overall diversity in the consumption of technologies in households, and recent research suggests that their incorporation into the domestic environment is affected by social and cultural differences. Indeed, it can be argued that households and families construct their technologies in different ways, creating private meanings (re-defining public ones) in their positioning, patterns of use and display. Equally, television, with its increasing range of potential uses and links to other technologies, is being conceived by those who market it as just another machine. Television, both medium and message, is becoming a key technology for the selling of other technologies and a focus (competing with telecommunications) for a whole range of projected domestically orientated goods and services.[14]

Our argument is that an understanding of the place of television both in society and in the household cannot ignore its contextualization by the market, technology or culture. This is not to say, however, that television is simply a technology like any other, or that a focus on it as technology will somehow exhaust its significance. There are differences as well as similarities between television and other technologies. The similarities revolve around these technologies' relative invisibility in use, as objects for consumption and in their capacity for reconstruction in the form of private display – in their appropriation as style. Their difference centres on what we would like to call their articulations, and their differential capacity within those articulations to change culture and society: to engage the user as audience or consumer.

Whatever the claims of the market, the materiality of the objects concerned cannot be ignored.[15] Television is technology (albeit in the last instance) and it is a technology which (like other communication and informing technologies) is articulated through two sets of meanings. The first set is the meanings that are constructed by both producers and consumers (and by consumers as producers) around the selling and buying of all objects and their subsequent use in a display of style, as a key to membership of community or sub-culture. The second set is the mediated meanings conveyed by those technologies which are open similarly to negotiation and transformation. The structuring of both, in the design and marketing of machines as commodities, and in the design of software and the creation of programme schedules and programme narratives, lays claim to the consuming 'modalities' of the relationship to television and to the general and specific rhetorics of television's engagement in everyday culture.[16]

In the remainder of the chapter we hope to present the outline of an argument which sustains and develops these initial perceptions and which illustrates what might be involved in pursuing them, both conceptually and empirically.

The problem of reading and the problem of the text

A significant issue now arises as a result of our attempt to re-contextualize the audience by placing it both within the domestic sphere and also within an environment containing a range of communications (and other) technologies. It is the issue of how we should characterize the audience's relationship to television (and, of course, also to other media).

There has been a certain amount of discussion concerning the possibility of a convergence of the 'uses and gratifications' and 'cultural studies' research trajectories.[17] We would like to suggest that such a discussion is beside the point, and that research on the television audience requires a substantial reformulation in the light of the relative failure of both these supposedly converging research trajectories to deal adequately with the complex social, psychological, ritual and ideological, active and passive dimensions of an audience's involvement with the medium.

This immediately raises the question of the applicability of the 'reading' model to the consumption of television. Ellis and Ang have both engaged in the debate[18] over television's dominant mode (or modes) of address, and over the extent to which television can be seen to offer 'single texts' to be consciously and attentively 'read' by a purposive viewer as opposed to being seen as a constant background flow of representations which receives little or no particular attention.

The point, of course, is that television is not uniform in this respect – modes of address vary across different genres of programming, as do modes of presentation, so that the single text/reader model which might (conceivably) be appropriate to a feature film will not necessarily do when it comes to a teatime magazine programme. Thus, the question may not be so much whether the 'reading' model applies to television (as such) as a question of when, for which categories of viewing, in which settings, and in relation to which types of programming, this model can usefully be applied.

Raising, as we have attempted to, the question of the applicability of the reading model is also, inescapably, to raise the question of the status of the text within media and communication studies. The most significant recent work in this respect has been that of Bennett and Woollacott, of Grossberg and of Browne,[19] all of whom have queried, in various ways, the viability of the concept of an independent text.[20]

Recently, Brunsdon[21] has responded to these developments with an argument in defence of the status of the text. She argues that the need to specify context and mode of viewing in any textual discussion, and even the awareness that these factors may be more determining of the experience of the text than any specific textual feature, does not, in and of itself, either eliminate the text as a meaningful category or render all texts 'the same'.[22] The fact that the text is only and always 'realized' in historically and contextually situated practices of reading does not demand that we collapse these categories into each other.[23]

In recognizing the complex nature of the domestic setting in which television is viewed one does not necessarily abandon concern with the texts it communicates. Rather, what is necessary is to examine the modes and varieties of viewing and attention which are paid to different types of programmes at different times of the day by different types of viewers. While it is against a baseline expectation of fragmented and distracted viewing that the variations in viewing behaviour must be traced, one does not necessarily thus conclude that intensive and attentive viewing (which, we would argue, *is* best analysed with reference to the text/reader model) never occurs.

The text/reader model, however, does now require some re-working. We would suggest that at least four dimensions to the relationship between television and its audience need to be taken into account. The first is that the meanings which are generated in the confrontation between television and audience are not confined to the viewing situation but are generated and sustained through the activities of daily life.[24]

The second has to do with media differences. Obviously, in dealing with television on its own, this is not a problem. But, as we have already suggested, television audiences are also radio audiences, computer and telephone users and readers of magazines, books and newspapers.[25] The contextualization of television within a domestic communication and information environment requires that we be more careful in identifying the specificity of each relationship.

Those who have given some attention to the different effects of media as such, from McLuhan[26] to Greenfield,[27] have pointed out that print, radio, television, video and the computer all require different skills and different modes of attention. This is not to say that the technologies themselves determine how they will be used, but that they create different possibilities for use.

The danger which we run, if these differences are ignored, is that we will reify the 'reading' metaphor. We do not respond to, or use, these different media in identical ways, yet we often persist with a single notion of 'reading' as a portmanteau term. The diversity of technologies and the many different creative possibilities which each engenders ought to be recognized in our characterization of our relationships to them. This can be done without sacrificing our interest in the specificities of particular programmes or items of software, and without sacrificing our appreciation of the differences between, say, radio and television, in different cultures and societies. We must also beware of over-privileging more 'visible' media to the neglect of others.

The third dimension of the relationship between an audience and television is one that has, particularly since the work of Collett and Lamb[28] and of Lull[29] become familiar. Since we watch television with different degrees of attention, and in conjunction, often, with other activities; since television is a domestic medium and our relationship to it is subject to the exigencies of our daily lives, we have to recognize what, for want of a better word, we have to call its 'modalities'. If we are to rethink the problem of 'reading' in relation to television or to other media, then we need to attend to the mechanisms of engagement: the ways in which, in our attention or inattention, the television audience incorporates, and in that incorporation constructs, the meanings which the medium offers.

This, we suggest, is the fourth dimension to any reconsideration of the notion of reading. At issue is a concern to understand the ways in which the varieties of the modes of address of media interact with the varieties of attention and variations in social and cultural circumstances. It is a concern with the 'how' of the relationship between the 'texts' and 'readers' of television. Silverstone has suggested that we bring to this problem some of the insights and modes of analysis of rhetoric.[30] To do so involves considering the television programme as a motivated bid for attention and action, more or less open to resistance or negotiation. It involves above all enquiring into both the general and the specific mechanisms of engagement that underlie and at the same time must qualify any understanding of the 'social act of reading' in relation to television. Such a perception, which rhetoric implies, commits us to preserving a model of the communication process which insists on an enquiry into the dynamics of production, textuality and response, without the need to grant, in any specific case, any one of those dimensions a necessary determinacy. Since television is both socially produced and socially received, we might legitimately enquire into the forms – the techniques of language and symbolization – which are involved in its mediation. For present purposes it is sufficient to indicate something of the generalized rhetorical processes which are involved. To do so involves not just considering television's textuality as rhetorical, but the relationship between text and audience as textual and therefore rhetorical.[31] What follows is inevitably schematic and very crude.[32]

The first dimension of rhetoric we are concerned with is homology, and it consists in the matching of textual and experienced temporalities.[33] As we have already suggested, the history of radio [34] and of television is a history of the creation of a communicating broadcast medium in such a way as to match, and to fit into, the domestic routines of its potential audience. The schedule on the one hand,[35] the narrativity of, for example, the soap opera on the other,[36] are both examples of rhetorical efforts to accommodate text to reader on a broad scale and, in the accommodation of both, to adjust and to fix the relationship.

A second dimension to the rhetoric of television is identification. Here there is a substantial literature in what might broadly be seen as the social psychology of television. One of the key texts is Horton and Wohl's paper on television as para-social interaction.[37] More recent excursions into these issues are Hobson's work on the *Crossroads* audience[38] and Ang's on *Dallas*.[39]

Identification implies not just a one-to-one correspondence between a

viewer and some favoured character, but also a more general identification, at a number of different levels, between what appears on the screen
and the lives, understandings or emotions of those who attend to it. This
does not apply only to the realist text. One can hardly imagine any
television text having any effect whatever without that identification.
Though, as suggested in Morley 1980, the rhetorical work of a text such as
Nationwide to create a space for the audience as family and to identify with
the image of the family constructed in the programme's own discourse is
not guaranteed success.[40] Its failures, of course, are particularly instructive. How identification is constructed textually, therefore, and how it is
responded to in the inter-textualities of everyday life, are questions for
empirical enquiry.

Yet another dimension of the rhetorical work of television, and one little
studied outside the realms of advertising, is the significance of metaphor. It
is a commonplace observation that television ads. provide children, in
particular, with a whole set of catch-phrases which often intrude into their
play or into their accounts of the world. The metaphors we live by, both as
adults and as children, are, as Lakoff and Johnson[41] argue, a major
constituent of daily thought and action.

The capacity of television to mobilize, extend, reinforce or transform the
metaphors of everyday life, and the ways in which its metaphors – from the
structuring of news on industrial relations, through concepts of the battle-
field, to stereotypical images of scientists or ethnic minorities – are taken
up and mobilized in the everyday discourse of its viewers would repay
careful and serious study. Lewis has argued for the significance of narrative
in television news as a similarly important dimension in getting its message
across.[42] In both cases (metaphor and narrative), it is the familiarity, the
commonplaces, of the content and form of our daily television texts on
which their claims to be heard are principally based.

Finally (at least as far as the present chapter is concerned), there are the
rhetorical operations of addition and suppression. At issue here is the
freedom of audiences to work with and transform the texts of television.
The work of Susan Smith[43] on newspaper crime-news and rumour in
Birmingham is instructive in this respect. Here the familiar issue is the way
in which a community reconstructs the news in terms of its own needs but
within an agenda set by the mass media. The media provide a framework
for the continuing processes of rumour and gossip to work their way
through the social and temporal structures of a community's everyday-life
experience. What is involved is the constant work of addition and/or
suppression, in the recreation of linked but increasingly attenuated narratives, prompted by the press in its capacity as an informer, but radically
reframed in 'perambulatory rhetorics of everyday life'.[44]

The model which is emerging, therefore, and one which might suggest
the amendment of the notion of reading by one of rhetoric, is that of the

'structured freedoms' of an audience's involvement with television. It is suggested that, taken together, the dimensions of media, the modalities of viewing, and the mechanisms of rhetorical engagement offer a more adequate account of that relationship, above all in their capacity to come to terms with the dynamics of the consumption and production of meaning at the heart of television's work in contemporary culture.

Television, technology and consumption

There are many parallels between the arguments just offered around the question of 'reading' and those that are increasingly surrounding the analysis of consumption in contemporary society. In this section, we consider television as an object of consumption, which, in its double articulation, is both meaningful in itself (in its marketing and in its deployment) and the bearer of meanings. Our aim is to understand television as one focus of a complex economy of meanings. The purchase and subsequent use of television, video, cable, satellite equipment, and their incorporation into the daily lives of their users (as technologies and as carriers of meanings), transform their status as commodities into objects of consumption. The goods bought, the meanings appropriated and transformed, are embedded in a social web of distinctions and claims for identity and status. If we are to make sense of the ways in which television is and might be used, then we need to understand the nature and consequences of the choices that are daily made in the public and private acts of consumption.

There are two points to be made here. The first is that all consumption involves the consumption of meanings; indeed, all consumption actually involves the production of meanings by the consumer:

> Within the available time and space the individual uses consumption to say something about himself, his family, his locality, whether town or country, on vacation or at home . . . Consumption is an active process in which all the social categories are being constantly refined.[45]

This argument emerges, though from a different perspective, in the work of Gershuny,[46] who attempts to identify the changing character of mass consumption, particularly in relation to the consumption of consumer durables. There has been, since the war, a demonstrable movement away from the public consumption of goods and services, towards the private consumption of technologies and private production of domestic services.[47] Although understood within an almost entirely utilitarian frame, consumption is presented as being a major component in an emerging self-service economy, and one which will be boosted by the new wave of information and communication technologies. Consumption, in this view, is production, and production must be understood as increasingly domesticated. Recent (and, predictably, future) changes in the provision of broad-casting involve financially informed choices, in which the selection of programmes (e.g. in the form of Pay-TV) will increasingly begin to look like the selection of goods. From this perspective, too, one can argue for a convergence between the consumption of television as medium and as message.[48]

There are, then, precise parallels between the consumption of objects and the consumption of 'texts'. Compare, for example, Hall's classic analysis of the work of decoding with some recent writing on the general character of consumption:

> Connotative codes are not equal among themselves. Any society/culture tends, with varying degrees of closure, to impose its classifications of the social and cultural and political world. These constitute a dominant cultural order, though it is neither univocal nor uncontested.[49]
>
> All . . . objects . . . are the direct product of commercial concerns and industrial processes. Taken together they appear to imply that in certain circumstances segments of the population are able to appropriate such industrial objects and utilize them in the creation of their own image. In other cases, people are forced to live in and through objects which are created through the images held of them by a different and dominant section of the population. The possibilities of recontextualization may vary for any given object according to its historical power or for one particular individual according to his or her changing social environment.[50]

As Daniel Miller argues, consumption has as one of its bases utility, and as one of its foundations human need, but neither utility nor need exhausts it. Consumption, as Douglas and Isherwood[51] and Sahlins[52] have also argued, is a general process of the construction of meaning. It is concerned, in Miller's words with 'the internalization of culture in every day life',[53] the result of a 'positive recontextualization' of the alienating possibilities of everyday life.

Miller focuses his own concerns on the theories of Bourdieu and of Douglas and Isherwood in developing a position on consumption as a cultural activity. Bourdieu is too insistent, Miller believes, on the divisive nature of consumption, on reducing consumption practices to social-class division, and he is insufficiently sensitive to the creativities and transform-ations of cultural work.[54]

Miller notes that Douglas and Isherwood's work similarly stresses the non-utilitarian character of consumption, examining goods in terms of their expressive, symbolic and orientational function in social life. But, he argues, their stress on the cognitive significance of goods leads to an under-estimation of their materiality and, above all, to an almost complete ignorance of the role of power, interest and ideology in defining and constraining their use.[55]

From the juxtaposition of these two views of consumption Miller offers an analysis which attempts to place it within a both subjective and objective frame, and to characterize goods, correlatively, as both symbolic and material. The key to understanding consumption is the interactive possibilities in play. The social differentiation of objects through consumption need not (indeed, in a world of mass consumption will not) simply be an expression of social divisions, or the power of the producer to define how a product will be used; nor indeed will it be necessarily defined or determined by the intrinsic properties of the object itself. Miller draws attention to the possibilities for the transformative work of consumption, but equally to the limits of the work in particular circumstances.

We have dwelled on Miller's argument because we think it provides, in this substantially under-theorized area, an important route not only into an understanding of the nature of consumption but also into the nature of the television audience. We are already aware of the audience's capacity to work creatively with the content of television. We are also aware of how important the communication of those meanings is for the maintenance of the group and of individual identities within it. Miller's argument allows us to recognize the same processes at work in all acts of consumption, and it seems to suggest that we can now look at the audience as multiply embedded in a consumer culture in which technologies and messages are juxtaposed, both implicated in the creation of meaning, in the creative possibilities of everyday life. Consumption, from this point of view is also a rhetorical activity.

We have attempted in this chapter to provide a framework for the redefinition and analysis of television in terms of its status as a domestic technology. This reconstitution has had two distinct ambitions. The first is to re-focus the problematic around the study of television in such a way as to contextualize it within a much wider and, we would claim, a more adequate socio-technical and cultural frame. The second is to draw in other domestic technologies – particularly those involved in the provision of information and communication – into this same socio-technical frame. At a conceptual level, we are offering what we believe to be a necessary challenge to many of the conventions (and some of the cornerstones) of current media and cultural studies as they bear on an understanding of the place and significance of television and other communication and information technologies in the modern world.

Chapter 10

The consumption of television as a commodity

The focus of this chapter is on how we are to understand the audience as consumer and the process of consumption of television at a point at which that process itself is being commodified – i.e. when the selection of programmes (in the form of pay-per-view or subscription services) begins to take a more closely parallel form to that of the purchase of consumer goods.

The 'commodification' of television

In *The Social Life of Things*, Appadurai (1986) offers an analysis of the modalities through which commodities, like persons, enjoy social lives. He is concerned with exploring how the circulation of objects in space and time is mediated by different 'regimes of value'. From this point of view, a commodity is defined as 'any thing intended for exchange'; the focus is not so much on the internal properties of the thing itself as on the nature of the exchange process. Thus, a commodity is not a certain type of thing; rather, Appadurai suggests, we should focus on the 'commodity potential' of all things and see things (biographically, as it were) moving in and out of the 'commodity state' over time. So, a 'commodity' is not a class of things (defined by internal properties) but, rather, one phase in the life of some things. Similarly, within this category, Appadurai notes that 'luxuries' are not a specific class of things, but, rather, that 'luxury' is a 'special register' of consumption, so that any particular commodity can move in and out of this 'register' over time (Appadurai 1986: 'Introduction').

One could argue that contemporary shifts in the financing of television, away from a flat-rate licence fee, towards further dependence on advertising finance and subscription (or pay-per-view) involve just such a process of the commoditization of television viewing, with concomitant shifts in the dynamics of the 'regime of value' through which exchange is achieved. It is also a process involving the enfranchisement (and disenfranchisement) of different groups (advertisers as opposed to viewers) in the determination of production mechanisms and in the modalities or capacities in which individual viewers relate to this process (as consumers rather than citizens, for example).

I will return to these issues at the end of the chapter. For the moment it is also necessary to note that the position of television, considered as an object of consumption, is already a complex one which needs to be considered as operating simultaneously, along a number of different dimensions. In the first place the television set (along with all the other technologies in the household) is already a symbolic object qua item of household furnishing, a choice (of design, style, etc.) which expresses something about its owner's (or renter's) tastes and communicates that choice, as displayed by its position in the household (cf. Bourdieu 1984 and Leal 1990).

This aspect of the process is perhaps most dramatically expressed in Gell's (1986) account of the Muria fishermen in Sri Lanka, where the richer villagers now often buy television sets, which are displayed as the centre-pieces of their personal collection of 'wealth signifiers', despite the fact that the lack of electricity supply makes the sets inoperable in any narrowly functional sense. None the less, the objects signify in powerful ways, just as would my own acquisition of a new flat-screen Japanese television, quite independently of whether or not I ever switched it on. Indeed, recent advertising campaigns, for flat-screen high-definition television sets, targeted at the up-market 'selective viewer', have taken precisely the theme of the 'less you watch, the higher standards you require when you *do* watch'. The symbolic function of objects is not a phenomenon exclusive to the ways of life of other people in strange places. All of which should also alert us to the fundamentally symbolic dimension of these forms of consumption, as opposed to an understanding of them as always/only desired for their 'rational'/functional uses (cf. Douglas and Isherwood 1980).

Take the well-known phenomenon of the numbers of home computers now back in their boxes, under the stairs in many households. How do we understand it? I would argue, in this case, that, in the first place, the attraction of the computer was what looked like the availability of a 'knowledge machine' (an updated/modern version of a set of encyclopaedias) which, in commodity form, made cultural capital more widely available. Second, for many consumers, the motivation to purchase the object was not simply rational; it was also to do with the acquisition of the computer as a totemic object ('I have the sign of the future in my house; my children are blessed'). Third, of course, having got it, it turned out that having the money to buy the object was not, in fact, enough. Making it 'work' depended also on the prior possession of certain other forms of cultural/technical know-how. Without that, the computer was liable to end up back in its box, under the stairs.

If television has to be understood as 'doubly articulated', in so far as its messages are themselves consumed (with meanings that are both pre-defined in design and marketing and negotiable – of which, more later), it also enables consumption. Through its combined messages it brings news of further consumption possibilities; and in some cases, through its interactive capacities, decisions to consume can now often be communicated, goods ordered, etc.

Thus, Robins and Webster have argued that television can usefully be considered as the 'fourth dimension of advertising', second-best only to having a salesman physically present, as a way for business to enter the homes of the nation through doors and windows no matter how tightly barred to deliver its message. Similarly, Conrad argues:

> the [television] set itself is a trophy of consumerism . . . as well as a theatre for the cavorting of consumer durables, on the game shows or in the ads. Watching TV, we're dually customers, of the medium (as spectators) and of the goods it's displaying (as potential customers). The screen is a shop window, the box a warehouse.
>
> (quoted in Robins and Webster 1986: 34)

However, it is a screen in a domestic context, and that context is no mere 'backdrop'. Rather, the material nature of the household (number of heated rooms etc.), along with the cultural rules for the allocation of space within the house (cf. Bourdieu 1972a), has to be understood as often determining how that screen is used, by whom and for what purposes. This is the 'black box' in most theories of consumption (of television or anything else); we know very little, it seems, of how consumption is actually practised in its primary context, behind the 'closed doors' of the household (cf. Silverstone, Morley *et al.* 1989).

Various trade commentators have pointed to the potential consequences of the trend towards individualized media delivery systems in the household, but some caution is needed here. There may be a number of television sets in the house, but whose rooms are they in? And who gets the old black and white set? As long as there is a main set in the most comfortable room, the question of 'what to watch' will remain a subject fraught with conflict and requiring delicate negotiating skills on the part of different household members, so the unit of consumption remains the household, not the individual (cf. negotiating of purchase decisions, etc.) and the material context of consumption exercises its own determinations on the process (cf. Spigel 1986 and 1992).

With the development of interactive services, of course, all of this reaches its apogee in programmes like CBS's *Home Shopping Club* in America. Desmond (1989) offers us an arresting account of viewing *Home Shopping Club*:

> The first time I tuned into the Home Shopping Club I couldn't get out of my chair for three hours. I sat stunned, mesmerised by the parade of neckchains, earrings, china birds, microwaves . . . It took every ounce of my will not to pick up the phone and dial . . . Jane, I said, remember

the anorexic state of your bank account. Still – two teak serving trays for
$10, minus my first-time shopper rebate of $5 = only $5! I didn't exactly
need teak trays . . . but . . . they were a bargain . . . At last, I thought,
the PBS slogan running through my mind, 'TV worth watching'.

(Desmond 1989: 340)

This, of course, is not only an 'American' phenomenon: Sky Television,
in the UK, now offers its 'Home Shopping TV network', under the slogan
'The Department Store you come home to'.

Consumption as a general process

In recent years anthropologists have had quite a lot to say about consumption; here I shall refer briefly to the frameworks offered by Douglas and
Isherwood (1980) and Miller (1988) for the analysis of consumption, as
well as to those sociologists such as Bourdieu (1984) and de Certeau
(1984). The polarities are simple: consumption as a material and as a
symbolic process; consumption as an active and creative and/or as a passive
and determined process (cf. de Certeau's metaphors of 'prosumption' or
'productive consumption'). Douglas and Isherwood offer us an analysis of
the symbolic dimension of consumption. They effectively take an idealist
position (not unlike that of Baudrillard (1988) which effectively defines
goods as 'information', as 'good to think with', in which consumption is
seen very much as an active process in which the individual 'says' things
about him or herself to others. To this extent their perspective is not
dissimilar to the early work of the sub-cultural theorists such as Hebdige
(1988a) in their concern with highlighting the non-utilitarian, symbolic and
communicative (or 'expressive') dimension of consumption. However, as
Miller (1988) argues, by the same token, Douglas and Isherwood's stress
on the cognitive significance of goods leads them to an underestimation of
their materiality, and leads them to ignore the role of power, interest and
ideology in defining and constraining the 'use' of goods.

Golding (1990: 91) suggests that it may also be worth reminding ourselves of Lockwood's tart (if over-materialistic) response to the *embourgeoisement* theorists of the 1960s: 'It is in any case sociology gone mad to
assume that because people want goods of this kind [consumer durables]
they [only] want them as status symbols. A washing machine is a washing
machine is a washing machine'.

Miller (1988) is very much concerned with consumption as a material
practice of 'work' through which commodities are transformed, in the
rituals of their incorporation into 'local' cultures. However, unlike Douglas
and Isherwood, Miller is very much alive to the question of power (and, for
instance, to the role of advertising and marketing in constructing 'preferred' images of objects and their appropriate uses).

To this extent Miller's perspective can be seen to share some ground with that of de Certeau, in so far as the latter is concerned with the 'perambulatory tactics' of everyday practices, in which people, in both their productive and their consumptive capacities, are credited with the ability to be 'creative' in their manipulation, for their own ends, of the resources available to them. Moreover, de Certeau is concerned to analyse this process not 'at the margins', in the occasional activities of minority/ spectacular sub-cultures, but in the everyday practices of mass culture. However, we should remember that de Certeau distinguishes sharply between the 'tactics' of the poor or subordinate groups and the 'strategies' of powerful institutions: from this perspective the point is, finally, that the 'creative' aspect of consumption is always operating by stealth, on momentarily 'stolen ground'. Thus, creative uses (tactics) of communications technologies are to be seen as operating on the ground established by the dominant images of these technologies, as presented through the discourses (strategies) of powerful institutions of design, marketing and advertising.

Which returns us, in a way, to Bourdieu, who reminds us, of course, of the deeply structured and historical nature of the process through which the resources (both symbolic and material) which consumers use to 'create meaning' are themselves distributed, in uneven and unequal ways, between different categories of people. So, if consumption can always be seen as an active process, it is also one that always moves within (or against) structural constraints. That is its dialectic. It is with the variety of those fundamental processes as they are 'worked out' by people in different social/cultural locations that we should be concerned. The question is that of the social distribution of the material and symbolic forms of 'capital' with which consumption is achieved (or 'performed').

Television and citizenship

A number of commentators have pointed to the fact that, as the availability of television programmes comes to depend, to an increasing extent, on people's ability to pay for them, the airways can no longer be considered as shared public resources. As the provision of information, education and entertainment passes into a 'regime of value' determined by the cash nexus, television's contributions to a public culture will be increasingly divisive, as between the 'information-rich' and the 'information-poor'. The much-heralded 'wider choices' offered by these new technologies will be available only to those who can afford to pay for them. To the extent that access to public information and cultural resources comes to depend on the capacity of citizens to pay, so their capacity to participate effectively in the public realm will be correspondingly differentiated.

Both Golding (1989) and Murdock (1990) have argued this case, focusing on the economic determinations of unequal access to information (cf. Schiller 1981, for the international version of this argument). As Golding puts it, commenting on the simple correlation of income levels with ownership media hardware (such as the telephone, video and computer),

> entrance to the new media playground is relatively cheap (as a percentage of total income) for the well-to-do, a small (and easy) adjustment in spending patterns. Conversely, for the poor (and this of course exacerbated in the UK by recent trends in income differentials) the price is a sharp calculation of opportunity cost, access to communication goods jostling uncomfortably with the mundane arithmetic of food, housing, clothing and fuel.
>
> (Golding 1989: 90)

Any mechanism of communication that costs money to use will necessarily produce inequalities of access across social and economic groups. What we see here, according to Golding, is the potential for the dramatic emergence of forms of 'attenuated citizenship, imposed by information poverty', especially in relation to television, given its centrality in the culture.

In Murdock's words, 'Given the steadily widening gap between the top and bottom income groups since 1979, the effect [of pay-per-view, subscription, etc.] is to deny the poorest members of the society access to the full range of resources they need for effective citizenship and full political participation' (Murdock 1990: 87). This is evidenced, in his view, by the 'reorientation of the BBC's view of its audiences . . . as consumers and honorary shareholders, wanting 'value for money' above all else'.

The concept of the 'information gap' may by simplistic, but the scenario of economic poverty retarding the ability to acquire cultural resources, which itself then leads to further disadvantage, is an all-too-plausible one.

The problem lurking here, though, is perhaps the over-materialist nature of the model: if it was only a question of financial limitations (rather than cultural ones) in the first place, then Bourdieu's work on the class composition of attendance at 'free' museums (1972b) would have been unnecessary and the profile of use of similar 'free' or subsidized services (such as swimming-pools, libraries, the health service, etc.) would not be as skewed as it, in fact, is in favour of the middle classes. The 'information gap' model may need to be redefined in more culturalist terms than those of its current formulation, as cultural barriers also have very material effects.

Television and popular taste

It has frequently been argued that the 'deregulation' of broadcasting and its increased reliance on advertising revenue will force the medium down market, and lead not only to a reduction in the opportunity for genuine viewer choice but also the end of 'quality television' as we know it. Of course, it is also increasingly recognized that, given advertisers' interests in targeting up-market segments of the population, this will not necessarily be the whole story, in so far as various forms of 'quality' or innovative programming may have to be sponsored in order to attract these 'desirable' groups. Nevertheless, so the argument runs, it is only rich minorities that will be served. That is certainly true, but there is a problem with the implied alternative model of public-service broadcasting, in so far as the 'public sphere' created by traditional broadcasting in the UK was itself always heavily structured by class (and region). That is the point of Connell's (1983) argument about the 'progressive' dimension of the impact of ITV in the 1950s, in so far as, both in its own programming and in terms of the extent to which the BBC was then forced to compete with it, ITV had a built-in drive to 'connect with the structure of popular taste' which no public-service institution necessarily has.

That also was the point, as I understood it, of the attempt within cultural studies to use a Gramscian notion of hegemony, rather than a notion of some imposed 'dominant ideology', to try to capture that interplay of cultural forces through which the 'popular' and the 'commercial' are related.

To move to another context, one could also argue that many of the more progressive developments in a whole range of public-welfare institutions over the last few years have precisely been the result of their beginning to take on board elementary considerations of marketing, premised on the need truly to serve their differentiated client bases, in something other than the traditional forms of 'universal provision'.

Linked to this issue is of course the further question of 'internationalization': the fear, in Milne's deathless phrase, that deregulation will lead to an endless supply of 'wall-to-wall *Dallas*', which will undermine our national culture and identity. To which, it seems to me, one reply is 'Whose national identity?'. The work of writers such as Worpole (1983) and Hebdige (1988b) on the extent to which such concepts of 'national culture' have always been heavily structured by metropolitan and class bias points to the fact that these 'foreign' cultural objects (from American crime fiction to Italian motor-scooters) have often functioned, for working-class people, as positive cultural icons, cultural resources which could be used to undercut the class structure of national taste, precisely by virtue of their 'vulgarity', as defined by established taste patterns.

Thus, Collins quotes a 'World Film News' survey from the 1930s which reported that cinema distributors in working-class areas of Scotland were

> on the whole, satisfied with the more vigorous American films . . . but practically unanimous in regarding the majority of British films as unsuitable for their audiences. British films, one Scottish exhibitor

writes, should rather be called English films, in a particularly parochial sense, they are more foreign to his audience than the products of Hollywood, over 6000 miles away.

(quoted in Collins 1988: 7)

From this perspective, we may better be able to understand how local cultures are produced, differentially, in their articulation with, and by means of their consumption of, global forms. By the same token, the process of commodification itself has contradictory effects on and in consumption–effects which will need to be researched in detail, in a variety of domestic contexts, rather than being assumed in advance.

Chapter 11

Private worlds and gendered technologies

Over the course of the last ten years or so, public debate in many of the advanced industrial countries of the West has often focused on questions concerning the impact and role of new information and communication technologies in transforming both society at large and the family in particular. Public discourse, from governmental papers, through business forecasting, to popular journalism, abounds with images of the increasingly privatized family, shut off from public life, turned in on itself, within a culture of DIY home improvement and privatized leisure, connected to the wider world only through the electronic forms of satellite/cable television and tele-shopping; this image has been articulated to both utopian and dystopian visions of various kinds. Moreover, this family itself is seen as increasingly fragmented internally – the 'multi-active cellular family' whose home is a 'multi-purpose activity centre' for the increasingly separate lifestyles of the individuals within it (cf. Tomlinson 1989). Much of this debate has been conducted in a frame of reference which takes technology as a (more or less) independent variable, which is then seen to have effects both on the family and on society at large. Thus, the new technologies are widely seen as portending the transformation both of relations within the family and of the overall relations between the private and public spheres of society.

Of course, in this day and age, no one wants to be seen as a technological determinist. Unfortunately, the theoretical disavowals of this position have not been reflected, in practice, by the abandoning of its premises in research in this field, where an agenda of 'how technology will change society' still persists. One might well draw a parallel here with developments in the more narrowly conceived field of media studies, which, over the last ten years or so, has gradually seen the abandonment of the theoretical problematic of the effects of the media, in favour of a concern with a rather more complex set of issues – as to how audiences (within the limits of their domestic and structural positions and with the limited set of cultural resources at their disposal as a result of their social positioning) actively make use of and interpret the symbolic products offered to them by the mass media. It is to those forms of mediation that we must address ourselves, not simply as they are applied to the consumption of mass media, but also as they are applied to the wider field of symbolic (and material) consumption practices through which a whole range of technologies is domesticated. New communications and information technologies have been argued to herald fundamental changes in the future of the family and social life. Different observers have pointed to the increasing capability of the home as site of leisure activities (video, cable, etc.), the growth of homeworking (computer, telephone services) and of interactive services (tele-shopping, tele-booking). But how much do we actually know about how these technologies are actually used? What do these technologies mean to their domestic users, and how are they incorporated into different household cultures? And, further, to what extent are they used in the ways and for the purposes which their designers and producers intended?

Clearly ICTs play a fundamental role in connecting the public and private worlds; in so doing they also transgress the boundaries of the household unit. Thus, questions arise as to how the use of ICTs is regulated in households of different types, with different cultures and values. Further questions arise as to how particular ICTs (which have the capacity to integrate and to isolate the household) are used in households with stronger or weaker boundaries, and as to the extent to which different types of social relations are mediated through various technologies in different types of household. Of course, over time, all these technologies acquire particular meanings and significances, through the ways in which they are used in domestic life. The issue, then, is exactly what do these technologies mean to their users, and how are different ICTs perceived and understood by different household members (for example, across divisions of gender and age)? Moreover, we have also to consider what role these private meanings have in determining how these technologies are used and what the role of socialization is in developing and transmitting technological competences, especially in relation to construction and maintenance of different forms of gendered subjectivities.

The public and the private

In attempting to develop an analysis of the domestic functions of communications and information technologies, we can usefully take, as one of our starting-points, Bourdieu's (1972a) analysis of the Berber house, in which he offers an exemplary model for the articulation of public and private space, and of domestic technologies within gender relations. While that analysis is, of course, culturally specific and clearly pertains to a pre-industrial rural society, I would wish to argue that a number of Bourdieu's insights remain pertinent to the analysis of these issues as they appear in urban and industrial societies.

In that analysis, Bourdieu formulates the relation between the domestic and the public as an 'opposition between female space and male space on the one hand, the privacy of all that is intimate, on the other, the open space of social relations' Bourdieu argues that the orientation of the house is fundamentally defined from the outside, from the point of view of the masculine, public sphere – as the 'place from which men come out', so that the house is 'an empire within an empire, but one that always remains subordinate' (Bourdieu 1972a: 101).

My argument is that, despite subsequent social and economic developments, in contemporary industrial societies, the division between public and private remains fundamentally articulated to gender relations. Thus Garmanikow and Purvis (1983b) note that the private realm continues to be outside the boundaries of the social, equated not only with the feminine, but also with the natural. Similarly, Fontaine observes that in our modes of social organization we retain a fundamental opposition between the public and private spheres, in which 'the former is [understood as] the realm of law and consists of the institutions of the state and the national economy, the latter is [seen as] the state of personal affection and moral duty' where there is a 'well established association of women with domestic life and men with the public world of competition and power' (Fontaine 1988: 268).

In his historical analysis, Zaretsky traces the process through which, as he puts it, with the transformation of the family from a productive unit to a unit of consumption, 'capitalist development gave rise to the idea of the family as a separate realm from the economy, [and] created a "separate" sphere of personal life, seemingly divorced from the mode of production'. As a result of this development, Zaretsky argues, 'The family became the major sphere of society in which the individual could be foremost – within it, a new sphere of social activity began to take shape: personal life' (Zaretsky 1976: 61).

In this connection, it is also important to note the arguments made by Hurtado, among others, concerning the specificty of the articulation of the public/private distinction with questions of race and ethnicity. Thus, Hurtado argues that 'the public/private distinction is relevant only for the white upper and middle classes, since historically the [American] state has intervened constantly in the private lives and domestic arrangements of the working class. Women of Color have not had the benefit of the economic conditions that underlie the public/private distinction . . . There is no such thing as a private sphere for people of Color except that which they manage to create and protect in an otherwise hostile environment' (Hurtado 1989: 849). Her point is well dramatized by the crisis of homelessness now being enacted on the streets of cities in the United States and elsewhere.

In his analysis of contemporary patterns of consumption, Tomlinson (1989) addresses the cultural and ideological dimensions of what he argues to be the increasing centrality of the home – and associated concerns with home-ownership and home improvements – within contemporary British society. He notes the familiar finding that for most people 80 per cent of leisure time is spent in the home (cf. Glyptis 1987), and further notes the growth of consumer spending on (and in) the home.

For Tomlinson, the central concern is with the development of the home as an autonomous or (increasingly) self-sufficient, contained consumer unit. He argues that what we see here is a continuing process of privatiza-tion, as home-based consumption represents a retreat from the public realm of community, and the private individual retreats into his (or her) house and garden (cf. Docherty *et al.* (1987), on the shift from cinema to television as the primary mode of film consumption).

Tomlinson argues that this represents not just a shift in patterns of consumption, but also a crucial ideological shift in the cultural meaning of the home. The home has become increasingly the site for 'an unpreceden-tedly privatised and atomised leisure and consumer lifestyle' (Tomlinson 1989: 10). For him, the key shift is one in which 'as the home fills up with the leisure equipment servicing the needs of the dispersed household members, it moves towards a new function. The Puritan notion of the home was as a Little Kingdom. The Victorian concept stressed Home as Haven: the late modern Elizabethan concept constructs the Home as Personalised Marketplace. It is where most of us express our consumer power, our cultural tastes' (10).

Certainly I would agree with Tomlinson in giving a central place to processes of domestic consumption. However, he articulates this analysis of the centrality of the home in contemporary culture to a somewhat one-sided vision of the cultural significance of this growth in privatized con-sumption. In this sense, he appears to offer a contemporary version of the *embourgeoisement* thesis which is prey to many of the shortcomings noted originally by Goldthorpe and Lockwood (1968).

The central point concerns the articulations of a set of parallel oppo-sitions – not only public/private, but also masculine/feminine; not only production/consumption, but also work/leisure. Our analysis of the uses of communications and information technologies must be integrated with an analysis of the shifting relations between these terms – and, indeed, must be concerned with the function of these technologies themselves in creating the possibility of such shifts. If we are to avoid the problematic 'naturaliz-ation' of the domestic (and its assumed connections to femininity, con-sumption and leisure), we must analyse its historical construction. In this connection, King (1980b), building on Thompson's (1967) work on the regulation of time in the development of industrial capitalism, offers an insightful analysis of the historical emergence both of leisure times ('the weekend') and leisure places (the home, the holiday cottage – 'a horizontal container for the consumption of surplus free time').

King's own analysis is principally concerned with class, and the differential development of free time for members of different classes. I should like to extend that analysis by also considering the question of gender and the differential relations of men and women to leisure, both as a temporal phenomenon ('after work') and as a spatial phenomenon (as sited routinely in the home or other places).

In *Everyday Television: 'Nationwide'* (1978), Brunsdon and I argued that, while the domestic sphere is also a sphere of domestic labour (the reproduction of labour power), it has come to be centrally defined as the social space within which individuality can be expressed – the refuge from the material constraints and pressure of the outside world, the last repository of the human values which are otherwise crushed by the pressure of modern life. The central point, it is argued (Brunsdon and Morley 1978: 78), is that the workings of this private sphere cannot effectively be understood without attention to the specific role of women and their central place in the domestic. As is noted in that analysis, the women and the home seem, in fact, to become each other's attributes, as evinced, among others by Ruskin: 'wherever a true wife comes, this home is always round her' (quoted in Brunsdon and Morley 1978: 78).

However, the point is not simply a historical one – rather, we see here an ideological construction of social domains and gender relations which retains a strong contemporary relevance – in so far as both the household itself and women's domestic labour within it continue to be conceived as the unchanging natural backcloth to the 'real' world of activity in the public sphere. The further point is, of course, that men and women are positioned in fundamentally different ways within the domestic sphere, If, for men, the home is fundamentally a site of leisure and recuperation from work, for women, whether or not they also work outside the house, it is also a site of work and responsibility. As the overall social location of 'leisure' moves increasingly into the home, the contradictions experienced by women in this sphere are correspondingly heightened (cf. Cowan 1989).

At the same time, I would argue that it is necessary to pay attention to the ways in which the private space of domestic life is socially constructed and articulated with political life. Zaretsky notes that historically 'the early bourgeois understood the family to be the basic unit of social order – "a little church, a little state" and the lowest rung on the ladder of social authority. They conceived society as composed not of individuals but of families' (Zaretsky 1976: 42). In a similar vein, Fontaine observes that in contemporary industrial societies 'households are also units in the political and economic organisation of society; as such they are part of the public domain. A legal address is an expected attribute of a citizen' (Fontaine 1988: 284). Thus, while the household enjoys privacy, which implies the right to exclude (unless the police have a warrant) and to enjoy autonomy of action, 'that privacy is as much a matter of social definition as the effect of thick walls' (280).

Moreover, as Donzelot (1979) argues, the family does not have a unique or unambiguous status. For certain (e.g. juridical) purposes it is private, while for others it is public. It is a site of intervention for various state-welfare agencies, whose intention to regulate child-rearing practices within the family, for example, is legitimated by references to the state's concern with the proper upbringing of future members of the national labour force (see Hodges and Hussain 1979). For Donzelot, the family is not simply a private institution, but also the point of intersection of a whole range of medical, judicial, educational and psychiatric practices – it is by no means a wholly private realm, somehow outside (or indeed setting the limits of) the social. In this sense the family is neither totally separate from nor opposed to the state; rather, the private is itself a (legally, juridically) constructed space, into which the state and other agencies can intervene, and whose very privacy is itself constituted and ultimately guaranteed by these institutions. This is not to suggest that the freedoms of the domestic space are somehow illusory, or ultimately reducible to their place within a history of regulation and power, in the way that Donzelot himself at times seems to do. Rather, it is to suggest that the latter perspective is a useful (and necessary) corrective of any analysis of domestic processes which remains blind to the history and social construction of that space.

We shall need to be attentive, in this context, to the incorporation of communication technologies within pre-existing social domains, particularly their incorporation within different gender domains, and also to the particular role of communications technologies in the construction and reconstruction of these domains. Haralovich offers a fascinating account of the role of the suburban family situation comedy on American television in the 1950s in 'the construction and distribution of social knowledge about the place of women' (Haralovich 1988: 39). She is concerned to analyse the inter-linkages between factors such as the roles of television representations of life-styles, government economies and housing policies, and the consumer-product industries in defining both the norms for a particular model of a 'healthy' life-style (a single-family, detached, suburban home in a stable, non-urban environment) and woman's place within that domain as a homemaker.

Her argument is precisely that television representations, in this respect, worked in close parallel to the material supports of housing policies – which were concerned to organize the interior space of the home so as to reinforce the gender-specific socializing functions of the family. Thus, she notes, in America in the 1950s 'the two national priorities of the post-war period – removing women from the paid labour force and building more housing – were conflated and tied to an architecture of home and neighbourhood that celebrates a mid-19th Century ideal of separate spheres for men and women' (ibid., 43).

Thus, we are returned to some of the concerns which my earlier discussion of Bourdieu was designed to indicate. Certainly not all contemporary television sit-coms are like the ones that Haralovich analyses (we have the 'divorce' sit-com, the 'single-parent' sit-com), but the nuclear family continues to play a central role in television discourses – which, in turn, continue to construct and circulate social knowledge about the appropriate forms of gender relations, and about the articulation of the domestic and the public spheres.

TECHNOLOGY AND GENDER

My argument is that we need a contextual understanding of the use and function of technologies, as they are incorporated both within the social organization of the relations between the public and private spheres and within the domestic sphere itself. This is also to focus, initially, on questions of 'how' rather than 'why' in relation to domestic technologies. To transpose Lindlof and Traudt's (1983) argument, it is also to say that the central theoretical and policy questions concerning the significance of the new technologies in the home cannot satisfactorily be framed, let alone answered, until a number of prerequisite questions concerning the uses and meanings of such technologies, for all family members, have been posed and investigated. In the first instance, this may lead us towards seemingly elementary considerations – such as the determining effect of the structure and size of the domestic space available to different families – which have been improperly neglected by researchers in this field to date. Thus, for example, it may be important to research the extent to which, for members of higher-density families with more restricted physical environments, the aural barriers afforded by the use of various communication media (from the television to the Walkman) may function as a way of creating personal 'space' in lieu of physical spatial privacy.

However, the domestic is not simply a physical space – it is also a socially organized space. Just as I argued earlier, following Bourdieu, that the public/private divide is closely articulated with gender relations, so, again following Bourdieu's lead, I turn to the significance of the gendered organization of domestic space within the private sphere – as a fundamental determinant of the take-up and use of different technologies by family members. As Bourdieu puts it, 'The opposition which is set up between the external world and the house only takes on its full meaning . . . if one of the terms of this relation, the house, is itself seen as being divided according to the same principles which oppose it to the other term' (Bourdieu 1972a: 104).

There is, of course, now a vast body of literature concerned with the

function of gender as a fundamental principle of social and cultural organization which it would be beyond the scope of this chapter to review. I shall
take only two central points from that literature. The first is that one of the
key concerns in this field has been the seeming invisibility of women and
their activities in traditional sociology. The second (and related) point is
that made by McRobbie and Garber in their analysis of girls' sub-cultures.
They argue that this 'invisibility' (within the public sphere of life on which
sociological analysis has been traditionally concentrated) is itself structurally generated by women's particular positioning in the domestic. Thus,
they argue,

> If women are marginal to the . . . cultures of work . . . it is because they
> are central and pivotal to a subordinate area, which mirrors, but in a
> complementary and subordinate way, the dominant masculine areas.
> They are marginal to work *because* they are central to the subordinate,
> complementary sphere of the family.
> (McRobbie and Garber 1976: 211 my emphasis – D.M.)

That centrality, I would argue, is of great consequence in determining
differential relations to domestic communications technologies for men and
women. We can begin by briefly exemplifying this argument by reference to
the significance of gender in organizing the domestic uses of one particular
technology, in this case television, as that is one area in which these
arguments have already been well developed. Hobson's work on housewives' television-viewing habits demonstrates that, for the women she studied, their sense of their home as a site of continuing domestic work and
responsibilities leads to a quite distinctive form of consumption of television
– in which viewing is, in the main, a fundamentally distracted and interrup-
ted activity for them. At its simplest, this suggests that men's and women's
differential positions in the domestic sphere – as, fundamentally, a site of
leisure for the one but, more contradictorily, a site of both leisure and work
for the other – determines their differential relation to television.

In the *Family Television* project, I argued that the gendering of technologies is most apparent in relation to video and that, on the whole, videos are
seen (like automatic control devices) as principally the possessions of
fathers and sons, occasionally of daughters, but least often of mothers. In a
similar vein, Rogge and Jensen (1988) refer to the world of the 'new media'
as principally a masculine domain. As Lull notes, the 'masculinization' of
the VCR

> is a logical extension of the masculine roles of installing and operating
> home equipment. They are the family members who develop user
> competency. Many new technologies are 'toys' for men [cf. Moores
> (1988), on radio] and they enjoy playing with them. So, the responsibil-
> ity becomes a kind of male pleasure. The operation of this equipment

. . . is a function that men are expected to perform for their families. The responsibilities, pleasures and functions that men have with all these pieces of equipment gives them some degree of control over them and over other family members along the way.

(Lull 1988: 28–9)

In her analysis of the use of home videos, Gray (1987a) begins by noting that the differential cultural positioning of men and women in the domestic sphere is relatively independent of (and resistant to) actual economic transformations (such as male unemployment or women going out to work). Regardless of such developments, the domestic is still largely seen as 'women's work', and this, Gray argues, strongly informs gender-based views of new technologies such as video. Thus, she follows both Cockburn (1985), in suggesting that new technologies have tended to reproduce traditional work-patterns across gender and Zimmerman (1983), in arguing that old ideas have largely become encoded in new technologies. From Gray's perspective, the use of all domestic technologies must be understood as being incorporated within the social organization of gender domains. The main structuring principle, she argues, is that technologies that are 'used for one off jobs with a highly visible end product (e.g., electric drill, saw, sander)' are understood as masculine while those 'used in the execution of the day to day chores with an end product that is often immediately consumed (e.g., cooker, washing machine, iron)' (Gray 1987a: 5) are understood as feminine.

The use (or non-use) of technologies is, as she argues, no simple matter of technological complexity. As she notes, while the women she studied did not use their domestic videos (or did not use particular functions, such as the time controls), relying instead on male partners or children, they routinely operated other, extremely sophisticated, pieces of domestic technology such as washing- or sewing-machines. The determining principle behind these women's felt alienation from the video seemed to be less to do with its technical complexity and more to do with its incorporation, alongside the television, into what they felt to be a principally masculine domain of domestic leisure – in which they felt they had no real place.

Appropriate technologies – for whom?

It is perhaps worth restating, at this point, the theoretical position being argued in relation to the 'gendering' of technologies. I am not advancing an 'essentialist' position which would interpret the empirical facts of different male and female patterns of use and involvement with technology as the inevitable result of the biological characteristics of the persons concerned (cf. the comments in chapter 6 on this). It is, in short, an argument about gender as a cultural category, rather than about sex as a biological category. I am concerned with the cultural construction of masculine and feminine positions, subjectivities and domains and the articulation (or disarticulation) of technologies into these culturally constructed domains. Different empirical persons who are biologically male or female may, of course, inhabit the cultural domains of masculinity and femininity in different ways. It is, however, the incorporation of technologies within these culturally defined patterns that is the critical issue.

As Kramarae (1988) notes, a whole set of issues is at stake here concerning which machines are called technologies: of technologies not only as machines, but also as social relations and communication systems; of the modes in which social relations are themselves structured and re-structured by technological systems; and of the role which the incorporation of technologies into gender domains plays, by defining both the meanings of the technologies and for whom their use is appropriate. The question is how to move beyond the simple description of existing patterns. Thus, Rothschild (1983) describes how the home computer can function to reinforce the gender division of labour, 'mother using it for recipes and household accounts, children – boys more than girls – using it for games . . . and dad using it both as an "adult toy" and possibly for professional work' (quoted in Baines 1989).

I shall return to the specific question of the gender determination of computer-use at the end of this section. For the moment, though, it is perhaps of more importance to pursue the theoretical point about how such differential patterns of use might be explained. In this connection, Baines (1989) argues for the usefulness of Bush's (1983) concept of techno-logical 'valences', as concerned with the culturally defined attributes (rather than the mechanically defined essential qualities) of technologies. Bush (1985: 155) argues that we must see social values, including those of gender, as embedded in technologies; and this is a factor determining their social use:

> Tools and technologies have . . . valence(s). . . . A particular technolo-gical system, even an individual tool, has a tendency to interact in similar situations in definable and particular ways . . . to fit in with certain social [and specifically gender – D.M.] norms . . . and to disturb others.

> (quoted in Baines 1989)

Rakow argues against any tendency to assume that technologies produce homogeneous effects. Rather, she suggests 'we should assume that the same technology may be used . . . by different people in different ways to different effects' (Rakow 1988a: 59). As posed, her arguments have both the strengths and the weaknesses of the established 'uses and gratifications' perspective in the study of the mass media (cf. Halloran's well-known injunction 'we should get away from thinking about what the media do to people and start thinking about what people do with the media'). The strength of the perspective lies in the acknowledgement of the potential openness or polysemy of both media products and technologies; the corresponding weakness lies partly in a tendency to overestimate this openness – and to neglect the inscription of powerful dominant meanings through the design, structuring and marketing of the products.

Rakow suggests that we should ask what role technologies play in constructing and maintaining gender relationships, seeing technology as 'a site where social practices are embedded . . . [which] . . . express and extend the construction of two asymmetrical genders' (ibid., 57) and crucially examining 'how certain values and meanings underlie the development of technologies, in particular, masculine and feminine assigned values and meanings about gender' (60).

Garmarnikow and Purvis (1983b: 5) suggest that the public/private split is a metaphor for the social patterning of gender. Rakow's central point is that this articulation also implies technologies. She argues:

> Practices involving technologies are constituted . . . in and through relations of gender. Who does what with a technology for what purpose is, at least in part, a cause and effect of gender. Consequently, not only a technology, but also a social practice involving it are associated by gender. Men are more likely than women to be owners and operators of cameras that take pictures of women. Women have their pictures taken and may be more likely to have responsibility for maintaining family ties and history through photographs. . . . Men speak, write and publish more in the public world of commerce, politics and ideas . . . but women write the family letters and make the family telephone calls.
>
> (Rakow 1988a: 67)

In a further paper, Rakow (1988b) extends her analysis of the mutual implications of technology and gender with particular reference to the telephone. She argues that the telephone is a technology that has been centrally implicated in managing the problems created by the physical separation of (feminine) activities in the private sphere from the predominantly masculine public sphere, by the isolation of the home and of women in that domestic space. Indeed, she claims that the very history of the telephone 'cannot be told without accounting for the gender relations within which . . . [it] . . . developed' (Rakow 1988b: 224). At an empirical level, the point is quite straightforward. As Mayer (1977: 23) reports, 'the most important single factor [determining how many single calls a household will make] is the presence of a woman'. This is, of course, not only an empirical fact, but also a cultural fact: the special role of the telephone in women's lives and the association of the telephone with women's talk ('gossip' or 'chatter') is condensed in the well-known stereotype of the woman who talks 'too much' on the phone. As Rakow notes, not only folklore but the phone companies' own marketing literature (after the initial period in which the networks seemed to disapprove of and discourage such social uses of the instrument) is replete with images of the woman user's 'peculiar addiction' to the phone.

However, I am, of course, concerned to offer an explanatory framework within which we might situate both the empirical facts and the cultural stereotypes. Maddox (1977) argues, quite simply, that women's particular attachment to the telephone, as a mode of symbolic communication (which to some large extent replaces physical movement: cf. Cowan (1989)) is to be explained by women's actual social position in relation to transport, housing and public space. Maddox cites three principal reasons for many women's heavy usage of the telephone: their confinement to the home while caring for children; their fear of crime in public spaces; and their physical separation from relatives, the maintenance of relations with whom they understand as being an integral part of their 'job description'. Both Rakow and Maddox note that, outside the home, womens' other principal involvement with the phone has been as operators and telephonists, paid to mediate communications, largely between men in the sphere of business.

The central argument is that the nature of many women's empirical use of this particular technology is an effect of their understanding of their gender-defined role, in combination with the social organization of space and the function of the telephone in managing physically dispersed social relations. Most women principally use this technology to discharge their responsibilities for maintaining family and social relations and for home-business transactions (calls to plumbers, dentists, babysitters, etc.). However, beyond this somewhat utilitarian perspective, Rakow (1988b: 207) also notes the important use of the phone for many housewives in alleviating their feelings of loneliness and isolation. In a similar vein, a number of housewives interviewed in the Brunel study of the household uses of ICTs were emphatic that the telephone is the key technology that they would hate to lose – because they see it (to use their repeated phrase) as a way of 'saving their sanity', given their felt sense of isolation in their homes.

Video games and computers: masculinized technologies?

Skirrow offers an analysis which is designed to explore the articulation of gender and technology in the case of video games. She starts from the empirical fact that, on the whole, these games are not played by girls or women, and accounts for this by means of an analysis of the extent to which the pleasures offered by these games are gender-specific. The issue is, then, the way in which the games fail to engage with (or are, indeed, more actively perceived as being at odds with) feminine cultural sensibilities. Once again, the argument is that the determining principle is the

articulation of specific technologies with the social and cultural organization of gender domains. Thus, Skirrow focuses on 'the relationship between a technologised sexuality and a sexualised technology' (Skirrow
1986: 142). In this particular case, Skirrow argues that 'video games are
particularly unattractive [to women] since they are part of a technology
which . . . is identified with male power, and they are about mastering a
specifically male anxiety in a specifically male way' (38).

Skirrow's analysis is principally concerned with the question of how this
particular technology has come to be identified with a masculine domain. It
is not a matter of machine design and hardware, in her view – rather, it is a
question of the ways in which the software and its marketing (the games
themselves, the advertising, the magazines) articulate the cultural meanings of the technology through a set of masculinized images. She notes that
popular culture is marked by a clear split along gender lines, and that the
games industry relies heavily in its marketing strategies on 'realizing'
familiar elements of popular culture in its own specific form, and that 'most
of these borrowings are from popular forms that appeal to boys' – principally action, adventure and horror genres – where the fundamental model
is that of the single (masculine) hero 'waging a personal battle against
overwhelming odds' (ibid., 120). As she observes, most of the adventure
games involve some kind of quest, and the narratives draw heavily on the
models of the exotic thriller, the travel story or science fiction – genres of
story that particularly appeal to boys, where there is a strong emphasis on
technology and technical inventions (rather in the James Bond mould) as
the solution to narrative problems.

I want to suggest that the model offered by Skirrow can also be applied
to understanding how (and why) the computer has primarily come to be
seen (and used) as a masculine technology, and how attempts to market
the home computer have largely ended up with its appropriation within the
masculine sub-division of that predominantly feminine domain. Just as
Moores (1988) argues that radio technologies were initially of interest
primarily to technically-minded male hobbyists (and just as Gray argues
that video was certainly understood initially as a 'masculine toy'), so
Haddon notes that initial interest in home computers in the UK was
primarily among 'adult male electronics enthusiasts who read *Wireless
World*, *Electronics Weekly*, etc . . . [who] wanted to explore the technology, how it worked' (Haddon 1988: 16). He notes the defensiveness of
the men concerned about being seen as 'playing around with toys' and
about references to consumer electronic retailers such as Curry's and
Dixon's as 'adult (male) toy shops'. Interestingly, Haddon's account of
subsequent attempts to market home computers in the UK (via notions
of 'user-friendliness' and the provision of documentation and instructions designed for the non-expert, which de-emphasized the computer's
status as technology) can be read as a (largely unsuccessful) attempt to

'de-masculinize' the home computer and thus enable it to break out of this narrow market. However, as Haddon notes, the non-experts, who were the new marketing strategists addressees, were still primarily implied to be lay*men* rather than women – whose involvement with home computers has, thus far, largely been confined to an indirect one in which, as part of their gender-defined responsibilities for the socialization of children, they are concerned to acquire home computers to secure perceived 'educational' advantage for their children.

This pattern of the masculinization of computer technology is no simple quirk of British culture. Similar patterns obtain in France, as reported in the work of Jouet and Toussaint (1987) and of Jouet (1988), who note that the majority of users both of home computers and of the 'Minitel' system are men (by a ratio of 3:1 in their findings). The problem, of course, is to understand why this is the case. In this connection, Turkle offers an extremely interesting analysis of the seeming rejection of computers by highly able female students at MIT and Harvard. The term Turkle uses to describe this phenomenon is not, for instance, 'computer phobia', but rather what she calls 'computer reticence' – which she characterizes as 'wanting to stay away, because the computer becomes a personal and cultural symbol of what a woman is not' (Turkle 1988: 41).

Where Skirrow is concerned to develop an analysis of the 'gender valence' of the specific pleasures offered by video games, as a means of understanding the social patterning of the use of that technology, Turkle attempts to develop an analysis of the motivating pleasures informing computer (and specifically computer 'hacker') culture. Turkle argues that one of the key satisfactions offered by getting involved with computers is that the involvement with an abstract formal system (as opposed to the ambiguities of interpersonal relationships) often functions as a safe retreat into a protective world – 'a flight from relationships with people to relationships to the machine' (Turkle 1988: 45), and she argues that this option (an intensive involvement with a world of things and formal systems) is particularly attractive to adolescent boys. However, beyond this, Turkle also argues that hacker culture is characterized by certain core values – a preoccupation with 'winning' and risks, or with dangerous learning strategies in which the hacker 'plunge[s] in first and tries to understand later' (49) – which, Turkle argues, are heavily identified with masculine cultural traits.

However, Turkle takes the argument a stage further, and offers valuable insights into the cultural processes in which the categories of gender act as filters which make particular technologies appear more or less 'appropriate' to individuals inhabiting differently gendered modes of subjectivity. McRobbie and Garber (1976) and Walkerdine (1988), among others, have offered analyses of the processes through which adolescent girls, in particular, often feel compelled to reject subjects (and objects) which they view as gender-coded in such a way as to compromise their sense of femininity (cf. Walkerdine 1988, on the debates on science and girls, and on mathematics and girls). It is for the same reasons, Turkle argues, that many women reject computers – because they perceive them as culturally coded as masculine. And identity, of course, is always centrally about difference (cf. Saussure 1974).

Turkle is concerned with the social construction of the computer as a masculine domain, as seen 'through the eyes of women who have come to see something important about themselves in terms of what computers are not' (Turkle 1988: 41). As she observes, women look at computers and see more than machines – they see those machines as predominantly mediated through what they perceive as a heavily masculine culture – and as a result they wish to differentiate themselves from this culture: because it would be threatening to their self-images to see themselves as 'a computer science type', and they 'don't want to be part of that world'. In short, Turkle argues, 'women use their rejection of . . . computer[s] . . . to assert something about themselves as women. Being a woman is [seen as] opposed to a compelling relationship with a thing [the computer] that shuts people out' (50).

I argued above that this analysis was concerned with cultural rather than biological categories. I would also sound one other note of caution. While gender is a vital dimension of the structuring of technologies' meanings and uses, it does not function in isolation. In the end, our concern must be to develop a mode of analysis in which the function of gender categories can be integrated along with (and at many points, as they cut across) other structuring categories – such as those of age, class and ethnicity (cf. my comments above on Ang and Hermes (1991) and on Hermes (1991)).

COMMUNICATIONS TECHNOLOGIES IN THE DOMESTIC SPHERE

In this section I shall focus principally on communications technologies (and, in particular, on broadcasting technologies), given the key role which they can be seen to play in articulating the spatial and temporal relations between the private and public spheres. My argument is that it is necessary to contextualize the development of communications technologies within the broader historical frame of the changing relations between public and private domains in contemporary culture, and to 'denaturalize' the now taken-for-granted and unobtrusive presence of various communications technologies within the domestic space of the household.

Moores (1988) offers an account of the troubled history of the introduction of radio into the home and argues that, while radio was gradually accommodated into the living-room – that space in the house designated to the unity of the family group – this accommodation was by no means unproblematic (cf. Boddy 1986, on initial anxieties as to whether the living-room was the appropriate location of the television set). As Moores points out, radio's entry into the living-room was 'marked by a disturbance of everyday lives and family relationships' (Moores 1988: 26). Indeed, the initial enthusiasm for the medium came largely from young, technically minded men – who were fascinated by the machine as a technology – and it was often resisted by women, for whom the unattractive mechanical appearance of the early sets (and their tendency to leak battery acid on to the furniture), combined with the fact that their husbands dominated their use, meant that, for many women, radio was at first an unattractive medium: ('only one of us could listen and that was my husband [using the earphones – D.M.]. The rest of us were sat like mummies' (respondent quoted in Moores 1988: 29)).

As Moores notes, radio signified something quite different for men and for women. For men, the 'wireless' was a 'craze', a 'miraculous toy' (cf. Gray 1987a, on video-recorders as 'women's work and boy's toys'); for women, it was, Moores argues, 'an ugly box and an imposed silence' (Moores 1988: 30–1) as reception was so poor that anyone talking in the room made it difficult for the (usually male) listener to follow the broadcast. It was only much later, with the development of loudspeakers to replace individual headphones, and the design of a new generation of radio sets marketed as fashionable objects of domestic furnishing, that radio gained its taken-for-granted place within the geography of the house – though, of course, its place in the sitting-room has now largely been taken by the television set, with the radio(s) now banished to the kitchen or the bedroom, in most houses, for personal rather than collective use – a good example of the 'career' of a technology in a parallel sense to that proposed by Appadurai (1986).

By extension, I would want to argue that similar processes have occurred in the contemporary entry of new communications technologies (e.g. video and computers) into the home – and that, again, their entry is likely to be marked by their differential incorporation into masculine and feminine domains of activity within the home. The work of Boddy (1986), Spigel (1986) and Haralovich (1988) offers a useful model for the analysis of the development and marketing of contemporary new technologies. In a close parallel to Moores's analysis, Spigel offers an account of the problematic nature of the introduction of television in America in the early 1950s. She is concerned primarily with the role of women's magazines in presenting 'the idea of television and its place in the home' (Spigel 1986: 3) to their female readers – who were of course, in their economic capacity, the key target group whom would-be television advertisers wished to reach and, in their social (gender-defined) role, the group seen to be responsible for the organization of the domestic sphere into which the television was to be integrated.

Spigel argues that, in the early 1950s, television was seen as potentially disrupting the internal arrangements of the home (just as radio had been in the earlier period) – disrupting patterns of child-rearing and marital relations, distracting housewives from the proper running of their homes, and necessitating a thorough re-arrangement of the moral economy of the household. Indeed, from the industry's point of view, problems were foreseen as to whether television, as a visual as well as an auditory medium (and thus, it was presumed, one which would require of its housewife viewers a degree of attention incompatible with the performance of their domestic tasks) could, in fact, be integrated into the patterns of daily domestic life. The introduction of television into the home did not take place as an easy, unruffled insertion of a new technology into the existing socio-cultural framework, not least because of concern that women would not be able to cope with the technological complexities of retuning the television set from one station to another (cf. recent debates about whether women can 'cope' with video and computer technologies). The industry's primary response was to offer other products as solutions to the problems which television was seen to create: thus, a wide variety of household appliances were marketed as 'solutions' to dilemmas posed by the television set. The crucial problem (from the advertisers' point of view) was how to bring the housewife into the unified space of the televiewing family. As Spigel notes, the electric dishwasher was marketed precisely as a technological solution to this problem – as it would 'bring the housewife out of the kitchen and into the living room, where she could watch TV with her family' (Spigel 1986: 8).

I wish to argue that our analyses must focus on how communications and information technologies came to be enmeshed in, and articulated with, the internal dynamics of the organization of domestic space (particularly with reference to gender domains) but also that they must be situated within a broader analysis of what Donzelot (1979) has described as 'the withdrawal to interior space'. This is a process in which communications technologies themselves have played a key role, as their domestication has increased the attractiveness of the home as a site of leisure (cf. Frith 1983).

In analysing all of these processes, I would want to insist on the extent to which the pre-existing social modes of organization of the home have exerted a determining effect on how communications and information technologies have been incorporated (or domesticated) into everyday life. However, there are other dimensions to these processes. At the same time, we need to be sensitive both to the various modes in which regulatory discourses have entered the domestic sphere and affected the development of these technologies (cf. contemporary debates about censorship and scheduling policies in broadcasting, anxieties about the moral dimension of some of British Telecom's new phone services, concern over domestic video and audio-tape 'pirating', etc.) In all of these areas we must also pay close attention to the effects of the dominant images of the (nuclear) family and its 'healthy' functioning held by producers and marketers – and to the determining effect of these images on the policies of powerful institutions.

Technologies, boundaries and domestication

It has been argued above that communications technologies play a crucial role in articulating the public and private spheres – hence the role of broadcasting in articulating the family and the nation into the 'national family'. In so far as, in contemporary Western societies, the home and family are considered to be a private shelter from public pressures, television and other communication technologies (e.g. the telephone) are problematic as they disrupt this separation of spheres. Thus, as Pool argues, the telephone has contradictory potential, in so far as while 'it invades our privacy with its ring . . . it [also] protects our privacy, by allowing us to transact affairs from the fastness of our homes' (Pool 1987: 4). Similarly, technological developments such as the video and the telephone answering-machine can both be seen as technical means for enhancing the family's (or individual's) ability to regulate the transgression of their domestic boundaries. In the case of the video, this works by enhancing the consumer's ability to manipulate broadcast schedules (by time-shift recording) so as to fit in more conveniently with domestic routines, and in the case of the telephone answering-machine, by enhancing the user's ability to screen out unwanted interruptions into their domestic space. Communications technologies are also problematic: their very capacity to break the boundaries of the family mean that they have always been seen as being in need of careful regulation – hence the longstanding concern with the danger of broadcasters transgressing standards of 'taste' and 'decency' in the most problematic sphere, inside the home. Moreover, new technologies themselves create new anxieties and calls for regulation. Thus, as Paterson (1987) argues, the development of home video technoloies quickly came to be seen as intensely problematic. The capacity of the video to offer individual family members (and particularly children – witness the scare about 'video nasties') an increased freedom to view uncertified material became the justification in the UK for a whole new round of state interventions designed to regulate this field of activity.

Certainly developments such as the proliferation of communication channels and cable and satellite networks offers the prospect of the fragmentation of the national audiences (and politics) which traditional broadcasting systems have created; we can also expect the development of miniaturized and portable 'delivery systems' and the further prospect of individualized consumption within the home (a double privatization). Lindlof and Meyer (1987) argue that the interactive capacities of recent technological developments fundamentally transform the position of the consumer. However, such arguments run the danger of abstracting these technologies' intrinsic capacities from the social contexts of their actual use (cf. Hymes's (1972) critique of Chomsky, for a parallel argument). In seeking to understand such technological developments, Bausinger raises the question of how these technologies are integrated into the structure and routines of domestic life – into what he calls 'the specific semantics of the everyday'. His basic thesis is that technologies are increasingly absorbed into the everyday ('everyone owns a number of machines, and has directly to handle technical products'), so that everyday routines themselves are constructed around technologies, which then become effectively invisible in their domestication. The end result, he argues, is the 'inconspicuous omnipresence of the technical' (Bausinger 1984: 346). The key point is to understand the processes through which communications and information technologies are 'domesticated' to the point where they become inconspicuous, if not invisible, within the home. The further point is then to focus on the culturally constructed meanings of these technologies, as they are produced through located practices of consumption.

AN ETHNOGRAPHIC PORTRAIT: THE DOMESTIC USES OF TECHNOLOGY

Below, I offer an account of the patterning and use of information and communication technologies in one of the first groups of families studied in the Brunel University research project into the uses of ICTs. The primary aim here is to offer insights into some of the key dynamics and processes in the family culture of this household, and to begin to demonstrate the context-specific ways in which technologies come to acquire particular meanings and thus to be used for different purposes by different people. Hopefully, these examples will serve at least to illustrate some of the issues addressed above[3].

The husband in this family is 48 and his wife 46; they have two children – a boy aged 15 and a girl of 12. The husband is a self-employed consultant in the market-research field; his wife works part time, as a sandwich-maker and cleaner in the cafeteria in a local school. They own a small house in a slightly down-market area of south-west London. The parents both left school at 15. Both vote Conservative. They have three televisions, the one with the remote control in their sitting-room, the others in the children's bedrooms; two computers: the son has a Sinclair in his room, and the father has an Amstrad with a printer, which he uses for work, in the front room, which is now converted into his office. There is a video in the sitting-room; an electric cooker, a refrigerator, an electric kettle, a toaster, a radio and a microwave (as well as the mother's clock) in the kitchen; and a washing-machine and spin-dryer in the utility room. The mother has an electric iron and a crimper. There are two phones: one in the sitting room, one in the office. The son has a hi-fi system and a Walkman; the daughter also has a hi-fi system, a radio and an under-used Walkman.

For some years this man had a relatively well-paid research job in the car industry, which he felt compelled to leave as a result of administrative and technological factors which seemed to marginalize his skills. His present work situation is rather unstable and, as a result, the family's rise from working-class to lower-middle-class status has halted. Indeed, their economic position is now quite precarious: they are somewhat fearful of their future prospects, and the woman has extended her part-time hours of work to increase the family's income. The organization of family activities is also affected by the fact that the man now works from home (the front-room has been converted into his office) and thus has a somewhat different perspective on home/work boundaries from the men in the other families researched in the project who go out to work.

The man sees his present difficult employment situation as the result of the imposition of a new form of short-term 'economic rationality' imposed in the company for whom he worked by 'accountants', through the medium of new technologies (especially computer databases), which were seen to replace (and thus marginalize) his personal research skills (built up through a network of 'personal contacts' in the relevant industries). The effects of this on the family have been complex. At the simplest level, the consequent fall in his earning capacity means that the family is not well-off and lacks the financial resources to engage in many forms of consumption. Thus, for instance, the children are encouraged to ensure that they mainly receive rather than make phone calls to their friends, and the wife has put on the wall a list of the cost per minute of calling the people they most often do phone. However, it is not only a matter of money, because (a) the man in particular also expresses moral disapproval of various forms of consumption; and (b) the controls exercised over telephone communication also relate to certain family rules about the boundaries and privacy of the household.

The man's anxieties about his loss of status in the external world also have effects within the household. On the one hand it would seem that, because he lacks external recognition, it is of particular importance to him to establish his position as head of the household by demonstrating his technological mastery (see below) inside the family. At the same time, although he is at home more than his wife, he seems to have refused to adjust his social role in the domain of domestic labour to recognize this fact: such domestic responsibilities as bringing in the milk-bottles, paying bills, cooking meals and washing up are still, as far as he is concerned, his wife's responsibility.

Boundaries: external and internal

In this family there is a stress on the importance of boundaries and control. Perhaps by way of compensation for his sense of lack of control over the outside world, the man is very concerned to regulate the functions of communication technologies in breaking the boundary between the private and public spheres. While there seems to be a low level of integration (for the parents) in the neighbourhood at large, there is a high level of integration within the family (evident both in visible expressions of closeness, and in a low level of gender-based separation in the parents' social life). The family displays a common pattern, in which the effective family unit (for leisure purposes such as watching television) is mother, father and daughter, based in the sitting-room, with the teenage son separated off – spending his time with his own ICTs in his bedroom.

The family's concern with regulating the cost of phone calls has already been noted. However, while some of the parents' anxieties are, no doubt, economic, broader issues concerning their ability to control and supervise their children do also seem to arise in this connection. The parents are proud of the fact that their daughter, on the whole, receives calls from, rather than makes calls to, her friends, and she asks permission before making a call out herself. However, they are deeply concerned about the stories they have read of teenagers using British Telecom's 'party lines', and running up huge bills for their parents to pay. They worry about leaving their children alone in the house for this reason, and are anxious that the introduction of tele-shopping facilities will exacerbate these temptations for their children. Similarly, they are concerned by the prospect of deregulated satellite television broadcasting bringing pornographic or violent programming within their children's grasp: '[They] have sets in their rooms and [we] can't know what they are watching all the time'. Thus, deregulation is not only a concern at the level of the disruption of national boundaries by transnational broadcasters: for this family at least, it is also a question of fear of the family's boundaries being transgressed.

Their parents' concern to regulate their children's use of ICTs is powerfully symbolized by the 'umbilical' principle of the electricity supply in this house: the only power point upstairs is in the parents' bedroom, from which wires are run into the children's rooms – and the children's electricity supply can thus be controlled directly by the parents. This, naturally, is a source of some tension, because, certainly for the son, part of the attraction of watching television in his room is his sense of this as a relatively unpoliced/unsupervised activity.

The parents explain that they feel they do need to 'supervise' their daughter's use of the phone, as noted earlier, but this is perhaps not only an economic issue. It is also a question of parental resentment of their daughter's incoming calls, as an intrusion into their domestic privacy – as events threatening a potentially fragile boundary, which they feel some need to reinforce. Thus, the daughter explains that her father doesn't like her friends ringing her so much 'because lots of people go too far . . . some of my friends do funny phone calls . . . they . . . dial your number and when you answer they start laughing . . . they do raspberries down the phone and my Dad doesn't like it'.

Unlike the majority of families studied in the course of the Brunel project, where it is the wife who uses the phone most, as a psychic life-line to alleviate her sense of isolation, the pattern is different in this family. Here the woman feels less need to use the phone in this way for her own purposes, as she goes out to work herself. In fact, she principally uses the phone as the medium for discharging what she sees as her familial obligations of keeping in touch with her and her husband's kin. Interestingly, even this has been a source of some tension: the list of telephone costs on the wall arose as a result of an occasion when her husband felt she spent 'too long' on the phone when speaking to his sister.

In this family it is the husband who uses the phone most, for business purposes, as he works from home. He insists, however, on a strictly limited definition of the phone – as a 'tool' for necessary contact 'passing information back and forth'. And even then he mistrusts the phone 'because it is so much easier to lie over the phone than it is face to face'. Beyond that, he regards it as an 'intrusion, it gets in the way . . . the phone rings when you don't want it to ring'. For this man the maintenance of internal boundaries is also important. Thus, he explains that he 'wouldn't have a telephone in the bedroom . . . unless someone was ill'.

Technology and control

The man's attitudes towards technology are complex and contradictory, but he expresses an overall sense of defeatism, or cynical resignation, as a result of the down-turn in his career – which leads to a broader sense of pessimism about the 'future' and a negative attitude to what he sees as the prevailing social uses of new technology.

To some extent his attitudes to domestic technology, which certainly are a powerful influence within the dynamics of this family, can be seen to be derived from his experience at work. He blames his own current difficulties on 'technology', given that he sees his own expertise as having been devalued and replaced by computerized information systems in the company for which he worked. Thus, his present position of insecure freelance employment has had powerful consequences on the family in two senses. Not only has it simply reduced their overall standard of living; 'technology' has also been constructed within this family's mythology as an inherently problematic and contradictory force.

He distinguishes strongly between the positive potential of technology and its regressive uses. Indeed, he has a distinct interest in communications technologies in themselves. Thus, not only has he mastered the operational use of his home computer (which he needs for his work), but he literally experiments with the family's microwave (putting different things in for different periods of time to 'see what happens to them'). However, the computer is an object of great ambivalence for him: while he has mastered it for his own purposes, he cannot communicate his mastery to other professionals in the field. He has a one-sided form of mastery of technology in which he has not learnt to externalize his knowledge and skills by acquiring the appropriate professional vocabulary and thus he has trouble gaining external recognition of his abilities.

Perhaps by way of rationalization of this inability, he also scorns the whole communicative/marketing dimension of business. He expresses disdain for all this 'wrapping things up' and for people who are 'only concerned about the presentation', which, as far as he is concerned, is little more than a set of 'con-tricks' in which, in order to be successful, you are required to 'call yourself' by a particular job-title or 'sign yourself off' in a certain way. In short, he thinks that the industry in which he works is improperly concerned with 'high falutin' names for things' which, for him, are 'only common sense'. He claims that he 'doesn't need those systems to tell me how to do it' and doesn't 'need those analytical techniques' because he has a richer and superior resource – years of personal experience. Unfortunately, this resource is not widely valued in the market in which he works, because nowadays 'they've dehumanized it'. 'They' are the accountants and computer specialists who failed to recognize the value of the 'contacts . . . built up over a long period' – personalized communication networks, built on trust; the problem being that, like this man, these people did not necessarily have 'formal qualifications' and so, in terms of 'modern ideas', they have been undervalued and their networks broken up.

In fact, in much of this man's talk there is a very strong theme of how depersonalization of information leads to loss of control and even to financial/moral ruin. He is very concerned about the ways in which technology 'has now taken over', and has 'dehumanized' skills of various sorts, destroying crafts and skills by its 'mechanical/logical' methods, 'once it has all been taken away from people and put in machines'. This, for him, is perhaps best symbolized by the telephone answering-machine. He will not leave messages on these machines, because it seems unnatural and improper to him that he should have to 'talk to the stupid machine . . . I don't like that robot type of thing . . . it's too impersonal'.

This man frequently expresses a distinctly fearful attitude towards the possibility of large organizations manipulating technology to take advantage of the individual in some way. In a general sense, he is fearful of the potential of ICTs for disembedding information from a human context –

this fear of loss of control concerns him greatly. Thus, he refuses to have a computerised credit card identification number because of the danger of someone else using it and leaving him responsible for the bill. He is deeply anxious about the possibility of errors in British Telecom's new computerized account system leading to the family being wrongly billed for phone calls they have not made. He is anxious about the misuse of personal data by the police and other agencies, 'Well, it's on computers, so [sic] sooner or later it's going to be misused' – an attitude that is meshed in with a fundamental view of the incompetent and corrupt nature of most large institutions. He is basically concerned that with 'the electronic thing, no one is really secure anymore' and is fearful of computer hackers because 'there's always someone who will find a way of getting through', and thus 'they' may, in his worst fears, end up being able to know 'exactly what is in your head'.

At key moments, his attitudes towards technology are paralleled by a generally more fearful relation to what he perceives as the depersonalizing dimensions of the 'modern' world: 'when you are in the middle of a modern shopping complex . . . it makes you feel small . . . so exposed . . . you're never quite sure what's expected of you'.

The organization of familial domains: space, gender, generation

Another dimension of familial organization in which we see here a concern for boundary maintenance is that of gender. In particular, it is clear that, within the home, the woman has responsibilities for a clear set of concerns. Thus, by way of dealing with their precarious financial position, she keeps the family finances in a set of books. It is she who knows all the names, ages and birthdays of her and her husband's kin and she who takes responsibility for managing kin relations – principally by the telephone. Indeed this is the principle significance of the telephone for her – as a way of conveying/receiving 'family news' and as a way of keeping tabs on her children (she requires then to phone her to let her know what they are doing if they are out late or otherwise have departed from their normal routines).

On the whole, she displays a fairly passive and accommodative attitude to the household ICTs. When her son is playing loud music in his room, her response is to 'want to disappear somewhere where you couldn't hear it'. Even her sense of her own pleasure in watching television ('I like all the soaps, of course, though I know deep down it's a lot of drivel') is expressed not only guiltily but also passively. Thus, what she likes about television is 'it makes me sit down and relax . . . I stop thinking about what I've got to do, the next job'. She does, of course, have her own domain, the kitchen, and there the radio is tuned to a local pop channel – which is her preferred station. Thus, within her own domain, she also has her own organization of time. In the kitchen she has her 'private clock', which she keeps 15–20 minutes fast 'so I'm always early . . . and I can have some time for myself'.

I have argued earlier that ICTs play an important part in the construction of internal and external boundaries and identities. Some part of this argument can be usefully exemplified if we focus on the differential relations to technology and space within the household that are demonstrated by the son and the daughter in this family. As noted earlier, the daughter spends little time in her own room – as opposed to watching television with her mother and father in the sitting-room. Conversely, the son spends most of his time in his own room, utilizing the ICT equipment which he has bought (with money earned from his Saturday job) and installed there (a pattern which is replicated in several of the families studied).

His mother refers to his room as 'his womb', and it certainly seems to function as a significant retreat for him. Here he can stay up late watching television (and possibly watching his preferred form of 'action movies', of which his parents disapprove). In the room he has a computer, a hi-fi and a television, and he is saving for a video. He and his friends are very interested in technology. He spends school lunchtimes at a friend's house playing video games. They often visit consumer electronic shops just to see 'what's new'; they read consumer electronic catalogues like magazines and will go to W. H. Smith's just to browse through the computer magazines. He is heavily dependent on technology to offer him a sense of 'something going on', preferably in the form of music (or, as his mother puts it, 'noise'). He says that he 'can't work without it . . . I like music, I don't like sitting and being dull. If I'm in my bedroom and that's all quiet, it feels like school and it depresses me'.

He wears his Walkman whenever he leaves the house, and takes it to school. He remarks that his classmates 'reckon my Walkman is my life-support system'. He says that he does 'feel lost without it . . . it just feels like I am not all there . . . As soon as I run out of batteries I'm down the shop, even if I've only got a pound left'. The other technology on which he is quite dependent is his Swatch: 'if my watch broke down I wouldn't know what to do . . . my other watch kept breaking, I was hopeless – I had to find people [at school] who had watches, to walk around with'.

Despite their contradictory attitudes towards technology, the parents encourage their children's acquisition of ICTs – both for rather undefined educational purposes and as a training in budgeting and saving. This works well with the son, but fails with the daughter. Her brother would be willing to give her his old ICT equipment as 'hand-me-downs' when he upgrades his systems, but her father insists that she save and buy them from her brother. However, the daughter, along with many teenage girls, is more interested in buying clothes and other such 'frivolous' things. Indeed, her very investment in femininity is at odds with the attitudes that would be required to engage more seriously with ICT (cf. McRobbie and Garber

1976; Turkle 1988). In fact, the daughter is both much less dependent on technology than her brother ('I plug in less than he does') and less concerned to differentiate herself from her parents by demarcating her own private space within the house.

Gendered technologies and technological competence/confidence

The contrast in attitudes towards different technologies displayed by the mother and by the son in the family are perhaps the most revealing. The son is positively disdainful of computers – as mere tools which he is well able to master: 'A computer's dumb, isn't it? . . . you've got to tell it what to do . . . it doesn't know what to do until you load something into it . . . . Say you programmed it to wash the dishes, and then put it in front of a car . . . it would wash an area the size of a dish . . . or just look at it and say . . . that's not the object I've been told to wash'. He has no fear of 'technical breakdowns' – 'I just do things as I do them, and if it goes wrong, it goes wrong' – which doesn't bother him, given his basic confidence in his ability to 'figure it out'. On the other hand, the son cannot operate the washing-machine and is frightened of 'touching the cooker', although he will now use the microwave because 'it's safer . . . because it's a closed system'.

Conversely, his mother, while being the only member of the household who can operate the washing-machine, cannot operate the video and is privately frightened of the computer. She has a very basic fear of uncontrollable technological muddles, 'with everything all wrong, twisted around. What do I do? Where do I go?'. She explains that she is 'not confident' with the computer 'it makes me feel uneasy, I'm afraid that if I touch a button I shouldn't, everything will go haywire . . . if I touch one button, it will go all wrong; that's the way I feel'. She is quite disinterested in the computer: 'It does completely nothing for me. The only time I use it is if [her husband] wants me to do something'. However, with technologies where she feels confident, and where she has a distinct interest in their uses, she will experiment: 'You take the washing-machine . . . if I can find a different way of getting the clothes better, I'll play around with it until I find out, like the microwave . . . I'll fiddle around with it until [I get] what I want'.

The gendered difference of such attitudes does not, of course, relate only to ICT or electronic technologies. The contrast here is clearest if we consider the attitudes of this woman and those of her son to modes of transport. Just as in the case of the computer, where the woman fears loss of control and consequent muddle, the idea of driving a car, she says, 'doesn't appeal to me at all, I'm scared of it . . . I have this fear of this monster in my hands'. For her son, his dream is 'to ride a motorbike . . . the feeling of speed . . . the wind in my face'.

Technological inheritances

Within families, of course, there are many forms of gender-based learning. Thus, in the example quoted above, the son's desire for the 'real thrill' of riding a motorbike is perhaps not unrelated to his father's claim that a cut-throat razor is really 'the only way to shave'. However, beyond this level of quite banal and predictable (though none the less powerful) forms of learning of the appropriate forms and symbols of gender identity, we can also identify some interesting processes when we look at the technological inheritance of attitudes and competences from father to son within this family.

I have already noted the son's easy confidence in his ability to 'figure out' technologies. The further point is that he takes a very much more 'adventurous' attitude than does his father. Indeed, he is quite (humorously) scornful of his father's logical approach – '*You*'d read the manual', he says, when asked by his father what he would do when confronted with an unknown machine or problem. For him, on the contrary, it is a matter of pride to 'figure it out' for himself without reference to any 'manual' (cf. Turkle 1988, on hackers' thrills of risk-taking). His attitude is that 'you've got to work around . . . and just try to work it out from there . . . work them out by using them . . . I never read the instructions . . . I'd rather figure it out for myself'.

In one sense, this can be seen as an advance in confidence in relation to technology on behalf of the young man, as compared to his father. But inheritances are complex equations, and his seeming bravado takes on another meaning if we note also that he 'hates reading' and is 'not very good at spelling' – which means that using the manual (or indeed the dictionary) is not, in fact, an easy option for him. This takes us back to the disjunction between his father's practical/operational skills and his own lack of communicative/linguistic skills. Perhaps this young man has inherited not only a certain interest in, an operational ability with, technology, but, much more precisely, a rather narrow and specifically limited operational form of technological competence, alongside, or perhaps as an integral part of, a particular masculine subjectivity.

Conclusion

Much of our theorizing about contemporary society – about the practices and cultures of everyday life – is informed less by an understanding of the detailed practices of real people as they go about their daily business than by an abstract theorizing that takes for granted, almost as much as we do ourselves in our daily lives, the forces and structures, the conflicts and contradictions, of quotidian reality.

The kind of portrait offered above, whilst by no means sufficient in itself, does at least provide a concrete starting-point for the investigation of household or domestic relationships: through consumption and use, to the design and marketing of the hardware and software of information and communication technologies. If we are to understand, better than we do now, the nature of the relationship between technological and social change, as it plays itself out in domestic life, then we need to know (to describe and account for) much more of how these technologies are actually used and what meanings they acquire in the course of their situated uses.

This, is, then, to focus on the significance of technology in people's lives, and more specifically on the particular significance of information and communication technologies on household and family relationships, both internal and external. The concerns are not just with the ways in which information and communication technologies mediate domestic space and time, and are implicated in shifting gender positions and identities, but also with the ways in which the consumption of technologies (and their messages) is implicated in the construction of individual and family identities, and in the relationship between their private and public worlds.

Part VI

Between the private and the public

Chapter 12

The construction of everyday life: political communication and domestic media

INTRODUCTION

In the study of political communicaticn, the analysis of the media's role in articulating the private and public spheres of society, and in the social construction of spheres of competence and understanding (and their differential distribution among the various sectors of the population), is of critical importance. By way of illustration of the issues at stake, I begin with the comments of a woman respondent, interviewed in my study of family viewing practices (Morley 1986), who was concerned to explain to me her strong preferences for local as opposed to national news, and her (to my mind, very cogent) reasons for being uninterested in the latter:

> Sometimes I like to watch the news, if it's something that's gone on – like where that little boy's gone and what's happened to him. Otherwise I don't, not unless it's local, only when there's something that's happened local . . . national news gets on my nerves . . . I can't stand *World in Action* and *Panorama* and all that. It's wars all the time. You know, it gets on your nerves. . . . What I read in the papers and listen to on the news is enough for me. I don't want to know about the Chancellor Somebody in Germany and all that. When I've seen it once I don't want to see it again. I hate seeing it again – because it's on at breakfast-time, dinner-time and teatime, you know, the same news all day long. It bores me. What's going on in the world? I don't understand it, so I don't listen to that. I watch – like those little kids [an abduction – D.M.] – that gets to me, I want to know about it. Or if there's actually some crime in [her local area – D.M.], like rapes and the rest of it, I want to read up on that; see if they've been caught and locked away. As for like when the guy says 'The pound's gone up' and 'the pound's gone down' I don't want to know about all that, 'cause I don't understand it. It's complete ignorance really. If I was to understand it all, I would probably get interested in it.
>
> (Morley 1986: 169)

Citizenship and audience membership

Merton and Lazarsfeld (1948) wrote of what they saw as the 'narcoticising dysfunction' of the media. They were concerned that exposure to a flood of information from the media might serve to 'narcoticize', rather than to 'energize', the audience, in the sense of motivating it to action:

> The individual reads accounts of issues and problems and may even discuss alternative lines of action. But this rather intellectualised, re- mote connection with organised social action is not activated. The interested and informed citizen can congratulate himself on his lofty state of interest and information and forget to see that he has abstained from decision and action. In short he takes his secondary contact with the world of political reality, his reading and listening and thinking, as a vicarious performance. He comes to mistake knowing about problems of the day for doing something about them. He is concerned. He is informed. And he has all sorts of ideas about what should be done. But, after he has gotten through his dinner and after he has listened to his favoured radio programs and after he has read his second paper of the day, it is really time for bed. In this peculiar respect, mass communi- cations may be included among the most respectable and efficient social narcotics.
>
> (quoted in Groombridge 1972: 72–3)

This view of the media as a 'narcotic'/ritual for the audience has been supported in more recent years by researchers such as that of Nordenstreng (1972), who quotes the results of an investigation into the media in Finland in the early 1970s, cf. p. 79 above. On the one hand, Nordenstreng *et al.* found that news broadcasts were among the most popular programmes, in that over 80 per cent of the Finnish population over the age of 15 followed at least one news broadcast a day. On the other hand, when they looked at 'comprehension' of these news broadcasts, by means of interviews immedi- ately after they had been shown, they found that 'in general, little if anything, is remembered of the content of the news', and even that 'the main thing retained from the news is that nothing special has happened'. (Nordenstreng 1972: 390). On this basis the investigators concluded:

> for most Finns, following the news is a mere ritual, a way of dividing up the daily rhythm, and a manifestation of alienation . . . many people follow the news because in this way they gain a point of contact with the outside world – a fixed point in life – while the content of the news is indifferent to them . . . [Thus] news programmes do not fulfil the function of transmission of information; they being to serve a different purpose whereby the following of news broadcasts becomes a ritual, a custom serving to maintain a feeling of security.
>
> (ibid., 391)

However, Groombridge, also writing in the early 1970s, suggested that, if this is the case, then it is because of the relatively powerless and alienated situation of the audiences:

this lack of power, this absence of cultural involvement is the underlying political fact behind all those studies and demonstrations of popular political ignorance. . . . Information does not motivate people [to action] . . . if they do not feel that they have an entrée to influence and power. It is fundamentally this gap, between the availability of information and the acknowledged opportunity to act on that information, which is responsible both for the way in which TV acts as a refracting window, rather than a reflecting window on the world, and for the paradoxical ignorance of the public.

(Groombridge 1972: 125)

As Groombridge goes on to argue, 'for most people, most of the time, it is not clear what, if anything can be done with the information received, so it is badly assimilated, if at all' (ibid., 175). Moreover, Groombridge continues, it is the audience's lack of power that conditions the way in which television addresses it, in news and current-affairs programmes. Because news has little real function, in terms of political control and economic decision-making, for most of those receiving it, he argues, it has tended to become an end-in-itself and has turned into a 'marketable commodity'.

In another debate concerning popular culture, Martin argued that, in a popular newspaper

Events (political, natural disasters, titbits, crime, all mixed up typographically) will all be presented in terms of some attitude that the reader will find it emotionally satisfying to adopt. This style of reporting will affect the kind of relationship which the reader feels him/herself to have with the reported world; it implies that without the colourful intervention of the newspaper there is no meaningful relationship between the events which it dramatises and the readers for whom the show goes on. In this respect the style has a hidden content. It speaks for readers whom it takes to be politically disenfranchised, for whom the news of political events is not about a world in which they feel they can meaningfully act.

(Martin 1973: 89–90)

In a review article on the press, the late Raymond Williams pointed to the sociological basis of this situation, in terms of the relationship between the 'mass public' and the political arena:

Compare any popular national paper with any ordinary evening or local paper. The amount of 'hard news' in the local paper is almost always much higher. Its presentation in the local paper is much closer to the minority than to the majority national press; in length of sentence, paragraph and article; in vocabulary, in the degree of headlining, angling, personalising. Yet the readers of the local papers are, in the majority, the same people as the readers of the national majority press. In a social situation which they are more in touch with, understand better and can respond to more directly in other ways, the style of the paper they are offered and expect is different. Minority national newspapers are written for people who can fairly regularly feel in this kind of relationship to the larger society. The popular synthesis, on the whole, is for those who do not feel this with any confidence, but who are then offered a connection in surrogate ways with a version of some national and international happenings, across a bridge of 'personalities' who function in a kind of analogy to actually known or observed persons.

(Williams 1970: 508–9)

New media: new relationships?

Of course, the impact of new communications technologies on this situation must also be considered. Writing at the end of the 1970s, one commentator noted: 'in its [fifty-]year history, the role of the TV receiver has not changed at all. Its sole function is to show programmes distributed from a central point for mass consumption, essentially TV is as it was when the BBC first started broadcasting from Alexandra Palace' (quoted in Webster and Robins 1979: 301).

However, as Webster and Robins argue, 'the development of viewdata, video equipment and new cable and TV services is bringing this phase in the history of television to a close' (ibid., 301). However, we need to see how the new media are integrated with the old. The significance of these technological changes must, of course, be analysed carefully. Gunter and Svennevig note evidence of the growth in the number of multi-television and multi-video households. As they put it, the question is:

Will families, through increased reliance on TV for different kinds of entertainment, be drawn closer together by the common source of amusement . . .? Or will there be a trend towards the increased acquisition of TV sets and accessory equipment (e.g. video recorders, home computers, etc) with each family member having access to a personal 'home entertainment system' which they use privately, resulting in increased isolation of family members from each other?

(Gunter and Svennevig 1987: 36)

In this changed context, a number of our working assumptions about television and its audiences may need to be considered afresh. However, I do not wish to argue that we only now need to consider these issues, simply as a result of technological changes in media-delivery systems. At a more fundamental level, I also want to argue that an understanding of the media's implication in the field of political communications needs to be reframed within the wider context of an analysis of the media's role in articulating the domestic/private and political/public spheres. I am aware that in arguing for the importance of the domestic context of media reception one runs the risk of being misinterpreted, as if to raise this issue was to abandon concern with wider societal questions of power, ideology and representation. However, I would want to resist this interpretation. Indeed, in *Everyday Television* Brunsdon and I (Brunsdon and Morley 1978) were concerned precisely with the links between the domestic and the political, manifested most clearly in *Nationwide*'s attempt to construct an image of the unified nation, built around the experiences that we are all assumed to share, as members of families. There is a strong tradition of thought which basically conceptualizes the family ('the private sphere') as precisely beyond/outside/constituting the limit of 'politics'. What I want to do here is to sketch in some of the ways in which television, as a specific discourse spanning this private/public divide, can be seen to articulate together domestic and national life. At one level, this is a question of understanding the organization of communications within the terms of the social organization of space. As Scannell puts it,

> the social spaces from within which and for which broadcasting produces its programmes and schedules . . . the places from which broadcasting speaks, and the places in which it is seen and heard, are relevant considerations in the analysis of communicative contexts that broadcasting establishes as part of the social fabric of modern life.
>
> (Scannell 1988: 15)

The question of the social organization of space also, and inescapably, involves questions of power and ideology. As Scannell also notes, in his historical analysis of the development of British broadcasting,

> It was no coincidence that Reith [the then Director-General of the BBC] had worked hard for years to persuade the King to speak, from his home and as head of his family, to the nation and empire of families, listening in their home on [Christmas] day. . . . It set a crowning seal on the role of broadcasting in bringing the nation together . . . the family audience, the Royal Family, the nation as family.
>
> (ibid., 19)

Modern mass democratic politics has its forum in the radically new kind of public sphere that broadcasting constitutes. In their historical analysis of the development of British broadcasting, Cardiff and Scannell (1987) focus on its crucial role in forging a link between the dispersed and disparate listeners and the symbolic heartland of national life, and on its role in promoting a sense of communal identity within its audience, at both regional and national levels. As they argue, historically the BBC can be seen to have been centrally concerned to supply its isolated listeners with a sense of the community they had lost, translated from a local to a national and even global level. Here we see precisely the concern to articulate the private and public spheres: to connect the family and the nation. As Cardiff and Scannell note, the audience has always been seen as composed of family units, as a vast cluster of families, rather than in terms of social classes or different taste publics. Lord Reith himself was most concerned with the possibilities that broadcasting offered of 'making the nation one man [sic]'. At its crudest level of operation, this can be seen in an Empire Day radio programme in 1935 (reported by Cardiff and Scannell) in which a mother is heard explaining to her daughter: 'The British Empire, Mary, is made up of one big family.' Mary asks, 'You mean a family like ours, Mummy?', and mother replies, 'Yes, darling. But very much larger.' The pervasive symbol of unification was, from the beginning, the family, connoting Mother Britain and her children in the Empire, as well as the Royal Family and each little family of listeners (Cardiff and Scannell 1987: 163)

This is no merely quaint or historical point. In a close parallel, Brunsdon and I (1978) argued that the central image of much contemporary current-affairs and magazine programming is precisely the family, and the nation as composed of families. In this type of broadcasting, the nuclear family is the unspoken premise of much programme discourse: not only is the programming addressed to a 'family audience', but this domestic focus accounts both for the content (human-interest stories) and for the dominant mode of presentation (the emphasis on the everyday aspects of public issues; 'So what will this new law mean for ordinary consumers?'). What is assumed to unite the audience, the 'nation of families', is its experience of domestic life.

The regulation of domestic pleasures

My interest here lies in clarifying the regulatory function of broadcasters' and policy-makers' images of the family, and in understanding how these regulatory discourses enter the domestic sphere. As Scannell (1988) and Frith (1983) have pointed out, the history of broadcasting is, to a significant degree, the history of the mobilization of a specific ideology of the family audience in the constitution of broadcasting practices.

This is, of course, not simply an image of the audience as composed of families, but, more specifically, and despite all the empirical evidence to the contrary, an image of the audience as composed of traditional nuclear-family units. It is this image of family life that remains central to broadcasting policy. Moreover, precisely in so far as broadcasting articulates the public and private spheres, it is at the same time a potentially 'dangerous' force, in need of regulation; it disrupts or transgresses the boundaries of the family household and its 'private universe'. In this connection, the centrality of the issue of censorship, in relation to broadcasting, was defined by the Annan Committee on Broadcasting (1977) in the following way, as consequent upon the fact that television is watched in the family:

> People watch and listen in the family circle . . . so that violations of the taboos of language and behaviour, which exist in every society, are witnessed by the whole family . . . in each others' presence. . . . These violations are more deeply embarrassing and upsetting than if they had occurred in the privacy of a book, or in a club, cinema or theatre.
>
> (Annan Committee 1977: 246)

Paterson (1987) argues that any contemporary analysis of the relationship between broadcasting and its audience needs to be set in the wider framework of the reordering of the private and public spheres in the period since World War Two. He notes specifically the increasing tendency for Welfare State professionals to concern themselves with family life – effectively a form of 'normalization' of state intervention into the private/domestic sphere.

As Paterson argues, in relation to broadcasting, the state's key concern, in the development of 'family viewing policy' was focused around the conjunction of the introduction of new technology in the home and a concern to ensure the provision of particular sorts of programmes at particular times which would not be unsuitable for children. These issues can usefully be seen within the context of Donzelot's (1979) analysis of the family. As Hodges and Hussain argue,

> Donzelot is . . . concerned with . . . policies relating to the maintenance of health, upbringing and education of children . . . it was the social concern with children which made family life and intra-familial relations a target of social intervention, and it was those interventions which ended up transforming the family.
>
> (Hodges and Hussain 1979: 89)

As Hodges and Hussain go on to argue, from Donzelot's perspective

> it is [the 'governmental' perception of] the systematic inability of [some] families . . . to perform the relevant functions [for the reproduction of the existing social order] which accounts for these interventions in the family.
>
> (ibid., 90)

Paterson (1987: 4) argues that, in the particular case of broadcasting, state concern in the recent period has focused precisely on the 'decline' of working-class families, the impact of divorce and the importance of child-care. Concern for the welfare of the child within the family (i.e. outside the direct control of the state) has acted as the central focus of concern.

As Paterson points out, the lobbyists of the National Viewers' and Listeners' Association (and other conservative pressure groups) focused their campaigns for greater regulation/classification of film/video material on the 'dangers' to children viewing in the home, the potentially unsuper-vised space. In particular, concern was generated about the absence of parental supervision of viewing among 'problem' families of various types. Thus, Paterson notes, it was argued: 'Parents of the working class were leaving their children alone with the video recorder while they went off to work, out at the pub or playing bingo, while the children of trendy middle class parents could watch anything, as controls on what they could see were minimal' (Paterson 1987: 6).

In this situation, Paterson argues, the growth of new technologies of communications, such as video, was seen to offer individual family members (children included – witness the scare about children viewing 'video nasties' at home) an increased freedom to schedule their own viewing, and in this 'derestricted' situation, the need for 'child protection' by the state was re-asserted and the problem of unsupervised home viewing was dealt with by imposing prohibitive restrictions on adults in order to protect the young.

The policing of domestic space is a relatively recent historical develop-ment. As Foucault points out, in his comments on the social organization of the working-class home,

> The house remains until the eighteenth century an undifferentiated space. . . . There are rooms – one sleeps, eats and receives visitors in them, it doesn't matter which. Then, gradually, space becomes specified and functional. . . . The working class family is to be fixed, by assigning it a living space with a room that functions as kitchen and dining room, a room for parents which is the space of procreation, and a room for children . . . one prescribes a morality for the family . . . the little tactics of the habitat,
>
> (quoted in Moores 1988: 26)

Broadcasting can be seen to play a crucial part in this process. Thus, as Moores notes, once established '. . . radio gradually came to address women as the 'centre' of its (daytime) audience. This singling out of the mother as the addressee of the radio broadcast can, of course, usefully be seen in the light of Donzelot's analysis of the move towards government through the family' (Moores 1988: 35). As Moores points out, the mother was addressed as the monitor of the domestic sphere and singled out as the main support in efforts to reform the family. She became the state's delegate, responsible for the moral and physical welfare of family members, the addressee of talks by doctors and educationalists on family and child health and welfare.

We see here, though, something more than a simple extension of a regulatory system (or proliferation of such systems, in Foucauldian terms): this was also a process involving a profound restructuring of social space, whereby broadcasters set about constructing the 'pleasures of the hearth' (see Frith 1983), and those pleasures were constructed around the central images of hearth and mother, interior space, family pleasure and domestic life.

Frith argues that the prime importance of radio broadcasting 'lay in its organisation of family life: what bound listeners together was where they listened' (Frith 1983: 110). He quotes a claim by the Marconi family (1923) that broadcasting had brought back the 'old fashioned family evening' and an advert by the Morley [sic] Radio company addressed 'To the Women of Britain', which notes approvingly that 'The Radio has undoubtedly helped you to keep your husbands and boys away from the club and kept them at home where they thus experience the benefits of your gentle charm and influence' (ibid., 110).

Similarly, Frith quotes the BBC's C. A. Lewis, as arguing in 1942:

> Broadcasting means the rediscovery of the home. In these days when house and hearth have been largely given up in favour of a multitude of other interests and activities outside, with the consequent disintegration of family ties and affections, it appears that this new persuasion may to some extent reinstate the parental roof in its old accustomed place, for all will admit that this is, or should be, one of the greatest and best influences in life.
>
> (quoted in Frith 1983: 110)

According to Frith, radio did more than make public events accessible, by bringing them into the home. More importantly, what was on offer was access to a community. As he puts it, what 'was (and is) enjoyable is the sense that you too can become significant by turning on the switch', and thus, while domestic listening might be 'a very peculiar form of public participation', it offers, above all else, that sense of participation in a national community (ibid.). But this is, of course, a domesticated national community, offering particular sorts of pleasures, and notably the plea- sures of familiarity, which, as Frith points out, came partly from the radio's organization of time, so that 'broadcasting provided a predictable rhythm to leisure, and partly from the use of repetition, the radio audience became the community of the catch phrase . . . expectations were always con- firmed and this, in the end, was the joy of listening' (ibid.; see also Rath 1986).

These joys, of course, have a profound temporal dimension. Time is not simply the medium in which societies exist; rather, specific modes of

organization of time can be seen to constitute a vital dimension of differentiation between one form of society and another.

The social construction of domestic time[1]

Scannell (1988) has argued that contemporary studies of communication
need to be reformulated in a number of respects. In the first instance, he
argues, the present overemphasis on television to the neglect of other
communications media is misplaced:

> The privileging of TV at the expense of radio in media studies has
> created a wholly artificial distinction, that has distracted attention from
> the ways in which both are routinely used by populations at different
> times in the day for different purposes . . . [i.e. through] the use of both
> media by people in the phased management of their daily routines . . .
> and the ways in which the schedules of both TV and radio . . . [are]
> unobtrusively arranged to fit in with, and structure, these routines.
>
> (Scannell 1988: 27)

Second, Scannell argues that, whether in relation to television or other
media, our analyses need to move away from their exclusive focus on
matters of representation, and to address the role of broadcasting in
relation to the arguably more fundamental matter of the social organization of time. Thus:

> Broadcasting, whose medium is time is profoundly implicated in the
> temporal arrangements of modern societies . . .
>   The fundamental work of national broadcasting systems goes beyond
> any ideological or representational role. Their primary task is the
> mediation of modernity, the normalisation of the public sphere and
> socialisation of the private sphere. This they accomplish by the continu-
> ous production and reproduction of public life and mundane life . . . not
> as separate spheres but as routinely implicated in each other . . .
> recognisable . . . and familiar. Modern mass democratic politics has its
> forum in the radically new kind of public sphere that broadcasting
> constitutes. At the same time radio and TV sustain, in individual,
> interpersonal and institutional contexts, the taken for granted accom-
> plishment of all the things we do every day in our lives.
>
> (ibid., 27–8)

Scannell follows Giddens (1979) in distinguishing between three inter-
secting planes of temporality ('clock time', 'life time' and 'calendrical
time') as different plans of temporality which permeate all aspects of
broadcast programmes and programming; and he argues for the particular
importance of broadcasting in synthesizing all the elements of a single

corporate national life, available to all, at the level of calendrical time. Thus, as he argues, the 'FA Cup Final, the Grand National, and the Last Night of the Proms, [which] . . . had previously been accessible as live and real events only to those immediately present, were transformed by the coming of radio, which made them available to anyone with a receiving set' (Scannell 1988: 5). Thus, as Scannell puts it, events such as the Grand National 'became and have remained, more than just sporting events. They have become . . . traditions, rituals, part of national life'. This form of broadcasting, Scannell argues, 'stitched together the private and public spheres . . . the events themselves . . . previously discrete [were] now woven together as idioms of a corporate national life [and] the BBC became perhaps the central agent of the national culture' (6). By playing this 'calendrical' role, broadcasting thus provides 'year in and year out . . . an orderly and regular progression of festivities, rituals and celebrations . . . that mark the unfolding of the broadcast year' (7).

Scannell is concerned with what he calls the 'unobtrusive ways in which broadcasting sustains the lives and routines, from one day to the next, year in, year out, of whole populations' (ibid.). This is, in effect, to pay attention to the role of the media in the very structuring of time. Scannell's focus, then, is on the role of national broadcasting media as central agents of national culture, in the organizing of the involvement of the population in the calendar of national life. Similarly, he analyses the way in which broadcast media constitute a cultural resource shared by millions and the way in which, for instance, long-running popular serials provide a 'past in common' to whole populations. Indeed, Lodziak (1987) has argued recently that it is at this level of analysis, the 'effect' of broadcasting on the organization of domestic time, rather than on any notion of the 'ideological effect' of television's content, that critical work in television studies should be focused. Lodziak's concern is the development of what he calls a 'political economy of time', which focuses on the media's role in articulating the temporal relations of the public and private spheres (Lodziak 1987: 135).

Cultural variations in time

Before I move on, to develop a line of analysis which is, in part, informed by Scannell's concerns (though rejecting his later attempt (Scannell 1989) entirely to displace questions of ideology by questions of ontology) a note of caution must be sounded. It would be quite possible to derive from Scannell's analysis a perspective which assumed that 'broadcasting times' simply imposed themselves on their audiences. Matters are, of course, not quite so simple as that. It is also a question of how different pre-existing cultural formulations of temporality determine how audiences relate to broadcast schedules, whether at the macro-level of variations in national or

regional cultures or at the micro-level of differences in family cultures
(differences themselves arising in part from divisions of class etc.). This is
simply to note, then, that these matters are culturally variable at both
macro- and micro-levels of analysis. In the former respect, the cross-
cultural comparisons in Lull's (1988) study are extremely helpful. Lull
notes that cultures have their own 'sense of time', which influences television viewing. Thus, he notes that the 'systematic, predictable pattern of
the Danish orientation towards time, including the schedule and viewing of
TV shows, is an extension of [a] very orderly culture' (Lull 1988: 10), and
contrasts this with the situation in Pakistan, where 'TV programmes often
appear . . . at times that differ from the published schedule, or fail to
appear at all [while] audiences are not surprised or angered by these
irregularities' (11).

However, as Lull, observes, while pre-existing cultural orientations
towards time may have an independent effect, in the long run television
itself also influences perceptions and uses of time. Thus, as he notes:
'mealtimes, bedtimes, sharetime, periods for doing homework . . . and
patterns of verbal interaction are influenced by the scheduling of TV
shows' (11). In particular, he reports Behl's (1988) research in India as
showing that television is 'transforming the lives of some rural Indian
families, by changing their routines away from regulation by nature to
regulation by the clock and by TV. . . . Sunday has become a "TV
Holiday" and "TV time" in the evening has replaced time that was previously used for transacting business . . . Parts of the day become redefined and structured around the scheduling of TV shows' (ibid., 244).

To move to the micro-level of analysis, Bryce's (1987) study of cultural
variations in 'family time and television use' is instructive. Bryce argues:
'The relationship between the family's use of time and TV raises many
questions which have not yet been addressed. The sequencing of viewing,
its place in the mesh of family activities, reflects a choice . . . a negotiation
process about which very little is known' (Bryce 1987: 123).

The question to be addressed, as far as Bryce is concerned, is that of the
temporal placement of television within the frame of family life. Bryce
argues that family uses of television need to be understood within the
context of family orientations towards time. This is because, according to
her argument, we need to see that family television-viewing behaviour is an
embedded reflection of the family's organization and orientation to its
social milieu. At its simplest, as Anderson suggests in his commentary
(1987) on Bryce's research, we need to see how 'families have negotiated
different concepts of time and how TV viewing has become incorporated
within those time concepts' (J. Anderson 1987: 167). Moreover, Bryce
argues that the study of family television viewing must begin with an
investigation of the overall structuring of time by families in relation to
what Kantor and Lehr (1975; quoted in Bryce 1987: 122) have described as

the family's mode of synchronization of their activities, their procedures for setting priorities, and their organization of time to meet family goals.

Bryce notes that, in the past, various diary studies have approached the question of differential time-use in families, but their limitation, as far as she is concerned, is their lack of attention to the process of time-allocation itself as opposed to its result. Thus, she argues that

> such studies have traditionally resulted in summaries of time allocation to various tasks, with little attention directed to the dynamic process through which families construct their individual days. . . . Time use studies . . . have documented . . . the amount of time the TV set is operated in homes, but very little about the nature of viewing or how it comes to occur.
>
> (Bryce 1987: 123)

In her own research Bryce is principally concerned to differentiate between her various families' behaviour by drawing on T. Hall's (1976) contrast between a monochronic orientation to time (linear and sequential organization of activity; heavy orientation to planning and scheduling; emphasis on clocks and calendars; closure-orientated emphasis on promptness) and a polychronic orientation (multiple concurrent activities; low planning/scheduling; little reference to clocks or calendars; process-orientated difficulty in meeting pre-set schedules). Bryce's point is that a family displaying one or other of these fundamentally different orientations towards time will consequently, and correspondingly, display a different mode of viewing behaviour in relation to television.

Thus, Bryce argues, families with a monochronic orientation to time will tend to display the following characteristics with regard to television:

(a) high planning and scheduling of television viewing;
(b) television watched between other activities;
(c) television viewing as singular activity;
(d) close visual attention.

Conversely, families with a polychronic orientation to time will display:

(a) little or no planning or scheduling of television viewing;
(b) television used as a 'clock' for other activities;
(c) television viewing as one of several concurrent activities;
(d) intermittent or sporadic attention to television.

Beyond doubt, Bryce here identifies a very important dimension of the differential orientation to time as a determinant of differential relations to television. However, the exact status of this contrastive dimension might be worth further scrutiny. In Bryce's account this difference is presented as an attribute of different families' rule-systems and internal cultures.

However, it should be noted that this same distinction can be interpreted in a different light, in which the monochronic/polychronic contrast can be seen as a matter of gender as much as a matter of family culture. Modleski (1984) attempts to account for the popularity of the soap-opera genre (featuring multiple narrative etc.) among housewives as a matter of its 'fit' with the polychronic rhythm of domestic labour (continuous different activities, interruptability, etc.). Similarly, in my own previous research (Morley 1986) the monochronic viewing mode seemed to be a characteristic of 'masculine' styles of viewing (planned viewing, concentrated attention, single activity) and the polychronic viewing mode to be the corresponding 'feminine' mode (unplanned viewing, concurrent activities, sporadic attention).

Bryce argues that, in a family with a monochronic orientation towards time, use of television is scheduled as a specific 'filler' activity at particular points within a framework set by other family activities. Conversely, in a family with a polychronic time orientation, 'rather than activities forming the frame and the TV the filler, TV [is] itself the frame [the television being on continually – D.M.] and other activities [are] scheduled around it' (Bryce 1987: 126). Thus, in one such family, baths were scheduled for 'the end of this show'; children's bedtime was defined as being at 'the end of *Little House on the Prairie*' (ibid., 126). Indeed, in this family, media schedules had taken over from clock-time as the standard of time-measurement against which other activities were defined. Thus, Bryce quoted the mother in this family as remonstrating with her children when trying to hurry them off to school by saying: 'You know that the second commercial means it's time to go' (ibid.).

Bryce observes that in the 'monochronic' family viewing was primarily an exclusive activity, involving relatively high levels of attention, that attempts to engage in any other activity while viewing were discouraged (127) and that talk was only permissible on subjects related to the programme being viewed. Conversely, in the 'polychronic' family 'doing something else while watching was the norm . . . [and] watching TV was often a part of the contextual background of family life, rather than an activity in and of itself (127), and attention levels were lower.

Part of the explanation here, according to Bryce, has to be located in the relative value given to achievement and effective time-use in different families. Thus, she notes that in the 'monochronic' family 'parents explicitly told their children that they should do one thing at a time and finish it before moving on to another; and the father reported concern that his children were 'wasting too much time' (ibid., 130–1).

Moreover, Bryce also notes the way in which the monochronic approach is supported/rewarded by the surrounding culture. Thus, the monochronic family studied 'succeed' more in fitting in with and participating effectively in wider social and community timetables of activity, whereas the members of the 'polychronic' family are 'often late for school, work and prearranged meetings' (ibid., 132). Similarly, Bryce reports some evidence that children from homes with a monochronic orientation to time were judged to cope more successfully in their entry to pre-school nursery, being evaluated by their teachers as more likely to succeed, as a result of the closer 'fit' between the demands of the school and the time orientation they had developed in their home life.

Clearly, Bryce's distinction between families with monochronic or with polychronic relations to time and television in some ways parallels Bernstein's (1971) distinction between families inculcating elaborated or restricted linguistic codes in their children, through their socialization practices. Certainly there is a paralleling of social consequences (in relation to schooling, as noted above, for example). It is not my intention to develop this analysis further here. Rather, my point in spending so much time in detailing Bryce's analysis is to offer a reminder of the need to maintain a sensitivity to these micro-levels of division and differentiation while we attend to the macro-questions of the media's own role in the social structuring of time. The fundamental issues at stake here can perhaps best be illuminated by reference to some historical perspectives on this question.

The broadcasting of time and the construction of imagined communities

Thompson (1967) has analysed the importance of the standardization of time as part of the process of synchronization of labour activity in the development of capitalism. In this connection, Thompson poignantly refers to the symbolism of time, and to the political struggles conducted around the definition and control of time in the labour process, when he quotes from the 'Law Book of the Crowley Iron Works' of 1700: 'it is therefore ordered that no person upon the account doth reckon by any other clock, bell, watch or dyall but the Monitor's which clock is never to be altered but by the clock-keeper' (quoted in Thompson 1967: 82 n. 84).

Giddens follows Mumford in arguing that 'the clock rather than the steam engine should be regarded as the prototype of the era of mechanical production' (Giddens 1979: 210). Questions of time inevitably also involve questions of power, questions of who has the power to define time, questions of the imposition of a standard or national time and of the relationship between time and modes of communication. Thus, as King argues, in his analysis of nineteenth-century British society 'with the diffusion of clocks and watches, urbanisation and the development of railways, there emerged a totally new orientation to and organisation of time, with "local time" being suppressed in favour of "London time"' (King 1980b: 198).

Time is intrinsically connected to communications (in both its physical and its symbolic sense). In a similar vein to King's analysis, Carey (1989) charts the emergence of standard national time in the US (adopted officially on 18 November 1883, according to Carey) as an effect of the need to synchronize the emerging national railway network. Rawlence (1985) analyses the significance of the institution of Greenwich Mean Time (and the development of accurate chronometers to maintain it) on the vessels of the British navy as a key factor in the organization of empire. Similarly, Cipolla (1978) demonstrates the significance of the clock as an organizing feature of the European colonization of Asia.

It is not simply that the analysis of communication needs to be situated in the context of an understanding of the spatio-temporal organization of society. It is also that modes of communication, both physical (e.g. the coming of the railways – see above) and symbolic (e.g. the coming of broadcasting), themselves transform these modes of social organization. In this context, it is vital to note the role of communications media, precisely as the medium of the extension of this new segmentation of time into the domestic sphere. This is in close parallel with the arguments of Scannell (1988) and Lodziak (1987) that the concern within media studies with questions of broadcasting's representational or ideological role should be supplemented by a parallel concern with broadcasting's role in the social organization of time.

As Seiter *et al.* (1989a) argue, the significance of Thompson's (1967) analysis lies in his demonstration that the 'rationalization' of time, which he traces in the sphere of industrial work, has also been extended to the domestic, the result being an increasing subjugation of the domestic sphere of reproduction to the segmented patterns of industrial production.

In studying broadcasting's contribution to what Lodziak (ibid.) calls the 'temporal organisation of relaxation', we must, of course, note that the relevant causal relations can run in (at least) two directions. Thus, we need to be attentive on the one hand to the ways in which, at both micro- and macro-levels, the organization of broadcasting is influenced by pre-existing cultural orientations to time, within the society at large, or within a particular sub-culture or family and, on the other hand, to the effect of broadcast schedules themselves on the organization of time. Broadcasting and other technologies of communication must be seen both as entering into already constructed, historically specific divisions of space and time, and also as transforming those pre-existing divisions.

Moores's historical analysis of the development of radio, referred to earlier, usefully points to the way in which broadcasting was responsible for bringing precise measurement of time into the home, via what he calls the 'domestication of standard national time' (Moores 1988: 67). Here we see the role of broadcasting in spanning the private and public spheres at its most elementary (and perhaps most ontologically significant?) level, where 'national' time can be relayed direct into the private sphere, thus providing all those who listen with the temporal authentication of their existence as members of a synchronized 'time-zone' or national community. Filson Young comments on the significance of the 'broadcasting of time' as both one of the 'most commonplace and regular features of the daily programme' but also 'one of the strangest of the new things' that broadcasting invented (quoted in Moores 1988: 38).

If one thinks for a moment of the insistence of the time-checks on many radio stations (in between the statutory announcement of the quarter- and half-hours) and of the ritual of the 'news on the hour' in the context of many radio listeners' habit of having the radio on all day, we begin to see that for many listeners one of the principal ways in which radio functions is as the national (and/or local) 'speaking' clock, which synchronizes their private activities with those of larger (local, national and international) communities. In a similar vein, Hartley has argued that 'television . . . is one of the prime sites upon which a given nation is constructed for its members' (Hartley 1987: 124). Hartley draws on Benedict Anderson's (1983) concept of the nation as an 'imagined community', the construct of particular discourses, and on Ellis's observation that broadcast television can be likened to 'the private life of the nation-state. . . . Incomprehensible for anyone who is outside its scope' (Ellis 1982: 5). In an age of international co-productions and satellite broadcasting, Ellis may perhaps be stretching the point, but if we take his comments alongside Scannell's argument about broadcasting's role in providing 'a past in common' to the members of its audience, then an interesting perspective begins to take shape concerning broadcasting's role in constructing the conditions of viable membership of the 'national community'.

Martin-Barbero (1988) points to the key role of the communications media in 'converting the masses into a people and the people into a nation'. He notes that in many Latin American countries it was above all the development of national broadcasting systems that provided the people of different regions and provinces with a first daily experience of the nation. As he argues, the construction and emergence of national identities cannot properly be understood without reference to the role of communications technologies. These technologies allowed people 'a space of identification': not just an evocation of a common memory, but rather 'the experience of encounter and of solidarity'. Thus, the nation is to be understood not simply as an abstraction, but as a lived experience made possible by broadcasting technologies, whose achievement was the 'transmutation of the political idea of the nation into lived experience, into sentiment and into the quotidian' (Martin-Barbero 1988: 455–6).

More prosaically, as Benedict Anderson puts it, 'An American will never meet, or even know the names of more than a handful of his fellow Americans. He has no idea of what they are up to at any one time. But he has complete confidence in their steady, anonymous, simultaneous activity' (B. Anderson 1983: 16).

Wherein lies this 'simultaneity'? Among other sources we can perhaps look to the regulation of simultaneous experience through television broadcast schedules. Where does this 'confidence' come from? In a parallel sense, Benedict Anderson (1983) points to the newspaper as a mechanism for providing imaginary links between the members of a nation. As Hartley puts it, newspapers are 'at one and the same time, the ultimate fiction, since they construct the imagined community, and the basis of a mass ritual or ceremony that millions engage in every day' (Hartley 1987: 123–4) Rath argues that it is no longer a case simply of the national community being constructed via broadcast television: we must also attend to the growing phenomenon of trans-border broadcasting, where 'frontiers of a national, regional or cultural kind no longer count; what counts much more is the boundary of the territory of transmission [where the] space of transmission cuts across . . . the geographies of power, of social life and of knowledge, which define the space of nationality of culture' (Rath 1986: 202–3).

Bausinger offers an interesting gloss on the role of the newspaper as a linking mechanism between the rituals of the domestic, the organization of the schedule of everyday life and the construction of the 'imagined community' of the nation. He comments on the nature of the 'disruption' caused when a morning edition of a newspaper fails to appear. His point concerns that which is missed. As he puts it, 'Is it a question . . . of the missing content of the paper? Or isn't it rather that one misses the newspaper "itself"? Because the newspaper is part of it (a constitutive part of the ritual of breakfast for many people), reading it proves that the breakfast time world is still in order' (Bausinger 1984: 334). And, of course, vice-versa. A similar point – and, indeed, a stronger one, given the necessary simultaneity of broadcast television-viewing – could be made in relation to the watching of evening news broadcasts for many viewers, where the fact of watching and engaging in a joint ritual with millions of others can be argued to be at least as important as any informational content gained from the broadcast (cf. Nordenstreng, cited above, pp. 79 and 252).

The further point, inevitably, concerns the significance of these arguments in the context of current and prospective changes in the structure of broadcasting. The proliferation of broadcast channels, cable and satellite is likely to move us towards a more fragmented social world than that of traditional national broadcast television. These new forms of communication may in fact play a significant part in deconstructing national cultures, and the 'rescheduling' potentialities of video and other new communications technologies may disrupt our assumptions of any 'necessary simultaneity' of broadcast experience. In a world of niche marketing and narrowcasting, many of us will have less and and less broadcast experience in common with anyone else. Our communities may, to that extent, be imagined along more fragmented lines.

However, if we follow Williams (1976) in believing that 'community' and 'communication' are indissolubly linked concepts, we can see the still resonant attraction of the invitation to switch on and 'join in' that broadcasting continues to offer us.

Silverstone (1988) has argued that our watching of television involves us in a rite of passage, away from and back to the mundane, in an often taken-for-granted, but none the less significant, immersion in the 'other-worldliness' of the screen:

> Our nightly news-watching is a ritual, both in its mechanical repetitiveness and . . . more importantly, in its presentation of the familiar and the strange, the reassuring and the threatening. In Britain, no major news bulletin will either begin without a transcendent title sequence [London at the centre of the planet Earth; Big Ben at the centre of the metropolis – D.M.] nor end without a 'sweetener' – a 'human interest story' to bring viewers decently back to the everyday. Indeed, the final shot is almost always of the . . . newsreaders, tidying their papers and soundlessly chatting to each other, thereby announcing the return to normality.
>
> (Silverstone 1988: 26)

Having begun with one viewer's account of her reasons for not watching national news programmes, I close with another's account of the importance of these broadcasts in structuring her household's domestic routine:

> When I'm writing I knock off to cook a very easy lunch, and then work until about five. Then Leslie knocks off, too, and always at six o'clock we sit down with a drink of gin and cinzano and watch the news with dear Sue Lawley and lovely Nicholas Witchell. We always have a date with them and they don't know us from Adam. She makes you feel so alright about everything, whatever the news is.
>
> ('A life in the day of Celia Fremlin', *Sunday Times*, 3 July 1988)

Chapter 13

Where the global meets the local: notes from the sitting-room

'For most people there are only two places in the world – where they live and their TV set.'

(DeLillo 1985: 66)

Soja (1989) argues that up till now time and history have occupied a privileged position in critical theory while, as Foucault puts it, 'Space was treated as the dead, the fixed, the undialectical, the immobile. Time, on the contrary, was richness, fecundity, life, dialectic' (quoted in Soja 1989: 4). Thus capitalism itself has been treated as a historical, but only incidentally geographical, process, the geography of which, when seen at all, has been recognized only as an external constraint or as an almost incidental outcome. Geography, for Marx himself, was little more than an 'unnecessary complication'. At the same time, as Soja notes, modern geography itself was 'reduced primarily to the accumulation, classification and theoretically innocent representation of factual material, describing the "areal differentiation" of the earth's surface – to the study of outcomes, the end products of dynamic processes best understood by others' (Soja 1989: 36–7).

Soja's own project involves the recognition of the fundamental distinction between space *per se* – space as a given, natural backdrop to human affairs – and the created space of social organization and production – the 'second nature' which is the proper object of a materialist interpretation of spatiality.

As Harvey observes,

Marx . . . Weber and Durkheim all . . . prioritise time and history over space and geography and, where they treat the latter at all, tend to view them unproblematically, as the stable context or site for historical action . . . The way in which spatial relations and geographical configurations are produced in the first place passes . . . unremarked, ignored.

(Harvey 1985: 141–2)

Moreover, as he also argues,

It is invidious to regard places, communities, cities, regions, or even nations as 'things in themselves' at a time when the global flexibility of capitalism is greater than ever. . . . Yet a global strategy of resistance and transformation has to begin with the realities of place and community.

(quoted in Robins 1989: 145)

Soja's declared aim is to spatialize the (conventional) historical narrative, to reveal 'how relations of power and discipline are inscribed into the apparently innocent spaciality of social life', and thus to transcend the 'fixed dead . . . Cartesian cartography of spatial science' (Soja 1989: 6–7) which sees only 'natural forms', susceptible to little beyond measurement and phenomenal description.

Foucault observes that 'the great obsession of the 19th Century was, as we know, history . . . [but] the present epoch will perhaps be above all the epoch of space' (Foucault 1986: 22). Jameson (1984) argues for the spatial specificity of the cultural logic of (postmodern) 'Late Capitalism'. As Soja notes, some years ago, John Berger argued: 'Prophesy now involves a geographical rather than historical projection; it is space, not time, that hides consequences from us' (quoted in Soja 1989: 22). It is in this context that we should heed Foucault's injunction 'A whole history remains to be written of *spaces* – which would at the same time be the history of *powers* . . . from the great strategies of geopolitics to the little tactics of the habitat (Foucault 1980b: 149).

I have, with Kevin Robins, elsewhere (see Morley and Robins 1989, 1990 and 1992) begun an exploration of the issues at stake once we try to think of communications processes within the terms of a postmodern geography, and once we begin to consider the role of communications in the ongoing construction and reconstruction of social spaces and social relations. At a meta-level Robins (1989) has argued that, in the present period, we are involved in fundamental processes of political and economic restructuring and transformation which presage (if not already reflecting) a shift beyond the Fordist system of accumulation and social regulation. Robins's central point is that, at the heart of these historical developments, is a process of radical spatial restructuring and reconfiguration which is 'at once a transformation of the spatial matrix of accumulation and of the subjective experience of, and orientation to, space and spatiality. Its analysis . . . demands a social theory that is informed by the geographical imagination' (Robins 1989: 145).

The point, for my present purposes, concerns the fact that the image industries, as Robins notes, are implicated in these socio-spatial processes in significant and distinctive ways. Thus, as Robins argues, 'issues around the politics of communication converge with the politics of space and place: questions of communication are also about the nature and scope of community' (ibid., 146). The further point, for the argument of this chapter, is

that such theoretical work as has begun to take on board these questions –
for instance, in the context of debates around satellite television and
cultural identity, has done so at a very abstracted level, principally in the
context of international geo-politics. However, the force of Foucault's
remarks quoted earlier is, of course, to remind us that the 'geographical
imagination', and its refocusing of the relation of communications and
geography, needs to be applied, as he puts it, to the 'little tactics of the
habitat' every bit as much as to the 'great strategies of geopolitics'. If one
of the central functions of communications systems is to articulate different
spaces (the public and the private, the national and the international) and,
necessarily, in so doing, to transgress boundaries (whether the boundary
around the domestic household, or that around the nation), then our
analytical framework must be capable of being applied at both the micro-
and the macro-level.

It is in this context that this chapter addresses the question of the place of
ethnographic studies of media consumption in the analysis of the simultaneous dynamic of globalization and localization in contemporary culture.
The key issue is that of the status of small-scale studies of micro-
process(es) in the analysis of these macro-issues. The argument of the
chapter is that it is precisely through such detailed 'domestic' or 'local'
studies, focused, in the first instance, on the 'politics of the sitting-room',
that we will most effectively grasp the significance of the processes of
globalization and localization (or homogenization and fragmentation)
which have been widely identified as central to contemporary (or even
'postmodern') culture.[1]

Clearly, any analysis which ultimately offers us *only* an understanding of
the micro-process of consumption in this or that domestic context, without
reference to the broader cultural (political and ideological) questions at
stake, is going to be, ultimately, of only limited value. That way lies the 'So
what?' problem – if we just pile up an endless set of descriptions of the
processes of consumption, however fine-grained our analyses. Conversely,
any analysis of these macro-processes which is not grounded in an adequate understanding of the complexities of the process of (principally
domestic) consumption runs the equal and opposite risk of being so over-
schematic as to hide all the differences that matter. Put another way, it is a
question of steering between the dangers of an improper romanticism of
'consumer freedoms', on the one hand, and a paranoiac fantasy of 'global
control' on the other. It is, as Murdock (1989b) argues, a question of
finding ways of combining interpretative studies of people's 'lifeworlds'
with attempts to map the contours of the wider formations that envelop
and organize them.

I shall attempt to address these issues, in the first instance by reviewing
some recent debates about the consumption of television and the 'activity'
of the television audience.

Romantic readings?

If for much of the 1970s the audience was largely ignored by many media theorists in favour of the analysis of textual and economic structures which were presumed to impose their effects on the audience, the 1980s, conversely, saw a sudden flourishing of 'audience' (or 'reception') studies. However, the more recent period has also seen a small but significant flurry of articles and papers questioning whether all (or, indeed, any) of this 'audience research' is getting us anywhere.[2]

On the one hand, there are the methodological difficulties pointed to by Feuer (1986), Hartley (1987) and Clifford and Marcus (1986), all of which raise doubts about the validity and viability of recent empirical audience research. A whole series of scholars has now argued that contemporary audience researchers, in their desire to avoid a 'hypodermic' effects model, have ended up uncritically celebrating the supposed 'creativity' of the audience and, in effect, endorsing the worst commercial products, on the grounds that if they are popular, then they are, *ipso facto*, good (cf. Ericson 1989; Schudson 1987; Gripsrud 1989; Brunsdon 1989). I shall not attempt to deal here with all of those critiques but will focus on those offered by Murdock (1989b), Morris (1988) and Willemen (1990). Murdock's argument is that

> In their eagerness to reassert the skillfulness of audiences . . . most proponents . . . of the 'new ethnography' have tended to skate round questions of power. As a result, the issue of the audience's relation to control within the media system is conspicuous by its absence . . . as are wider questions about the way these relations are structured in turn by the unequal distribution of material and symbolic resources.
>
> (Murdock 1989b: 228–9)

In a somewhat similar vein, Morris (1988) acidly sums up what she takes to be the cosy (old-fashioned) 'cultural studies' orthodoxy in relation to the audience and the question of 'reading'. As she notes, many versions of this 'theory' have now been offered – from Fiske's (1987a) notion of a 'reader's liberation movement', through Nava's (1987) analyses of the 'contradictions of consumerism', to Chambers's (1986) accounts of counterhegemonic forces in popular culture, all extolling the creative energies of the much-maligned consumers of popular culture. As far as Morris is concerned, the 'Ur-thesis' of this kind of cultural studies runs perilously close to the banal observation that, as she puts it, 'people in modern mechanised societies are complex and contradictory; mass cultural texts are complex and contradictory; therefore people using them produce complex and contradictory culture' (Morris 1988: 24–5).

I would agree with Morris that some of this work is indeed problematic, but for a rather different reason from that which she adduces. For me, it is the lack of a sufficiently sociological dimension to Fiske's or Chambers's work that is the problem. Certainly, if, as Morris notes, our analyses finally say only that 'it's always complex and contradictory', then that is a banal observation. The point, however, is, in my view, an *empirical* one: the question is one of understanding (and here I continue to believe that Bourdieu has much to offer in this respect) just *how* 'complex' or 'contradictory' it is, for *which* types of consumers, in *which* social positions, in relation to *which* types of texts or objects. The 'distinctions' are all, in this respect, and if Fiske and Chambers can be faulted for failing to help us see them, Morris seems not even to realize that they are what we need to look for. Everything might simply be 'complex and contradictory' at one level of abstraction – but the banality of that observation is, to my mind, ultimately a function of the level of (over-)abstraction of Morris's argument, and of the lack in her own analysis, of an explicitly sociological perspective. In this connection, Nice's comments on the significance of Bourdieu's work in the sociology of culture remain relevant. As Nice puts it,

> Those who seek to expel sociology . . . in favour of a strictly internal analysis of what happens on the screen, or how the viewing subject is articulated, can only do so on the basis of an implicit sociology which, in so far as it ignores the social relations of the differential distribution of cultural competences and values, is an erroneous sociology, the more insidious for being unrecognised.
>
> (Nice 1978: 24)

Willemen has argued that many 'left cultural commentators' have made the 'tragic mistake' of 'conniving' with the capitalist logic of 'multinational commodification' of culture. Willemen's specific point is that my own *Family Television* book, for instance, is vitiated by the 'lack of attention to the capitalist logic overdetermining cultural production' (Willemen 1990: 109) in so far as, he claims, I 'construe the site of plurivocality, the space for resistance, as a space only invested by the power relations that obtain *within* family or peer group situations' (my emphasis), ignoring the powerful pre-structuring agency of capitalist cultural production in setting all the significant boundaries to what people can do within these structures. Willemen argues that this work focuses wrongly on 'the way the TV as a piece of sound-and-image emitting furniture is used in interpersonal relations, that is, the immediate commodity aspect of the use of TV' (ibid., 109) to the detriment of these broader questions. Thus, according to Willemen, the consequence is an analysis of 'the uses of TV-as-furniture' which is improperly substituted for an analysis of 'the things people can, and more importantly, cannot do with TV discourses', where the analysis of all the important issues of cultural power is consequently sidestepped (ibid.).

For my part, I think that the notes of caution sounded by Murdock are entirely appropriate. In the research which Silverstone, Hirsch and I have conducted on the 'Household Uses of Information and Communication Technology, for example, we have been concerned not simply with the 'creative' abilities of consumers, but also with how such 'abilities' are manifested in a situation in which (a) the symbolic and material resources required for various forms of cultural consumption are themselves unequally distributed; and (b) such consumption practices are working in, through (and occasionally against) the powerful discourses of design, marketing, advertising and education, which have constructed the dominant definitions of these technologies and their 'appropriate' uses. This, as I understand it, is the point of de Certeau's distinction between the 'strategies' of the powerful and the 'tactics' of the weak. The weak are not totally powerless, but, given their lack of control over institutions and resources, they have to operate in the margins (temporal and spatial) left (defined) by those who do control such institutional resources.

Micro- and macro-issues

Willemen's critique is more problematic. This arises from a misperception on his part – it is clearly not the case that the only power relations relevant to the process of consumption are those that obtain *'within* family or peer group situations'. In the case of the *Family Television* study (Morley 1986), for example, and its focus on gender relations, these are not simply an 'internal' factor of family life. Rather, the argument is that the gender roles adopted within the family, which then function as the immediate determinants of viewing practices, are themselves structured by the dominant public discourses of gender within the particular culture being researched (cf. Althusser 1972, on 'overdetermination').

Willemen's argument in fact operates within a structuralist (and indeed, over-determinist) perspective which entirely reduces the micro to an effect of the macro (and reduces people to the function of 'tragers' of their structural positions), rather than seeing structures as only themselves reproducible through agency (cf. Giddens 1979, on 'structuration'). As for the charge that *Family Television* (and, by implication, the later HICT study) is *only* concerned with the 'uses of TV-as-furniture' in interpersonal relations, Willemen would be quite right to be concerned if that were the exclusive focus of the research. However, the whole point of the research is that it is attempting to integrate this level of analysis (and its consequent focus on the complexities of the immediate processes of domestic consumption), with the analysis of the 'broader questions' to which Willemen refers. The argument is rather that these 'broader questions' have to be approached via this 'necessary detour' into the detail of domestic consumption, if we are in fact to understand their pertinence.

To do otherwise is finally to relegate the domestic context of television consumption, once more, to the status of mere backdrop – to be 'recognized' and then immediately forgotten, as if this context had no effectivity of its own. As Slack puts it, 'more often than not "context" is invoked as a sort of magical term, as if by claiming to take context into consideration, one could banish the problems of its specificity' (Slack 1989: 329). The question is precisely one of addressing contextual specificity in relation to broader structural factors. In fact, one might reasonably argue (*pace* Willemen) that, at least in contemporary Western Europe, attention to the 'commoditization' (cf. Appadurai 1986) of television and to its transformation, as it is further incorporated into this particular 'commodified' regime of value, would in fact be very timely, in relation to the pressing political questions towards which Willemen gestures.

The objective, from this point of view, is not to substitute the one (micro-)level of analysis for the other (macro-)level, but, rather, to integrate the analysis of the 'broader questions' of ideology, power and politics (what Hall (1988a) has described as the 'vertical' dimension of communications) with the analysis of the consumption, uses and functions of television in everyday life (the 'horizontal' dimension of communications, in Hall's terms). It is not a question, finally, of understanding simply television's ideological (or representational) role, or simply its ritual (or socially organizing) function, or the process of its domestic (and more broadly social) consumption. It is a question of how to understand all these issues (or dimensions) in relation to each other.

From this perspective, the challenge lies precisely in the attempt to construct a model of television consumption which is sensitive to both the 'vertical' dimension of power and ideology and the 'horizontal' dimension of television's insertion in, and articulation with, the context and practices of everyday life. Silverstone and I have argued elsewhere (Morley and Silverstone 1990) that we need to develop a 'double focus' on television viewing, so that, for instance, we can understand viewing as, *simultaneously*, a ritual whose function is to structure domestic life and provide a symbolic mode of participation in the national community *and* an active mode of consumption and production, *and* as a process operating within the realm of ideology. To debate whether we should regard television viewing as either one or the other is to miss the point. Thus, for example, news watching is not to be understood as *either* 'mere ritual' (cf. Nordenstreng 1972) *or* a process of transmission of ideological (or cultural) categories (cf. Morley 1980), but precisely as operating along both dimensions at once. Indeed the notion of 'mere ritual' is itself problematic, for, as Silverstone (1981) and others have argued, an understanding of the rituals of television is an essential component of any understanding of its place in everyday life and, as such, a crucial aspect of ideology. Our objective, therefore, ought to be the production of analyses of the specific relationships of particular audiences to particular types of media content which are located within the broader framework of an analysis of media consumption and domestic ritual. These analyses, of course, must be sensitive to empirical variation.

Communications technologies: scenarios of the future

In this section of the chapter, I want to try to make a number of arguments concerning (a) the question of the 'effects' of communications technologies; (b) the ways in which these technologies have been claimed to be responsible for *both* the 'fragmentation' and the 'homogenization' of contemporary culture; and (c) how abstract (and technologically determinist) futuristic scenarios of this kind need to be informed by the analysis of the economic, social and cultural determinations of technology's impact, 'take-up' and use.

Erni argues bluntly that 'in the context of the enormous changes in television technology' (such as the increasing use of video technology and the development of 'television–computer–telephone hybrids') audience research work focused on broadcast television 'becomes somewhat obsolete' (Erni 1989: 39). In a not dissimilar vein, Lindlof and Meyer (1987) argue that the 'interactive' capacities of recent technological developments fundamentally transform the position of the consumer. As they put it,

> with increasing adoption of technological add-ons for the basic media delivery systems, the messages can be edited, deleted, rescheduled or skipped past with complete disregard for their original form. The received notion of the mass communications audience has simply little relevance for the reality of mediated communication.
>
> (Lindlof and Meyer 1987: 2)

The technological advances are often seen to have transformative (if not utopian) consequences for the television audience. Thus, in the Italian context, RAI's publicity claims:

> The new telematic services, video recorders and video discs . . . will make a more personal use of the medium possible. The user will be able to decide what to watch when he [*sic*] wants. It will be possible, then, to move beyond that fixed mass audience which has been characteristic of TV's history: everybody will be able to do his [*sic*] own programming.
>
> (quoted in Connell and Curti 1985: 99)

The problem, of course, is that many of these arguments run the danger of abstracting these technologies' intrinsic 'capacities' from the social contexts of their actual use. In understanding such technological developments, we could usefully follow Bausinger in his concern with the question of how these technologies are integrated into the structure and routines of domestic life – into what he calls 'the specific semantics of the everyday'. His basic thesis is that technologies are increasingly 'absorbed' into the everyday ('everyone owns a number of machines, and has directly to handle technical products'), so that everyday routines themselves are constructed around technologies which then become effectively 'invisible' in their domestication. The end result, he argues, is the 'inconspicuous omnipresence of the technical' (Bausinger 1984: 346). The key point is to understand the processes through which communications and information technologies are 'domesticated' to the point where they become inconspicuous, if not 'invisible' within the home. The further point is then to focus on the culturally constructed meanings of these technologies, as they are 'produced' through located practices of consumption. I will return to these points later in the chapter. First, however, I want to point to the parallel between these arguments about the individualizing effects of these new communications technologies and those 'postmodern' scenarios which simultaneously point to their homogenizing effects.

Let us begin with the well-known postmodern theorist Marshall McLuhan, who, of course, argued that the effect of television and computer technology was to erase time–space differences and to herald a new audio-visual age of global *Gemeinschaft*. Thus, McLuhan and Fiore (1967) argued:

> Electric circuitry has overthrown the regime of 'time' and 'space' and pours upon us incessantly and continually the concerns of all other men . . . Ours is a brand new world of 'allatonceness'. 'Time' has ceased, 'space' has vanished. We now live in a global village.
>
> (quoted in Ferguson 1989: 163).

In recent years, writers such as Carey (1989), drawing on, among other sources, the work of Innis (1951), have rightly drawn our attention to the historical role of communications systems, both physical and symbolic (cf. also de la Haye 1979) in transforming our senses of space and time. Thus, at one point, for example, Carey speaks of the

> United States [as] the product of literacy, cheap paper, rapid and inexpensive transportation and the mechanical reproduction of words – the capacity, in short, to transport not only people but a complex culture and civilisation from one place to another . . . between places that were radically dissimilar in geography . . . and . . . climate . . . the eclipsing of time and space.
>
> (Carey 1989: 2–3)

Carey is concerned with, among other things, the role of communications in the construction of empire and the administration of power. Thus, Carey notes, the economic influence not only of the coming of the railways but, more dramatically perhaps, of the coming of the telegraph, which 'permitted for the first time, the effective separation of communication from transportation . . . allowing messages to be separated from the physical movement of objects' (ibid., 203), thus freeing communication from the constraints of geography, and to that extent 'making geography irrelevant' (217) and 'diminishing space as a differentiating criterion in human affairs' (222).

In order to make my task easier here, rather than attempting to deal with Carey's carefully nuanced historical work on the mutual influence of communications technologies and social development, I shall choose as an example of contemporary scenario-writing Meyerowitz's (1985) fascinating (if overblown) analysis of the impact of electronic media on social behaviour, in transforming the 'situational geography of human life'. Meyerowitz's concern is with the way in which electronic media have undermined the traditional relationship between physical setting and social situation, to the extent that we are 'no longer "in" places in quite the same way' (Meyerowitz 1989: 333), as these media 'make us . . . audiences to performances that happen in other places and give us access to audiences who are not physically present' (Meyerowitz 1985: 7). Meyerowitz's central argument is that these new media re-define notions of social position and of 'place', divorcing experience from physical location.

He argues that the electronic media have transformed the relative significance of live and mediated encounters, bringing 'information and experience to everyplace from everyplace', as 'state funerals, wars . . . and space flights are dramas that can be played on the stage of almost anyone's living room' (ibid., 118) and, in Horton and Wohl's (1956) terms, viewers develop forms of 'para-social interaction' with media figures and 'stars' they have never met. In this way, these media, according to Meyerowitz, create new 'communities' across their spaces of transmission, bringing together otherwise disparate groups around the 'common experience' of television, in a process of cultural 'homogenisation of here and there'. Thus, argues Meyerowitz, television acquires a similar status to that of the weather, as a basis of common experience and source of conversation, as a sort of 'metaphysical arena' (ibid., 146), so that 'to watch TV is to look into . . . the [common] experience: . . . to see what others are watching'. Thus, Meyerowitz argues,

> the millions who watched the assassination of JFK . . . were in a 'place' that is no place at all . . . the millions of Americans who watch TV every evening . . . are in a 'location' that is not defined by walls, streets or neighbourhoods but by evanescent 'experience' . . . more and more, people are living in a national (or international) information-system rather than [in] a local town or city.
>
> (Meyerowitz 1985: 145–7)

Postmodern geography and the 'generalized elsewhere'

It is in this sense, Meyerowitz argues, that the electronic media are destroying our sense of locality, so that 'places are increasingly like one another and . . . the singularity . . . and importance of . . . locality is diminished' (Kirby 1989: 323). This may be to overstate the case, as Meyerowitz admits in his reply to Kirby, but, minimally, the function of these electronic media is certainly likely to 'relativize' our sense of place – so that 'locality is no longer necessarily seen as the centre stage of life's drama' (Meyerowitz 1989: 330). That centre stage is, then, according to Meyerowitz, taken by national television in the home, bringing us news of the 'generalized elsewhere' of other places and 'non-local' people and their simultaneous experiences – thus undermining any sense of the primacy of 'locality', as the 'unifying rhetorical space of daily TV extends into the living rooms of everyone' (Berland 1988: 47).

As Meyerowitz notes, part of the point is that, for instance, access to non-local people (for instance, via the telephone) is often faster and simpler than access to physical neighbours. The 'community' is thus 'liberated from spatial locality' and many intimate ties are supported by the telephone rather than by face-to-face interaction (cf. the telephone advertisement: 'Long distance is the next best thing to being there'). Thus, it seems, we should no longer conceive of community so much in terms of a local clustering of relationships as in terms of types of social relationship, whether local or distant – a 'psychological neighbourhood' or a 'personal community' as a network of (often non-local) ties (Wellman 1979; quoted in Meyerowitz 1989). Thus, 'community' is transformed: living physically near to others is no longer necessarily to be tied into mutually dependent communication systems; conversely, living far from others is no longer, necessarily, to be communicationally distant. Thus, it seems, locality is not simply subsumed in a national or global sphere; rather, it is increasingly bypassed in both directions – experience is both unified beyond localities and fragmented within them.

Such fragmentation, however, is rarely random; nor is it a matter of merely individual differences or 'choices' (cf. Morley 1980). Rather, it is a question of the socially and culturally determined lines of division along which fragmentation occurs. Central among these lines is, of course, that of gender. Both in the HICT research described earlier and in that of others in the field, there is an increasing recognition of the 'gendering' of technologies such as the telephone, which is an effect of the socially organized positioning of gendered categories of persons across the public/private division. As Garmarnikow and Purvis (1983b) note, the public/private split can, of course, itself be seen as a fundamental metaphor for the patterning of gender. 'Place' and 'placelessness' can certainly be seen to be (among other determinations) highly gendered experiences.

The vision of an 'emergent placelessness' (cf. Berland 1988: 147) offered (celebrated?) by a number of postmodern commentators can be criticized on a number of different counts. On the one hand, it offers little recognition of the particular operations of power, in so far as what emerges across this electronic ('placeless') network is what Mattelart *et al.* identify as the 'time of the exceptional and the spectacular, the product of an international industrial entertainment culture' (Mattelart *et al.* 1987: 97) – a heavily standardized televisual language which will tend to disqualify and displace all others. On the other hand, as Ferguson (1989) argues, the 'techno-orthodoxist' world view, which proclaims that satellite and other new ICTs have effectively reduced time/space differences to insignificance, is badly over-abstracted. Principally, this is because the argument has little empirical grounding and operates at a level of abstraction which does not permit us to answer questions about *how* these media shift our everyday understandings of time and space, or about *which* media-forms influence *which* people in *which* ways in their conceptualization of duration and distance (cf. Bryce 1987). What is needed, in this respect, is 'qualitative research into *how* electronic communications magnify [or otherwise – D.M.] time–space imperatives and *which* forms produce *which* kind of intended and unintended consequences' (Ferguson 1989: 171).

If the homogenization of space and time in contemporary culture has not yet abolished all differences, still we must attend to the need to construct a properly postmodern geography of the relations between communications and power and the contemporary transformations of the public and private spheres. As Ferguson notes, despite the grand claims of the techno-orthodoxist 'homogenizers', it remains true that 'just as they have differential access to new and old communication media, so do different cultures, social groups and national sources of power perceive, categorise and prioritise temporal and spatial boundaries differently' (ibid., 153). To take a 'European' example, rather than speculating, in the abstract, as to whether or not we are seeing the emergence of a unified 'European culture' under the impact of pan-European media, it may be more instructive to ask to what extent, for which groups (e.g. teenage viewers of satellite-television music channels, Euro-businesspersons, etc.) such a 'European' perspective is emerging (cf. Collins 1990).

Rather than presuming a uniform effect in which, from a crudely technologically determinist perspective, new ICTs impose new sensibilities on peoples across the globe, it may be more realistic to conceive of them as overlaying the new upon the old (cf. Rogge and Jensen, in Lull 1988). Thus, a new technology such as the home computer may often be principally 'made sense of' via its integration into the very old 'technology' of the peer-gossip network. Rather than the new media promoting a 'boundless media-land of common understandings', a variety of senses of 'temporal elasticity and local indeterminacy' may be the more likely result, where 'formerly finite absolutes take on a notably relativist character . . . and old certainties . . . [are undermined, to some extent by] new ambiguities' (Ferguson 1989: 155). This seems both a more realistic (cf. Miller, 1992) and a richer perspective from which to analyse the interaction of local definitions and larger communications systems. As Miller (ibid.) argues in his analysis of the consumption of American soap opera in Trinidad, the 'local' is not to be considered as an indigenous source of cultural identity, which remains 'authentic' only in so far as it is unsullied by contact with the global. Rather, the local is often itself produced by means of the 'indigenization' (or 'domestication') of global or 'foreign' resources and imputs.

Massey makes the point eloquently, in her critique of the widespread tendency to counterpose a concept of the local (usually conflated with the concrete) with that of the global (usually conflated with the abstract). As she puts it,

> the . . . world economy is no less concrete than a local one [it] is 'general' in the sense of being a geographically large-scale phenomenon, to which can be counterposed internal variations. But it is also, un-equivocally, concrete as opposed to abstract . . . Those who conflate the local with the concrete . . . are confusing geographical scale with processes of abstraction in thought . . . [and] those who make this mistake then frequently . . . confuse the study of the local with description, which they oppose to theoretical work . . . this argument . . . [confuses] . . . the dimensions concrete–abstract and local–general . . . The 'local' . . . is no less subject to, nor useful for theorisation than big, broad, general things. The counterposition of general and local is quite distinct from the distinction between abstract and concrete.
>
> (Massey 1991a: 270–1)

If 'geography matters', and if place is important, this is not only because the character of a particular place is a product of its position in relation to wider forces, but also because that character, in turn, stamps its own imprint on those wider processes. Moreover, places are not static or fixed, easily definable, or bounded entities into which external forces somehow (improperly or problematically) intrude, as those working in the Heideggerian tradition would often seem to imply. This is simply the theoretical correlative of Marx's observation that people are not 'in' society as an object is in a box, and of Voloshinov's concept of the 'social individual'. As Massey argues, places are to be seen as themselves processes; they are frequently riven with internal conflicts and divisions (they are not internally homogenous) and are perhaps best seen not as 'bounded areas' but as 'spaces of interaction' in which local identities are constructed out of resources (both material and symbolic) which may well not be at all local in their origin. But then perhaps, as Miller (op. cit.) observes, we should define 'authenticity' *a posteriori*, rather than *a priori*, as a matter of local consequences, rather than of local origins. Similarly, to the extent that imported television programmes penetrate local meaning systems, rather than thereby 'homogenizing' diverse cultures, their principal effect may be a rather variable one – in so far as they introduce a relativizing perspective, as an 'uncertainty principle' which may work to undermine established and dominant frameworks of meaning in a variety of ways (cf. Hebdige 1988b and Worpole 1983, on the effects of 'foreign' cultural artefacts in undermining the hierarchies of national taste cultures; but cf. also Chen 1990, on the significance of the fact that the 'foreign' is so often represented by the 'American').

From the sitting-room to the (inter)nation(al)

In recent years, one line of criticism of researchers such as Lull, Silverstone and myself has been that, in our concern with the domestic context of television-viewing, we were busy conducting an ill-considered (if not hasty) 'retreat' into the private realm of the 'sitting-room' and away from the important 'public' issues of power, politics and policy which constitute the proper subjects of the study of communication. I shall argue that this critique is misguided, on a number of counts. It is not only that the average sitting-room (in my experience) is the site of some very important political conflicts – it is, among other things, one of the principal sites of the politics of gender and age. It is also that, in my view, the sitting-room is exactly where we need to start from, if we finally want to understand the constitutive dynamics of abstractions such as 'the community' or 'the nation'. This is especially so if we are concerned with the role of communications in the continuous formation, sustenance, recreation and transformation of these entities. The central point precisely concerns television's role in connecting, for example, the 'familiar' or domestic, and the national and international spheres, and in sustaining both the image and the reality of the 'national family' and of various trans-national 'communities'.

From this perspective, one of the key functions of broadcasting is the creation of a bridge between the public and the private, the sacred and the profane, the extraordinary and the mundane. Thus, as Silverstone argues,

> In Durkheimian terms, television provides a forum and a locus for the mobilisation of collective energy and enthusiasm, for example, in the presentation of national events, from coronations to great sporting fixtures, and it also marks a consistently defined but significant boundary in our culture between the domestic and taken-for-granted world and that of the unreachable and otherwise inaccessible world of . . . show business, Dallas and the moon landings.
>
> (Silverstone 1988: 25)

In a similar vein, Chaney (1983) analyses the role of broadcasting in enabling the public to participate in the collective life of the nation. As Chaney points out, a 'nation' is a very abstract collectivity, in so far as it is too big to be experienced directly by the individual. To that extent, the 'we-feeling' of community has to be continually engendered by opportunities for identification, as the sense of 'nation' is manufactured. Chaney is particularly concerned with the role of mass media in relaying civic rituals (coronations, royal weddings, etc.). As he notes, if such rituals are 'dramatizations' of the nation as symbolic community, then the infinite reproduceability of media performance makes the 'audience' for them possible on a scale previously unimaginable (Chaney 1983: 121). Recalling Silverstone's definition of television's role in establishing 'the space of intimate distance' (1988: 23), Chaney analyses the 'quasi-democracy of intimate access' (cf. Dayan and Katz 1987: 88 'TV is that which abolishes distance') created by the presence of the television camera, 'representing' the public in the most intimate moments of symbolic ritual. At the heart of the process is an ambivalence, in which public figures are simultaneously humanized through vicarious observation (and the camera often gives the audience at home a closer view than those physically present – D.M.) but also distanced through the dramatic conventions of media presentation (Chaney 1986: 121).

Chaney is concerned with the spectacular character of ceremonial occasions, arguing finally (in a curious reversal of Ellis (1992) comments on broadcast television as the 'private life of the nation state') that 'spectacular forms of mass communication are the public life of a mass culture' (Chaney 1986: 132). Contrary to the established view that 'ritual' is less significant in secularized industrial societies than it was in earlier times, Chaney argues that, because of the scale and nature of these societies (where the entire citizenry simply cannot be personally acquainted and a sense of collective identity must be continually invented), ritual becomes more salient as a mode of dramatizing (indeed, constituting) 'community'. Thus, Chaney notes that 'collective ceremonies have patently not disappeared from the calendar of institutional identity and reproduction; indeed they have been made more accessible and less arcane through their dramatisation as media performances' (132). This is, in some part, a question of 'access' – thus, Chaney notes the significance of the radio broadcasting of George VI's coronation in 1937 in involving a huge proportion of the national public, who 'spent the day listening in and thus partaking in the central events' (Jennings and Madge 1937; quoted in Chaney 1986: 129). However, it is not only a question of access. Thus, in his earlier article, Chaney notes that, in the end, the media's role transforms these events, so that 'national festivals . . . become . . . media occasions, rather than occasions to which the media have access' (ibid., 134).

It is also a question, as Stam (1983) argues, of understanding the specific form of the pleasure offered to the viewer by television, and in particular by television 'news' in its most general sense. Stam is concerned with what he calls the 'metaphysics of presence' of television and the ways in which television news promotes 'the regime of the fictive "we"' (39) as a 'community'. Stam's argument is that 'epistemophilia' (the pleasure of knowing) can offer only a partial account of the motivation of news viewing. Beyond this, argues Stam, we must attend to the ways in which the pleasures offered are narcissistic and are 'designed to enhance the self-image of His or Her Majesty the Spectator' (27). The principal point, argues Stam, is that, television transforms us into 'armchair imperialists' and 'audio-visual masters of the world' (25). In this respect, Stam argues, while 'live' television is only a small portion of all broadcast television, it 'sets the tone' for much of what television offers. As he puts it, television

> allows us to share the literal time of persons who are elsewhere. It grants us . . . instantaneous ubiquity. The telespectator of a lunar landing becomes a vicarious astronaut . . . The viewer of a live transmission, in fact, can in some respects see better than those immediately present on the scene.
>
> (ibid., 24)

It is this 'interfacing' of the public and the private that concerns us here. On the one hand, the audience for such national events is usually atomized, either attending individually or in small groups such as the family or peer group. On the other hand, each such group sits in front of a television set emitting the same representations of this 'central' event. The 'public' is thus experienced in the private (domestic) realm: it is 'domesticated'. But at the same time the 'private' itself is thus transformed or 'socialized'. The space (and experience) created is neither 'public' nor private in the traditional senses.

In unravelling these connections, the work of Dayan and Katz (1987) on the representation of the royal wedding of 1981 on British television may be of some help. Drawing on Austin's (1962) theory of 'performative' speech acts, Dayan and Katz are concerned to analyse television's role in constructing (literally 'performing') media events such as the royal wedding. In this connection, they argue, television should be seen not as 'representing' the event but as constructing the experience of it for the majority of the population. Television, they argue, is not so much reporting on the event as actively involved in 'performing' it. Television is not simply transmitting such an event (or commenting on it) but is bringing it into existence.

General de Gaulle's concept of television as the face of the government in the sitting-room can, of course, be argued to apply only to broadcasting under quite particular conditions, specifically where broadcasting is allowed very little autonomy from direct governmental control. However, if we take our lead from the work of Chaney and Dayan and Katz (see above), we can not only begin to see the crucial role of television in articulating 'governmental' (cf. Foucault 1980) or 'public' with domestic space; we can also pose the more fundamental question as to the extent to which it still makes sense to speak of broadcast media as 'reporting' on political developments. The problem is that to pose the question this way is to presume that there exists some separate realm of 'politics' on which television then, subsequently, reports. In an age when international sporting events are routinely arranged to suit the convenience of broacasting schedules and acts of war are timed with reference not so much to military requirements as to maximizing PR advantage, this may seem obvious. The fundamental issue is of some long standing. As early as 1974, Pateman argued a similar point in relation to electoral politics. His point was that television can only 'cover' an election when the campaign has an existence independent of the presence of television, and that nowadays these campaigns no longer have any such existence, being principally designed and planned – in terms of 'photo-opportunities', 'sound-bites', etc. – with reference to their televisualization. Thus, Pateman argues, 'we do not have television coverage of an election, we have a television election' (1974). Pateman's point can be extended well beyond the specific field of 'elections' to cover 'politics' in a much more general sense: for the majority of the population, 'politics' is principally a 'media event', and their participation in this realm is a heavily mediated one.

We are back, once again, with the politics of 'being there'. This is, increasingly, a complex issue. The *Guardian*'s South Africa correspondent, David Beresford, offered a telling account (*Guardian*, 17 April 1990) of his attempt to report Nelson Mandela's speech in Cape Town on his release from prison – where 'being there' physically unfortunately entailed being unable to see or hear Mr Mandela. This Beresford accounts as an experience of 'being there and not being there' where being the 'man on the spot' has the perverse effect of being unable to witness the images available to the rest of the global village. In a similar vein, Dayan and Katz refer to the seemingly puzzling (but increasingly common) behaviour of those physically present at public events who, if they can, also take with them a portable television, so they too can see 'what is happening'. Physical contiguity does not, then, necessarily equate with effective participation; and, of course, vice versa.

From this angle we could also usefully reconsider the debates that arose concerning the television spectaculars of the 1980s – from 'Band Aid/Live Aid' onwards. Meyerowitz comments: 'Live Aid was an event that took place nowhere but on TV, the ultimate example of the freeing of communications experience from the 'restraint of social and physical passage'. Many commentators have been critical of the ways in which such 'trans-national' broadcasts expressed a 'mythology' of international (if not universal) community. However, in a very important sense this was no 'mythical' achievement. If a sense of community was created, this may have had something to do with the fact that all over the world millions of people were (in reality) watching these 'simultaneous' broadcasts – and, to that extent, in Dayan and Katz's terms, participating quite effectively in a 'diasporic ceremony' which was anything but illusory.

The question that Dayan and Katz pose is what happens to public ceremonies when, instead of being attended in person, they are delivered to us at home. As they note, being physically distanced from the ceremonial forms and isolated from each other, television audiences do not form 'masses' or 'crowds' except in an abstract, statistical sense (cf. Ang 1991). The question they pose is that of whether we can still speak of a public event when it is celebrated at home – and whether we can speak of a collective celebration when the collectivity is scattered (cf. Siskind 1992). As they note, under these conditions:

> The very hugeness of the audiences had paradoxically transposed the celebration into an intimate register. Ceremonial space has been reconstituted, but in the home. Attendance takes place in small groups congregated around the television set, concentrating on the symbolic centre, keenly aware that myriads of other groups are doing likewise, in a similar manner, and at the same time.
>
> (Dayan and Katz 1987: 194)

The analogy which Dayan and Katz offer is that of the Jewish Passover 'Seder' ritual – a collective ceremony without a central 'cultic temple', which translates the public celebration into 'a multiplicity of simultaneous, similarly programmed, home-bound, micro-events' (ibid., 195). Thus, Dayan and Katz imply, the television audience, as a dispersed community, can usefully be seen as being regularly united (both by its occasional viewing of special events and by its regular viewing of the 'news' or favourite soap operas) through precisely this kind of 'diasporic ceremony'. While 'media events' such as a televised royal wedding clearly constitute a special case, in which this issue is brought into particular prominence, this model can clearly be extended to the quotidian level – so that the regular viewing of the nightly television news or of a long-running soap opera can be seen in the same light – as a discourse which constitutes collectivities through a sense of 'participation' and through the production of both a simultaneity of experience and a sense of a 'past in common' (cf. the debates on 'popular memory': Wright 1985).

The production of cultural identities

In this connection, Schlesinger (1987) has rightly argued that the conventional question concerning the 'effects' of new information and communication technologies (satellite television etc.) on cultural (or 'national') identities is mal-posed. His argument is that we should, rather, invert the terms of the question: rather than starting with a set of supposedly 'pre-given' objects ('national cultures') and investigating the 'effects' which communications technologies have on them, we should begin by posing the question of identity itself and ask what importance 'communications' of various sorts might have in its constitution.

In a similar vein, Donald (1988) argues that we should focus our analyses on the apparatuses of discourses, technologies and institutions which produce cultures. As he suggests, from this perspective, the 'nation' is an effect of these cultural technologies, not their point of origin. A nation is not reflected in or expressed through its culture: rather, it is cultural apparatuses (among other things) that produce the nation. The point is increasingly well taken, as demonstrated by the essays collected in Rutherford 1990 and Bhabha 1990, the latter directly addressing the question of the relationship between 'nation' and 'narration' and focusing on the 'performativity' of language and discourse in constructing the narratives of national and cultural identities. Clearly, the point applies at both micro- and macro-levels – just as we should, then, be concerned with the role of communications technologies in the constitution of national identity, so with the analysis of the role of these technologies in the construction of identities at the domestic level.

One of the critical issues, as argued earlier, concerns the relationship between community and geography, when, as Rath (1986) puts it, we increasingly live in a 'television-geography', where the invisible electronic networks defined by spaces of transmission (and distribution) cut across established geographical boundaries. By way of indication of some of the issues involved in developing this work further, we can also usefully refer to the work of Gillespie (1989), who offers an insightful analysis of the role played by the video-recorder in the negotiation of ethnic identities among Asians in Britain (who utilize the video to arrange regular showings of Indian films and similar material unavailable on broadcast television in Britain – a process which can be found among other ethnic groups (Turks, Moroccans, etc.) in other European countries). In this way, new communications technologies are mobilized in the (re-)creation and maintenance of traditions and of cultural and ethnic identities which transcend any easy equation of geography, place and culture, creating symbolic networks throughout the various communities of the diaspora. The point here is that such groups have, thus far, usually appeared in the research frame on the understanding that theirs is a particularly problematic position – as 'immigrants'. In this respect Hall (1988b) usefully reminds us of the increasing centrality of the 'migrant' experience throughout contemporary culture, even if we might still want to distinguish between 'voluntary' and 'involuntary' cosmopolitans (cf. Hannerz 1990; Hebdige 1990).

If the traditional *equation* of community with geographical boundary and physical place is something which we simply have to ditch in order to understand contemporary culture and communications, this is *not* to say that these terms will have *no* effective relation – simply that it is increasingly misleading to reduce the former to either of the latter. As long ago as 1933, the art historian and psychologist Rolf Arnheim foresaw the social consequences of television as a means of distribution:

> it renders the object on display independent of its point of origin, makes it unnecessary for spectators to flock together in front of an 'original' . . . it takes the place of other means of distribution . . . Thus TV turns out to be related to the motor car and the aeroplane – as a means of transport for the mind.
>
> (quoted in Rath 1985: 199)

As I said in the Introduction, I am finally interested in articulating the analyses of micro- and macro-processes in relation to the simultaneous processes of homogenization and fragmentation, globalization and localization in contemporary culture. Certainly, as we enter the era of narrowcasting and audience segmentation, it may well be (*pace* Scannell) that many of us will have less broadcast 'experience' in common with anyone else – and anyway video allows us both to time-shift broadcast materials so as to consume them at times that fit our 'private' schedules, and to consume non-broadcast materials – so the model of a 'necessary simultaneity' of shared social experience, provided by broadcasting, becomes problematic. However, at the same time, new developments in broadcasting (whether the occasional Global Totemic Festivals of the 'Live Aid' variety or the regular construction of a Europe-wide youth audience for music programming) begin to combine us into not just national but international collectivities, especially as the supply of programmes to national broadcasting systems is increasingly dominated by a small number of transnational corporations. But then, as Coca Cola put it, 'we are not a multi-national, we are a multi-local' (cf. D. Webster 1989; Robins 1989).

Even more confusingly, we have yet to recognize the full implications of globalization for commercial strategies, not least the emergence of the 'decentred' or 'polycentric' corporation, operating increasingly with an 'equidistance of perspective' (Kenichi Ohmae; quoted in Robins 1991: 26), and treating all strategic markets with the same attention as the 'home' market. Ohmae sees Honda, operating in Japan, Europe and North America as a typical case, where, 'the very word "overseas" has no place in Honda's operating vocabulary, because the Corporation sees itself as equidistant from all its key customers' (ibid.). What is required, in this context, is an analysis which can deal both with the global/local dynamic of these cultural processes at a substantive level and with the need to articulate the micro- and macro-dimensions of our analyses, so as both to ground our theories, and to theorize our ground, in an attempt more effectively to connect our analyses of the domestic, the local, the national and the inter- or trans-national aspects of communications.

Notes

INTRODUCTION

The reader's attention is drawn to two distinct works referred to throughout this book: the *Nationwide* audience study, and the book based on this research project entitled *The 'Nationwide' Audience* (D. Morley, London: British Film Institute, 1980).

1 In this connection, it is worth noting that, while the 'deconstructionist' project has rapidly come to be equated with a certain kind of 'anything goes' attitude to textual interpretation, this kind of laxity is quite at odds with the actual practice of both de Man and Derrida, for example. Norris (1991) interestingly quotes both of these 'deconstructionists' on this point. First, de Man argues that 'reading is an epistemological event prior to being an ethical or aesthetic value. This does not mean that there can be a true reading, but that no reading is conceivable in which the question of its truth or falsehood is not primarily involved' (quoted Norris 1991: 154). Second, Norris quotes from Derrida's acrimonious debate with John Searle, concerning Austin's philosophy of the speech act, where Derrida argues quite simply that Searle's 'definition of the deconstructionist is false (that's right: false, not true) and feeble: it supposes a bad (that's right: bad, not good) and feeble reading of numerous texts, first of all mine, which therefore must be finally read or re-read' (Derrida; quoted ibid., 158).

2 PSYCHOANALYTIC THEORIES: TEXTS, READERS AND SUBJECTS

1 This article was originally based on work undertaken with Charlotte Brunsdon to extend the theoretical terms of the argument in *Everyday Television: 'Nationwide'* (BFI 1978), particularly in relation to the problem of audiences. This version also incorporates comments from Dorothy Hobson, Adam Mills and Alan O'Shea, and was extensively revised for publication by Stuart Hall.
2 For an attempt to develop a psychoanalytic perspective which avoids the problems of universalism and abstraction referred to above, see Walkerdine (1987). For detailed comments on this, see Morley (1989).

3 INTERPRETING TELEVISION: THE *NATIONWIDE* AUDIENCE

1 This programme analysis was completed and written up for publication by Charlotte Brunsdon and David Morley (*Everday Television: 'Nationwide'*, London: British Film Institute, 1978). The subsequent audience research was

conducted by David Morley, supported by a grant from the British Film Institute, and published as *The 'Nationwide' Audience*, London: British Film Institute, 1980.

4   *THE 'NATIONWIDE' AUDIENCE*: A CRITICAL POSTSCRIPT

In writing this chapter I am indebted to a range of people for their critical comments on the earlier work – among them John Corner, Philip Schlesinger, Tony Trew, James Donald, Adam Mills, Stuart Hall and Charlotte Brunsdon.

1 F. Parkin, *Class, Inequality and Political Order*, London: Paladin, 1971; see especially chapter 3. Parkin's model was adapted and developed in relation to the media audience in Stuart Hall, 'Encoding and decoding in TV discourse' CCCS, University of Birmingham, 1973.
2 See the formulation in S. Hall *et al.*, 'The unity of current affairs television', WPCS no. 9, CCCS, and in C. Brunsdon and D. Morley *Everyday Television: 'Nationwide'*, London: British Film Institute, 1978.
3 S. Hall, 'Once more round preferred readings', mimeo, CCCS, 1978.
4 See V. Voloshinov, *Marxism and the Philosophy of Language*, London: Academic Press, 1973.
5 For these points, I am particularly indebted to Tony Trew.
6 See S. Neale, 'Propaganda', *Screen* 18:3, (1977).
7 See G. Kress and R. Hodge, *Language as Ideology*, London: Routledge & Kegan Paul, 1979, and R. Fowler *et al.*, *Language and Control*, London: Routledge & Kegan Paul, 1979.
8 See, in particular, the work of Bourdieu published in *Media, Culture and Society*, 2:3 (1980).
9 See Parkin, op. cit., and Hall, op. cit.
10 See R. Dyer, 'Victim: hermeneutic project', *Film Form*, Autumn 1977, 19–21.
11 See T. Ryall, 'The notion of genre', *Screen* 11:2 (1970).
12 See A. Mattelart and S. Sieglaub, *Communications and Class Struggle*, Vol. 1, New York: International General, 1979, and P. Cohen and D. Robbins, *Knuckle Sandwich*, Harmondsworth: Penguin, 1979.
13 See 'Recent developments in English studies', in S. Hall *et al.*, *Culture, Media and Language*, London: Hutchinson, 1981.
14 See English Studies Group, op. cit., p. 239.
15 C. Brunsdon, '*Crossroads*: notes on soap-opera', paper to Rutgers University Conference 'Perspectives on TV and Video Art', 1981.
16 D. Hobson, 'Housewives and the mass media', in S. Hall *et al.*, *Culture, Media and Language*.
17 P. Corrigan and P. Willis, 'Cultural forms and class mediators', *Media Culture and Society* 2:2.
18 See S. Suleiman and I. Crossman (eds), *The Reader in the Text*, Princeton, NJ: Princeton University Press, 1980, p. 32.
19 D. Hymes, 'On communicative competence', in J. Pride and J. Homes (eds) *Socio-Linguistics*, Harmondsworth: Penguin, 1972.

7   FROM *FAMILY TELEVISION* TO A SOCIOLOGY OF MEDIA CONSUMPTION

1 Many of these observations derive from critical comments offered by Valerie Walkerdine in response to the *Family Television* project. I am grateful to her for these contributions.

8 TOWARDS AN ETHNOGRAPHY OF THE TELEVISION AUDIENCE

1 Some sections of this chapter also appear in 'Communication and context: anthropological and ethnographic perspectives on the media audience', co-authored with R. Silverstone, in N. Jankowski and K.B. Jensen (eds), *A Handbook of Qualitative Methodologies for Mass Communication Research*, London: Routledge, 1991.

2 See Trinh T. Minh-ha's *Woman Native, Other*, Bloomington: Indiana University Press, 1989, for a further discussion of these issues, especially in relation to S. Adoltevi's argument: 'Today . . . the only possible ethnology is the one which studies the anthropophagous behaviour of the white man' (Adoltevi, *Negritude and Negrologues*, Paris: Union Générale d'Etudes, 1972; quoted in Minh-ha, op. cit., p. 73). Minh-ha explores the metaphors of anthropology as 'gossip about gossip', and of interpretation – as an attempt to 'grasp the marrow of native life' – as itself a cannibalistic rite.

3 For a more extended review of the literature on Orientalism (and on 'Orientalism-in-reverse'), see D. Morley and K. Robins, 'Techno-orientalism: futures, foreigners and phobias', *New Formations* 16 (Spring 1992).

4 For an interesting exploration of the possibilities of 'ethno-semiotics', see J. Fiske 'Ethnosemiotics: some personal and theoretical reflections', *Cultural Studies* 4:1, (January 1990).

5 Geertz is referring once again to the conceptual issues raised by Ryle's famous example of the difficulties involved in interpreting such a seemingly simple event as the movement of a human eyelid (as indicating, for example, either an involuntary twitch or a conspiratorial signal to a friend, etc.). Geertz's original discussion of these matters is to be found in his *Interpretation of Cultures*, New York: Basic Books, 1973, pp. 6–7. See also Carr, op. cit., on this point. For an interesting critique of the relativist and textualist perspectives which have influenced the field of cultural studies in the wake of Rorty's influential (1978) reading of Derrida, and for a spirited defence of a critical realist position, see Norris (1991).

6 For a detailed discussion of the methodological procedures employed in the HICT study, see R. Silverstone, E. Hirsch and D. Morley, 'Listening to a long conversation: an ethnographic approach to the study of information and communication technologies in the home', *Cultural Studies* 5:2 (May 1991).

7 But see my comments in the Introduction here, in support of Corner's (1991) observations on the corresponding dangers of radical contextualism.

9 DOMESTIC COMMUNICATION: TECHNOLOGIES AND MEANINGS

1 This is an edited version of a paper written with R. Silverstone, which appeared in *Media, Culture and Society*, 12:1 (1990). The paper arose from our work on a project entitled 'The Household uses of Information and Communication Technologies', conducted at Brunel University's Centre for Research in Innovation, Culture and Technology, under the directorship of Roger Silverstone, as part of the research Programme in Information and Communication Technology funded by the Economic and Social Research Council. The research involved a detailed ethnography of the technological and cultural dynamics of life within twenty families in south-east England, focusing on questions of ICT use, and patterns of media consumption in a context of technological and social change. Further details of the study are reported in R. Silverstone, E. Hirsch and D. Morley, 'Information technology and the moral economy of the household', in R. Silverstone and E. Hirsch (eds),

Consuming Technologies, London: Routledge, 1992, and in R. Silverstone, 'Beneath the bottom line: households and information and communications technologies in an age of the consumer', PICT Policy Research Paper no. 17 (1991). Further details of the project (which continues) are available from Professor Roger Silverstone, now at the Department of Media Studies, Sussex University.

2 See B. Gunter and M. Svennevig, *Behind and In Front of the Screen*, London: John Libbey, 1987, p. 79.

3 See ibid., p. 84, on the role of video and computer technology in displacing conflict over programme choice into conflict over alternative uses of the television set.

4 See ibid., p. 86.

5 As one trade commentator notes, 'Whereas in 1980 TV was a family mechanism, it now provides a more personal service for each of the various members of the household. Consequently, specific segments and programmes are now being identified as the sole domain for discrete audiences', *Marketing Review*, June 1987, p. 15; quoted in R. Paterson, 'Family perspectives on broadcasting policy', paper to BFI Summer School, 1987.

6 P. Palmer, *The Lively Audience*, London: Allen & Unwin, 1987.

7 See S. Moores, 'The box on the dresser: memories of early radio', *Media, Culture and Society* 10 (1988), and S. Frith, 'The pleasures of the hearth', in J. Donald (ed.), *Formations of Pleasure*, London: Routledge & Kegan Paul, 1983.

8 Lindlof and Meyer, op. cit., p. 2.

9 J. Bryce 'Family time and television use', in T. Lindlof, (ed.), *Natural Audiences*, Norwood, NJ: Ablex, 1987, p. 137.

10 ibid.

11 My argument is that, given the sheer amount of time in which the television set is 'on' in the main living-room of most Western households, television viewing (and other uses of domestic communication technologies) will be most productively examined in and through its integration with a variety of domestic practices. A number of examples can be offered which may illuminate the point: both Palmer, op. cit., and Leoncio Barrios (see his essay in J. Lull (ed.), *World Families Watch Television*, Newbury Park and London: Sage, 1988) have examined the variety of ways in which children integrate their television viewing into their play activity. In a similar vein, Lull points to the integration, for many adolescents, of television viewing (or music) and homework and, for many families, the integration not only of viewing and eating, but of specific programme 'slots' and specific mealtimes (cf. Lull, op. cit., pp. 4 and 14–15). Similarly, Traudt and Lont offer a useful analysis of the ways in which parental monitoring of children's television viewing needs to be seen as a key mode of their socialization practices (see P. Traudt and C. Lont, 'Media logic in use', in Lindlof (ed.), *Natural Audiences*, pp. 170 ff.; see also P. Simpson (ed.), *Parents Talking Television*, London: Comedia, 1987).

12 See J. Lull's 'Conclusion' to Lull, op. cit.; E. Medrich 'Constant television: a background to daily life', *Journal of Communication* 26:3 (1979); R. Kubey, 'Television use in everyday life', *Journal of Communication*, Summer 1986; C. Lodziak, *The Power of Television*, London: Frances Pinter, 1987.

13 D. Noble; quoted in B. Keen, 'Play it again Sony: home video technology', *Science as Culture* 1:9 (1988).

14 e.g., Michael Green, Chairman of Carlton Communications, one of the most successful of the new generation of television entrepreneurs, was quoted as follows: 'The philosophy that has driven me is that the television set is an underutilised force. Half of modern video's output is not theatrical or entertainment,

it is useful: how-to-do-it tapes, kid's tapes. Did you know that there are more video outlets in Britain than bookshops? It is today's form. I think of television as a manufacturing process. What is the difference between a television programme and this lighter?', *The Independent*, 30 March 1988.

15 D. Miller, *Material Culture and Mass Consumption*, Oxford: Blackwell, 1988.

16 As Silverstone has argued elsewhere, 'we ought to be interested in the relationship between public and private "texts", in the parallel and competing rhetorics (and mythologies) of the relatively powerful and the relatively powerless, in the cultural stratification of everyday life. And in this stratified world we need to establish how much room there is for doing what and by whom, in the transformations of fashion into style, commodities into objects, and broadcasts into action and gossip. It is in these transformations that we can gain a measure of the strengths and weaknesses of contemporary culture and its asymmetries. And it is this formulation, rather than the classic "who says what in which channel to whom and with what effect" which should now orient out research' (quoted in R. Silverstone, 'Television and everyday life: towards an anthropology of the television audience', in M. Ferguson (ed.), *Public Communication: The New Imperatives*, London: Sage, 1990).

17 See, for example, Schroder 1987; Jensen 1987; Jensen and Rosengren 1990 in bibliography.

18 See J. Ellis, *Visible Fictions*, London: Routledge, 1982 and Ang 1987.

19 T. Bennett and J. Woollacott, *Bond and Beyond*, London: Macmillan, 1987; L. Grossberg, 'The in-difference of television', *Screen* 28:2 (1987); N. Browne, 'Political economy of the television supertext', *Quarterly Review of Film Studies* 9 (1984).

20 See also Silverstone, op. cit.

21 C. Brunsdon, 'Text and audience', in E. Seiter *et al.* (eds), *Remote Control*, London: Routledge, 1989.

22 ibid.

23 ibid.

24 James Anderson rightly points to the way in which 'the interpretive process of meaning construction does not end with the process of reception. . . . Meaning construction . . . is an ongoing process which reaches well beyond the moment of reception . . . we also (re)interpret media content retrospectively in the subsequent uses we have for it. Interpretation certainly begins in the practices of reception. . . . But further interpretation awaits an occasion in which media content is seen to have some utility' (J. Anderson, 'Commentary on qualitative research', in Lull, op. cit., p. 167).

25 The theoretical background to this point is developed in Pêcheux's concept of 'interdiscursive space' (see M Pêcheux, *Language, Semantics and Ideology*, London: Macmillan, 1982).

26 M. McLuhan, *Understanding Media*, London: Routledge & Kegan Paul, 1964.

27 P. Greenfield, *Mind and Media*, Harmondsworth: Penguin, 1984.

28 P. Collett and R. Lamb, 'Watching people watching television', report to the Independent Broadcasting Authority, 1986.

29 See J. Lull, 'The social uses of television', *Human Communication Research* 6:3 (1980).

30 See Silverstone, op. cit.

31 See R.H. Brown, *Society as Text: Essays on Rhetoric, Reason, and Reality*, Chicago: University of Chicago Press, 1987.

32 See Silverstone, op. cit., for a fuller treatment of these issues.

33 P. Ricoeur, *Time and Narrative*, Vol. 1, Chicago: University of Chicago Press, 1984.

34 See Boddy 1986, and Scannell 1988 in bibliography.
35 See Paterson 1987 in bibliography.
36 See C. Geraghty, 'The continuous serial', in R. Dyer *et al.* (eds), *Coronation Street*, London: British Film Institute, 1980; and D. Hobson, *Crossroads: Drama of a Soap Opera*, London: Methuen, 1982.
37 D. Hobson and R. Wohl, 'Mass communication and para-social interactions', *Psychiatry* 19:3 (1956): 215–29.
38 See Hobson 1982 in bibliography.
39 See I. Ang, *Watching 'Dallas'*, London: Methuen, 1985.
40 See Morley 1980 in bibliography.
41 G. Lakoff and M. Johnson, *Metaphors We Live By*, Chicago: University of Chicago Press, 1980.
42 J. Lewis, 'Decoding television news', in P. Drummond and R. Paterson (eds), *Television in Transition*, London: British Film Institute, 1985.
43 S. J. Smith, 'News and the dissemination of fear', in J. Burgess and J. R. Gold (eds), *Geography, the Media and Popular Culture*, London: Croom Helm, 1985.
44 M. de Certeau, *The Practice of Everday Life*, Berkeley: University of California Press, 1984.
45 M. Douglas and B. Isherwood, *The World of Goods: Towards an Anthropology of Consumption*, Harmondsworth: Penguin, 1980.
46 J. Gershuny, 'The leisure principle', *New Society*, 13 February 1987; J. Gershuny and I. Miles, *The New Service Economy*, London: Frances Pinter, 1983.
47 Cf. R. Pahl, *Divisions of Labour*, Oxford: Blackwell, 1984.
48 See N. Garnham 'Contribution to a political economy of mass communication', in R. Collins *et al.*, (eds), *Media, Culture and Society: A Critical Reader*, London: Sage, 1986. See also Hartley, op. cit., and J. Fiske, *Television Culture*, London: Methuen, 1987.
49 S. Hall, 'Encoding/decoding television discourse', reprinted in S. Hall *et al.* (eds) *Culture, Media, Language*, London: Hutchinson, 1981.
50 Miller, *Material Culture*, p. 175.
51 See Douglas and Isherwood, *The World of Goods*.
52 M. Sahlins, *Culture and Practical Reason*, Chicago: University of Chicago Press, 1976.
53 Miller, op. cit., p. 212.
54 ibid., p. 156.
55 ibid., pp. 145–6.

11 PRIVATE WORLDS AND GENDERED TECHNOLOGIES

1 This paper has benefited from Roger Silverstone's comments on an earlier draft, for which I am grateful. Parts of the paper draw on material previously used in a Brunel University Discussion Paper, 'Families, technologies and consumption', written jointly with Roger Silverstone, Andrea Dahlberg, and Sonia Livingstone. Other parts draw on material from 'Families and their technologies: two ethnographic portraits', written jointly with Roger Silverstone, which appeared in T. Putnam and C. Newton (eds), *Household Choices*, London: Futures Publications, 1990.
2 For the rationale for choosing to work with nuclear families (as the project did) rather than with any other types of household, see Morley and Silverstone 1990 in bibliography.
3 For a discussion on the methodological issues necessarily at stake in ethno-

graphic work of this type, see Silverstone, Hirsch and Morley 1991 in bibliography.

12 THE CONSTRUCTION OF EVERYDAY LIFE

1 For a fascinating collection of essays exploring the social construction of temporality, see John Hassard (ed.), *The Sociology of Time*, London: Macmillan, 1990.

13 WHERE THE GLOBAL MEETS THE LOCAL

1 The theoretical backdrop to the approach taken in this chapter is derived in some part from the work of Fernand Braudel (see especially his *Civilisation and Capitalism: The Perspective of the World*, London: William Collins, 1988). Most particularly, my emphasis here is on attempting to transcend the sterile dichotomy, characterized by Immanuel Wallerstein, between, on the one hand, the limitations of the 'idiographic', empirical, 'concrete' perspective of both narrative history and classical anthropology and, on the other hand, the absurdities of the 'nomothetic' approach which has traditionally dominated the social sciences in their search for the transcendental laws of social life (see Wallerstein's *Unthinking Social Science*, Cambridge: Polity Press, 1991, for an exposition of this argument). The attempt made here to reconceptualize the relation of the 'micro-' and the 'macro-' levels of analysis (to relate 'event', 'conjuncture' and 'structure', in Braudel's terms) is in many ways parallel to that offered by the analyses collected together in K. Knorr-Cetina and A.V. Cicourel (eds), *Advances in Social Theory and Methodology: Toward an Integration of Micro- and Macro- Sociologies*, London: Routledge & Kegan Paul, 1981.

2 See Seaman (1992) for a recent critique of 'active audience theory' which entirely fails to grasp the original point of the analysis of popular culture and media audiences. In the wake of the emerging critique of 'populism' in cultural studies, the pendulum of intellectual fashion seems to be swinging fast. A number of voices, besides Seaman's, can now be heard issuing clarion calls for a return to the 'old certainties' of political economy and conspiracy theory and to models of imposed 'dominant ideologies' which seem to be quite innocent of any recognition of the complexities of the concept of hegemony.

Bibliography

Abercrombie, N. and Turner, B. (1978) 'The dominant ideology thesis', *British Journal of Sociology* 29(2).
Abercrombie, N. *et al.* (1984) *The Dominant Ideology Thesis*, London: Allen & Unwin.
Acland, C. (1989) [Review of *Family Television*], *Journal of Film and Video* 41(3).
Allen, R. (ed.) (1987) *Channels of Discourse*, London: Routledge.
Althusser, L. (1971) 'Ideology and ideological state apparatuses', in L. Althusser, *Lenin and Philosophy*, London: New Left Books.
—— (1972) *For Marx*, Harmondsworth: Penguin Books.
Anderson, B. (1983) *Imagined Communities*, London: Verso.
Anderson, J. (1987) 'Commentary on qualitative research', in T. Lindlof (ed.) *Natural Audiences*, Norwood, NJ: Ablex.
Anderson, J. and Avery, R. (1988) 'The concept of effects', *Journal of Broadcasting and Electronic Media* 32.
Ang, I. (1985) *Watching 'Dallas'*, London: Methuen.
—— (1987) 'On the politics of empirical audience studies', paper presented to 'Rethinking the Audience' symposium, Blaubeuren, West Germany.
—— (1989) 'Wanted: audiences', E. Seiter *et al.* (eds) *Remote Control*, London: Routledge.
—— (1990) 'Culture and communication', *European Journal of Communications* 5(2–3).
—— (1991) *Desperately Seeking the Audience*, London: Routledge.
Ang, I. and Hermes, J. (1991) 'Gender and/in media consumption', in J. Curran and M. Gurevitch (eds) *Mass Media and Society*, London: Edward Arnold.
Ang, I. and Morley, D. (1989) 'Mayonnaise culture and other European follies', *Cultural Studies* 3(2).
Annan Committee (1977) *Report of the Committee on the Future of Broadcasting*, London: HMSO.
Arnheim, R. (1933; reprinted 1958) *Film as Art*, London: Faber & Faber.
Appadurai, A. (1986) *The Social Life of Things*, Cambridge: Cambridge University Press.
Austin, J. (1962) *How to Do Things with Words*, Oxford: Oxford University Press.
Baines, S. (1989) 'Approaches to home automation', unpublished paper, Center for Urban Regional Development Studies, Newcastle upon Tyne.
Bandura, B. (1961) 'Identification as a process of social learning', *Journal of Abnormal and Social Psychology* 63(2).
Barkin, S. and Gurevitch, M. (1987) 'Out of work and on the air', *Critical Studies in Mass Communication* 4.
Barrington-Moore, Jr (1967) *The Social Origins of Dictatorship and Democracy*,

Harmondsworth: Penguin.

Barthes, R. (1972) *Mythologies*, London: Paladin.

—— (1977) 'The death of the author', in R. Barthes, *Image: Music: Text*, London: Fontana.

Bassett, G. and Wiebe, Z. (1991) 'Television viewing contexts and television genres', paper presented to International Television Studies Conference, London.

Baudrillard, J. (1988) *Selected Writings*, Cambridge: Polity Press.

Bausinger, H. (1984) 'Media, technology and everyday life, *Media, Culture and Society* 6(4).

Behl, N. (1988) 'Television and tradition in an Indian village', in J. Lull (ed.) *World Families Watch Television*, Newbury Park and London, Sage.

Bennett, T. and Woollacott, J. (1987) *Bond and Beyond: The Political Career of a Popular Hero*, London: Macmillan.

Berelson, B. (1952) *Content Analysis in Communication Research*, Glencoe, Ill.: Free Press.

Berkowitz, L. (1962) 'Violence and the mass media', Paris Stamford Studies in Communication, Stamford, NY: Institute for Communication Research.

Berland, J. (1988) 'Placing television', *New Formations* 4.

Bernstein, B. (1971) *Class, Codes and Control*, Vol. 1, London: Paladin.

Bernstein, R. (1978) *The Restructuring of Social and Political Theory*, Philadelphia: University of Pennsylvania Press.

Beynon, H. (1973) *Working for Ford*, Harmondsworth: Penguin.

Beynon, H. and Nicholls, T. (1977) *Living with Capitalism*, London: Routledge.

Bhabha, K. H. (ed.) (1990) *Nation and Narration*, London: Routledge.

Billig, M. (1987) *Arguing and Thinking*, Cambridge: Cambridge University Press.

Blumler, G., Gurevitch, M. and Katz. E. (1985) 'Reaching out: a future for gratifications research', in K. Rosengren *et al.* (eds) *Media Gratifications Research*, Beverly Hills, Calif.: Sage.

Bobo, J. (1988) '*The Color Purple*: Black women as cultural readers', in E. Pribram (ed.) *Female Spectators*, London: Verso.

Boddy, W. (1986) 'The shining centre of the home' in P. Drummond and R. Paterson (eds) *Television in Transition*, London: British Film Institute.

Bourdieu, P. (1972a) 'The Berber house', in M. Douglas (ed.) *Rules and Meanings*, Harmondsworth: Penguin.

—— (1972b) 'Cultural reproduction and social reproduction', in R. Brown (ed.) *Knowledge, Education and Cultural Change*, London: Tavistock.

—— (1984) *Distinction*, London: Routledge.

Bourdieu, P. and Passeron, J. C. (1977) *Reproduction in Education, Society and Culture*, London: Sage.

Brecht, B. (1966) 'The anecdotes of Mr Keuner', in B. Brecht, *Tales from the Calendar*, London: Methuen.

Brodie, J. and Stoneman, L. (1983) 'A contextualist framework for studying the influence of television viewing in family interaction', *Journal of Family Issues* 4(2).

Browne, N. (1984) 'Political economy of the television supertext', *Quarterly Review of Film Studies* 9.

Brunsdon, C. (1981) '*Crossroads*: notes on a soap opera', *Screen* 22:4.

—— (1986) 'Women watching television', *MedieKulture* 4.

—— (1989) 'Text and audience' in E. Seiter *et al.* (eds), *Remote Control*, London: Routledge.

—— (1990a) 'Television: aesthetics and audiences' in P. Mellencamp (ed.) *The Logics of Television*, Bloomington: Indiana University Press.

—— (1990b) 'Problems with quality', *Screen* 31(1).

Brunsdon, C. and Morley, D. (1978) *Everyday Television: 'Nationwide'*, London: British Film Institute.

Brunt, R. (1973) 'The spectacular world of Whicker', *Working Papers in Cultural Studies* (University of Birmingham) 3.

Brunt, R. and Jordin, M. (1986) 'Constituting the television audience: a problem of method', paper presented to International Television Studies Conference, London, July 1986.

Bryce, J. (1987) 'Family time and television use', in T. Lindlof (ed.) *Natural Audiences*, Norwood, New Jersey: Ablex.

Budd, B., Entman, R. and Steinman, C. (1990) 'The affirmative character of American cultural studies', *Critical Studies in Mass Communication* 7(2).

Bulmer, M. (ed) (1975) *Working Class Images of Society*, London: Routledge.

Bush, C. G. (1983) 'Women and the assessment of technology', in J. Rothschild (ed.) *Machina ex Dea*, New York: Pergamon Press.

Butler, J. (1990) *Gender Trouble*, London: Routledge.

Byars, J. (1991) *All that Hollywood Allows: Re-Reading Gender in 1950s Melodrama*, London: Routledge.

Cardiff, D. and Scannell, P. (1987) 'Broadcasting and national unity', in J. Curran *et al*. (eds) *Impacts and Influences*, London: Methuen.

Carey. J. (1989) *Culture as Communication*, London: Unwin Hyman.

Carr, E. H. (1967) *What is History?*, Harmondsworth: Penguin.

Carragee, K. (1990) 'Interpretive media study', *Critical Studies in Mass Communication* 7(2).

Castells, M. (1983) 'New historical relationships between space and society', *Space and Society* 1(1).

Chambers, I. (1974) 'Roland Barthes: structuralism/semiotics', *Working Papers in Cultural Studies* (University of Birmingham) 6.

—— (1986) *Popular Culture: The Metropolitan Experience*, London: Methuen.

Chaney, D. (1972) *Processes of Mass Communication*, London: Macmillan.

—— (1983) 'A symbolic mirror of ourselves: civic ritual in mass society', *Media, Culture and Society* 5(2).

—— (1986) 'The symbolic form of ritual in mass communication', in P. Golding *et al*. (eds) *Communicating Politics*, Leicester: Leicester University Press.

Chen, K. H. (1990) 'Postmarxism', Taiwan: Institute of Literature, National Tsing-Hua University.

Cipolla, C. (1978) *Clocks and Culture*, New York, Norton.

Clifford, J. (1986) 'Partial truths', in J. Clifford and G. Marcus, *Writing Culture*, Berkeley: University of California Press.

Clifford, J. and Marcus, G. (1986) *Writing Culture*, Berkeley: University of California Press.

Cockburn, C. (1985) *Machinery of Dominance: Women, Men and Technical Know-How*, London: Pluto Press.

Cohen, P. and Gardner, C. (eds) (1984) *It Ain't Half Racist Mum*, London: Comedia/Routledge.

Collet, P. and Lamb, R. (1986) 'Watching people watching television', report presented to the Independent Broadcasting Authority, London.

Collins, R. (1988) 'National culture: a contradiction in terms?' paper presented to International Television Studies Conference, London, July 1988.

—— (1990) *Satellite Television in Western Europe*, London, John Libbey Books.

Condit, C. (1989) 'The rhetorical limits of polysemy', *Critical Studies in Mass Communication* 6(2).

Connell, I. (1983) 'Commercial broadcasting and the British Left', *Screen* 24(6).

—— (1985) 'Blaming the Meeja', in L. Masterman (ed.) *Television Mythologies*, London: Comedia/Routledge.

Connell, I. and Curti, L. (1985) 'Popular broadcasting in Italy and Britain', in P. Drummond and R. Paterson (eds) *Television in Transition*, London: British Film Institute.

Corner, J. (1991) 'Meaning, genre and context: the problematics of 'public knowledge' in the new audience studies', in J. Curran and M. Gurevitch (eds) *Mass Media and Society*, London: Edward Arnold.

Corrigan, P. (1983) 'Film entertainment as ideology and pleasure', in J. Curran and V. Porter (eds) *The British Film Industry*, London: Weidenfeld & Nicolson.

Counihan, M. (1973) 'Orthodoxy, revisionism and guerilla warfare in mass communications research', mimeo, University of Birmingham.

Cowan, R. S. (1989) *More Work for Mother*, London: Free Association Books.

Coward, R. (1977) 'Class, culture and the social formation', *Screen* 19(4).

Critcher, C. (1978) 'Structures, cultures and biographies', in S. Hall and T. Jefferson (eds), *Resistance through Rituals*, London: Hutchinson.

Cubitt, S. (1985) 'The politics of the living room', in L. Masterman (ed.) *Television Mythologies*, London: Comedia/Routledge.

Curran, J. (1976) 'Content and structuralist analysis of mass communication', Open University Social Psychology Course, D305, Milton Keynes: Open University Press.

—— (1990) 'The "new revisionism" in mass communications research', *European Journal of Communications* 5(2–3).

Curran, J. and Gurevitch, M. (eds) (1991) *Mass Media and Society*, London: Edward Arnold.

Dayan, D. and Katz, E. (1987) 'Performing media events', in J. Curran *et al.* (eds) *Impacts and Influences*, London: Methuen.

de Certeau, M. (1984) *The Practice of Everyday Life*, Berkeley: University of California Press.

de la Haye, Y. (1979) *Marx and Engels on the Means of Communication*, New York: International General.

de Lauretis, T. (1987) *Technologies of Gender*, Bloomington: Indiana University.

de Sola Pool, I. (1977) (ed.) *The Social Impact of the Telephone*, Cambridge, Mass.: MIT Press.

DeLillo, D. (1985) *White Noise*, London: Picador.

Desmond, J. (1989) 'How I met Miss Tootie: the home shopping club', *Cultural Studies* 3(3).

Deutscher, I. (1977) 'Asking questions', in M. Bulmer (ed.) *Social Research Methods*, London: Macmillan.

Docherty, D. *et al.* (1987) *The Last Picture Show*, London: British Film Institute.

Donald, J. (1988) 'How English is It?', *New Formations* 6.

—— (1989) *Fantasy and the Cinema*, London: British Film Institute.

Donzelot, J. (1979) *The Policing of Families*, London: Hutchinson.

Downing, J. (1974) 'Some aspects of the presentation of industrial and race relations in the British media', Ph.D. thesis, London School of Economics, University of London.

Douglas, M. and Isherwood, B. (1980) *The World of Goods*, Harmondsworth: Penguin.

Dreitzel, H. (1972) 'Introduction' to H. Dreitzel (ed.) *Recent Sociology* 2, London: Macmillan.

Drummond, P. and Paterson, R. (eds) (1985) *Television in Transition*, London: British Film Institute.

Drummond, P. and Paterson, R. (eds) (1988) *Television and its Audiences*,

London: British Film Institute.

Durkheim, E. (1938) *The Rules of Sociological Method*, Glencoe, Ill.: Free Press.

Dyer, R. (1977) 'Victim: hermeneutic project', *Film Form* 1(2).

Eco, U. (1972) 'Towards a semiotic enquiry into the television message', *Working Papers in Cultural Studies* (University of Birmingham) 3.

Elliott, P. (1972) *The Making of a Television Series*, London: Constable.

—— (1973) 'Uses and gratifications: a critique and a sociological alternative', mimeo, Centre for Mass Communications Research, University of Leicester.

Ellis, J. (1977) 'The institution of the cinema', *Edinburgh 1977 Television Festival Magazine*.

—— (1992) *Visible Fictions*, London: Routledge.

Ericson, S. (1989) 'Theorising popular fiction', in M. Skovmand (ed.) *Media Fictions*, Aarhus: Aarhus University Press.

Erni, J. (1989) 'Where is the audience?', *Journal of Communication Enquiry* 13(2).

Evans, W. (1990) 'The interpretive turn in media research', *Critical Studies in Mass Communication* 7(2).

Feher, M. and Kwinter, S. (eds) (1987) *The Contemporary City*, Cambridge, Mass.: MIT Press.

Ferguson, M. (1989) 'Electronic media and the redefining of time and space', in M. Ferguson (ed.) *Public Communication*, London: Sage.

Feuer, J. (1986) '*Dynasty*', paper presented to International Television Studies Conference, London.

—— (1989) 'Narrative form in American network television', in C. McCabe (ed.) *High Theory/Low Culture*, Manchester: Manchester University Press.

Fiske, J. (1984) 'Television quiz shows and the purchase of cultural capital', *Australian Journal of Screen Theory* 13–14.

—— (1986) 'Television: polysemy and popularity', *Critical Studies in Mass Communication* 3.

—— (1987a) *Television Culture*, London: Methuen.

—— (1987b) 'British cultural studies and television', in R. Allen (ed.) *Channels of Discourse*, London: Methuen.

—— (1989) 'Moments of television', in E. Seiter *et al.* (eds) *Remote Control*, London: Routledge.

—— (1990) 'Ethnosemiotics', *Cultural Studies* 4(1).

Fontaine, J. S. (1988) 'Public or private? The consitution of the family in anthropological perspective', *International Journal of Moral and Social Studies* 3(3).

Forgacs, D. (1985) [Review of E. Laclau and C. Mouffe, *Hegemony and Socialist Strategy*], *Marxism Today*, May 1985.

Foucault, M. (1980a) 'The eye of power', in C. Gordon (ed.) *M. Foucault: Power/Knowledge*, New York: Pantheon.

—— (1980b) 'Questions on geography', in C. Gordon (ed.) *M. Foucault: Power/Knowledge*, New York: Pantheon.

—— (1986) 'Of other spaces', *Diacritics* 16.

Frith, S. (1983) 'The pleasures of the hearth', in J. Donald (ed.) *Formations of Pleasure*, London: Routledge.

—— (1990) [Review article], *Screen* 31(2).

Frow, J. (1991) 'Michel de Certeau and the practice of representation', *Cultural Studies* 5(1).

Garmarnikow, E. and Purvis, J. (1983a) *The Public and the Private*, London: Heinemann Educational Books.

—— (1983b) 'Introduction' to E. Garmarnikow and J. Purvis (eds) *The Public and the Private*, London: Heinemann Educational Books.

Geertz, C. (1973) 'Thick description', in C. Geertz, *The Interpretation of Cultures*,

New York: Basic Books.

—— (1988) *Works and Lives: The Anthropologist as Author*, Cambridge: Polity Press.

Gell, A. (1986) 'Newcomers to the world of goods: consumption among the Muria Gonds', in A. Appadurai (ed.) *The Social Life of Things*, Cambridge: Cambridge University Press.

Gerbner, G. (1964) 'Ideological perspectives in news reporting', *Journalism Quarterly*, 41(4).

Gewertz, D. and Errington, E. (1991) 'We think, therefore they are? On occidentalising the world', *Anthropological Quarterly*, 64(2).

Giddens, A. (1979) *Central Problems in Sociological Theory*, London: Hutchinson.

Giglioli, P. (ed.) (1972) *Language and Social Context*, Harmondsworth: Penguin.

Gillespie, M. (1989) 'Technology and tradition', *Cultural Studies* 3(2).

Gilroy, P. (1989) 'Cruciality and the frog's perspective', *Third Text* 5.

Glaser, B. and Strauss, A. (1968) *Grounded Theory*, London: Weidenfeld & Nicolson.

Glasgow Media Group (1976) *Bad News*, London: Routledge.

Gledhill, C. (1978) 'Recent developments in film criticism', *Quarterly Review of Film Studies* 3(4).

—— (1988) 'Pleasurable negotiations', in E. Pribram (ed.) *Female Spectators*, London: Verso.

Glyptis, S. (ed.) (1987) *Leisure and the Home*, Loughborough: Leisure Studies Association.

Golding, P. (1989) 'Political communication and citizenship', in M. Ferguson (ed.) *Public Communications*, London: Sage.

Goldthorpe, J. and Lockwood, D. (1968) *The Affluent Worker*, 3 vols, Cambridge: Cambridge University Press.

Goodhart, G. J. (1975) *The Television Audience: Patterns of Viewing*, London: Saxon House.

Goodman, I. (1983) 'Television's role in family interaction', *Journal of Family Issues*, June 1983.

Gorrell-Barnes, G. (1985) 'Modern systems theory and family therapy', in M. Rutter and L. Herzov (eds) *Modern Child Psychiatry*, London: Tavistock Books.

Gray, A. (1987a) 'Behind closed doors: women and video', in H. Baehr and G. Dyer (eds) *Boxed in: Women on and in Television*, London: Routledge.

—— (1987b) 'Reading the audience', *Screen* 28(3).

Gripsrud, J. (1989) 'High culture revisited', *Cultural Studies* 3(2).

Groombridge, B. (1972) *Television and the People*, Harmondsworth: Penguin.

Grossberg, L. (1983) 'Cultural studies revisited', in M. Mander (ed.) *Communication in Transition*, New York: Praeger.

—— (1987) 'The In-difference of television', *Screen* 28(2).

—— (1988) 'Wandering audiences, nomadic critics', *Cultural Studies* 2(3).

Grossberg, L., Nelson, C., Treichler, P. (eds) (1992) *Cultural Studies*, London: Routledge.

Gunter, B. and Svennevig, M. (1987) *Behind and in Front of the Screen: Television and Family Life*, London: John Libbey.

Haddon, L. (1988) 'The home computer: the making of a consumer electronic', *Science and Culture* 2.

Hall, S. (1973a) 'Encoding/decoding in television discourse', reprinted in S. Hall *et al.*, (eds) (1981) *Culture, Media, Language*, London: Hutchinson.

—— (1973b) 'The determinations of news photographs', *Working Papers in Cultural Studies* (University of Birmingham) 3.

—— (1974) 'Deviancy, politics and the media', in P. Rock and M. McIntosh (eds)

Deviance and Social Control, London: Tavistock.

—— (1977) *Notes on 'The Spectacle'*, mimeo, Centre for Contemporary Cultural Studies, University of Birmingham.

—— (1978) 'Some problems with the ideology/subject couplet', *Ideology and Consciousness* 3.

—— (1980) 'Cultural studies and the Centre', in S. Hall *et al.* (eds) *Culture, Media, Language*, London: Hutchinson.

—— (1982) 'The rediscovery of ideology', in M. Gurevitch *et al.* (eds) *Culture, Society and the Media*, London: Methuen.

—— (1986) 'On postmodernism and articulation', *Journal of Communication Inquiry* 10(2).

—— (1988a) [Introductory Address, International Television Studies Conference, Institute of Education, London, July 1988].

—— (1988b) 'New ethnicities', in K. Mercer (ed.) *Black Film, British Cinema*, London: Institute of Contemporary Arts.

—— (1990) 'Cultural studies, now and in the future', paper presented to conference of that title, University of Illinois, April 1990. Reprinted in L. Grossberg *et al.* (eds)(1992).

Hall, S., Connell, I., and Curti. L. (1981) 'The unity of current affairs television', in T. Bennett *et al.* (eds) *Popular Television and Film*, London: British Film Institute/Open University Press.

Hall, S. and Jefferson, T. (eds) (1978) *Resistance through Rituals*, London: Hutchinson.

Hall, S. *et al.* (eds) (1981) *Culture, Media, Language*, London: Hutchinson.

Hall, T. (1976) *Beyond Culture*, New York: Anchor/Doubleday.

Halloran, J. (1970a) *The Effects of Television*, London: Panther.

—— (1970b) *Demonstrations and Communications*, Harmondsworth: Penguin.

—— (1975) 'Understanding television', *Screen Education* 14.

Hammersley, M. and Atkinson, P. (1983) *Ethnography: Principles and Practice*, London: Tavistock Books.

Hannerz, U. (1990) 'Cosmopolitans and locals in world culture', in M. Featherstone (ed.), *Global Culture*, London: Sage.

Haralovich, M. (1988) 'Suburban family sit-coms and consumer product design', in P. Drummond and R. Paterson (eds) *Television and its Audience*, London: British Film Institute.

Hardy, P., Johnston, C. and Willemen, P. (1976) 'Introduction', *Edinburgh 1976 Television Festival Magazine*.

Harris, N. (1971) *Beliefs in Society*, Harmondsworth: Penguin.

Hartley, J. (1987) 'Television audiences, paedocracy and pleasure', *Textual Practice* 1(2).

Hartmann, P. and Husband, C. (1972) 'The mass media and racial conflict', in D. McQuail, (ed.) *Sociology of Mass Communication*, Harmondsworth: Penguin.

Hartsock, N. (1987) 'Rethinking modernism', *Cultural Critique* 7.

Harvey, D. (1985) 'The geopolitics of capitalism', in D. Gregory and J. Urry (eds) *Social Relations and Spatial Structures*, London: Macmillan.

—— (1989) *The Condition of Postmodernity*, Oxford: Basil Blackwell.

Hassard, J. (1990) *The Sociology of Time*, London: Macmillan.

Heath, S. and Skirrow, G. (1977) 'Television: a world in action', *Screen* 18(2).

Hebidge, D. (1979) *Subculture: The Meaning of Style*, London: Methuen.

—— (1988a) *Hiding in the Light*, London: Comedia/Routledge.

—— (1988b) 'Towards a cartography of taste', in D. Hebidge, *Hiding in the Light*, London: Comedia/Routledge.

—— (1990) 'Fax to the future', *Marxism Today*, January 1990.

Hermes, J. (1991) 'Media, meaning and everyday life', paper presented to International Television Studies Conference, London, July 1991.

Hill, J. (1979) 'Ideology, economy and the British cinema', in M. Barrett *et al.* (eds) *Ideology and Cultural Production*, London: Croom Helm.

Hirst, P. (1976) 'Althusser's theory of ideology', *Economy and Society*, November 1976.

Hobson, D. (1982) *'Crossroads': Drama of a Soap Opera*, London: Methuen.

Hodges, J. and Hussain, A. (1979) 'La police des familles' [review article], *Ideology and Consciousness* 6.

Horton, D. and Wohl, R. (1956) 'Mass communications and para-social interaction', *Psychiatry* 19.

Hoyles, M. (ed.) (1977) *The Politics of Literacy*, London: Writers and Readers Publishing Cooperative.

Hurtado, A. (1989) 'Relating to privilege: seduction and rejection in the subordination of white women and women of colour', *Signs: Journal of Women in Culture and Society* 14(4).

Hymes, D. (1964) 'Towards ethnographies of communication', reprinted in P. Giglioli (ed.) (1972) *Language and Social Context*, Harmondsworth: Penguin.

—— (1972) 'On communicative competence', in J. Pride and J. Holmes (eds) *Sociolinguistics*, Harmondsworth: Penguin.

Innis, H. (1951) *The Bias of Communication*, Toronto: University of Toronto Press.

Jameson, F. (1984) 'Postmodernism: the cultural logic of late capitalism', *New Left Review* 146.

Jensen, K.B. (n.d.) *The Politics of Polysemy*, mimeo, Centre for Mass Communication, University of Copenhagen.

—— (1987) 'Qualitative audience research: toward an integrative approach to reception', *Critical Studies in Mass Communication* 4.

Jensen, K. B. and Rosengren, K. (1990) 'Five traditions in search of an audience', *European Journal of Communications* 5(2–3).

Johnston, C. (1979) 'The subject of feminist film', in *Edinburgh Television Festival Papers*.

Jouet, J. (1988) 'The social uses of micro-computers in France', paper presented to International Association of Mass Communication Researchers Conference, Barcelona, July 1988.

Jouet, J. and Toussaint, Y. (1987) 'Telematics and the private sphere: the case of the French videotext', paper presented to Data Communication Conference, Université Libre de Bruxelles, May 1987.

Kantor, D. and Lehr, W. (1975) *Inside the Family*, New York: Harper & Row.

Katz, E. (1959) 'Mass communications research and popular culture', *Studies in Public Communication* 2.

Katz, E. and Lazarsfeld, P. (1955) *Personal Influence*, New York: Free Press.

Keddie, N. (ed.) (1973) *Tinker, Tailor: The Myth of Cultural Deprivation*, Harmondsworth: Penguin.

King, A. (1980a) *Buildings and Society*, London: Routledge.

—— (1980b) 'A time for space and a space for time', in A. King (ed.) *Buildings and Society*, London: Routledge.

Kirby, A. (1989) 'A sense of place', *Critical Studies in Mass Communication* 6(3).

Klapper, J. (1960) *The Effects of Mass Communication*, Glencoe, Ill.: Free Press.

Knorr-Cetina, K. (1989) 'The micro-social order', in N. Fielding (ed.) *Actions and Structures*, London: Sage.

Kramarae, C. (ed.) (1988) *Technology and Women's Voices*, London: Routledge.

Kubey, T. (1986) Television use in everyday life', *Communication*, Summer 1986.

Kumar, K. J. (1988) 'Indian families watching television', paper presented to International Television Studies Conference, London, July 1988.

Labov, W. (1970) 'The Logic of Non-Standard English' in N. Keddie (ed.) *Tinker, Tailor: The Myth of Cultural Deprivations*, Harmondsworth: Penguin.

Laclau, E. (1977) *Politics and Ideology*, London: New Left Books.

Lazarsfeld, P. *et al.* (1944) *The People's Choice*, New York: Columbia University Press.

Leal, O.F. (1990) 'Popular taste and erudite repertoire: the place and space of TV in Brazil', *Cultural Studies* 4(1).

Lemish, D. (1982) 'The rules of viewing television in public places', *Journal of Broadcasting* 26(4).

Lewis, J. (1983) 'The encoding/decoding model: criticisms and redevelopments', *Media, Culture and Society* 5.

—— (1992) *The Ideological Octopus*, London: Routledge.

Lewis, J. *et al.* (1986) *The Audience for Community Arts*, London: Comedia.

Liebes, T. and Katz, E. (1991) *The Export of Meaning*, Oxford: Oxford University Press.

Lindlof, T. (ed.) (1987) *Natural Audiences*, Norwood, NJ: Ablex.

Lindlof, T. and Meyer, T. (1987) 'Mediated communication: the foundations of qualitative research' in T. Lindlof (ed.) *Natural Audiences*, Norwood, NJ: Ablex.

Lindlof, T. and Traudt, P. (1983) 'Mediated communication in families', in M. Mander (ed.) *Communications in Transition*, New York: Praeger.

Lodziak, C. (1987) *The Power of Television*, London: Frances Pinter.

Lull, J. (1980) 'The social uses of television', *Human Communications Research* 6(3).

—— (1982) 'How families select television programmes: a mass observational study', *Journal of Broadcasting* 26.

—— (1987) 'Audience, texts and contexts', *Critical Studies in Mass Communication* 4.

—— (1991) *Inside Family Viewing*, London: Routledge.

—— (ed.) (1988) *World Families Watch Television*, Newbury Park and London: Sage.

McArthur, C. (1981) 'Historical drama', in T. Bennett *et al.* (eds) *Popular Television and Film*, London: British Film Institute/Open University Press.

McCabe, C. (1981), 'Days of hope', in T. Bennett, *et al.* (eds) *Popular Television and Film*, London: British Film Institute/Open University Press.

MacIntyre, A. (1963) 'A mistake about causality in the social sciences', in P. Laslett and W.G. Runciman (eds) *Philosophy, Politics and Society, II*, Oxford: Blackwell.

McLuhan, M. (1964) *Understanding Media*, London: Routledge & Kegan Paul.

McLuhan, M. and Fiore, Q. (1967) *War and Peace in the Global Village*, New York: Bantam Books.

McRobbie, A. (1982) 'The politics of feminist research', *Feminist Review* 12.

McRobbie, A. and Garber J. (1976) 'Girls and subcultures', in J. Clarke *et al.* (eds) *Resistance through Rituals*, London: Hutchinson.

Maddox, B. (1977) 'Women and the switchboard', in Sola de Pool (ed.) *The Social Impact of the Telephone*, Cambridge, Mass.: MIT Press.

Mann, M. (1970) 'The social cohesion of liberal democracy', *American Sociological Review*, June 1970.

—— (1973) *Consciousness and Action among the Western Working Class*, London: Macmillan.

Marcus, G. and Fischer, M. (1986) *Anthropology as Cultural Critique*, Chicago:

University of Chicago Press.

Martin, G. (1973) 'The press', in D. Thompson, (ed.) *Discrimination and Popular Culture*, Harmondsworth: Penguin.

Martin-Barbero, J. (1988) 'Communication from culture', *Media, Culture and Society* 10.

Marx, K. (1973) *Grundrisse*, trans. Martin Nicolaus, Harmondsworth: Penguin.

Mascia-Lees, F. E. *et al.* (1989) 'The postmodernist turn in anthropology: cautions from a feminist perspective', *Signs* 15(1).

Massey, D. (1991a) 'The political place of locality studies', *Environment and Planning (A)* 23(2).

—— (1991b) 'Flexible sexism', *Environment and Planning (D): Society and Space* 9(1).

Mattelart, A. and Dorfmann, A. (1979) *How to Read Donald Duck*, New York: International General.

Mattelart, A. *et al.* (1987) *International Image Markets*, London: Comedia.

Mayer, M. (1977) 'The telephone and the uses of time', in Sola de Pool (ed.) *The Social Impact of the Telephone*, Cambridge, Mass.: MIT Press.

Medrich, E. (1979) 'Constant television: a background to everyday life', *Journal of Communication* 26(3).

Mercer, K. (1990) 'Black art and the burden of representation', *Third Text* 10.

Merton, R. (1946) *Mass Persuasion*, New York: Free Press.

Merton, R. and Kendall, P. (1955) 'The focussed interview', in P. Lazarsfeld and M. Rosenberg (eds), *The Language of Social Research*, New York: Free Press.

Merton, R. and Lazarsfeld, P. (1948) 'Communication, taste and social action', in L. Byron (ed.), *The Communication of Ideas*, New York: Cooper Square.

Meyerowitz, J. (1985) *No Sense of Place*, New York: Oxford University Press.

—— (1989) 'The generalised elsewhere', *Critical Studies in Mass Communication* 6(3).

Miller, D. (1988) *Material Culture and Mass Consumption*, Oxford: Basil Blackwell.

Miller, D. (1992) 'The young and the restless in Trinidad', in R. Silverstone and E. Hirsch (eds), *Consuming Technologies*, London: Routledge.

Mills, A. and Rice, P. (1982) 'Quizzing the popular', *Screen Education* 41.

Mills, C. W. (1939) 'Language, logic and culture', in C. W. Mills, *Power, Politics and People*, New York: Oxford University Press.

Modleski, T. (1984) *Loving with a Vengeance*, London: Methuen.

—— (ed.) (1986) *Studies in Entertainment*, Bloomington: Indiana University Press.

—— (1990) *Feminism without Women*, London: Routledge.

Moores, S. (1988) 'The box on the dresser: memories of early radio', *Media, Culture and Society* 10(1).

Moorhouse, H. and Chamberlain, C. (1974) 'Lower class attitudes to the British political system', *Sociological Review* 22(4).

Morley, D. (1974) 'Reconceptualising the media audience', stencilled paper, Centre for Contemporary Cultural Studies, University of Birmingham.

—— (1976) 'Industrial conflict and the mass media', *Sociological Review*, 24(2).

—— (1980) *The 'Nationwide' Audience*, London: British Film Institute.

—— (1981a) '*The "Nationwide" Audience*: a critical postscript', *Screen Education* 39.

—— (1981b) 'Texts, readers and subjects', in S. Hall *et al.* (eds), *Culture, Media, Language*, London: Hutchinson.

—— (1986) *Family Television*, London: Comedia/Routledge.

—— (1989) 'Changing paradigms in audience studies', in E. Seiter *et al.* (eds), *Remote Control*, London: Routledge.

—— (1990a) 'Behind the ratings', in J. Willis and T. Wollen (eds), *Neglected Audiences*, London: British Film Institute.

—— (1990b) 'The construction of everyday life', in D. Swanson and D. Nimmo (eds) *New Directions in Political Communication*, Newbury Park and London: Sage.

—— (1991a) 'Where the global meets the local', *Screen* 32(1).

—— (1991b) 'The consumption of media' [review article] *Journal of Communication* 41(2).

Morley, D. and Robins, K. (1989) 'Spaces of identity', *Screen* 20(4).

Morley, D. and Robins, K. (1990) 'No place like Heimat', *New Formations* 12.

—— (1992) 'Techno-orientalism', *New Formations* 16.

Morley, D. and Silverstone, R. (1990) 'Domestic communications', *Media, Culture and Society* 12(1).

—— (1991) 'Communication and context', in N. Jankowski and K. B. Jensen (eds) *A Handbook of Qualitative Methodologies for Mass Communication Research*, London: Routledge.

Morris, M. (1988) 'Banality in cultural studies', *Block* 14; reprinted in P. Mellencamp (ed.) *Logics of Television*, Bloomington; Indiana University Press, 1990.

Murdock, G. (1973) 'Mass media and the construction of meaning', in N. Armistead (ed.) *Reconstructing Social Psychology*, Harmondsworth: Penguin.

—— (1989a) 'Cultural studies: missing links', *Critical Studies in Mass Communications* 6(4).

—— (1989b) 'Critical Inquiry and audience activity', in B. Dervin *et al.* (eds) *Rethinking Communication*, Vol. 2, Newbury Park and London: Sage.

—— (1990) 'Television and citizenship', in A. Tomlinson (ed.) *Consumption, Identity and Style*, London: Comedia.

Murdock, G. *et al.* (1989) 'Home computers: the social construction of a complex commodity', *International Review of Sociology* (forthcoming).

Naumann, M. (1973) *Gesellschaft–Literatur–Lesen*, Berlin: Aufbau-Verlag.

Nava, M. (1987) 'Consumerism and its contradictions', *Cultural Studies* 1(2).

Neale, S. (1977) 'Propaganda', *Screen* 18(3).

Newcomb, H. and Hirsch, P. (1984) 'Television as a cultural forum', in W. Rowland and B. Watkins (eds) *Interpreting Television*, Newbury Park: Sage.

Nice, R. (1978) 'Pierre Bourdieu: a "vulgar materialist" in the sociology of culture', *Screen Education* 28.

Nicholls, T. and Armstrong, P. (1976) *Workers Divided*, London: Fontana.

Nightingale, V. (1986) 'What's happening to audience research?', *Media Information Australia* 39.

Nordenstreng, K. (1972) 'Policy for news transmission', in D. McQuail (ed.) *Sociology of Mass Communication*, Harmondsworth: Penguin.

Norris, C. (1991) *Deconstruction: Theory and Practice*, rev. edn., London: Routledge.

Nowell-Smith, G. (1977) 'Editorial', *Screen* 18(3).

O'Connor, A. (1989) 'The problem of American cultural studies', *Critical Studies in Mass Communication* 6(4).

Ohmae, K. (1989) 'Managing in a borderless world', *Harvard Business Review* 67(3).

Open University (1981) *Course U203 Popular Culture*, Milton Keynes: Open University Press.

Parkin, F. (1971) *Class Inequality and Political Order*, London: Paladin.

—— (ed.) (1974) *The Social Analysis of Class Struggle*, London: Tavistock Books.

—— (1979) *Marxism and Class Theory: A Bourgeois Critique*, London: Tavistock Books.

Pateman, T. (1974) *Television and the February 1974 General Election*, London: British Film Institute.

Paterson, R. (1987) 'Family perspectives on broadcasting policy', paper presented to British Film Institute Summer School.

Pêcheux, M. (1982) *Language, Semantics and Ideology*, London: Macmillan.

Peters, M. (1987) [Review of *Family Television*], *Initiatives* (SEFT), April 1987.

Piepe, A. *et al.* (1975) *Television and the Working Class*, London: Saxon House.

Pollock, F. (1955) 'Empirical research into public opinion', reprinted in P. Connerton (ed.) *Critical Sociology*, Harmondsworth: Penguin, 1976.

Poulantzas, N. (1971) *Political Power and Social Classes*, London: New Left Books.

Press, A. (1991) *Women Watching Television*, Philadelphia: University of Pennsylvania Press.

Pride, J. and Holmes, J. (1972) *Sociolinguistics*, Harmondsworth: Penguin.

Rabinow, P. (1977) *Reflections on Fieldwork in Morocco*, Berkeley: University of California Press.

Radway, J. (1984a) 'Interpretative communities and variable literacies', *Daedalus*, Summer 1984.

—— (1984b) *Reading the Romance*, Chapel Hill: University of North Carolina Press; British edition, London: Verso Books, 1987.

—— (1988) 'Reception study', *Cultural Studies* 2(3).

Rakow, L. (1988a) 'Gendered technology, gendered practice', *Critical Studies in Mass Communication* 5.

—— (1989b) 'Women and the telephone, the gendering of a communications technology', in C. Kramarae (ed.) *Technology and Women's Voices*, London: Routledge.

Rath, C.D. (1985) 'The invisible network: television as an institution in everyday life', in P. Drummond and R. Paterson (eds) *Television in Transition*, London: British Film Institute.

—— (1988) 'Live/life: television as a generator of events in everyday life', in P. Drummond and R. Paterson (eds) *Television and its Audience*, London: British Film Institute.

Rawlence, C. (ed.) (1985) *About Time*, London: Jonathan Cape.

Richards, I. (1960) 'Variant readings and misreading', in T. Sebeok (ed.) *Style in Language* Cambridge, Mass.: MIT Press.

Riley, D. (1988) *Am I That Name? Feminism and the Category of 'Women' in History*, London: Macmillan.

Riley, J. and Riley, M. (1959) 'Mass communication and the social system', in R. Merton (ed.) *Sociology Today*, New York: Free Press.

Robins, K. (1989) 'Reimagined communities', *Cultural Studies* 3(2).

—— (1991) 'Tradition and translation', in J. Corner and S. Harvey (eds) *Enterprise and Heritage*, London: Routledge.

Robins, K. and Webster, F. (1986) 'Broadcasting politics', in *Screen* 27(3–4).

Rogge, J. U. and Jensen, K. (1988) 'Everyday life and television in West Germany', in J. Lull (ed.) *World Families Watch Television*, London: Sage.

Rorty, R. (1978) 'Philosophy as a kind of writing', *New Literary History*, X.

Rosen, H. (1972) *Language and Class*, Bristol: Falling Wall Press.

Rosengren, K. (1985) 'Growth of a research tradition', in K. Rosengren *et al.* (eds) *Media Gratifications Research*, Beverly Hills, Calif.: Sage.

Ross, A. (1988) 'All in the family', *Camera Obscura* 16.

Rothschild, J. (ed.) (1983) *Machina ex Dea*, New York: Pergamon Press.

Runciman, W. (1983) *A Treatise on Social Theory*, Vol. 1, Cambridge: Cambridge University Press.

Rutherford, J. (ed.) (1990) *Identity: Community, Culture, Difference*, London: Lawrence & Wishart.

Ryle, G. (1949) *The Concept of Mind*, New York: Barnes & Noble.

Said, E. (1978) *Orientalism*, Harmondsworth: Penguin.

Sangren, S. (1988) 'Rhetoric and the authority of ethnography', *Current Anthropology*, 29.

Saussure, F. de (1974) *Course in General Linguistics*, London: Fontana.

Scannell, P. (1988) 'Radio times: the temporal arrangements of broadcasting in the modern world', in P. Drummond and R. Paterson (eds) *Television and its Audience*, London: British Film Institute.

—— (1989) 'Public service broadcasting and modern public life', *Media, Culture and Society*, 11.

Schiller, H. (1981) *Who Knows? Information in the Age of the Fortune 500*, Norwood, NJ: Ablex.

—— (1988) 'The erosion of national sovereignty by the world business system', in M. Taber (ed.) *The Myth of the Information Revolution*, London: Sage.

Schlesinger, P. (1987) 'On national identity', *Social Science Information* 26(2).

Schroder, K. (1987) 'Convergence of antagonistic traditions?', *European Journal of Communications* 2.

Schudson, M. (1987) 'The new validation of popular culture: sense and sentimentality in Academia', *Critical Studies in Mass Communication* 4(1).

Schutz, A. (1963) *Collected Papers*, I, Den Hague: Martins Nijhoff.

Seaman, W.R. (1992) 'Active audience theory: pointless populism', *Media, Culture and Society* 14.

Seiter, E. (1990) 'Making distinctions in television audience research', *Cultural Studies* 4(1).

Seiter, E. *et al.* (1989a) 'Introduction', in E. Seiter *et al.* (eds) *Remote Control*, London: Routledge.

Seiter, E. *et al.* (1989b) 'Towards an ethnography of soap opera viewers', in E. Seiter *et al.* (eds) *Remote Control*, London: Routledge.

Silverstone, R. (1981) *The Message of television*, London: Heinemann.

—— (1988) 'Television, myth and culture', in J. Carey (ed.) *Media, Myths and Narratives*, London: Sage.

—— (1989) 'Television: text or discourse?' *Science as Culture* 6.

—— (1990a) 'Television and everyday life: towards an anthropology of the television audience', in M. Ferguson (ed.) *Public Communication: The New Imperatives*, London: Sage.

—— (1990b) 'Communication is a carp', working paper, Centre for Research in Innovation, Culture and Technology, Brunel University.

Silverstone, R., Hirsch, E. and Morley, D. (1990) 'Information and communication technologies and the moral economy of the household', discussion paper for Centre for Research in Innovation, Culture and Technology, Brunel University. Reprinted in R. Silverstone and E. Hirsch (eds) (1992) *Consuming Technologies*, London: Routledge.

—— (1991) 'Listening to a long conversation: an enthnographic approach to ICT in the home', *Cultural Studies*, 5(2).

Silverstone, R., Morley, D. *et al.* (1989) 'Families, technologies and consumption', working paper, Centre for Research in Innovation, Culture and Technology, Brunel University.

Siskind, J. (1992) 'The invention of Thanksgiving: a ritual of American nationality', *Critique of Anthropology* 12(2).

Skirrow, G. (1986) 'Hellivision: an analysis of video games', in C. McCabe (ed.) *High Theory/Low Culture*, Manchester: Manchester University Press.

Slack, J. D. (1989) 'Contextualising technology', in B. Dervin *et al.* (eds), *Rethinking Communication*, Vol. 2, London: Sage.

Soja, E. (1989) *Postmodern Geographies*, London: Verso.

Spigel, L. (1986) 'Ambiguity and hesitation: discourses on television and the housewife in women's magazines', paper to International Television Studies Conference, London, July 1966.

—— (1992) *Make Room for TV: Television and the Family Ideal in Post-war America*, Chicago: University of Chicago Press.

Spivak, G. (1988) 'Can the subaltern speak?', in C. Nelson and L. Grossberg (eds) *Marxism and the Interpretation of Cultures*, Urbana: University of Illinois Press.

Stam, R. (1983) 'Television news and its spectator', in E. Kaplan (ed.) *Regarding Television*, Vol. 2, New York: American Film Institute.

Thompson, E. P. (1967) 'Time, work-discipline and industrial capitalism', in *Past and Present* 38.

Tomlinson, A. (1989) 'Home fixtures: doing it yourself in a privatised world', in A. Tomlinson (ed.) *Consumption, Identity and Style*, London: Comedia/Routledge.

Towler, R. (1985) 'Beyond head counting', paper to the Royal Television Society Convention, Cambridge.

Turkle, S. (1988) 'Computational reticence: why women fear the intimate machine', in C. Kramarae (ed.) *Technology and Women's Voice*, London: Routledge.

Turner, G. (1990a) *British Cultural Studies*, London: Unwin Hyman.

—— (1990b) 'It works for me: British cultural studies, Australian cultural studies, Australian film', paper presented to 'Cultural studies: now and in the future' conference, University of Illinois, April, 1990. Reprinted in L. Grossberg *et al.* (eds) (1992).

Voloshinov, V. (1973) *Marxism and the Philosophy of Language*, New York: Academic Press.

Walkerdine, V. (1987) 'Video replay: families, films and fantasy', in J. Donald and C. Kaplan (eds) *Formations of Fantasy*, London: Methuen.

—— (1988) *The Mastery of Reason: Cognitive Development and the Production of Rationality*, London: Routledge.

Wallman, S. (1984) *Eight London Households*, London: Tavistock Books.

Webster, D. (1989) 'Cocacolonisation and national cultures', *Overhere* 9(2).

Webster, F. and Robins, K. (1979) 'Mass communications and information technology' in R. Miliband and J. Saville (eds) *Socialist Register*, London: Merlin.

Wellman, B. (1979) 'The community question', *American Journal of Sociology* 84.

Willemen, P. (1978) 'Notes on subjectivity', *Screen* 19(1).

—— (1990) [Review of J. Hill *Sex, Class and Realism: British Cinema 1963–1965*], in M. Alvarado and J. O. Thompson (eds) *The Media Reader*, London: British Film Institute.

Williams, R. (1970) 'The local press', *The Listener*, 15 October 1970.

—— (1976) *Keywords*, London: Fontana.

Williamson, J. (1986) 'The problems of being popular', *New Socialist*, September 1986.

Willis, P. (1978) *Learning to Labour*, London: Saxon House.

—— (1981) 'Notes on method', in S. Hall *et al.* (eds) *Culture, Media, Language*, London: Hutchinson.

Wober, M. (1981) 'Psychology in the future of broadcasting research', *Bulletin of the British Psychological Society* 34.

Wolf, M. *et al.* (1982) 'A rules-based study of television's role in the construction of social reality', *Journal of Broadcasting* 26(4).

Woods, R. (1977) 'Discourse analysis: the work of Michel Pêcheux', *Ideology and Consciousness* 2.

Woolfson, C. (1976) 'The semiotics of workers' speech', *Working Papers in Cultural Studies* (University of Birmingham) 9.

Worpole, K. (1983) *Dockers and Detectives*, London: Verso.

Wright, P. (1975) *On Living in an Old Country*, London: Verso.

—— (1985) *On Living in an Old Country*, London: Verso.

Wright, R. (1960) 'Functional analysis and mass communication', *Public Opinion Quarterly* 24.

Zaretsky, E. (1976) *Capitalism, the Family and Personal Life*, London: Pluto Press.

Zimmermann, J. (1983) *The Technological Woman*, New York: Praeger.

Index

Abercrombie, N. *et al*.: on 'dominant ideology thesis' 20, 24
Abercrombie, N. and Turner, B.: on media studies 7
address: mode of 65–7, 84–5, 112, 113, 206
advertising: and metaphor 209
age: as structuring factor 125
Allen, R.: *Channels of Discourse* 6
Althusser, L. 24, 136; on family/school couplet 70; influence on cultural studies 7; on interpellation 62; and relative autonomy concept 55; on unconscious nature of ideology 121
Anderson, B.: on nation as 'imagined community' 267–8
Anderson, J.: on family use of time and television viewing 262; on naturalistic perspective 185–6; on rules of family viewing 184
Anderson, J. and Avery, R.: on interpretative research 36
Ang, I.: on context of viewing 184; on *Dallas* 208; on ethnography 27; in favour of particularization 187–8; on gender 8, 15, 147; on purpose of empirical study 181; on quantitative research 175, 177, 179; on ratings discourse 175; on role of researcher 31; on viewing and non-viewing 197
Ang, I. and Hermes, J. 169; on dispersion of power 25; on 'gender essentialism' 160–1
Ang, I. and Morley, D.: on context of cultural studies 2
Annan Committee on Broadcasting (1977) 257
anthropology: postmodern 189;

research into consumption 216–17; *see also* ethnography
anti-racism: perspective on cultural studies 8
Appadurai, A.: on 'career' of technology 236; *The Social Life of Things* 213
Arnheim, Rolf: on social consequences of television 289
audience: assumptions made about 84; characterizing relationship to television 206; and citizenship 252–4; definition of 'common sense' terms 98; discourses available to 87, 92; as element of mass communications 77–8; ethnography of *see* ethnography; as a fiction 178; and 'generalised other' 95; granting privileged status to 180; as passive consumers 18; positioning of 84–5; process of interpretation/decoding *see* decoding; sub-cultures within 87–90; *see also* audience research
audience research 6–7; 'hypodermic' model 273; micro- and macro- issues 275–7; and nature of texts 119; 'new revisionism' 22–6; obsolence of 277; problems of quantitative methods 174–7; questioning of 273–5; role of hindsight 23–4
Australia, cultural studies 3
autonomy: and determination 55–7; relative 55

Baines, S.: on technological 'valences' 230
Bandura, B.: on 'acting-out' 50